MTG

NCERT at your FINGERTIPS

QUESTIONS EXTRACTED FROM EACH LINE OF LATEST NCERT TEXTBOOK

SCIENCE

by

MTG Editorial Board

CLASS 7

MTG Learning Media (P) Ltd.

New Delhi | Gurugram

Published by : **MTG Learning Media (P) Ltd., New Delhi**

Corporate Office : Plot 99, Sector 44 Institutional Area, Gurugram, Haryana-122003
Phone : 0124 - 6601200. Web : mtg.in Email : info@mtg.in

Regd. Office : 406, Taj Apt., Ring Road, Near Safdarjung Hospital, New Delhi-110029

Information contained in this book has been obtained by mtg, from sources believed to be reliable. Every effort has been made to avoid errors or omissions in this book. In spite of this, some errors might have crept in. Any mistakes, error or discrepancy noted may be brought to our notice which shall be taken care of in the next edition. It is notified that neither the publishers nor the author or seller will be responsible for any damage or loss of action to anyone, of any kind, in any manner, therefrom.

Printed by Akash Press, New Delhi.

Preface

NCERT at your Fingertips series is particularly designed as per the latest CBSE guidelines to help the learners build a strong foundation for achieving future goals.

As we know NCERT books are the primary resource books; learners must be well-equipped with them in order to excel academically. At the same time, in this age of knowledge, it is essential to broaden the subject knowledge to be ready for future opportunities.

Keeping this in mind, **NCERT at your Fingertips series** (classes 6 to 12) provides a comprehensive set of questions that not only thoroughly covers NCERT syllabus but also offers challenging and application-based questions for future competitive exam-related focussed study.

The powerful set of features of this series that makes it an invaluable resource for both learners and teachers are-

- **NCERT Notes :** Chapterwise student-friendly NCERT Notes for quick and easy revision.
- **Practice Corner :** Includes
  - Huge variety of questions like Topicwise MCQs, True-False, Fill in the blanks, Figure based questions, Column matching questions, VSA type questions framed from each and every line of NCERT Science textbook.
- As per the latest CBSE guidelines, **Competency Based Questions, Case/Source Based Questions** are included. Questions are labelled as per the **cognitive levels** issued by CBSE for assessment and evaluation to provide evidence of students' knowledge and ability.

  Cognitive Levels :

  Remembering R Understanding U Applying Ap Analysing An Evaluating Ev Creating Cr
- **NCERT Exemplar Problems :** Includes NCERT Exemplar MCQs.
- **Assertion & Reason Corner :** Includes questions for an edge in your preparation.
- **Exam Corner :** Includes MCQs, VSA, SA-I, SA-II, LA and Case Based Questions.
- **Gyaan & Jigyasa** and their quick-witted conversations make learning enjoyable and explorative.
- **Hints & Explanations :** Solutions for each exercise are provided.

We, at MTG have put in great effort and care to bring these books error-free, yet criticisms or suggestions are always welcome from our readers. This will help us to improve and serve you better. Kindly e-mail your views to *editor@mtg.in.*

Wishing you all the success!

MTG Editorial Board

Rationalisation of Content in NCERT Textbooks*

In view of the COVID-19 pandemic, it is imperative to reduce content load on students. The National Education Policy 2020, also emphasises reducing the content load and providing opportunities for experiential learning with creative mindset. In this background, NCERT has undertaken the exercise to rationalise the textbooks across all classes.

The following table contains information about contents which have been dropped and hence are not to be assessed.

Class-7

Chapter	Page No.	Dropped Chapters
Chapter 3: Fibre to Fabric	24-34	Full chapter
Chapter 7 : Weather, Climate and Adaptations of Animals to Climate	68-79	Full chapter
Chapter 8: Winds, Storms and Cyclones	80-95	Full chapter
Chapter 9: Soil	96-107	Full chapter
Chapter 16: Water: A Precious Resource	193-205	Full chapter

*NCERT has issued rationalised content for the current academic year so, these chapters are not covered in this book.

CONTENTS

1 Nutrition in Plants

NCERT Notes

- All living organisms require food as it provides energy to carry out various life activities.
- The process of taking in food and its utilisation by the body for various life processes is called **nutrition**. The various components of food are carbohydrates, proteins, fats, vitamins, minerals, roughage and water. These are called nutrients which are necessary for our body.

1.1 Mode of Nutrition in Plants

- Plants are the only organisms that can prepare food for themselves by using water, carbon dioxide and minerals. The raw materials are present in their surroundings.
- Living organisms exhibit two main modes of nutrition (i) Autotrophic nutrition and (ii) Heterotrophic nutrition.
  (i) Autotrophic nutrition (auto – self; trophos – nourishment) : The mode of nutrition in which organisms synthesise or prepare their own food with the help of simple inorganic substance is called as autotrophic nutrition. Such organisms are called as autotrophs or producers, *i.e.*, green plants and algae.

+ Plants are autotrophs. The cells of green leaves and young stems of plants have green structures called **chloroplasts**. They are green due to the presence of chlorophyll.
  - **Chlorophyll** absorbs solar energy and converts it into chemical energy.
  - **Thylakoids** are disc-like structures present in the chloroplast.
  - **Grana** are stacks of thylakoids inside the chloroplasts.
  - **Stroma** is the fluid matrix in a chloroplast.

  (ii) Heterotrophic nutrition (heteros – other; trophos – nourishment) : The mode of nutrition in which organism obtain their food from plants or other animals is called heterotrophic nutrition. Such organisms are called heterotrophs, *e.g.*, all animals, non-green plants, fungi, most bacteria, etc.

1.2 Photosynthesis- Food Making Process in Plants

- Leaves are the food factories of plants.

- Green plants synthesise their food by the process of photosynthesis (photo : light; synthesis : to combine, *i.e.*, Synthesis of food in the presence of sunlight). It is a unique process on earth. During this process, solar energy of sun is captured by chlorophyll of leaves and converted into chemical energy.
- Tiny pores present on the surface of leaves which are called **stomata**, surrounded by guard cells. Stomata help in taking of carbon dioxide (CO_2) from air.
- Water and minerals present in soil are absorbed by the roots and transported to the leaves by xylem vessels. It forms continuous path. Which run like pipes throughout the root, the stem, the branches and the leaves.
- During photosynthesis, chlorophyll containing cells of leaves in the presence of sunlight, use carbon dioxide and water to synthesise carbohydrates.

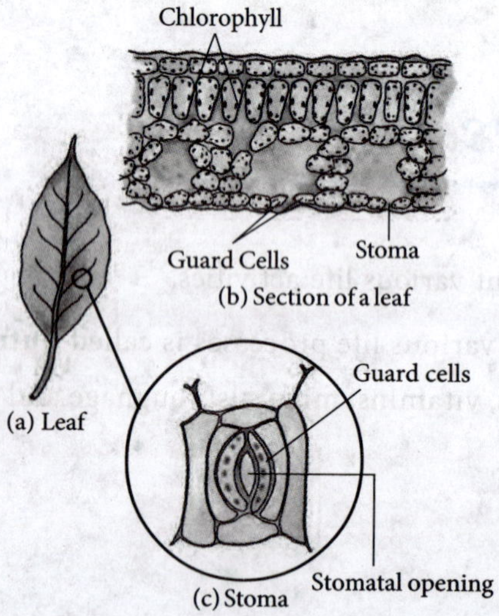

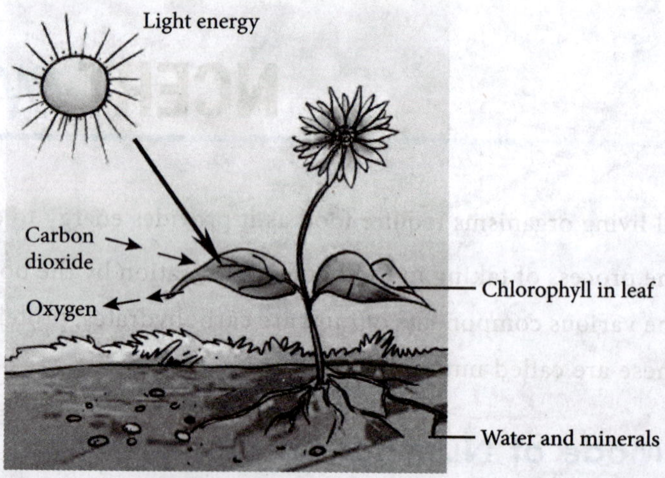

Fig.: Process of photosynthesis

- Chemical reaction for photosynthesis is as follows :

$$6\,CO_2 + 6H_2O \xrightarrow[\text{Chlorophyll}]{\text{Sunlight}} C_6H_{12}O_6 + 6O_2$$

Carbon dioxide (from air) + water (from soil) —Sunlight / Chlorophyll→ Carbohydrate (Food stored in plants) + Oxygen (Released in air)

- Photosynthesis also takes place in green stems and in green branches. The desert plants have scale or spine-like leaves to reduce loss of water by transpiration. These plants have green stems which carry out photosynthesis.

To demonstrate that light is necessary for photosynthesis.

Materials required – A healthy potted plant, a petri dish, a beaker containing water, forceps, a water bath, a piece of wire gauze, a tripod, a burner, alcohol, a strip of black paper, iodine solution and clips.

Procedure

- Take the potted plant and keep it in a dark place for 2-3 days so that the leaves get destarched.
- Cover a part of one of its leaves with the strip of black paper using the clips. Make sure that you cover both the sides of the leaf.
- Now place this plant in sunlight for 4-6 hours.
- Pluck the selected covered leaf and remove the black paper covering it.
- Place this leaf in the beaker containing water and boil it for 5-10 minutes.
- Take out the leaf and now boil it in alcohol, using water bath. This removes the chlorophyll.

- Take out the leaf and wash it with water.
- Place this leaf in the petri dish and put a few drops of iodine solution on it. Now observe the change in colour.

Observation – The part of the leaf which was covered with black paper strip turned yellow-brown (did not turn blue-black) whereas the exposed part turned blue-black in colour.

Conclusion – The covered region did not perform photosynthesis, and no starch was formed and open region of leaves perform photosynthesis and formed starch in the presence of light. This show that sunlight is essential for photosynthesis.

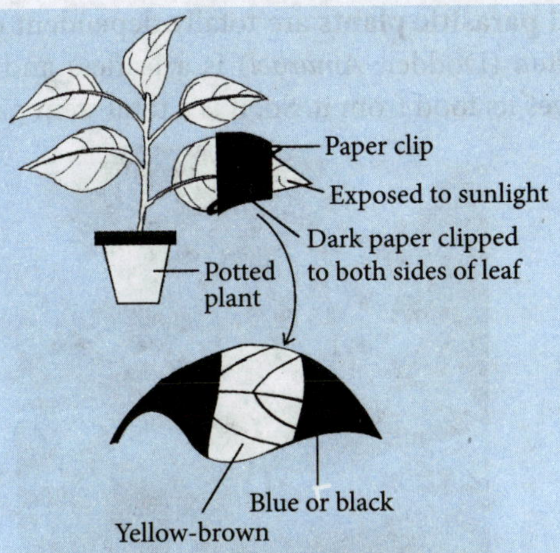

Fig.: Experiment showing light is required during photosynthesis

- In the absence of photosynthesis, there would not be any food. The survival of almost all living organisms directly or indirectly depend upon the food made by the plants.
- During the process, oxygen is released. The carbohydrates (glucose) ultimately get converted into starch. The presence of starch in leaves indicates the occurrence of photosynthesis.
- We always say that the green parts of the leaf contained the pigment chlorophyll but the leaves other than green also have chlorophyll. The large amount of red and brown and other pigments mask the green colour. Photosynthesis takes place in these leaves also.
- Algae is autotrophic organism which appears as green patches in ponds or stagnant water bodies. It has chlorophyll pigments and can prepare their own food by photosynthesis.

Synthesis of Plant Food other than Carbohydrates

- Plants synthesise carbohydrates through the process of photosynthesis. The carbohydrates are made of carbon, hydrogen and oxygen. These are used to synthesise other components of food such as proteins and fats. Proteins are nitrogenous substances, that contain nitrogen abundance is gaseous form in the air and which cannot be absorbed directly by plants. Soil has certain bacteria that convert gaseous nitrogen into usable form and release it into soil. These are absorbed by the plants along with water to make proteins and vitamins.
- We know buildings are made up of bricks. Similarly bodies of living organisms are made of tiny units called cells. Cells can be seen only under microscope. Some organisms are made of only one cell called unicellular organism, *e.g., Amoeba*. The thin outer boundary of cell is called cell membrane or plasma membrane. Most cells have distinct, centrally located spherical structure called nucleus which was discovered by Robert Brown. The nucleus is surrounded by jelly like substance called cytoplasm.

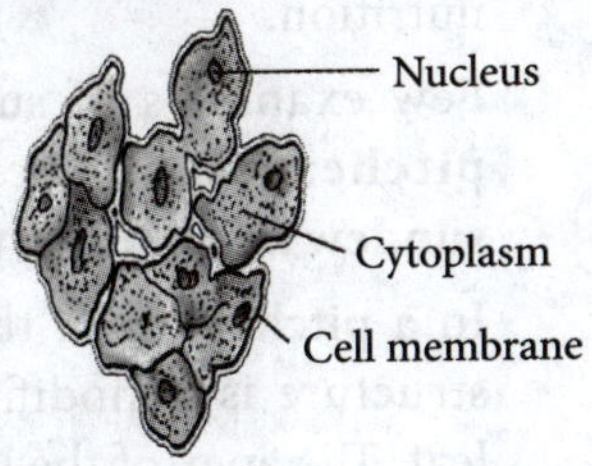

Fig.: Cell

1.3 Other Modes of Nutrition in Plants

- There are some plants which do not have chlorophyll. They cannot prepare their own food. They depend directly or indirectly upon green plants for their nutrition. This mode of nutrition is called heterotrophic nutrition.
- Parasitic plants and insectivorous plants are included under heterotrophic mode of nutrition.

Parasitic Plants

- A parasite is an organisms that lives in or on the body of another organisms and derives nutrients from it (host). Mosquitoes, bed bugs, lice and leeches that suck our blood are also parasites. Parasitic plants develop special root like structures called haustoria which penetrate the stem of the host plant and deprive it of valuable nutrients. They can be categorised into two :

- **Total parasitic plants** are totally dependent on their host for their food and no longer need green leaves., *e.g.*, *Cuscuta* (Dodder, *Amarbel*) is a leafless and rootless parasitic plant that cannot perform photosynthesis and derives its food from it. So, it is a total stem parasite and total root parasite is *Rafflesia*.

(a)

(b)

Fig.: (a) *Cuscuta* (Amerbel) on host plant, (b) *Rafflesia*

Rafflesia – The largest single flower in the world is a total root parasite. It grows on the roots of host plant. Its stem is highly reduced to fine threads growing in the roots of the host plant from where it sucks its food.

Fig.: Mistletoe

- **Partial parasitic plants** possess green leaves and can synthesise their carbohydrate food by themselves through photosynthesis. However, they depend on the host plant for water and minerals, *e.g.*, Mistletoe.

Insectivorous Plants

- Insectivorous plants feeds insects. They are green and synthesise their own food by the process of photosynthesis but they also feed on insects to obtain their nitrogen nutrition.

  Few examples of such plants are **pitcher plant, venus flytrap, sundew** and **bladderwort**, etc.

  In a pitcher plant, the pitcher like structure is a modified part of the leaf. The apex of the leaf forms a lid which can open and close the mouth of the pitcher. When an insect lands in the pitcher, the lid closes and the trapped insect gets entangled into the hair. The insect is digested by the digestive juices secreted in the pitcher and its nutrients are absorbed.

(A)

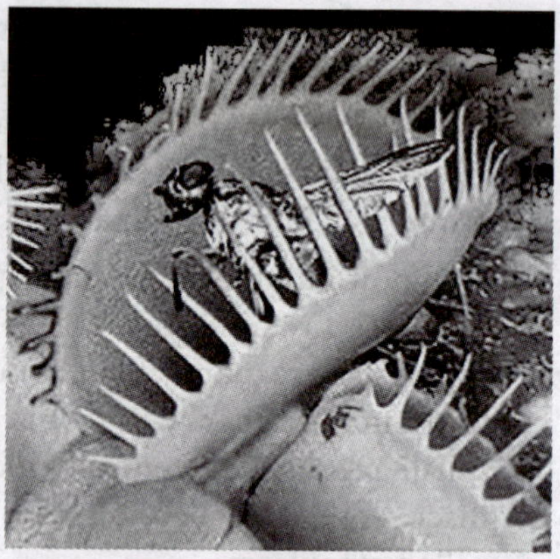

(B)

Fig.: (A) Pitcher plant, (B) Venus flytrap

1.4 Saprotrophs

- Saprotrophs are the organisms that obtain their nutrition from dead and decaying organic matter by releasing digestive juices on them and covert them into soluble form and it is called saprotrophic nutrition.

Fungi

- They are the saprotrophic organisms which are more abundant in warm and humid areas. The white cottony mass of fine thread that grows on stale bread, fruits, pickles, leather goods is fungus called **bread mould**.

- Mushrooms are also an example of fungus that are edible and form a delicacy whereas some varieties of fungi are poisonous, can cause disease in crops and humans.
- Fungi reproduce through spores. Spores always floats in the air. When these spores landed on some moist organic matter, they germinate and form a mesh of fine threads.
- Some fungi are used in medicines.

To observe fungi growing on a food material

- Take a slice of bread and moisten it with water. Leave it in a moist warm place for 2-3 days. You will observe the growth of white, green, or brown coloured thread-like structures or patches on the surface of bread. This organism is a fungus called bread mould. It is a saprotroph. You can observe it with a magnifying glass or under a microscope to view the spore bearing thread like structures.

Fig.: Fungi growing on bread

Symbiosis

- Symbiosis is a special mode of nutrition. When two organisms live together and mutually help to each other, their association is called symbiosis or symbiotic relationship. For example : lichen, mycorrhiza. Lichens shows the symbiotic relationship between an alga and a fungus that live together and mutually beneficial to each other.
- Alga provides food to fungus and, in return fungus provides shelter, water and minerals to alga.
- Mycorrhiza is a symbiotic relationship between fungus and roots of higher plants. Plants provide nutrients to the fungus and, in return, the fungus provides water and certain nutrients.

1.5 How Nutrients are Replenished in the Soil

- Plants require nutrients for their growth. They absorb these nutrients from the soil. Continuous growing of crops in the field make it deficient in vital nutrients like Nitrogen (N), Phosphorus (P) and Potassium (K). Such nutrients need to be added to enrich the soil and enrichment can be done in the following ways:
  - Farmers should add manures and fertilisers to increase the soil fertility.
  - After a crop is harvested, the soil becomes deficient in nitrogen. Farmers may grow leguminous crops (*e.g.* pulses, peas, beans, etc.), to replenish nitrogen in the soil because *Rhizobium* bacteria present in roots of legume crops add soluble nitrogenous compounds in the soil to be absorbed by plants.
- *Rhizobium* bacteria and roots of legumes show a kind of symbiotic relationship. This association has great significance for farmers. It can reduce the use of nitrogenous fertiliser where leguminous plants are grown.

Practice Corner

Extracted from NCERT

Assessment is complementary part of the learning process. It gives you a total insight whether the learning outcomes have been achieved or not. After going through the corresponding NCERT Textbook chapter, attempt these questions in exam like environment. Give yourself one mark for correct answer. A table is given at the end, that will help you plan your next step.

All the Best!

1.1 Mode of Nutrition in Plants

NCERT Page 1

A. Select the correct option.

1. Which of the following is not required by the plants to prepare their food?
   (a) carbon dioxide (b) water
   (c) chlorophyll (d) oxygen. U

2. Which of the following are called autotrophs?
   (a) Animals (b) Microorganisms
   (c) Plants (d) Insects U

3. The mode of nutrition in which organisms make food themselves from simple substances is called ____________ nutrition.
   (a) autotrophic (b) heterotrophic
   (c) saprotrophic (d) parasitic An

4. Select the incorrect statement(s).
   (i) Plants can make their own food.
   (ii) Animals including humans cannot make their own food.
   (iii) Raw materials used by plants to make their food are water, oxygen and carbon dioxide.
   (a) (ii) and (iii) (b) Only (iii)
   (c) (i) and (ii) (d) (i) and (iii) An

B. Fill in the blanks.

5. ____________ is the mode of taking food by an organism and its utilisation by the body.

6. ____________ takes readymade food prepared by the plants.

7. The organisms that takes readymade food prepared by plants are known as ____________.

8. Different nutrients required by our body are ____________, ____________, ____________, ____________ and ____________.

9. Humans and animals are directly or indirectly dependent on ____________.

1.2 Photosynthesis- Food Making Process in Plants

NCERT Page 1-4

A. Select the correct option.

10. Which of the following are known as the 'food factories' of the plants?
    (a) Leaves (b) Stems
    (c) Roots (d) Flowers An

11. Tiny pores present on the surface of the leaves of plants are called
    (a) chlorophylls (b) stomata
    (c) guard cells (d) nucleus. U

12. Green pigment present in the leaves of plants is called
    (a) guard cell (b) starch
    (c) chlorophyll (d) stoma. U

13. The ultimate source of energy for all living organisms is/are
    (a) oxygen
    (b) plants
    (c) sun
    (d) microorganisms. U

14. Select the correct statements.
    (i) Carbohydrates are made of carbon, hydrogen and oxygen
    (ii) Fertilisers are rich in nitrogen.
    (iii) Plants can absorb nitrogen directly present in the atmosphere.
    (iv) Plants cannot synthesise fats and proteins.
    (a) (i), (ii) and (iv) (b) (i), (ii) and (iii)
    (c) (i) and (ii) (d) (i) and (iv) Ap

15. Plants can synthesise
    (a) Protein (b) Carbohydrate
    (c) Fat (d) all of these R

16. The chemical equation for photosynthesis is as follows :

$$X + Water \xrightarrow[Y]{Sunlight} Carbohydrate + Z$$

What are the identities of X, Y and Z?

	X	Y	Z
(a)	Carbon dioxide	Chlorophyll	Oxygen
(b)	Oxygen	Chloroplast	Carbon dioxide
(c)	Carbon dioxide	Chloroplast	Glucose
(d)	Oxygen	Chlorophyll	Carbon dioxide

Cr

17. Atmospheric carbon dioxide is absorbed by the plants with the help of
(a) *Rhizobium* (b) stomata
(c) xylem (d) stroma. An

B. Fill in the blanks.

18. In plants, the process of synthesis of food takes place in the ________ and the phenomenon is called ________.
19. The food prepared by plants is stored as ________.
20. Algae contains ________ which make them appear green in colour.
21. ________ capture the solar energy and store in the plant in the form of food.
22. During photosynthesis, plants use sunlight, carbon dioxide and ________ to synthesise ________.
23. The gaseous nitrogen is converted into a usable form and released into the atmosphere by the ________ present in the soil.
24. The simplest carbohydrate made as food by photosynthesis is ________.

C. State True (T) or False (F) for the given statements.

25. A plant having red leaves cannot perform photosynthesis. ☐
26. Chlorophyll helps the leaves to capture carbon dioxide from the atmosphere. ☐
27. During photosynthesis, plant takes in carbon dioxide and release oxygen. ☐
28. Plants use carbon dioxide and water to synthesise proteins. ☐
29. Desert plants perform photosynthesis with the help of their green stems. ☐
30. Guard cells are externally surrounded by the stomata. ☐
31. The presence of starch in green leaves indicates the occurrence of photosynthesis. ☐
32. Cactus has spine-like leaves to reduce the loss of water. ☐
33. Vessels form a continuous path from the roots to each part of the plant for the passage of nutrients. ☐
34. Algae are usually slimy, green seen as patches on stagnant water bodies. ☐

D. Figure based questions.

A leaf of a potted plant was covered with a black paper and kept under the sun as shown. After 2-3 hrs, iodine test was performed on the leaf.

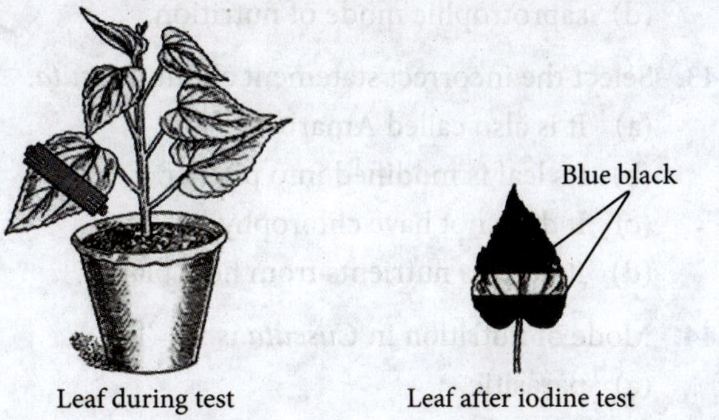

35. Write down the result of the iodine test.
36. What conclusion can you draw from the given experiment?

1.3 Other Modes of Nutrition in Plants

NCERT Page 4-5

A. Select the correct option.

37. Which of the following is an insectivorous plant?
(a) *Cuscuta* (b) Pitcher plant
(c) Mushroom (d) Cactus R
38. Which of the following is autotrophic?
(a) Amarbel (b) Mosquito
(c) Bed bugs (d) Algae An
39. The pitcher-like structure in pitcher plant is the modified
(a) stem (b) branch
(c) leaf (d) flower. R

40. __________ is a parasitic plant.
(a) Mushroom
(b) Pitcher plant
(c) Cactus
(d) *Cuscuta* R

41. __________ present inside the pitcher of the pitcher plant helps in trapping insects.
(a) Hair
(b) Mucous
(c) Digestive enzymes
(d) Nectar U

42. The mode of nutrition in which an organism cannot prepare its own food and depends on other organisms for its nutrition is referred to as
(a) autotrophic mode of nutrition
(b) heterotrophic mode of nutrition
(c) symbiotic mode of nutrition
(d) saprotrophic mode of nutrition. U

43. Select the incorrect statement about *Cuscuta*.
(a) It is also called Amarbel.
(b) Its leaf is modified into pitcher.
(c) It does not have chlorophyll.
(d) It derives nutrients from host plant. An

44. Mode of nutrition in *Cuscuta* is
(a) parasitic
(b) saprophytic
(c) symbiotic
(d) autotrophic. Ap

45. Select the mismatched pair.
(a) Venus flytrap – An insectivorous plant
(b) Black bread mould – A saprotroph
(c) *Rafflesia* – A total parasite
(d) *Rhizobium* – An autotroph U

46. Insectivorous plants are
(a) chemotrophs
(b) total parasites
(c) total heterotrophs
(d) autotrophs. U

47. Select the mismatched pair.
(a) Yeast – A parasite
(b) Bladderwort – Insectivorous plant
(c) Mistletoe – A partial parasite
(d) Bacteria – Saprophyte An

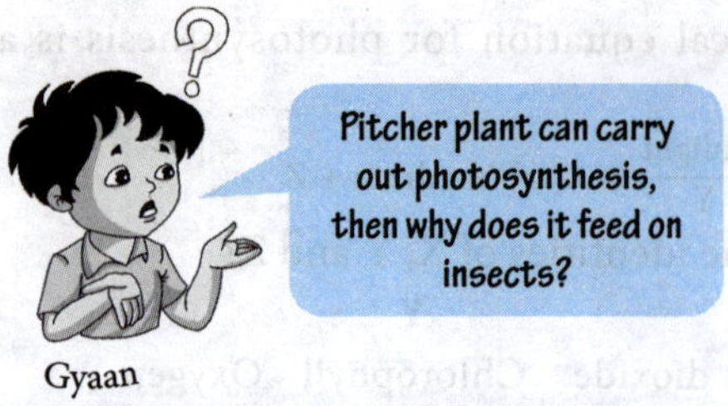

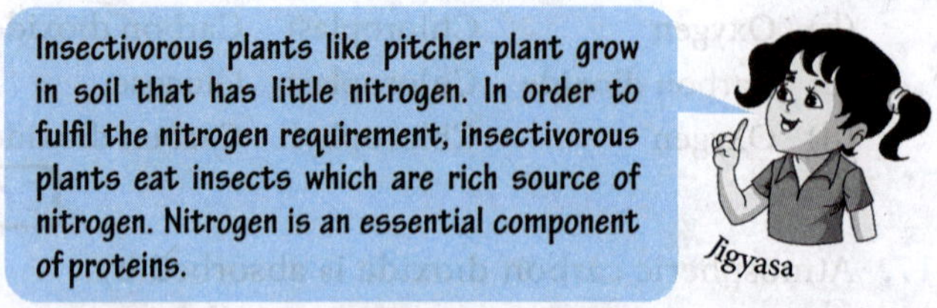

B. Passage based question.

48. Plants can synthesise their own food. However, some plants such as *Cuscuta* cannot make their own food because they lack __________. Such plants depend on the __________ plant on which they are climbing and take the valuable nutrients from them. Such types of plants are called __________. The mode of nutrition used by them is __________.

C. Figure based questions.

Direction (Q.No. 49 and 50) : Refer to the given figure and answer the following questions.

49. Identify the plant.

50. Identify mode of nutrition in this plants.

D. State True (T) or False (F) for the given statements.

51. Pitcher plant does not have chlorophyll. ☐

52. Like humans and animals, some plants also use heterotrophic mode of nutrition. ☐

53. The plant on which *Cuscuta* plant climbs is called parasite. ☐

54. Insect-eating plants are called insectivorous plants. ☐

55. Amarbel can secrete digestive juices to dissolve the insects they trap for nutrition. ☐

56. Pitcher plants form a bag-like structure with a lid by modifying their branches for trapping insects. ☐

57. Louse is a parasite as it sucks our blood. ☐

1.4 Saprotrophs

NCERT Page 5-7

A. Select the correct option.

58. The fluffy umbrella-like structures growing on rotting wood on rainy days is
(a) mushroom (b) pitcher plant
(c) bacteria (d) algae. U

59. Which of the following organisms takes nutrients in solution form from dead and decaying matter?
(a) Pitcher plant
(b) Fungi
(c) Mushroom
(d) Both (b) and (c) An

60. Lichen is an association of
(a) an alga and a fungus
(b) a green plant and a fungus
(c) a green plant and an alga
(d) bacteria and legume plant. R

61. Select the incorrect statement(s) about fungi.
(i) They lack chlorophyll.
(ii) They can grow only on dead and decaying matter.
(iii) They can cause diseases in crops and humans.
(iv) They are used in medicines.
(a) (i) and (iv) (b) Only (iv)
(c) (i), (ii) and (iv) (d) Only (ii) An

62. Symbiotic relationship is one, in which
(a) organisms feed on dead and decaying organic matter
(b) organisms trap and feed on insects
(c) two organisms live together and get benefited from each other
(d) one organism grows as parasite on the body of other. U

63. Some organisms secrete digestive juices over the decaying matter and absorb nutrients from it. This is called ______ mode of nutrition.
(a) autotrophic (b) saprotrophic
(c) parasitic (d) symbiotic U

64. A symbiotic relationship exists between bacteria and
(a) fungi
(b) leguminous plant
(c) lichen
(d) both (a) and (b) An

65. Select the correct statement about symbiosis.
(a) Both the organisms are benefited.
(b) Only one organisms is benefited.
(c) One gains and the other loses.
(d) No one is benefited. An

B. State True (T) or False (F) for the given statements.

66. Fungi lack green pigment and cannot make their own food. ☐

67. In a symbiotic relationship, only one organism is benefited. ☐

68. Mushroom is an autotroph. ☐

69. Symbiotic relationship exists only between fungi and algae. ☐

70. Some fungi can live in the roots of trees. ☐

71. In an association, the alga provides food to the fungus while the fungus provides shelter, water and minerals to the alga. ☐

C. Fill in the blanks.

72. Fungi can grow well in ______ and ______ weather.

73. Fungi can secrete ______ which converts dead and decaying matter into a solution.

74. Growth of fungi increases during ______ season.

75. In ______ relationship, organisms live together and share shelter and nutrients.

76. Fungal spores germinate and grow when they land on ______ and ______ surfaces.

77. Some fungi can live in the roots of trees where the tree provides ______ to the fungus and, in return, receives help from it to take up ______ and ______ from the soil.

D. Figure based questions.

Direction (Q.No. 78 and 79) : Refer to the given figure and answer the following questions.

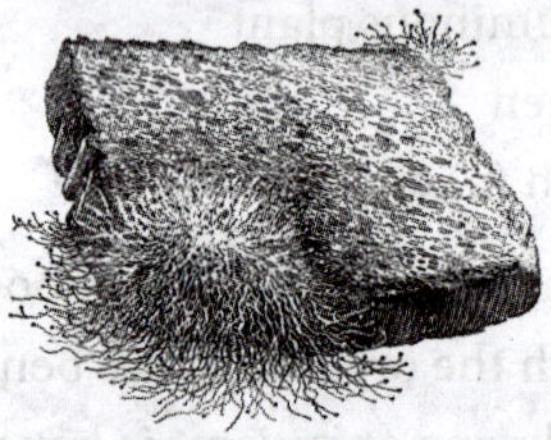

78. What are these cotton-like threads spread on the piece of bread?

79. What type of mode of nutrition such organisms have?

Direction (Q.No. 80 and 81) : Refer to the given figure and answer the following questions.

80. Name the organism.

81. Identify the mode of nutrition.

1.5 How Nutrients are Replenished in the Soil

NCERT Page 7-8

A. Select the correct option.

82. Fertilisers increase soil fertility by
(a) adding nutrients to soil
(b) adding oxygen to soil
(c) removing microbes from soil
(d) removing excess of moisture from soil. An

83. __________ can trap atmospheric nitrogen and convert it into soluble form.
(a) Mushroom
(b) *Rhizobium*
(c) Algae
(d) Both (a) and (b) R

84. *Rhizobium* lives in the roots of
(a) mango
(b) *moong*
(c) neem
(d) lotus. An

85. Select the incorrect statement(s) regarding *Rhizobuim*.
(i) It cannot make its own food.
(ii) It causes deficiency of nitrogen in the soil.
(iii) It lives in the roots of leguminous plants.
(iv) They shows symbiotic relationship.
(a) (i) and (ii)
(b) (ii) and (iv)
(c) (i) and (iv)
(d) Only (ii) An

86. Farmers do not need to add nitrogen fertiliser to the soil in which __________ are growing.
(a) fungi
(b) algae
(c) leguminous plants
(d) pitcher plants U

87. Which of the following options contains leguminous crops only?
(a) Rice, wheat and maize
(b) Wheat, rice and peas
(c) Peas, beans and maize
(d) Peas, beans and gram R

88. Soil nutrients can be replenished by
(a) growing leguminous plants.
(b) adding manure.
(c) adding fertiliser.
(d) all of these U

B. Passage based questions.

89. Fill in the blanks in the given passage.

Due to continuous absorption of nutrients from the soil by the plants, the soil become deficient in nutrients. __________ are added to the soil to enrich it with nutrients. They contain nutrients such as __________, __________, __________, etc. Plants require a lot of nitrogen to make __________. Plants cannot use the atmospheric nitrogen as such, and need it in a __________ form. This form of nitrogen is provided by the bacterium called __________. It fixes atmospheric nitrogen and convert it into usable form. This usable form can be easily absorbed by the plants. This nitrogen fixing bacterium lives in the roots of __________.

C. Figure based questions.

90. Tick the images of the plants that have *Rhizobium* in their roots.

Gram

Papaya

Peas

Groundnut

Mango

Cherry

Rajma

Moong

Water melon

PROGRESS CHECK

Check your score! If your score is

> 95%	EXCELLENT !	- Move on to the next chapter. You have mastered this chapter. Concepts are certainly on your fingertips.
95-85%	VERY GOOD !	- Revise once more thoroughly. Recognise your mistakes and work on them. You will master this chapter.
84-75%	GOOD!	- Work on your weak areas, master them and come back to this chapter in a few days.
74-65%	MEDIOCRE!	- Understand your weak areas and work on strengthening your concepts. Devote more time to master this chapter.
< 65%	NOT SATISFACTORY!	- This is where you fall behind from scoring well. Give special attention to this chapter. Work on clearing concepts and common errors.

NCERT Exemplar Problems

This section contains MCQs of **'NCERT Exemplar Problems'** Book.

1. Organisms which prepare food for themselves using simple naturally available raw materials are referred to as
(a) heterotrophs (b) autotrophs
(c) parasites (d) saprophytes.

2. In the absence of which of the following, will photosynthesis not occur in leaves?
(a) Guard cells (b) Chlorophyll
(c) Vacuole (d) Space between cells

3. Which of the following statements is/are correct?
(i) All green plants can prepare their own food.
(ii) Most animals are autotrophs.
(iii) Carbon dioxide is not required for photosynthesis.
(iv) Oxygen is liberated during photosynthesis.
Choose the correct answer from the options below.
(a) (i) and (iv) (b) (ii) only
(c) (ii) and (iii) (d) (i) and (ii)

4. Pitcher plant traps insects because it
(a) is a heterotroph
(b) grows in soils which lack in nitrogen
(c) does not have chlorophyll
(d) has a digestive system like human beings.

5. The term that is used for the mode of nutrition in yeast, mushroom and bread mould is
(a) autotrophic (b) insectivorous
(c) saprophytic (d) parasitic.

6. When we observe the lower surface of a leaf through a magnifying lens we see numerous small openings. Which of the following is the term given to such openings?
(a) Stomata (b) Lamina
(c) Midrib (d) Veins

7. Two organisms are good friends and live together. One provides shelter, water and nutrients while the other prepares and provides food. Such an association of organisms is termed as
(a) saprophytic (b) parasitic
(c) autotrophic (d) symbiotic.

8. Which of the following raw material is available in the air for photosynthesis?
(a) Oxygen (b) Carbon dioxide
(c) Nitrogen (d) Hydrogen

12. Select the incorrect statement regarding the organism shown in the given figure.

(a) It can synthesise its own food.
(b) It feeds on dead organic matter.
(c) It is a fungus.
(d) Some of its varieties are edible whereas some are poisonous.

13. A mutually beneficial relationship between two living organisms is called ________, and an example of this is ________.
(a) parasitism, mycorrhiza
(b) predation, mycorrhiza
(c) symbiosis, lichens
(d) parasitism, lichens

14. Select the correctly matched pair.
(a) Lichen – Parasitic relationship
(b) Fungi – Autotrophic
(c) Algae – Saprotroptic
(d) Sundew – Insectivorous

15. Which of the following statement is correct regarding the given structure?

(a) It is the insect-catching organ of a parasitic plant.
(b) It is the modification of leaf.
(c) It is the pitcher of plant Venus flytrap.
(d) It is the haustorium of a parasitic plant.

B. Fill in the blanks.

16. The stacks of thylakoids are called ________.
17. Amarbel produces special sucking parts called ________.
18. In *Nepenthes*, ________ is modified to form pitcher.
19. Insectivorous plants obtain ________ by eating insects.
20. ________ are the two bean-shaped cells that controls opening and closing of ________ in the leaves of plants.
21. *Rafflesia* is a/an ________ plant.
22. Heterotrophs are also called as ________.
23. ________ is a free-living bacteria that can fix atmospheric nitrogen.
24. ________ converts energy of the sun to make food for the plants.
25. The plant from which a parasitic plant derive its nutrients is called ________.
26. ________ is the thin outer membrane enclosing a cell.
27. Algae are ________ while fungi are ________.
28. Tapeworm is a ________.
29. Like pitcher plant, fungus can also produce ________ to convert their food into solution.
30. Amarbel is a common hindi name of ________.

C. State True (T) or False (F) for the given statements.

31. Unlike animals, plants never show heterotrophic mode of nutrition.
32. Insectivorous plants have both autotrophic and heterotrophic mode of nutrition.
33. *Rhizobium* bacteria are found in the root nodules of gram plants.
34. Mushroom grows in fresh soil.
35. Mistletoe is a partial parasite.
36. Glucose produced in leaves ultimately changes into starch.
37. Sundew is a carnivorous plant.
38. The fluid matrix in the chloroplast is called thylakoid.
39. Saprotrophs are green in colour due to presence of chlorophyll.

40. Autotrophs are dependent on bacteria for obtaining nitrogen as nutrition. ☐

41. Saprotrophs can synthesize their own food. ☐

42. Yeast and mushrooms are autotrophic organisms. ☐ U

43. In symbiotic relationship, only one organism is benefited always. ☐ U

44. During photosynthesis, carbon dioxide and water are used to make carbohydrates. ☐

45. Water and minerals are absorbed by the roots of plants from the soil. ☐

46. Leaves of desert plants are modified into spines to reduce the process of photosynthesis. ☐

47. Mistletoe is a partial heterotroph. ☐

48. Bacteria convert animal dung and other organic waste into manure. ☐ An

49. *Cuscuta* plants do not have chlorophyll, so they cannot synthesize their own food and die. ☐

50. Mushrooms can grow on decayed materials. ☐

D. Figure based questions.

51. After harvesting, the land of a farmer becomes deficient in nutrients. Select the plant from the given figures that will be grown by the farmer to replenish the soil with nutrients. Write down the reason for your choice.

Rose plant ☐

Pea plant ☐

Mango plant ☐ An

E. Match the columns.

52. Match the columns.

	Column I		Column II
A.	Conducts food from leaves to other parts of the plant	(i)	Symbiosis
B.	The process by which plants prepare their food	(ii)	Parasites
C.	Organisms that feed on dead and decaying organic matter	(iii)	Lichen
D.	An association of two organisms where both are benefited	(iv)	Chlorophyll
E.	Organisms that derive nutrition from their host	(v)	Phloem
F.	Green coloured pigment in plants	(vi)	Photosynthesis
G.	An association between a fungus and an alga	(vii)	Xylem
H.	Conducts nutrients from the roots to the leaves	(viii)	Saprophytes

VERY SHORT ANSWER TYPE QUESTIONS (VSA)

A. Answer the following questions in one or two words.

53. Name two chief modes of nutrition in organisms. R

54. What are the raw materials required for photosynthesis?

55. Give two examples of saprotrophic organisms.

56. Name two plants that exhibit partially heterotrophic mode of nutrition.

57. Name two leguminous plants.

58. A section of a leaf is shown below. Observe it carefully and label the different parts.

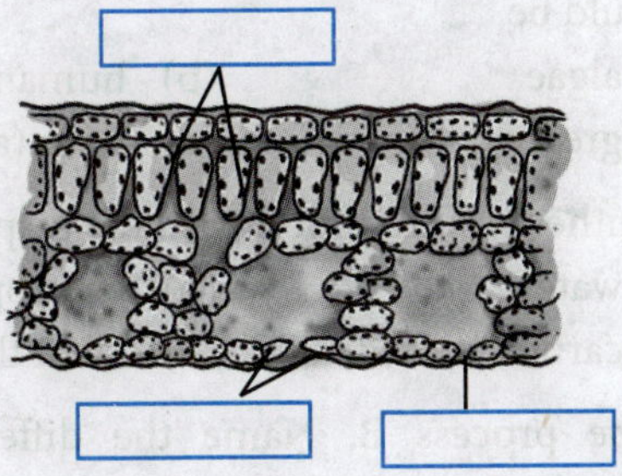

59. Where does the synthesis of food in a plant usually take place?

B. Circle the odd one out. Give reason for your choice.

60. Algae, Mushroom, *Cuscuta*, Mistletoe Ap
61. Carbon dioxide, Water, Starch, Chlorophyll
62. Lichen, Pitcher plant, Sundew, Venus flytrap
63. Human, Dog, Bird, Mango
64. *Azotobacter*, *Rhizobium*, Mushroom R

SHORT ANSWER TYPE QUESTIONS-I (SA-I)

65. Define the term 'photosynthesis'. Where does it take place in plants? An
66. Write down the difference between autotrophs and heterotrophs.
67. Define :
    (a) Thylakoids
    (b) Host
    (c) Mycorrhiza
    (d) Symbiosis
68. Write some benefits of fungi.
69. Why are leaves called the "food factories" of plants?
70. Gardener adding fertiliser into the soil in the given figure. Why?

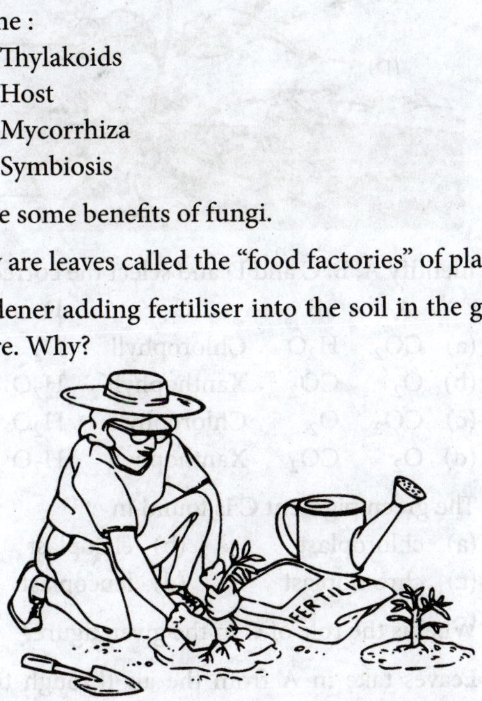

71. Identify the process taking place in the figure given below. Write down the raw materials required and the products obtained during this process.

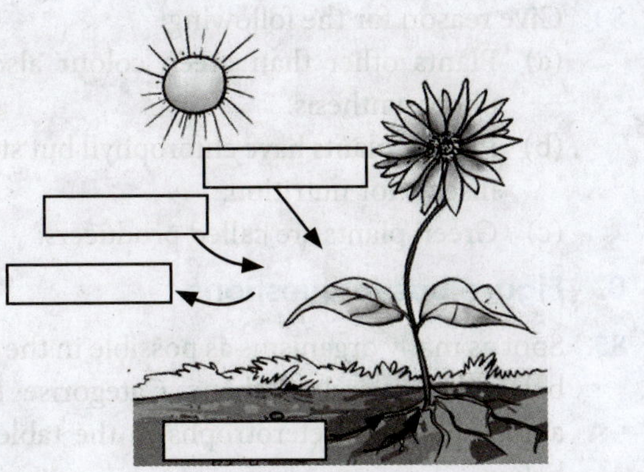

72. Identify the given figure and write its role during photosynthesis.

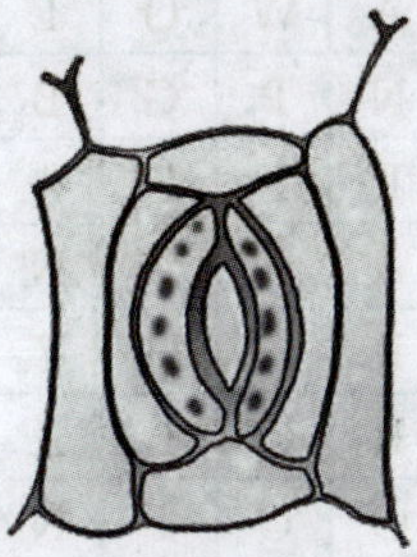

73. Write down the differences between algae and fungi.

SHORT ANSWER TYPE QUESTIONS-II (SA-II)

74. Why is photosynthesis important for the survival of organisms on the earth? An
75. What are conducting tissue? Name the two types of conducting tissues found in plants. Also write their functions.
76. What is the role of bacteria and fungi in cleaning our environment?
77. Explain why fertilisers and manures are needed in the fields from time to time?

LONG ANSWER TYPE QUESTIONS (LA)

78. How do plants synthesise foods other than carbohydrates? An
79. How do saprotrophs obtain their food? U
80. What are lichens? Describe the symbiotic relationship of lichens.
81. Write a note on the symbiotic association between leguminous plants and *Rhizobium*?
82. Explain the mechanism of trapping and eating insects by the pitcher plant with the help of diagram.
83. How are nutrients replenished in the soil? An

84. Give reason for the following:
(a) Plants other than green colour also perform photosynthesis.
(b) Pitcher plants have chlorophyll but still they eat insects for nutrition.
(c) Green plants are called producers.

B. Figure based questions.

85. Spot as many organisms as possible in the grid given below by encircling them. Categorise them into autotrophs and heterotrophs in the table provided below.

S	P	C	J	D	J	E	M	S	M
B	B	A	W	O	L	L	O	U	A
U	L	N	P	G	B	E	N	N	N
T	E	P	E	D	A	P	K	F	G
T	O	A	A	A	N	H	E	L	O
E	P	R	C	H	Y	A	Y	O	R
R	A	R	O	L	A	N	R	W	A
F	R	O	C	I	N	T	O	E	N
L	D	T	K	A	F	J	S	R	G
Y	O	O	G	Z	O	D	E	Q	E

Autotrophs	Heterotrophs

CASE BASED QUESTIONS (CBQs)

Case I : Read the given passage and answer the following questions :

All living organisms require energy to carry out life processes. Life processes include, respiration, excretion, response to stimuli, reproduction, growth and development. Energy is obtained from food through process B. Plants can synthesise their own food hence called as C, while animals are directly or indirectly dependent on plant to fulfil their food requirement thus, called as D.

86. The components required for process B are
(a) proteins and fats
(b) carbohydrates
(c) vitamins and minerals
(d) all of these.

87. C could be
(a) algae (b) humans
(c) green plants (d) both (a) and (c).

88. C synthesises their food with the help of
(a) water (b) chlorophyll
(c) carbon dioxide (d) all of these

89. Define process B. Name the different types of process B.

90. Why B is important for living organism?

Case II : Read the given passage and answer the following questions :

The process, by which green plants make their own food from A and B in the presence of sunlight and green pigment C, is called photosynthesis. During the process of photosynthesis, D is released.

The process can be represented in the form of equation :

$$A + B \xrightarrow[C]{\text{Sunlight}} \text{Carbohydrate} + D$$

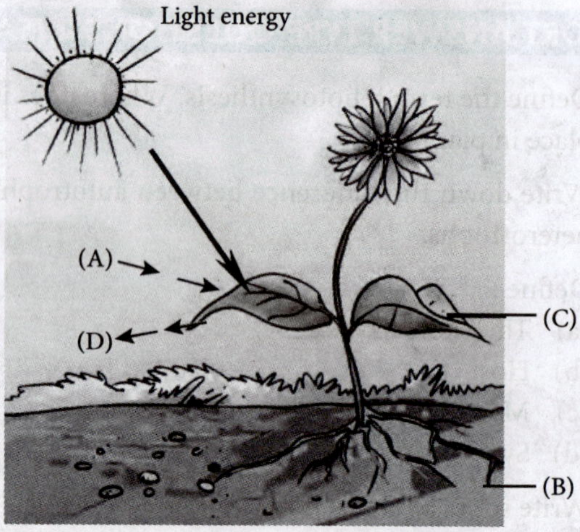

91. Identify A, B, C and D and select the correct option.

	A	B	C	D
(a)	CO_2	H_2O	Chlorophyll	O_2
(b)	O_2	CO_2	Xanthophyll	H_2O
(c)	CO_2	O_2	Chlorophyll	H_2O
(d)	O_2	CO_2	Xanthophyll	H_2O

92. The green pigment C is found in
(a) chloroplast (b) elaioplast
(c) chromoplast (d) leucoplast

93. What is the role of C in the given figure?

94. Leaves take in A from the air through tiny pores called
(a) Ostia (b) Stomata
(c) Porins (d) Stomium

95. Does the process of photosynthesis will occur, if the given plant is placed inside the bell jar having KOH crystals in petridish?

Case III : Read the given passage and answer the following questions :

P is a type of plant that lives in or on the body of another organism and derives nutrients from it. Q are green and synthesise their food *via.* photosynthesis but they also feed on insects to obtain their nitrogen nutrition. R is a special association in which two different kinds of organisms live together for shelter and nutrients, *e.g.*, lichens. Bacteria like S live in the roots of leguminous plants, provide the soluble form of nitrogen to leguminous plants and get food and shelter in return.

96. Amarbel is the example of ________.

(a) R (b) P
(c) S (d) Q

97. Why do Q feed on insects?

98. S helps to replenish the soil nutrients. S could be
(a) *Streptomyces* (b) *Amoeba*
(c) *Rhizobium* (d) All of these.

99. Match column I with column II and select the correct option from the given codes.

A. P	(i) Mycorrhiza
B. Q	(ii) *Rafflesia*
C. R	(iii) Sundew

(a) A – (i), B – (ii), C – (iii)
(b) A – (iii), B – (ii), C – (i)
(c) A – (ii), B – (iii), C – (i)
(d) A – (i), B – (iii), C – (ii)

100. Identify Q and mention its one characteristic.

ANSWER KEY

Practice Corner

1. (d) 2. (c) 3. (a) 4. (b) 5. Nutrition 6. Animals/Humans/Heterotrophs
7. heterotrophs 8. fats, proteins, carbohydrates, vitamins, minerals 9. plants 10. (a)
11. (b) 12. (c) 13. (c) 14. (c) 15. (d) 16. (a) 17. (b) 18. leaves, photosynthesis
19. starch 20. chlorophyll 21. Leaves 22. water, carbohydrates 23. bacteria
24. glucose 25. False 26. False 27. True 28. False 29. True 30. False 31. True
32. True 33. True 34. True 37. (b) 38. (d) 39. (c) 40. (d) 41. (a) 42. (b)
43. (b) 44. (a) 45. (d) 46. (d) 47. (a) 48. chlorophyll, host, parasites, parasitic mode of nutrition
49. Pitcher plant 51. False 52. True
53. False 54. True 55. False 56. False 57. True 58. (a) 59. (d) 60. (a) 61. (d)
62. (c) 63. (b) 64. (b) 65 (a) 66. True 67. False 68. False 69. False 70. True
71. True 72. hot, humid 73. digestive juices 74. rainy 75. symbiotic 76. wet, warm 77. food, water, minerals 80. Mushroom 81. Saprophytic mode of nutrition
82. (a) 83 (b) 84. (b) 85. (d) 86. (c) 87. (d) 88. (d)
90. Gram, peas, groundnut, rajma, moong

NCERT Exemplar Problems

1. (b) 2 (b) 3. (a) 4. (b) 5. (c) 6. (a) 7. (d) 8. (b)

A & R Corner

1. (d) 2. (a) 3. (a) 4. (d) 5. (b) 6. (a) 7. (c) 8. (d) 9. (b) 10. (d)
11. (a) 12. (c) 13. (b) 14. (c) 15. (a)

Exam Corner

1. (c) 2. (a) 3. (b) 4. (b) 5. (a) 6. (c) 7. (c) 8. (d) 9. (b) 10. (c)
11. (c) 12. (a) 13. (c) 14. (d) 15. (b) 16. grana 17. haustoria 18. leaf
19. nitrogen 20. Guard cells, stomata 21. parasitic 22. consumers 23. *Azotobacter*
24. Chlorophyll 25. host 26. Cell membrane 27. autotrophic, saprotrophic
28. parasite 29. digestive juices 30. *Cuscuta* 31. False 32. True 33. True 34. False.
35. True 36. True 37. True 38. False. 39. False. 40. True 41. False. 42. False. 43. False.
44. True 45 True 46. False 47. True 48. True 49. False 50. True 86. (d) 87. (d) 88. (d)
91. (a) 92. (a) 94. (b) 96. (b) 98. (c) 99. (c)

2 Nutrition in Animals

NCERT Notes

- Plants can make their own food by the process of **photosynthesis**, but animals are directly or indirectly dependent on plants to fulfill their food requirement and hence are **heterotrophic** in their mode of nutrition.
- Animals break down the complex food into simpler forms in their body by the process of **digestion**. Their body gets the required nutrition through three main steps:
  - Nutrient requirement
  - Mode of intake of food
  - Utilisation in the body

2.1 Different Ways of Taking Food

- The method of taking in food is different in different organisms.
  - Sucking – Bees and humming birds suck the nectar of plants whereas the human and many other animals feed on mother's milk. Lice adhere to the animals and suck their blood. Whereas mosquitoes have a long trunk-like mouth to suck the blood of humans.
  - Capturing and swallowing – Eagle capture the prey, uses its strong beak to tear the flesh and then swallows it. The jaws of many snakes enable them to swallow animals that may be much larger than the size of their head.
  - Scraping – Snail feed on small insects by the mode of scraping.
  - Siphoning – Butterflies usually feed on nectar of flower by siphoning. The tongue or proboscis is a tube like structure which extend and siphon water and nectar during feeding.
  - Filter feeders – Filter feeders filter water through specialised teeth, mouth parts, etc., discarding the water and keeping hold of small sized food particles. Examples include flamingo and ducks.

+ Starfish are marine invertebrates. They typically have a central disc and five arms. When the starfish feeds on animals covered by hard shell of calcium carbonate, it opens the shell of the prey animal and then pops out its stomach through its mouth to engulf the soft animals inside the shell and releases enzymes to digest it. The stomach then goes back into the body and food is slowly digested.

2.2 Digestion in Humans

- The food that we eat passes through a long muscular tube (called the alimentary canal) present inside our body. This tube begins at the mouth and ends at the anus.

- Parts of alimentary canal are :
  - Buccal cavity
  - Oesophagus (Food pipe)
  - Stomach
  - Small intestine
  - Large intestine
  - Rectum
  - Anus

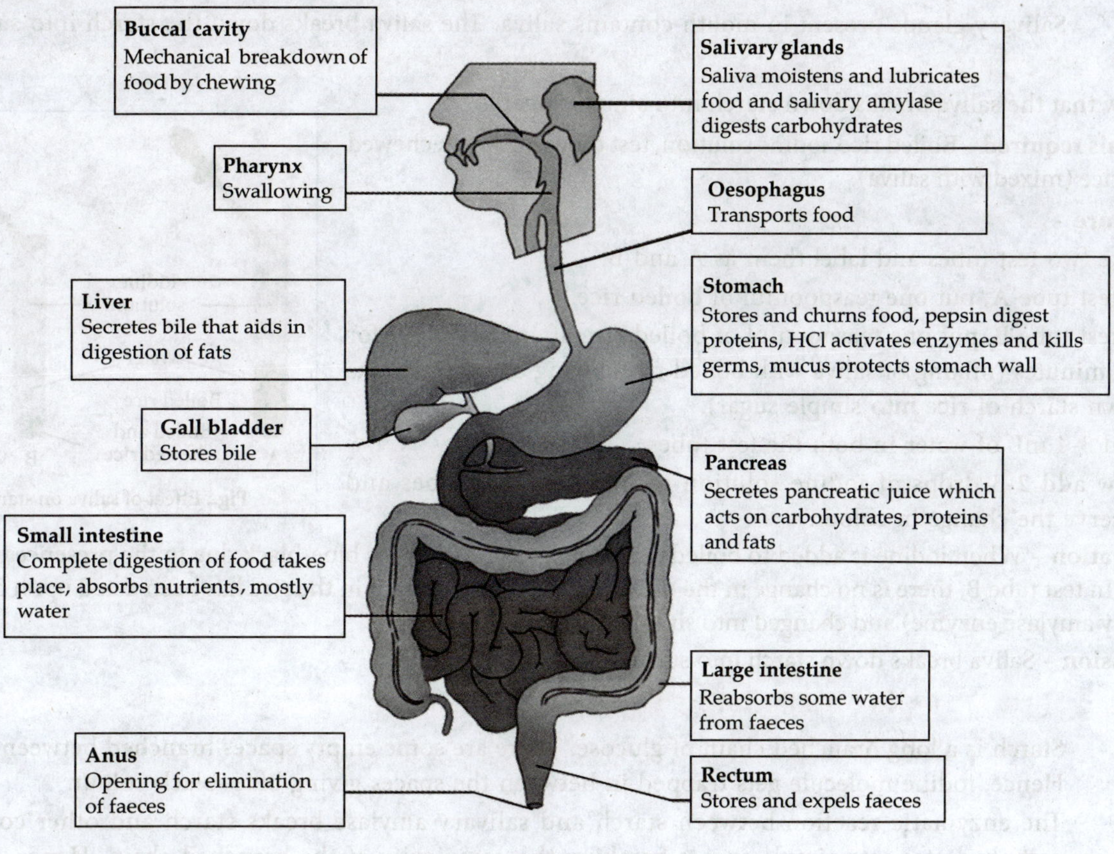

Fig.: Human digestive system

- Besides these parts, there are three digestive glands associated with the process of digestion of food. These are:
  - Salivary glands
  - Pancreas
  - Liver
- The alimentary canal, along with these associated digestive glands, form the overall digestive system.
- The digestive juices secreted by our internal organs, *e.g.*, stomach, liver, small intestine etc., contain enzymes which break down the complex food materials into simpler ones to make it readily absorbable.

The Mouth and Buccal Cavity

- The inner side of mouth which contains teeth, tongue and salivary glands is called **buccal cavity**.
- The process of taking food in the body is called ingestion.
- The first set of teeth are 20 small teeth, known as milk teeth.
- The second set of 32 large teeth which eventually replaces the milk teeth are called permanent teeth.

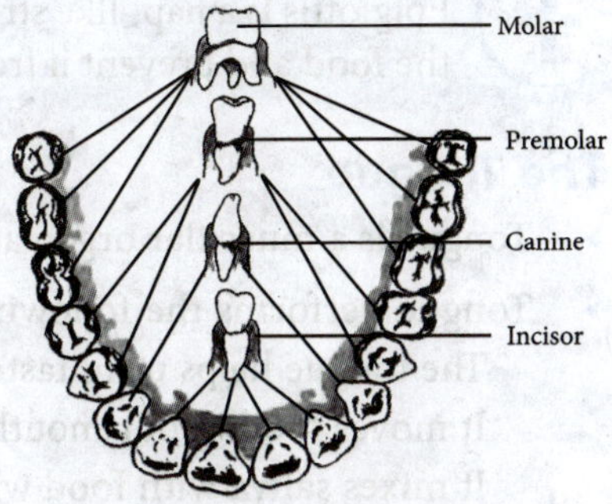

Fig.: Arrangement of teeth and different types of teeth

- Humans have four different types of teeth that perform different functions :
  - Incisors – Used for biting and cutting.
  - Canines – Used for piercing and tearing.
  - Premolars and molars – Used for crushing and grinding the food.
  - There are 8 incisors, 4 canines, 8 premolars and 12 molars in the mouth of an adult human.

+
- Enamel is the hardest substance in the human body that covers the outer portion of the teeth. It is made up of mineral salts of calcium and magnesium which can withstand quite high pressure.
- Salivary glands present in mouth contains saliva. The saliva breaks down the starch into sugars.

To show that the saliva breaks down starch into simple sugars.

Materials required – Boiled rice, iodine solution, test tubes, dropper, chewed boiled rice (mixed with saliva).

Procedure –

- Take two test tubes and label them as A and B.
- In test tube A, put one teaspoonful of boiled rice.
- In test tube B, put one teaspoonful of boiled rice after chewing it for 3-5 minutes (mixing of saliva with boiled rice during chewing breaks down starch of rice into simple sugar).
- Add 3-4 mL of water in both the test tubes.
- Now add 2-3 drops of iodine solution in both the test tubes and observe the change in colour.

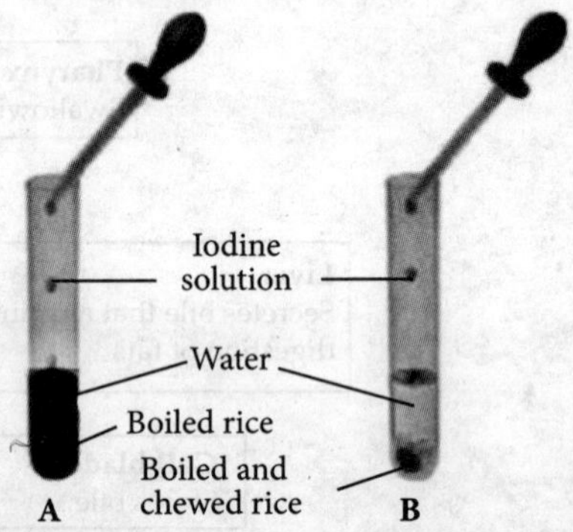

Fig.: Effect of saliva on starch

Observation – When iodine is added to boiled rice in test tube A, it turns blue-black due to the presence of starch in rice. In test tube B, there is no change in the colour as the starch present in the rice has been acted upon by saliva (salivary amylase enzyme) and changed into simple sugars.

Conclusion – Saliva breaks down starch into sugars.

+
- Starch is a long branched chain of glucose. There are some empty spaces branched between them. Hence, iodine molecule gets trapped in between the spaces giving blue–black colour.
- The enzymatic reaction between starch and salivary amylase breaks starch and other complex carbohydrates into simple sugars breaking the complexity of the branched chain. Hence, iodine molecule is not trapped in between and this is the reason why chewed rice fails to respond to iodine test.

- Harmful bacteria present in mouth breaks down the sugar present in the left over food and release lactic acid which gradually damages the teeth. This is called **tooth decay**.
- Choking sensation or hiccups occur when food particles enter the windpipe running adjacent to the food pipe.

+ Epiglottis is a flap–like structure present at the top of the windpipe. It closes the windpipe when we swallow the food and prevent it from entering into larynx.

The Tongue

- Tongue is a muscular organ attached to the floor of the buccal cavity.
- Tongue performs the following functions :
  - The tongue helps us to taste the food.
  - It moves food in our mouth between the teeth for chewing.
  - It mixes saliva with food while chewing.
  - It helps us to swallow the food.

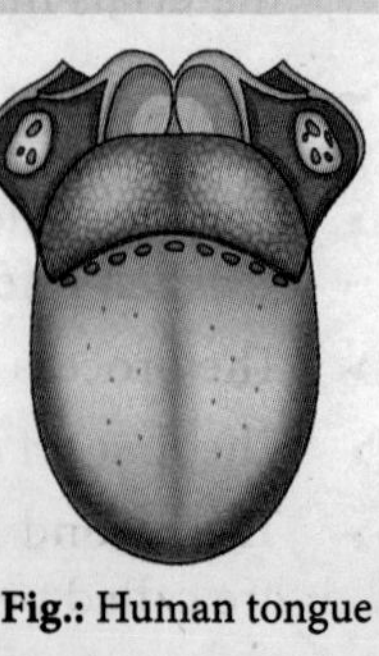
Fig.: Human tongue

The FoodPipe/Oesophagus

- The foodpipe is a long, narrow and muscular tube that connects the buccal cavity to the stomach.
- The muscles of oesophagus gently push food down to the stomach in a wave like action (contraction and relaxation) called **peristalsis**.

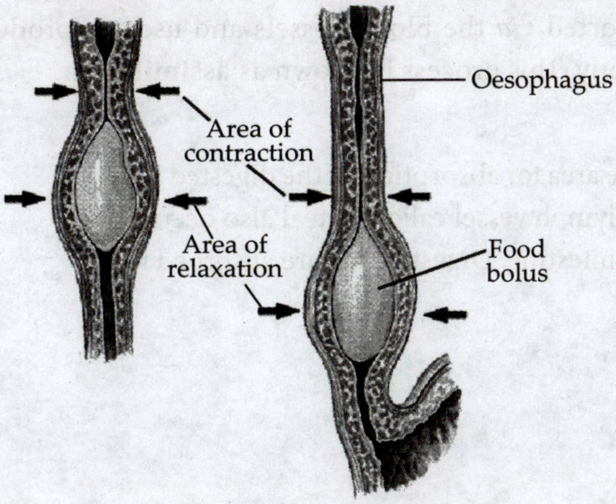

Fig. : Movement of food in oesophagus through peristalsis

The Stomach

- It is the widest organ of alimentary canal which receives food from food pipe at one end and opens into small intestine at the other end.
- The gastric juice contains :
  - Mucus which protects the lining of stomach from the action of enzymes and acids.
  - Hydrochloric acid (HCl) which kills bacteria that enter stomach along with food. It also makes acidic medium in stomach and help the digestive juices to act.
  - Digestive enzymes help to break down the proteins into simpler substances.

The Small Intestine

- It is the longest part of alimentary canal, about 7.5 metres long.
- The digestion of food is completed in small intestine.
- Secretions from liver and pancreas are poured into small intestine. Besides, it also secretes intestinal juice which completes digestion of all components of food.
  - Carbohydrates are digested to simple sugars like glucose.
  - Proteins are broken down to amino acids.
  - Fats are broken down into fatty acid and glycerol.

Liver

- **Liver** is the largest, reddish brown gland situated in upper part of the abdomen on right side. It secretes bile juice (an alkaline juice) which does not contain any enzyme but helps to break fats into tiny droplets that can be digested and absorbed easily.
- The bile secreted by liver is stored in a hollow pear-shaped organ **gall bladder.**

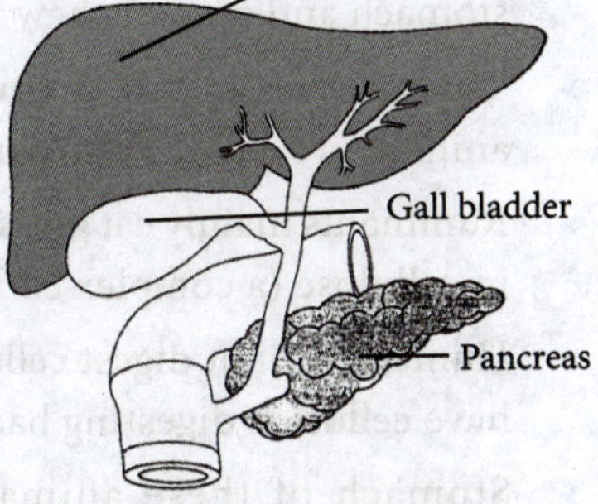

Fig.: Human liver, gall bladder and pancreas

Pancreas

- **Pancreas** is a leaf shaped cream coloured gland, present below the stomach that secretes pancreatic juice. The pancreatic juice acts on carbohydrates, fats and proteins and changes them into simpler forms.

Absorption of Digested Food in the Small Intestine

- The digested food is absorbed by thousands of finger like outgrowths in the inner walls of the small intestine known as **villi**.
- Each villus has a network of thin small blood vessels close to its surface.
- The absorbed food is transported *via* the blood vessels and used to produce energy and to build complex substances required by the body. This process is known as **assimilation**.

Villi increase the surface area for absorption of the digested food. A minute blind-ended lymph vessel called lacteal also occurs in each villus of the small intestine. Digested fats are absorbed into the lacteals.

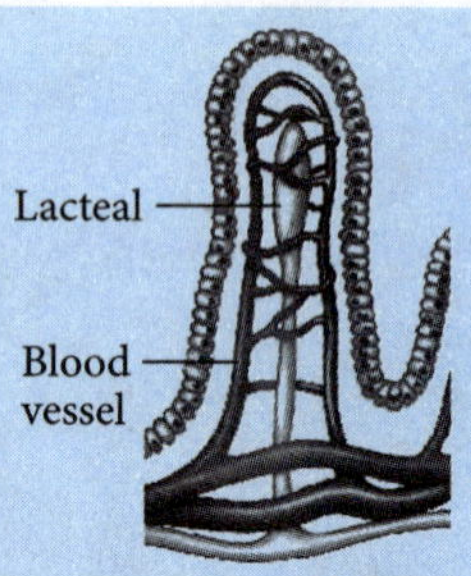

Fig.: Villus

Large Intestine

- Undigested and unabsorbed food passes into large intestine.
- The large intestine is about 1.5 m long. It is wider and shorter than small intestine.
- Its function is to absorb water and salts from the undigested food material.
- The left over waste part of food passes to the rectum and stored there as faecal matter which are eliminated through anus by the process of **egestion**.

- Diarrhoea is the condition of frequent passing of loose or liquid stools due to infection, food poisoning or indigestion.
- ORS (Oral Rehydration Solution), a solution of boiled and cooled water with a pinch of salt and sugar dissolved in it, is quick and effective remedy for diarrhoea.

2.3 Digestion in Grass Eating Animals

- Cud chewing herbivore animals also called ruminants. *e.g.*, cow, sheep, camel, buffalo and giraffe chew continuously. These animals bite off their food, chew it a little, swallow it and store it in a part of stomach. Here, food gets partially digested and is called cud.
- Later, the food is brought back into mouth from stomach and animal chew it for a second time.
- This process is called **rumination** and these animals are called **ruminants**.
- Ruminants mainly eat grass and leaf that are rich in cellulose (a complex carbohydrate).
- Humans cannot digest cellulose, as they do not have cellulose digesting bacteria.
- Stomach of these animals consists of four chambers :

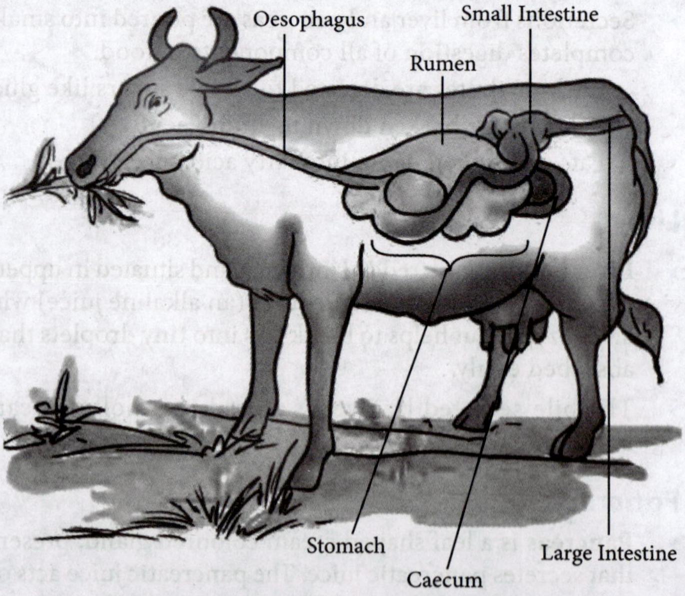

Fig.: Digestive system of ruminant

- Rumen – A large sac like structure which harbours large population of bacteria which helps in the digestion of cellulose.
- At resting stage of animal, the cud is brought back into the mouth and is chewed further. Since digestion occurs in rumen only, it is called the true stomach of ruminants.
- Reticulum – The second chamber in which the food moves from rumen.
- Omasum and Abomasum – The completely chewed food is passed to these chambers and ultimately to intestine for complete digestion.

➤ Horses and rabbits have a large sac-like structure called **caecum** which harbours cellulose digesting bacteria to digest the cellulose.

2.4 Feeding and Digestion in *Amoeba*

➤ *Amoeba*, a microscopic, unicellular organism possess false feet for the movement and capture of food, known as **pseudopodia**.

➤ When *Amoeba* comes in contact with food, it produces pseudopodia around it to trap the food in food vacuole.

➤ Digestive juices are secreted into the vacuole to digest the food and the undigested food is expelled by the process of egestion.

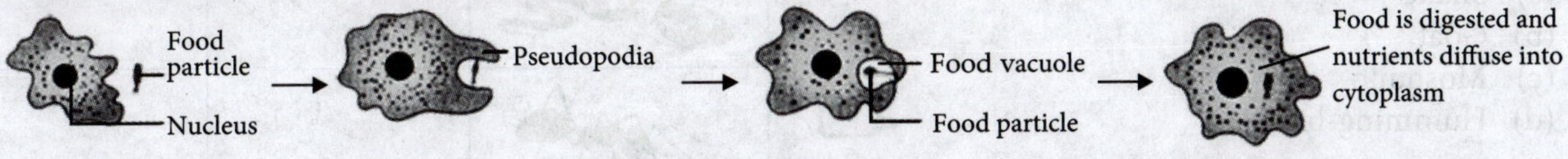

Fig.: Feeding and digestion in *Amoeba*

Amoeba possess contractile vacuole for maintaining water and salt balance in its cell. If an *Amoeba* is placed in distilled water, its contractile vacuole works faster and if a freshwater *Amoeba* is placed in salt solution, the contractile vacuole disappears.

Practice Corner

Extracted from NCERT

Assessment is complementary part of the learning process. It gives you a total insight whether the learning outcomes have been achieved or not. After going through the corresponding NCERT Textbook chapter, attempt these questions in exam like environment. Give yourself one mark for correct answer. A table is given at the end, that will help you plan your next step.

All the Best!

2.1 Different Ways of Taking Food

NCERT Page 11-12

A. Select the correct option.

1. Which of the following animals swallows its food?
   (a) Snake
   (b) Goat
   (c) Mosquito
   (d) Humming-bird
   U

2. What is the mode of intake of mosquito?
   (a) Sucking (b) Chewing
   (c) Swallowing (d) Gnawing
   R

3. Humming-birds ________ the nectar of plants.
   (a) swallow (b) suck
   (c) capture (d) scrape
   R

B. Fill in the blanks in the given passage.

4. Plants make their own food by the process of ________. Animals depend on plants directly or indirectly for nutrition. Animal nutrition includes nutrient requirement, ________ of food and its ________ in the body. The mode of taking food into the body varies in different organisms. ________, ________, ________ and ________ are some of the modes of intake of food into the body by different animals.

C. Figure based questions.

5. Identify the animals shown below and write down the kind of food they eat and their mode of feeding.
   U

Animal	Kind of food	Mode of feeding

6. Identify the organism in the image given below and explain how it takes in food from the surrounding.

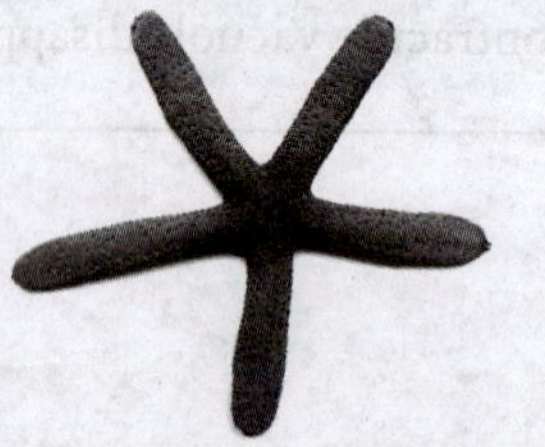

2.2 Digestion in Humans

NCERT Page 12-17

A. Select the correct option.

7. Which of the following is not a part of the buccal cavity?
   (a) Teeth
   (b) Tongue
   (c) Oesophagus
   (d) Salivary glands
   U

8. ________ teeth are used for tearing and piercing.
   (a) Incisor (b) Canine
   (c) Premolar (d) Molar
   R

9. ________ is the process of using the absorbed nutrients by the body cells for producing energy and for growth of the body.
   (a) Digestion (b) Absorption
   (c) Assimilation (d) Defecation
   R

10. Match the columns and select the correct option.

Column I		Column II
A. Mechanical breakdown of food by chewing	(i)	Stomach
B. Passage that connects mouth to stomach	(ii)	Gall bladder
C. Chemical digestion of protein starts	(iii)	Mouth
D. Stores bile	(iv)	Oesophagus

(a) A – (iii), B – (iv), C – (i), D – (ii)
(b) A – (iii), B – (iv), C – (ii), D – (i)
(c) A – (iv), B – (iii), C – (i), D – (ii)
(d) A – (ii), B – (iii), C – (iv), D – (i) An

11. The liver and pancreas, release their secretions into
(a) large intestine (b) small intestine
(c) stomach (d) oesophagus. R

12. Inner lining of the stomach does not secrete
(a) digestive juice
(b) mucus
(c) saliva
(d) hydrochloric acid. U

13. Which of the following options shows the correct sequence of the flow of food from mouth to anus?
(a) Mouth → Oesophagus → Stomach → Small intestine → Large intestine → Anus
(b) Mouth → Large intestine → Oesophagus → Stomach → Small intestine → Anus
(c) Mouth → Small intestine → Large intestine → Oesophagus → Stomach → Anus
(d) Mouth → Stomach → Small intestine → Large intestine → Oesophagus → Anus U

14. Digestion of food does not take place in
(a) small intestine (b) stomach
(c) large intestine (d) mouth. R

15. Part of the digestive system which helps in the formation of faeces is the
(a) large intestine (b) gall bladder
(c) small intestine (d) anus. U

16. Which of the following does not help during egestion of undigested food in humans?
(i) Rectum and anus
(ii) Stomach and liver
(iii) Small intestine and gall bladder
(iv) Large intestine and rectum
(a) Only (i)
(b) Only (iv)
(c) (ii) and (iii)
(d) (i), (iii) and (iv) U

17. Hydrochloric acid in stomach
(i) helps in the digestion of proteins.
(ii) kills bacteria present in ingested food.
(iii) converts starch into sugars.
(iv) provides an alkaline medium in the stomach.
(a) (ii) and (iv) (b) (i) and (ii)
(c) (ii) and (iii) (d) Only (ii) An

B. Fill in the blanks.

18. Saliva breaks down the _________ present in food into sugars.

19. Small intestine is about _________ long.

20. During the act of swallowing, the passage of _________ is closed to guide food into _________.

21. _________ and _________ are absorbed from the undigested food in the large intestine.

22. Bile helps in the digestion of _________ present in food.

23. The colour of a solution containing water and chewed boiled rice will not change when _________ solution is added.

24. The first set of teeth that grows during infancy is called _________.

25. _________ is a condition in which a person passes watery stool frequently.

26. _________ helps to mix saliva with the food during chewing.

27. The finger-like projections in the small intestine are called _________.

C. State True (T) or False (F) for the given statements.

28. Food which we eat passes through a continuous canal called digestive tract. ☐

29. The process of taking digested food into the blood vessels is called assimilation. ☐

30. Egestion of undigested food occurs from large intestine. ☐

31. Digestion of carbohydrates begins in the buccal cavity. ☐

32. Each villus has a network of thin and small blood vessels close to its surface. ☐

33. Pancreatic juice acts only on the fats present in food. ☐

34. Large intestine is wider and longer than the small intestine.

35. The stomach is like a flattened C-shaped bag.

36. Canines are used for chewing and grinding of food.

37. Food gets digested gradually while passing through the various parts of alimentary canal.

D. Figure based questions

38. Given figure shows arrangement of different types of teeth in adult human. Label the types of teeth in the boxes provided.

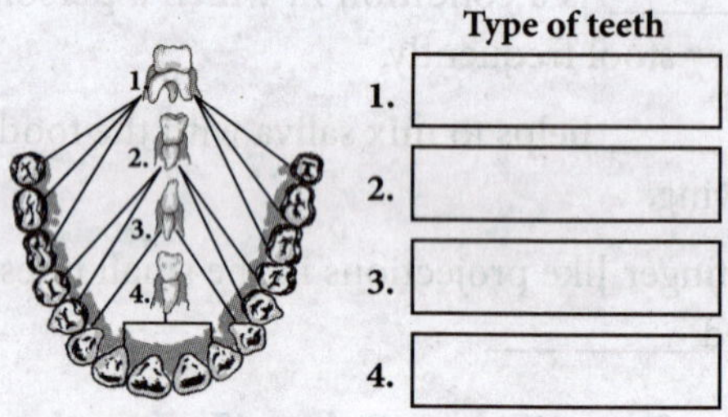

39. Given figure shows the human digestive system. Label its different parts in the boxes provided.
(a) Identify and label the digestive organ and gland 1 and 2 respectively in the box provided.
(b) Identify and label the digestive organs 3 and 4 respectively in the box provided.

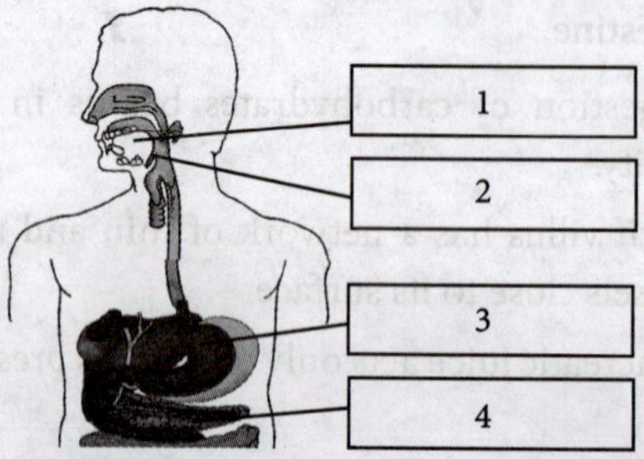

2.3 Digestion in Grass-Eating Animals

NCERT Page 17-18

A. Select the correct option.

40. Which of the following option enlist some ruminants?
(a) Human, Lion, Goat
(b) Goat, Cow, Camel
(c) Buffalo, Deer, Dog
(d) Cow, Buffalo, Pig **U**

41. Rumen is present between
(a) oesophagus and small intestine
(b) small intestine and large intestine
(c) oesophagus and stomach
(d) stomach and small intestine. **An**

42. Cows and buffaloes can digest grass due to the presence of ________ in their stomach.
(a) bacteria
(b) digestive juices
(c) hydrochloric acid
(d) bile juice **R**

43. Which of the following statements is correct regarding digestion in ruminants?
(a) Ruminants swallow food quickly and store it temporarily in rumen.
(b) When ruminants stop feeding, cud returns to the buccal cavity in small lumps to be chewed again.
(c) Ruminants are able to digest cellulose present in grass.
(d) All of these **U**

44. The part of the stomach where grass-eating animals store their swallowed food is the
(a) rumen (b) small intestine
(c) large intestine (d) rectum **R**

45. The partially-digested food inside the stomach of grass-eating animals is called
(a) bolus (b) cud
(c) cellulose (d) starch. **R**

B. Fill in the blanks.

46. The process where the partially digested food from stomach is returned back to the mouth and then chewed again, is called ________.

47. Cellulose is a type of ________.

48. A large sac-like structure in the stomach of ruminants where digestion of grass takes place is called ________.

49. Cud-chewing animals are also called as ________.

50. Animals like cows, buffaloes, etc., store the partially digested food in the __________.

C. Figure based question.

51. Label the different parts of the digestive system of ruminants.

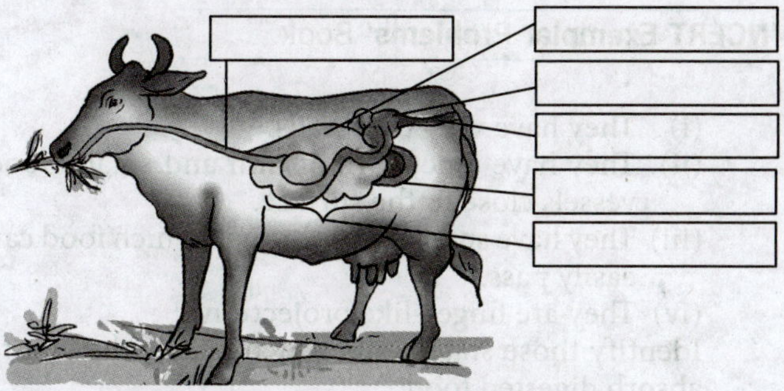

2.4 Feeding and Digestion in *Amoeba*

NCERT Page 18-19

A. Select the correct option.

52. Finger-like projections in *Amoeba* are called
(a) vacuoles (b) pseudopodia
(c) villi (d) caecum. R

53. *Amoeba* has
(i) a cell membrane
(ii) a dense nucleus
(iii) many vacuoles
(iv) only one pseudopodia.
(a) (i) and (iv) (b) (ii) and (iv)
(c) (iii) and (iv) (d) (i), (ii) and (iii) U

54. *Amoeba* uses its __________ to take in food.
(a) false feet (b) tentacles
(c) villi (d) skin R

55. *Amoeba* is a/an
(a) microscopic organism
(b) single-celled organism
(c) organism found in pond water.
(d) all of these U

56. *Amoeba* has small bubble-like structures in its cytoplasm called
(a) vacuoles (b) nucleus
(c) pseudopodia (d) cilia. R

B. Fill in the blanks.

57. Food is digested inside the food vacuole in *Amoeba* by secreting __________.

58. Digested food absorbed by *Amoeba* is used for __________, __________ and __________.

59. The undigested residue of food is expelled outside the body of *Amoeba* by the __________.

60. __________, also called false feet, help in movement and capture of food.

61. Cell structure of *Amoeba* consists of a __________, a round dense __________ and many __________.

62. When *Amoeba* senses food, it __________ it with the help of __________.

63. *Amoeba* is a microscopic __________ celled organism.

C. Figure based questions.

The given figure shows the steps involved in the intake and digestion of food by *Amoeba*.

64. Write down these steps in the space provided.

65. Identify the labelled part Y.

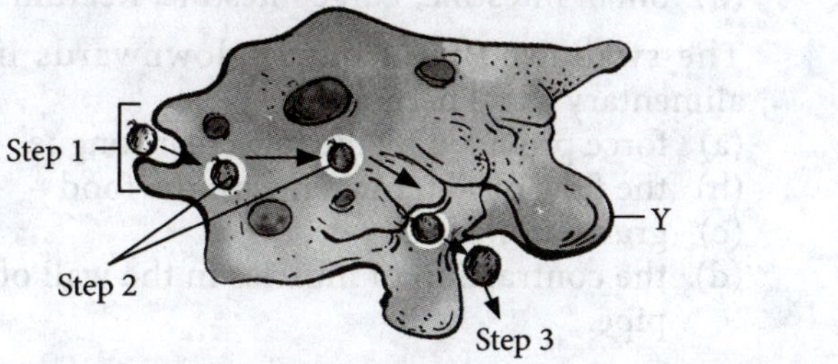

Step 1 : __________
Step 2 : __________
Step 3 : __________

PROGRESS CHECK

Check your score! If your score is

> 95%	EXCELLENT !	Move on to the next chapter. You have mastered this chapter. Concepts are certainly on your fingertips.
95-85%	VERY GOOD !	Revise once more thoroughly. Recognise your mistakes and work on them. You will master this chapter.
84-75%	GOOD!	Work on your weak areas, master them and come back to this chapter in a few days.
74-65%	MEDIOCRE!	Understand your weak areas and work on strengthening your concepts. Devote more time to master this chapter.
< 65%	NOT SATISFACTORY!	This is where you fall behind from scoring well. Give special attention to this chapter. Work on clearing concepts and common errors.

NCERT Exemplar Problems

This section contains MCQs of **'NCERT Exemplar Problems'** Book.

1. Given below from (i) to (iv) are some food items.
(i) Boiled and mashed potato
(ii) Glucose solution
(iii) A slice of bread
(iv) Mustard oil
Which of the above will give blue-black colour when tested with iodine?
(a) (i) and (ii) (b) (i) and (iii)
(c) (ii) and (iii) (d) (iii) and (iv)

2. Which of the following pair of teeth differ in structure but are similar in function?
(a) Canines and incisors
(b) Molars and premolars
(c) Incisors and molars
(d) Premolars and canines

3. Read carefully the terms given below. Which of the following sets is the correct combination of organs that do not carry out any digestive functions?
(a) Oesophagus, Large intestine, Rectum
(b) Buccal cavity, Oesophagus, Rectum
(c) Buccal cavity, Oesophagus, Large intestine
(d) Small intestine, Large intestine, Rectum

4. The swallowed food moves downwards in the alimentary canal because of
(a) force provided by the muscular tongue
(b) the flow of water taken with the food
(c) gravitational pull
(d) the contraction of muscles in the wall of food pipe.

5. The acid present in the stomach
(a) kills the harmful bacteria that may enter along with the food
(b) protects the stomach lining from harmful substances
(c) digests starch into simpler sugars
(d) makes the medium alkaline.

6. The finger-like outgrowths of *Amoeba* help to ingest food. However, the finger-like outgrowths of human intestine help to
(a) digest the fatty food substances
(b) make the food soluble
(c) absorb the digested food
(d) absorb the undigested food.

7. Read the following statements with reference to the villi of small intestine.
(i) They have very thin walls.
(ii) They have a network of thin and small blood vessels close to the surface.
(iii) They have small pores through which food can easily pass.
(iv) They are finger-like projections.
Identify those statements which enable the villi to absorb digested food.
(a) (i), (ii) and (iv) (b) (ii), (iii) and (iv)
(c) (iii) and (iv) (d) (i) and (iv)

8. The false feet of *Amoeba* are used for
(a) movement only
(b) capture of food only
(c) capture of food and movement
(d) exchange of gases only.

9. The enzymes present in the saliva convert
(a) fats into fatty acids and glycerol
(b) starch into simple sugars
(c) proteins into amino acids
(d) complex sugars into simple sugars.

10. Cud is the name given to the food of ruminants which is
(a) swallowed and undigested
(b) swallowed and partially digested
(c) properly chewed and partially digested
(d) properly chewed and completely digested.

11. Choose the correct order of terms that describe the process of nutrition in ruminants.
(a) Swallowing → partial digestion → chewing of cud → complete digestion
(b) Chewing of cud → swallowing → partial digestion → complete digestion
(c) Chewing of cud → swallowing → mixing with digestive juices → digestion
(d) Swallowing → chewing and mixing → partial digestion → complete digestion

12. Cellulose-rich food substances are good source of roughage in human beings because
(a) human beings do not have cellulose digesting enzymes
(b) cellulose gets absorbed in the human blood and converts into fibres
(c) the cellulose-digesting bacteria convert cellulose into fibres
(d) cellulose breaks down into smaller components which are egested as roughage.

A&R Corner

Directions : In the following questions, a statement of assertion is followed by a statement of reason. Mark the correct choice as :
(a) If both assertion and reason are true and reason is the correct explanation of assertion.
(b) If both assertion and reason are true but reason is not the correct explanation of assertion.
(c) If assertion is true but reason is false.
(d) If both assertion and reason are false.

1. **Assertion :** Liver is the largest gland in the body.
Reason : Liver is situated in the lower part of abdomen.

2. **Assertion :** Villi are finger-like outgrowths present in the inner walls of small intestine.
Reason : Villi increases the surface area for absorption of food.

3. **Assertion :** Ruminants feed on cellulose rich food.
Reason : Ruminants possess longer small intestine.

4. **Assertion :** *Amoeba* constantly change its shape and position.
Reason : *Amoeba* is multi-celled organism.

5. **Assertion :** The stomach of ruminants consists of three chambers.
Reason : Ruminants need very little time for feeding.

6. **Assertion :** Incisors are front teeth.
Reason : Incisors are used for crushing and grinding of food.

7. **Assertion :** Most of the protein digestion occurs in stomach.
Reason : The acidic environment of stomach helps in protein digestion.

8. **Assertion :** In starfish, the stomach pops out through mouth to feed on animal covered by hard shell.
Reason : Stomach engulf the soft animals inside the shell and release enzymes to digests it.

9. **Assertion :** Each tooth is embedded in separate socket in gums.
Reason : Permanent set of teeth last throughout the life.

10. **Assertion :** The chemical digestion of food in mouth is done by saliva.
Reason : Saliva contains enzymes for digestion of fats.

11. **Assertion :** Butterflies suck nectar from flowers.
Reason : Butterflies take in food by siphoning.

12. **Assertion :** Oral rehydration therapy is given to the patients suffering from diarrhoea.
Reason : Oral rehydration therapy decreases chances of human deaths from dehydration.

13. **Assertion :** Human beings cannot eat and digest cellulose.
Reason : The enzymes required for digestion of cellulose are absent in humans.

14. **Assertion :** Milk teeth are the first set of teeth that erupt during infancy.
Reason : Milk teeth are 32 in number.

15. **Assertion :** Bile is secreted from the gall bladder.
Reason : Bile plays an important role in the digestion of fats and carbohydrates.

Exam Corner

This section comprises of different types of questions:

- **Objective Type Questions :** These are **one mark** questions.
- **Very Short Answer Type Questions (VSA) :** These are **one mark** questions.
- **Short Answer Type Questions-I (SA-I) :** These are **two marks** questions.
- **Short Answer Type Questions-II (SA-II) :** These are **three marks** questions.
- **Long Answer Type Questions (LA) :** These are **five marks** questions.
- **Case Based Questions (CBQs) :** These are case study/passage based questions.

OBJECTIVE TYPE QUESTIONS

A. Select the correct option.

1. Which teeth in the given figure are incorrectly labelled?

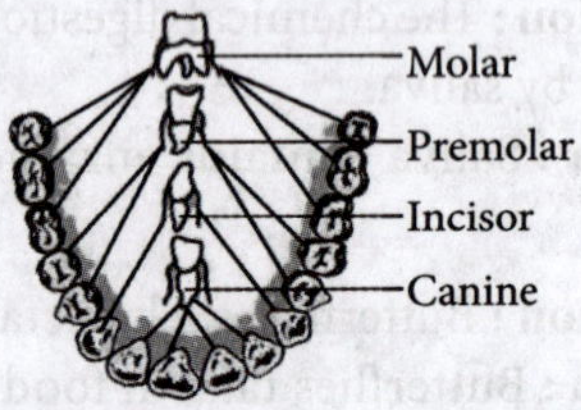

(a) Incisor and canine
(b) Canine and premolar
(c) Premolar and molar
(d) Canine and molar U

2. ________ are the pointed teeth present in our mouth.
(a) Canines (b) Incisors
(c) Molars (d) Premolars

3. Complete digestion of food takes place in the
(a) stomach (b) small intestine
(c) large intestine (d) rectum.

4. Which of the following statements is not true?
(a) Mode of taking food into the body varies in different organisms.
(b) Bees and humming birds suck the nectar of flowers.
(c) *Hydra* catches food with the help of its tentacles.
(d) Lice and mosquitoes chew their food by grinding with teeth.

5. The dental formula for adult human beings is
(a) 2123/2123 (b) 3142/3143
(c) 2102/2102 (d) 3131/3121 R

6. *Amoeba* is a single-celled organism, which sends out one or more finger-like projections called ________ for movement and capture of food.
(a) food vacuole
(b) pseudopodia
(c) cilia
(d) contractile vacuole

7. The teeth that are used for biting an apple are
(a) incisors (b) canines
(c) premolars (d) molars. Ap

8. Select the incorrect statement out of the following.
(a) Large intestine is called large because its length is greater than small intestine.
(b) Minerals and vitamins do not need to be broken down during digestion.
(c) Mucus of stomach protects the lining of stomach from the action of enzymes and acids.
(d) Small intestine is smaller in diameter than large intestine.

9. Given lists contain characteristics of organ A and organ B of human body.

Organ A	Organ B
– Food is completely digested here.	– Water absorption takes place here.
– The substance produced is carried to all parts of the body.	– The substance produced is expelled out of the body.

Refer to the characteristics and select the option which correctly identifies organ A and B.

	Organ A	Organ B
(a)	Small intestine	Oesophagus
(b)	Stomach	Large intestine
(c)	Large intestine	Liver
(d)	Small intestine	Large intestine

An

10. Which of the following is called the true stomach in ruminants?
(a) Abomasum (b) Omasum
(c) Rumen (d) Reticulum

11. Select the correct match(es).

(i) Digestion – Breakdown of food into simpler forms

(ii) Assimilation – Expulsion of undigested food from the body

(iii) Absorption – Utilisation of absorbed food

(iv) Egestion – Release of digested food from the body.

(a) Only (i) (b) Only (iv)

(c) (iii) and (iv) (d) (ii) and (iii)

12. Complete the given analogy.

________ : Cellulose : : Human : Starch

(a) Lion (b) Cow

(c) Cat (d) Pigeon

An

13. Select the correct statements.

(i) The liver secretes bile juice which is stored in gall bladder.

(ii) Teeth help in mixing food with saliva.

(iii) There are 32 teeth in human adult.

(iv) Each child possesses 10 milk teeth.

(a) (i) and (ii) (b) (i) and (iii)

(c) (i), (iii) and (iv) (d) (i) and (iv)

14. In assimilation,

(i) glucose is used during cellular respiration.

(ii) bile is used to make fatty acids.

(iii) amino acids are used for building and repairing of body parts.

(iv) glycerols are used to build new proteins.

(a) (i) and (iii) (b) (i), (ii) and (iii)

(c) (i), (ii) and (iv) (d) (ii) and (iii)

U

15. Select the incorrect statements.

(i) Papillae are a part of small intestine.

(ii) There are finger-like projections in the large intestine called villi.

(iii) Pancreas secretes bile juice and mucus.

(iv) Abomasum in ruminants possesses micro-organisms that digest cellulose.

(a) (i) and (iii)

(b) (ii) and (iii)

(c) (i) and (iv)

(d) (i), (ii), (iii) and (iv)

16. Study the flow chart given below.

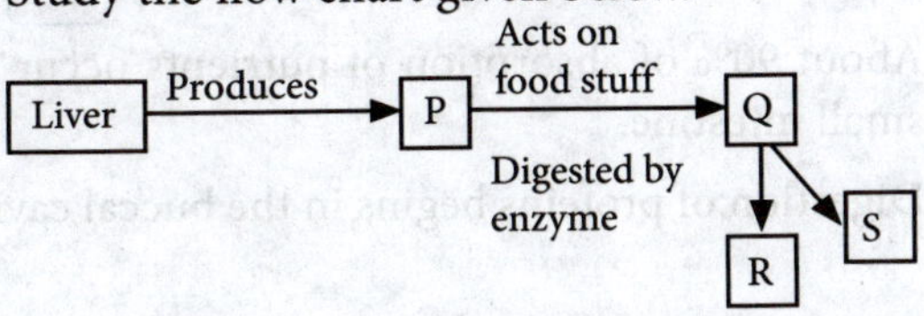

Select the correct option for P, Q, R and S.

	P	Q	R	S
(a)	Digestive juice	Proteins	Fatty acids	Glycerol
(b)	Bile	Fats	Fatty acids	Glycerol
(c)	Bile	Proteins	Amino acids	Peptides
(d)	Digestive juice	Fats	Glucose	Amino acids

Ap

17. Given is a match of number and role of different teeth present in an adult human. Select the correct match(es).

	Teeth	Number (Total)	Role
(i)	Incisors	12	Biting and cutting
(ii)	Canines	4	Tearing and piercing
(iii)	Premolars	8	Chewing and grinding
(iv)	Molars	8	Crushing and grinding

(a) (ii) and (iii) (b) Only (iv)

(c) (i) and (iii) (d) (iii) and (iv)

18. Inside our stomach,

(i) the mucus protects the inner lining of stomach from the action of HCl.

(ii) partial digestion of food occurs.

(iii) fats are converted to tiny droplets.

(iv) no further digestion of carbohydrates occurs due to the acidic condition in it.

(a) (ii) and (iii) (b) (i), (ii) and (iv)

(c) Only (ii) (d) Only (iv)

19. Select the incorrect statement(s).

(i) Food is pushed down the oesophagus with the help of the movement of its wall.

(ii) Proteins are digested in the stomach completely.

(iii) Digestion starts from the buccal cavity of the digestive system.

(iv) The third molars in adults are referred to as wisdom teeth.

(a) (ii) and (iii) (b) Only (ii)

(c) (ii), (iii) and (iv) (d) (ii) and (iv)

U

20. The simple form of nutrients obtained after digestion gets absorbed in (I). The remaining matter goes into the (II) where excess of (III) is absorbed. The remaining waste is called (IV) and it is pushed into the rectum where it is stored before releasing through anus.

Read the above paragraph and select the correct option for (I), (II), (III) and (IV).

	(I)	(II)	(III)	(IV)
(a)	small intestine	rectum	water	urine
(b)	stomach	small intestine	nutrients	faeces
(c)	large intestine	small intestine	water	bolus
(d)	small intestine	large intestine	water	faeces

B. Fill in the blanks.

21. Animals are called __________, as they are directly or indirectly dependent on plants for food.

22. __________ are sharp, pointed teeth, used for tearing food. U

23. __________ secretes __________ that aids in the digestion of fats.

24. The muscles of oesophagus gently push food down to the __________ in a wave-like action called __________.

25. During digestion, carbohydrates get broken down into __________, fats into __________ and __________, and proteins into __________.

26. __________ is the process of using the absorbed nutrients by the body for producing energy and for growth of the body.

27. The large intestine is __________ and __________ than the small intestine.

28. __________ are able to digest cellulose due to the presence of cellulose-digesting bacteria present in the __________ of their stomach.

29. The __________ of the small intestine increase the surface area for absorption of digested food.

30. The condition in which watery stools are passed out from the body is called __________.

31. *Amoeba* feeds with the help of __________ while *Hydra* feeds with the help of __________. R

32. The semi-digested food that is chewed again by ruminants is called __________.

33. Digestion mainly occurs in __________ and __________.

34. Saliva is secreted by the __________ present in our mouth which can convert __________ into __________.

35. Stomach of ruminants is divided into four parts namely, __________, __________, __________ and __________.

36. The __________ sucks up the blood of animals with its proboscis.

37. Small intestine receives secretions from the __________ and __________ and also secretes its own intestinal juice. U

38. __________ are the animals which can bring back the swallowed food to the mouth to chew again.

C. State True (T) or False (F) for the given statements.

39. Tongue helps in mixing the saliva with food. ☐

40. Bile breaks up fat into tiny droplets that can be digested more easily. ☐

41. Complete digestion of food occurs in large intestine. ☐

42. Oesophagus transfers food from mouth to stomach. ☐

43. Digestion of starch begins in the stomach and completes in small intestine. ☐

44. Direction of the peristaltic movement is reversed during vomiting. ☐

45. During assimilation, digested food passes into the blood in humans. ☐

46. There are different taste buds present on the surface of our tongue. ☐

47. Pancreatic juice acts only on proteins ☐. U

48. Villi help in digestion of food in small intestine. ☐

49. *Amoeba* feeds with the help of its villi. ☐

50. Digestion of starch takes place only in the stomach. ☐

51. Saliva helps in the breaking down of proteins into amino acids. ☐

52. Like cattle, humans can also digest cellulose. ☐

53. Epiglottis prevents the entry of food into windpipe. ☐

54. Food moves down the oesophagus to the stomach in a wave-like action called peristalsis. ☐

55. Glucose is broken down into carbon dioxide and water during digestion. ☐

56. Stomach is the largest gland in our body. ☐ R

57. About 90% of absorption of nutrients occur in the small intestine. ☐

58. Digestion of proteins begins in the buccal cavity. ☐

D. Match the columns.

59.

Column I	Column II
A. Stores undigested food for egestion	(i) Absorption
B. Passage of food in soluble form into blood	(ii) Rectum
C. Provides acidic medium for digestive juices	(iii) Hydrochloric acid
D. Breaking down of food into simpler compounds	(iv) Small intestine
E. Receives bile, pancreatic juice and secretes intestinal juice	(v) Digestion

(a) A–(ii), B–(i), C–(iii), D–(v), E–(iv)
(b) A–(ii), B–(iii), C–(i), D–(v), E–(iv)
(c) A–(i), B–(iv), C–(ii), D–(iii), E–(v)
(d) A–(iv), B–(i), C–(iii), D–(v), E–(ii)

60.

Column I	Column II
A. Protects inner lining of the stomach	(i) Fats
B. Utilisation of absorbed nutrients to produce energy	(ii) Assimilation
C. Broken down into fatty acids and glycerol after digestion	(iii) Egestion
D. Expulsion of undigested food from body	(iv) Mucus

(a) A–(ii), B–(i), C–(iii), D–(iv)
(b) A–(i), B–(iv), C–(iii), D–(ii)
(c) A–(iv), B–(ii), C–(i), D–(iii)
(d) A–(iv), B–(ii), C–(iii), D–(i) U

E. Figure based question.

61. Observe the images given below and answer the questions that follow:

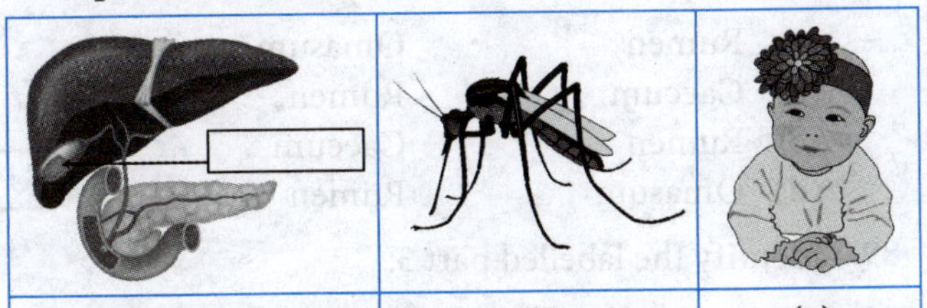

(a) (b) (c)

(i) Label the part of digestive system shown in figure (a) and write its function.
(ii) What is the kind of food and mode of feeding of the organism shown in figure (b)?
(iii) Name the type of set of teeth present in the girl shown in the figure (c).

VERY SHORT ANSWER TYPE QUESTIONS (VSA)

A. Answer the following in one or two words.

62. Write the names of any two glands associated with the digestive system.
63. Write the names of any two chambers of the stomach of ruminants. R
64. Write the function of molar teeth.
65. Write the name of the J-shaped organ of the alimentary canal.
66. Write the name of the large cream-coloured gland which is located just below the stomach.
67. Unscramble the words with the help of the given clues.

	Scrambled words	Clues	Words
(i)	A I O P D O D U P S E	Help *Amoeba* to feed nearby food	______
(ii)	I R V L E	Largest gland in the body	______
(iii)	S E P A O H U G S O	Muscular pipe that pushes food from mouth to stomach	______
(iv)	M R I U A N S T N	Have a complex stomach of four chambers	______
(v)	T E H O R T O P H E S R	They depend on plants for food	______

SHORT ANSWER TYPE QUESTIONS-I (SA-I)

68. Define: (a) rumination, (b) peristalsis.
69. What is the difference between assimilation and absorption? U
70. Write a note on the functions of human tongue.
71. What is the function of epiglottis in our body?
72. Briefly discuss the structure of stomach.

SHORT ANSWER TYPE QUESTIONS-II (SA-II)

73. Write four differences between milk teeth and permanent teeth.
74. What is the function of : (a) hydrochloric acid, (b) saliva, (c) bile juice?
75. How does villi help during absorption? An

76. How tooth decay is caused? How can we prevent tooth from decaying?

LONG ANSWER TYPE QUESTIONS (LA)

77. With the help of a labelled diagram, describe the process of ingestion in *Amoeba*? U

78. Draw a neat and labelled diagram of human digestive system.

79. How the food gets digested in different parts of the digestive tract of humans?

80. Give reason for the following statements.
(a) Oral Rehydration Solution (ORS) is given to the patient suffering from diarrhoea.
(b) Well-chewed rice does not give a positive iodine test.
(c) Humans cannot digest cellulose like cattle.
(d) We should not talk while eating food. An

CASE BASED QUESTIONS (CBQs)

Case I : Read the given passage and answer the following questions :

The digestive tract and the associated glands together constitute the digestive system. A part of alimentary canal of human which starts from the mouth and ends at the anus is given below.

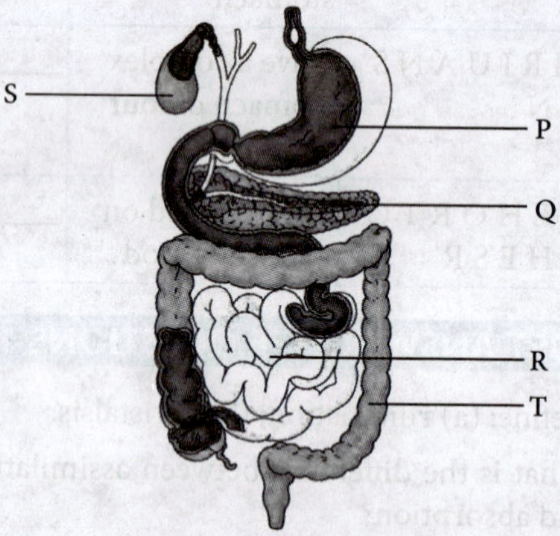

81. The widest and the longest portion of alimentary canal respectively are
(a) P and R (b) Q and P
(c) P and Q (d) R and P

82. In which part does the partial digestion of food occur?
(a) R (b) Q
(c) P (d) S

83. Select the incorrect statement.
(a) The liver secretes bile juice which is stored in S.
(b) The complete digestion of food takes place in R.
(c) The inner surface of Q has villi to increase the surface area for absorption.
(d) Bile helps in neutralisation of HCl of semi-solid food that comes from P.

84. What is the function of part T?

85. Explain how the digestive juice found in S help in digestion?

Case II : Read the given passage and answer the following questions :

The plant eating mammals like ruminants possess a unique digestive system that allows them to better use energy from fibrous plant material than other herbivores. Given below is the alimentary canal of a ruminant.

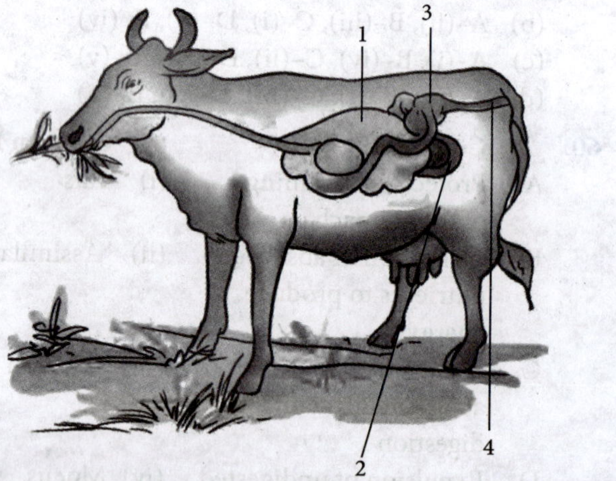

86. In which part does partially chewed food get stored?
(a) 1 (b) 2
(c) 3 (d) 4

87. Identify the sac like structure in horses which contains cellulose digesting bacteria.
(a) 3 (b) 4
(c) 2 (d) 1

88. Which option correctly identifies the labelled parts? U

	1	2
(a)	Rumen	Omasum
(b)	Caecum	Rumen
(c)	Rumen	Caecum
(d)	Omasum	Rumen

89. Identify the labelled part 3.

90. Give examples of animals which possess given type of digestive system.

Case III : Read the given passage and answer the following questions :

An experimental set up is done to test the presence of X in two samples, (i) boiled rice and (ii) boiled and chewed rice.

The two test tubes with label A and B are given here.

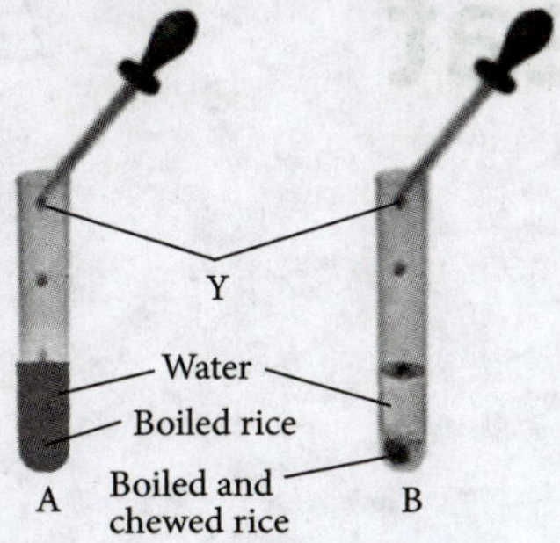

91. Name the solution Y poured in test tube A and B.

92. Given experiment is done to test the presence of X in the test tube A and B. Identify X.

93. How will we detect the presence of X in test tubes A and B?

94. Give the test result for test tube A and B after pouring the solution Y.

95. What conclusion can be drawn from above experiment?

ANSWER KEY

Practice Corner

1. (a) **2.** (a) **3.** (b) **7.** (c) **8.** (b) **9.** (c) **10.** (a) **11.** (b) **12.** (c) **13.** (a)
14. (c) **15.** (a) **16.** (c) **17.** (b) **18.** starch **19.** 7.5 m **20.** Windpipe, foodpipe
21. Water, salts **22.** fat **23.** iodine **24.** milk teeth **25.** Diarrhoea **26.** Tongue **27.** villi
28. True **29.** False **30.** False **31.** True **32.** True **33.** False **34.** False **35.** False **36.** False **37.** True
40. (b) **41.** (a) **42.** (a) **43.** (d) **44.** (a) **45.** (b) **46.** rumination **47.** carbohydrate
48. rumen **49.** ruminants **50.** rumen **52.** (b) **53.** (d) **54.** (a) **55.** (d) **56.** (a)
57. digestive juices **58.** growth, maintenance, multiplication **59.** vacuole **60.** Pseudopodia
61. cell membrane, nucleus, vacuoles **62.** engulfs, pseudopodia **63.** single

NCERT Exemplar Problems

1. (b) **2.** (b) **3.** (a) **4.** (d) **5.** (a) **6.** (c) **7.** (a) **8.** (c) **9.** (b) **10.** (b)
11. (a) **12.** (a)

A & R Corner

1. (c) **2.** (a) **3.** (b) **4.** (c) **5.** (d) **6.** (c) **7.** (a) **8.** (a) **9.** (b) **10.** (c)
11. (a) **12.** (b) **13.** (a) **14.** (c) **15.** (d)

Exam Corner

1. (a) **2.** (a) **3.** (b) **4.** (d) **5.** (a) **6.** (b) **7.** (a) **8.** (a) **9.** (d) **10.** (c)
11. (a) **12.** (b) **13.** (b) **14.** (a) **15.** (d) **16.** (b) **17.** (a) **18.** (b) **19.** (b)
20. (d) **21.** heterotrophs **22.** Canines **23.** Liver, bile **24.** stomach, peristalsis
25. sugars, fatty acids, glycerol, amino acids **26.** Assimilation **27.** wider, shorter **28.** Ruminants, rumen
29. villi **30.** diarrhoea **31.** pseudopodia, tentacles **32.** cud **33.** stomach, small intestine
34. salivary glands, starch, sugars **35.** rumen, reticulum, omasum, abomasum **36.** mosquito **37.** liver, pancreas
38. Ruminants **39.** True **40.** True **41.** False **42.** True **43.** False **44.** True **45.** False **46.** True
47. False **48.** False **49.** False **50.** False **51.** False **52.** False **53.** True **54.** True **55.** False **56.** False
57. True **58.** False **59.** (a) **60.** (c) **62.** Liver, Pancreas **63.** Rumen, Abomasum
64. Crushing and grinding food **65.** Stomach **66.** Pancreas **81.** (a) **82.** (c) **83.** (c) **86.** (a)
87. (c) **88.** (c) **91.** Iodine solution **92.** Starch

3 Heat

NCERT Notes

3.1 Hot and Cold

- **Heat** is a form of energy. It flows from a region of higher temperature to a region of lower temperature.
  - Heat can be converted into other forms of energy.
  - It is measured in joule.
  - It can change the state of matter.
  - Matters expand on heating.

+ Heat is a form of energy which produces the sensation of warmth. It flows whenever there is temperature difference between two bodies.

3.2 Measuring Temperature

- **Temperature** is a measure of degree of hotness or coldness of an object.
  - Temperature is measured by a device known as thermometer.
  - The science of measurement of temperature is known as thermometry.
- Temperature is usually measured in degree **celsius** (°C). For scientific work, kelvin temperature scale is used.
- The normal temperature of a human body is 37°C.

Formulae used for conversion

Scale	Celsius	Kelvin	Fahrenheit
Formula	$°C = K - 273.15$ $°C = (°F - 32) \times \frac{5}{9}$	$K = °C + 273.15$ $K = (°F - 32) \times \frac{5}{9} + 273.15$	$°F = °C \times \frac{9}{5} + 32$

3.3 Laboratory Thermometer

- **Thermometer** works on the principle of expansion of liquids on heating to measure temperature.
- Types of thermometers:
  - **Mercury thermometer** can measure a wide range of temperatures as mercury has high boiling point (~ 357°C) and low freezing point (–39°C).

- There is a kink in the thermometer which holds the mercury.
- **Alcohol thermometer** is safe to use and easily available. It has a low freezing point (–115°C) and therefore, can be used to measure very low temperatures.
- **Clinical thermometer** ranges from 35°C to 42°C. It is used for measuring human body temperature.
- **Laboratory thermometer** is used to measure the temperature of other objects like hot water, milk, etc. Its range varies but usually in between –10°C and 110°C.

Mercury expands immediately after coming in contact with heat since it is a good conductor of heat. The mercury is non-adhesive to the glass.

3.4 Transfer of Heat

- Heat transfer from one body to another can take place by the process of conduction, convection and radiation.
  - **Conduction** is that process of heat transfer in which heat is transferred from a hot body to cold body, provided that there is no gap between the two bodies. Movement of molecules does not take place.
  - **Convection** is that process of heat transfer in which heat is transferred by the actual movement of molecules. Transfer of heat in liquids and gases takes place by convection. Sea breeze and land breeze are the examples of convection currents in gases.
  - During the day time, land gets heated faster than the water. The air over the land becomes hotter and rises up. The cooler air from the sea rushes in the land to take place of hotter air. The warm air from the land moves towards the sea to complete the cycle. The air from the sea is called sea breeze. At the night time, it is exactly reverse. The water cools down more slowly than the land. So, the cool air from the land moves towards the sea. This is called land breeze.
  - **Radiation** does not require any material medium for the transfer of heat. In this process, heat is directly transferred from one body to another. It is the fastest mode of transfer of heat.

3.5 Kinds of Clothes We Wear in Summer and Winter

- Materials which allow heat to be conducted through them easily are called **good conductors** of heat for example, aluminium, iron and copper.
- Materials which do not allow heat to be conducted through them are called **insulators**. For example, wood and plastic.
- Light colours are good reflectors and poor absorbers of heat, whereas dark colours are good absorbers and poor reflectors of heat.
- Woollen clothes keep us warm during winter as wool is a poor conductor of heat and it has air trapped in between the fibres.
- The thermos flask minimizes transfer of heat by conduction, convection and radiation. The silver coating on the inner surface of bottle prevents heat transfer by radiation, the vacuum between its double wall prevents heat transfer by convection and the thinness of the glass wall stops heat leaving and entering the flask by conduction.

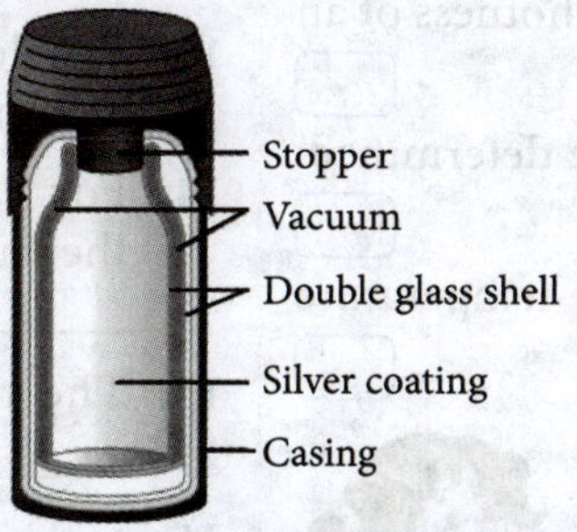

The spatula used in cooking is generally made of wood as it thermally insulates the hotness of cooking vessel reaching the hands of a cook, thereby protecting the hands from getting burnt.

Practice Corner

Extracted from NCERT

Assessment is complementary part of the learning process. It gives you a total insight whether the learning outcomes have been achieved or not. After going through the corresponding NCERT Textbook chapter, attempt these questions in exam like environment. Give yourself one mark for correct answer. A table is given at the end, that will help you plan your next step.

All the Best!

3.1 Hot and Cold

NCERT Page 24-25

A. Select the correct option.

1. The degree of hotness or coldness of a body is measured by
   (a) thermometer (b) ammeter
   (c) barometer (d) odometer
   R

2. A reliable measure of the hotness of an object is called its
   (a) pressure (b) speed
   (c) density (d) temperature.

3. Which of the following is/are the effect(s) of heating?
   (i) Motion of an object
   (ii) Chemical change in an object
   (iii) Change in state of matter
   (iv) Expansion or contraction of an object
   (a) (i) and (ii)
   (b) (i), (ii), (iii) and (iv)
   (c) (ii), (iii) and (iv)
   (d) Only (i)
   An

B. Fill in the blanks.

4. One calorie is nearly equal to ______ joule.

C. State True (T) or False (F) for the given statements.

5. Touching is a reliable measure of the hotness of an object. ☐
6. Temperature of any object cannot be determined. ☐
7. Thermometer is used to measure the temperature of any object. ☐

The first steam engine was invented by Thomas Savery. Its principle was based on the transformation of heat energy into mechanical energy.

Jigyasa

3.2 Measuring Temperature

NCERT Page 25-27

A. Select the correct option.

8. The normal body temperature measured using a clinical thermometer on the Celsius scale is
   (a) 37°C (b) 45°C
   (c) 57°C (d) 67°C
   R

9. The range of temperature on a clinical thermometer is
   (a) 37° C to 45°C (b) 32°C to 45°C
   (c) 35° C to 42°C (d) none of these
   Ap

10. ______ is the boiling point of water on the Fahrenheit scale.
    (a) 273°F (b) 212°F
    (c) 312°F (d) 100°F

11. Which of the following is not a scale of temperature?
    (a) Celsius scale (b) Fahrenheit scale
    (c) Richter scale (d) Kelvin scale

12. When a solid melts, the temperature remains same even though heat is being supplied because
    (a) the molecules are moving faster
    (b) the molecules are far apart
    (c) the solid is not absorbing any heat
    (d) the heat is being used to break up the intermolecular bonds.

B. Fill in the blanks.

13. The device used for measuring the temperature of a human body is ______.
14. For the correct measurement on a clinical thermometer, the mercury level should be below ______.
15. The range of a clinical thermometer in °F is ______.
    U
16. ______ is a metal used in thermometer.
17. The difference between lower fixed point and upper fixed point is divided into ______ parts on a Celsius scale.

18. The minimum possible temperature is ________ K.

19. SI unit of temperature is ____________.

C. State True (T) or False (F) for the given statements.

20. Temperature of hot milk can be measured by clinical thermometer.

21. The temperature of human body could be slightly higher or slightly lower than 37°C.

22. A temperature of 32°C can be measured on a clinical thermometer.

23. Thermometer should be washed before and after use.

24. 310 K is the normal temperature of human body.

25. – 40°C and – 40° F are identical temperatures.

3.3 Laboratory Thermometer

NCERT Page 27-29

A. Select the correct option.

26. The range of a laboratory thermometer is
    (a) 10°C to 110°C (b) –110°C to –10°C
    (c) –110°C to 10°C (d) –10°C to 110°C

27. Mercury is not used in
    (a) clinical thermometers
    (b) laboratory thermometers
    (c) digital thermometers
    (d) all of these

28. A ________ prevents the mercury level from falling on its own.
    (a) kink (b) bulb
    (c) thread (d) glass tube

29. ________ are the features of a clinical thermometer.
    (i) Short temperature range
    (ii) kink in glass tube
    (iii) Alcohol filled glass bulb
    (iv) Wide temperature range
    (a) (i) and (iii) (b) (iii) and (iv)
    (c) (ii) and (iii) (d) (i) and (ii)

30. Thermometer senses the temperature by which one of the following liquids?
    (a) Hydrocarbon based fluid
    (b) Sulphur based fluid
    (c) Potassium based fluid
    (d) None of these

B. State True (T) or False (F) for the given statements.

31. Mercury is a toxic substance.

32. The temperature of a human body can be measured by a laboratory thermometer.

33. A kink is not present in a laboratory thermometer.

C. Figure based question.

34. In the given figure, fill in the blanks with the parts of the thermometer.

A : ____________________

B : ____________________

The highest and lowest temperatures of the previous day are measured by the maximum-minimum thermometer (Alcohol - mercury thermometer) in which two tiny spring-loaded steel markers pushed by a mercury column record the two temperatures.

Jigyasa

3.4 Transfer of Heat

NCERT Page 29-31

A. Select the correct option.

35. Transfer of heat takes place
    (a) from an object at lower temperature to an object at higher temperature.
    (b) from an object at higher temperature to an object at lower temperature.
    (c) when the temperature of both objects is same.
    (d) none of these

36. When one end of an iron rod is heated, its other end also gets heated. It is due to the
    (a) insulation of heat (b) radiation of heat
    (c) convection of heat (d) conduction of heat.

37. Convection of heat takes place in
    (a) solids only (b) gases only
    (c) liquids only (d) liquids and gases.

38. Identify the odd one out.
    (a) Wooden ruler, rubber gloves
    (b) Silver chain, plastic wrap
    (c) Needle, ceramic bowl
    (d) Sand paper, stainless steel spoon

39. The handles of cooking vessels are covered with plastic or wood because

(a) it is customary
(b) they are attractive
(c) they are good conductors of heat
(d) they are bad conductors of heat.

40. By which process does the Sun's heat reach the Earth?
(a) Convection (b) Transpiration
(c) Radiation (d) Conduction

41. The phenomenon involved in the formation of sea breeze and land breeze is
(a) conduction (b) convection
(c) radiation (d) none of these

42. Which of the following conditions lead to the blowing of sea breeze in coastal areas?
(i) Day time
(ii) Night time
(iii) Hot land and cold sea
(iv) Cold land and warm sea
(a) (i) and (iv) (b) (ii) and (iii)
(c) (ii) and (iv) (d) (i) and (iii)

43. Aluminium is a better conductor of heat than wood. It is so because
(a) aluminium has a higher specific heat capacity than wood
(b) aluminium has a higher mass than wood
(c) aluminium has a higher density than wood
(d) aluminium has more free electrons than wood.

44. Which of the following is mode transfer of heat in fluids?
(a) Conduction (b) Radiation
(c) Compression (d) Convection

45. When hot tea is poured suddenly into a glass tumbler, it cracks because
(a) tea has chemicals which react with glass tumbler
(b) glass expands unevenly around the place of contact with the tea
(c) glass cannot resist heat
(d) cannot be explained.

46. Cooling always accompanies evaporation because
(a) the escaped molecules return to the liquid
(b) the more energetic molecules leave the liquid
(c) the air molecules cool the liquid surface
(d) there are fewer liquid molecules left in the liquid.

47. When a copper plate having a hole in middle is heated at its centre position, then the diameter of the hole would
(a) remain same (b) always increase
(c) always decrease (d) none of these

48. Aadvik has difficulty in opening the metal lid of a glass jar of peanut butter. His mother asked him to place the lid of the jar in hot water. The reason was that the hot water will cause the
(a) glass jar to expand more than the metal lid expands
(b) metal lid to expand more than the glass jar expands
(c) metal lid to contract and the glass jar to expand
(d) metal lid to expand and the glass jar to contract.

B. Fill in the blanks.

49. In vacuum, transfer of heat takes place by the process of ____________.

50. Water and air are ____________ conductors of heat.

51. The handles of cooking utensils are made of ____________.

52. Transfer of heat takes place in solids by the process of ____________.

53. Solids ____________ on heating and contract on ____________.

54. Density of a liquid ________ on heating.

55. The conduction of heat is more effective when the molecules are ____________

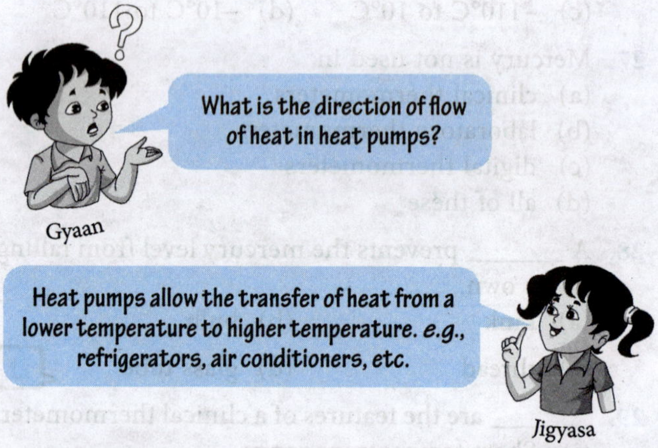

C. State True (T) or False (F) for the given statements.

56. House are made of building materials like bricks, mud and grass as these are good conductors of heat.

57. Aluminium is an insulator of heat.

58. Conduction and convection do not require any medium but radiation requires a medium for heat to flow.

59. Heat increases the temperature of a body.

60. Copper and iron are good conductors of heat.

61. All hot objects emit radiant energy. U

62. A good conductor of heat is not necessarily a good conductor of electricity.

63. As the water kept at room temperature heats up, its volume decreases.

D. Figure based questions.

I. Study the given figures carefully and answer the following questions.

(a) (b)

64. What is the cause behind the wind in coastal areas?

65. Name the wind in figure (a) and figure (b).

66. Explain the reason behind the convection current.

II. Explain the primary mode of heat transfer in each case.

67. From flame to the vessel

68. From hot coffee to the edge of the spoon

69. To the water in the vessel

70. From hot coffee to the air above

3.5 Kinds of Clothes We Wear in Summer and Winter

NCERT Page 32-33

A. Select the correct option.

71. The woolen clothes keep us warm during winter because
(i) wool is a conductor
(ii) wool is an insulator
(iii) wool traps air
(iv) wool absorbs heat quickly.
(a) (i) and (ii) (b) (ii) and (iii)
(c) (i) and (iii) (d) (iii) and (iv)

72. A polished, silvery surface is a
(a) poor absorber and good radiator of heat
(b) good absorber and good reflector of heat
(c) good absorber and bad radiator of heat
(d) poor absorber and good reflector of heat. U

73. Petrol storage tanks are not painted black because
(a) black is a good absorber of radiation
(b) black is bad conductor of heat
(c) black is good conductor of heat
(d) black is bad emitter of radiation. U

B. Fill in the blanks.

74. The water in the black container becomes ______ than that in white container after exposing to the Sun.

75. Black colour is a ______ absorber of heat.

76. We prefer ______ coloured clothes in summer and ______ coloured clothes in winter.

77. Sweating causes cooling by ______. R

C. State True (T) or False (F) for the given statements.

78. Black object absorbs more heat radiations than a white object.

79. Wool is a poor conductor of heat.

80. Silver colour absorbs minimum heat radiation.

D. Figure based question.

81. Write the reasons due to which a thermos flask maintains the temperature of its content.

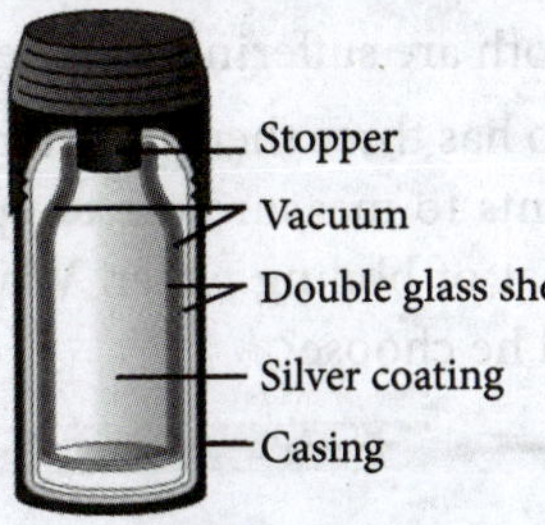

Cr

PROGRESS CHECK

Check your score! If your score is

> 95%	EXCELLENT !	Move on to the next chapter. You have mastered this chapter. Concepts are certainly on your fingertips.
95-85%	VERY GOOD !	Revise once more thoroughly. Recognise your mistakes and work on them. You will master this chapter.
84-75%	GOOD!	Work on your weak areas, master them and come back to this chapter in a few days.
74-65%	MEDIOCRE!	Understand your weak areas and work on strengthening your concepts. Devote more time to master this chapter.
< 65%	NOT SATISFACTORY!	This is where you fall behind from scoring well. Give special attention to this chapter. Work on clearing concepts and common errors.

NCERT Exemplar Problems

This section contains MCQs of **'NCERT Exemplar Problems'** Book.

1. A marble tile would feel cold as compared to a wooden tile on a winter morning, because the marble tile
(a) is a better conductor of heat than the wooden tile.
(b) is polished while wooden tile is not polished.
(c) reflects more heat than wooden tile.
(d) is a poor conductor of heat than the wooden tile.

2. A beggar wrapped himself with a few layers of newspaper on a cold winter night. This helped him to keep himself warm because
(a) friction between the layers of newspaper produces heat.
(b) air trapped between the layers of newspaper is a bad conductor of heat.
(c) newspaper is a conductor of heat.
(d) newspaper is at a higher temperature than the temperature of the surrounding.

3. Paheli and Boojho measured their body temperature. Paheli found her's to be 98.6 °F and Boojho recorded 37°C. Which of the following statement is true?
(a) Paheli has a higher body temperature than Boojho.
(b) Paheli has a lower body temperature than Boojho.
(c) Both have normal body temperature.
(d) Both are suffering from fever.

4. Boojho has three thermometers as shown in figure. He wants to measure the temperature of his body and that of boiling water. Which thermometer(s) should he choose?

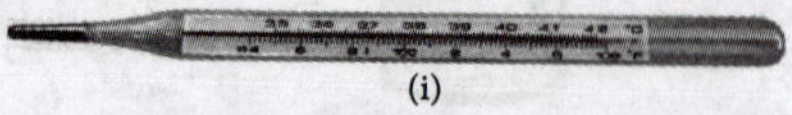
(i)

(ii)

(iii)

(a) Thermometer (i) or (iii) for measuring body temperature and (ii) for measuring the temperature of boiling water.
(b) Thermometer (i) for measuring temperature of both.
(c) Thermometer (ii) for measuring temperature of both.
(d) Thermometer (iii) for measuring temperature of both.

5. Four arrangements to measure temperature of ice in beaker with laboratory thermometer are shown in figure (a, b, c and d). Which one of them shows the correct arrangement for accurate measurement of temperature?

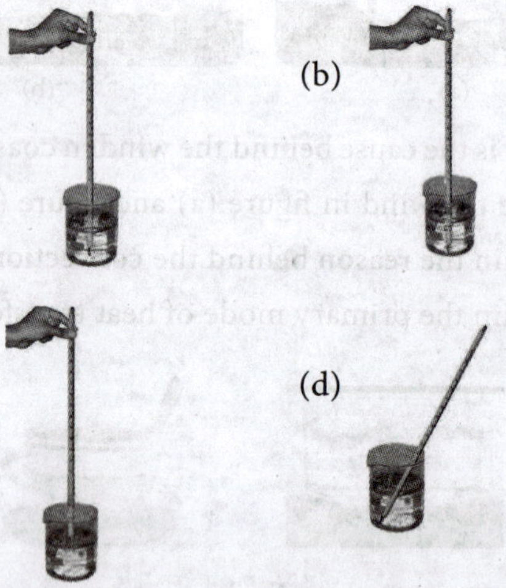

6. Figure (a–d) shows a student reading a doctor's thermometer. Which of the figure indicates the correct method of reading temperature?

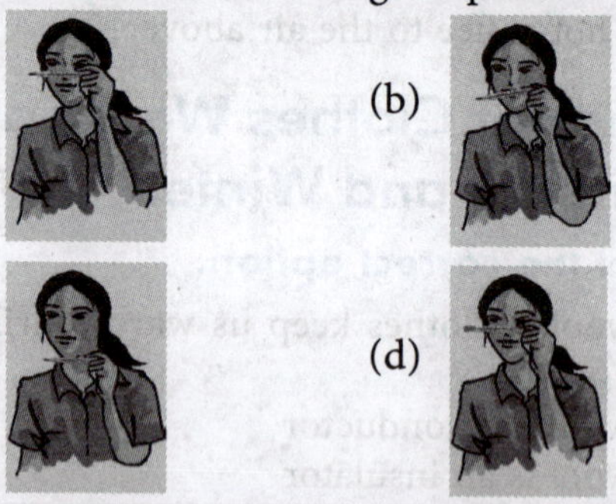

7. Figure (a–d) shows the readings on four different thermometers. Indicate which of the reading shows the normal human body temperature?

A&R Corner

Directions : In the following questions, a statement of assertion is followed by a statement of reason. Mark the correct choice as :
(a) If both assertion and reason are true and reason is the correct explanation of assertion.
(b) If both assertion and reason are true but reason is not the correct explanation of assertion.
(c) If assertion is true but reason is false.
(d) If both assertion and reason are false.

1. **Assertion :** Heat energy is transferred from one body to another due to a temperature difference between them.
Reason : Heating a substance causes a rise in temperature. U

2. **Assertion :** Various modes by which heat can flow are conduction, convection and radiation.
Reason : Heat always flows from a larger object to a smaller object.

3. **Assertion :** Sea breeze blows during daytime.
Reason : The air above the sea is hot and moves toward land. An

4. **Assertion :** Two bodies at the same temperature may contain different amounts of heat.
Reason : Two bodies may require different amounts of heat to maintain or require same temperature.

5. **Assertion :** The flow of heat energy from one body to the other depends upon the amount of heat energy in them.
Reason : Heat flows from lower temperature of the body to higher temperature of the body.

6. **Assertion :** Temperature is a measure of degree of hotness of our body.
Reason : We use a clinical thermometer to measure the degree of hotness of body. R

7. **Assertion :** A clinical thermometer has a scale in the range of 37 °C to 45 °C.
Reason : The normal temperature of human body is 40 °C. R

8. **Assertion :** In a room containing air, heat can go from one place to another by radiation only.
Reason : In conduction, heat is transferred from one place to other by actual motion of heated material.

9. **Assertion :** Radiation is a method of transfer of heat.
Reason : The process of heat transfer that does not require any medium is called radiation.

10. **Assertion :** Water boils faster in a vessel having copper bottom.
Reason : Copper is the best conductor of heat. U

Exam Corner

This section comprises of different types of questions:

- **Objective Type Questions :** These are **one mark** questions.
- **Very Short Answer Type Questions (VSA) :** These are **one mark** questions.
- **Short Answer Type Questions-I (SA-I) :** These are **two marks** questions.
- **Short Answer Type Questions-II (SA-II) :** These are **three marks** questions.
- **Long Answer Type Questions (LA) :** These are **five marks** questions.
- **Case Based Questions (CBQs) :** These are case study/passage based questions.

OBJECTIVE TYPE QUESTIONS

A. Select the correct option.

1. Trishu served some hot soup in a metal bowl. She carried the bowl with her bare hands to the dining table. What she did was unwise because the heat from the soup would
   (a) transfer through the air and burn her hand
   (b) melt the bowl and the soup would burn her hand
   (c) cause her hand to perspire and the bowl would slip from her hand
   (d) transfer through the metal bowl and burn her hand.

2. Which one of the following is not a good conductor of heat?
   (a) Aluminum
   (b) Tungsten
   (c) Steel
   (d) Sand **R**

3. A dog pants with its tongue sticking out on hot day. The reason is that
   (a) it is a genetic disease found in few animals like dogs
   (b) saliva vaporises, cooling the tongue
   (c) producing more saliva cools down the body temperature
   (d) it is a habit.

4. Process of change of state from liquid state to gaseous state is called
   (a) boiling
   (b) sublimation
   (c) condensation
   (d) freezing. **R**

5. Which of the following is true?
   (a) Sea breeze blows during day when the land is cooler than the sea.
   (b) Land breeze blows during day when the sea is cooler than the land.
   (c) Land breeze blows during night when the land is cooler than the sea.
   (d) Sea breeze blows during night when the sea is cooler than the land. **U**

B. State True (T) or False (F) for the given statements.

6. SI unit of temperature is Kelvin. ☐
7. Heat transfer to stainless steel spoon from hot milk is an example of conduction. ☐
8. Our body gives off heat to the atmosphere and receives heat from the atmosphere by radiation. ☐
9. Wooden objects will feel warmer than metallic objects to touch in winter. ☐
10. There is no limit to maximum temperature. ☐

C. Match the columns.

11.

Column I	Column II
(i) Temperature	(P) Good absorbers
(ii) Heat transfer in air	(Q) Vacuum
(iii) Absence of any medium	(R) Bad radiators
(iv) White coloured surfaces	(S) Convection
(v) Black coloured surfaces	(T) Measure of coldness or hotness

An

VERY SHORT ANSWER TYPE QUESTIONS (VSA)

A. Convert the following as per direction:

12. 45°C into °F ________
13. 67°C into K ________
14. 95°C into °F ________
15. 105 K into °C ________
16. 99 K into °F ________ Ap

B. Write one word for each of the following:

17. Heat energy transferred from one material to another by direct contact ________
18. Cause of expansion in solid, liquid and gas ________
19. A thermometer that does not use mercury ________
20. The principle on which a thermometer works ________
21. The liquid used in thermometers in very cold places ________ U

SHORT ANSWER TYPE QUESTIONS-I (SA-I)

22. Write any two advantages of using mercury in thermometer.
23. Why does convection not take place in solids?
24. Differentiate between conductors and insulators of heat.
25. Why does the heating coil of the kettle is always placed near the bottom?
26. What is thermal expansion?

SHORT ANSWER TYPE QUESTIONS-II (SA-II)

27. Why do we prefer light-coloured clothes in summer and dark-coloured clothes in winter?
28. What precautions should be taken while using a clinical thermometer?
29. Define:
    (i) Conduction
    (ii) Convection
    (iii) Radiation
30. What do you mean by lower fixed point and upper fixed point on temperature scales? Write these points on different temperature scales.
31. Why do we wear woolen clothes in winter?

LONG ANSWER TYPE QUESTIONS (LA)

32. Differentiate between heat and temperature.
33. How do sea breeze and land breeze form? Explain with diagram.
34. Draw a labeled diagram of a clinical thermometer and explain its construction.
35. Give reason for the following:
    (i) An ice box is constructed with a double wall.
    (ii) A clinical thermometer has the range 35°C – 42°C.
    (iii) Silver is good conductor of heat and electricity but water is a good conductor of electricity only.
    (iv) Bullock carts have wooden wheels with metal rims of smaller size. How fitting is done?

CASE BASED QUESTIONS (CBQs)

Case I : Read the given passage and answer the following questions :

The clinical thermometer given below is used to measure the temperature of human body. The liquid used is mercury which is non-adhesive to the thermometer tube (capillary). The liquid expands on heating (rises in tube) and contracts on cooling (drops down in tube) exhibiting different temperatures indicated by the calibrations of the thermometer.

Clinical Thermometer

36. What is the lower fixed point of clinical thermometer?
    (a) 35 °C (b) 42 °C
    (c) 32 °C (d) 45 °C
37. What is the range of clinical thermometer?
    (a) 32 °C – 42 °C
    (b) 94 °F – 108 °F
    (c) 32 °C – 45 °C
    (d) 35 °F – 108 °F R
38. What is normal temperature of human body?
    (a) 36 °C (b) 100 °F
    (c) 98.6 °F (d) 37 K R
39. ________ is to prevent the back flow of mercury into thermometer bulb when the thermometer bulb is removed from the mouth of a patient.
    (a) Bulb (b) stem
    (c) Kink (d) Bubble

Case II : Read the given passage and answer the following questions :

Heat transfer from one object to another can take place by the process of conduction, convection and radiation. The heat always flow from hot body to cold body.

40. Which is the fastest mode of heat transfer?

41. What is the consequence of convection process.

42. Name the process by which heating takes place in a solid.

43. Why silver is a better conductor of heat than rubber.

ANSWER KEY

Practice Corner

1. (a) **2.** (d) **3.** (c) **4.** 4.184 **5.** False **6.** False **7.** True **8.** (a) **9.** (c) **10.** (b) **11.** (c)
12. (d) **13.** Clinical thermometer **14.** 35°C **15.** 94-108 **16.** Mercury **17.** Hundred
18. 0 **19.** Kelvin **20.** False **21.** True **22.** False **23.** True **24.** True **25.** True **26.** (d) **27.** (c)
28. (a) **29.** (d) **30.** (a) **31.** True **32.** False **33.** True **34.** A-Bulb; B-Mercury **35.** (b) **36.** (d)
37. (d) **38.** (a) **39.** (d) **40.** (c) **41.** (b) **42.** (d) **43.** (d) **44.** (d) **45.** (b) **46.** (b) **47.** (b)
48. (b) **49.** radiation **50.** bad/poor **51.** insulator **52.** Conduction **53.** Expands, Cooling
54. Decreases **55.** Closely packed **56.** False **57.** False **58.** False **59.** True **60.** True **61.** True **62.** True
63. False **65.** Land breeze, Sea breeze **67.** Conduction **68.** Conduction **69.** Convection
70. Convection **71.** (b) **72.** (d) **73.** (a) **74.** warmer **75.** Good **76.** Light, Dark
77. Evaporation **78.** True **79.** True **80.** True

NCERT Exemplar Problems

1. (a) **2.** (b) **3.** (c) **4.** (a) **5.** (a) **6.** (a) **7.** (c)

A & R Corner

1. (b) **2.** (c) **3.** (c) **4.** (b) **5.** (c) **6.** (b) **7.** (d) **8.** (d) **9.** (b) **10.** (a)

Exam Corner

1. (d) **2.** (d) **3.** (b) **4.** (a) **5.** (c) **6.** True **7.** True **8.** True **9.** True **10.** True
11. (i)-T; (ii)-S; (iii)-Q; (iv)-R; (v)-P **12.** 113°F **13.** 340.15 K **14.** 203°C **15.** –168.15°C
16. –281.47°F **17.** Conduction **18.** Heating **19.** Digital thermometer **20.** Thermal Expansion
21. Alcohol **36.** (a) **37.** (b) **38.** (c) **39.** (c)

4 Acids, Bases and Salts

NCERT Notes

Materials are classified in numerous ways depending upon their characteristics. One such method classifies substances into acids, bases and salts. Acids and bases play a major role in chemistry because most of the chemical reactions are acid-base reactions.

4.1 Acids and Bases

- Different solutions can be classified as acids, bases and salts. All these classes have distinct properties and chemical behaviour.
- Generally, acids are defined as substances with sour taste whereas bases are defined as substances with bitter taste. Bases have a soapy touch. Acids are soluble in water and yield large amount of heat when they are dissolved in water. All bases are not soluble in water. Water soluble bases are known as alkalies Hence, all alkalies are bases but all bases are not alkalies. The solutions of both acids and bases conduct electricity. When acids are dissolved in water, they generally release hydrogen ions (H^+) whereas when bases are dissolved in water, they release hydroxide ions (OH^-).

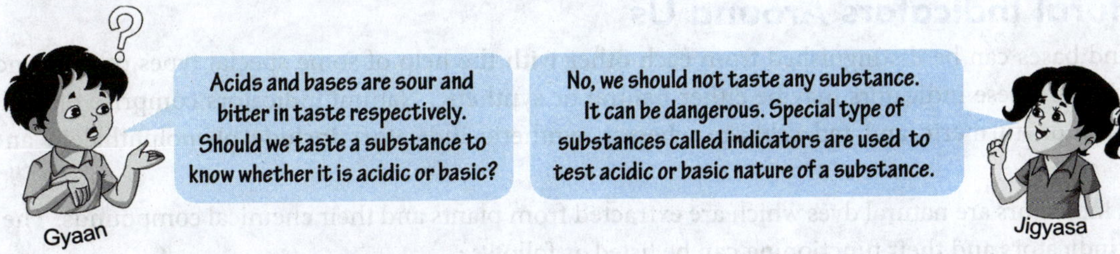

- Some common acids and bases can be tabulated as follows :

Sources	Acids
Lemon, orange	Citric acid
Vinegar	Acetic acid
Curd	Lactic acid
Tamarind	Tartaric acid
Apple	Malic acid
Spinach	Oxalic acid

Common Name of Base	Chemical Name
Caustic soda	Sodium hydroxide
Caustic potash	Potassium hydroxide
Milk of magnesia	Magnesium hydroxide
Slaked lime	Calcium hydroxide

- **Organic acids** are the naturally occurring acids, found in plants and animals. They are weak acids. **Inorganic (mineral) acids** are prepared from the minerals of the earth's crust. They are generally strong acids except carbonic acid.
- Depending on the amount of water present in it, an acid is **concentrated** or **dilute**. If small amount of water is present, the acid is **concentrated** and if large amount of water is present, the acid is **dilute**. A concentrated acid can be diluted by adding water to it and a dilute acid can be concentrated by evaporating the water from it. Remember, never add water to acid, always add acid to water.
- Acids which dissociate completely in water and produce more H^+ ions are called **strong acids**. Acids which do not dissociate completely in water and produce much less H^+ ions are called **weak acids.**

+ Soaps and fats in our body contain fatty acids. Cells of our body contain an important acid DNA (deoxyribonucleic acid) which is responsible to pass characters from one generation to other.

- Bases which dissociate completely in water and produce more OH^- ions are called **strong bases**. Bases which do not dissociate completely in water and produce much less OH^- ions are called **weak bases.**
- **Basicity of an acid** is the number of replaceable hydrogen atoms in a molecule of an acid. On the basis of this, acids are monobasic acids *e.g.*, HCl, CH_3COOH, etc., dibasic acids *e.g.*, H_2SO_4, H_2CO_3, etc., tribasic acids *e.g.*, H_3PO_4, etc.
- **Acidity of a base** is the number of hydroxyl groups present in a molecule of a base. On the basis of this, bases are monoacidic bases *e.g.*, NaOH, KOH, etc., diacidic bases *e.g.*, $Mg(OH)_2$, $Ca(OH)_2$, etc., triacidic bases *e.g.*, $Al(OH)_3$, etc.
- Acids and bases are used as laboratory reagents. They are used for manufacturing of several products which are an integral part of our daily lives like paper, rayon, textiles, paints, soaps, fertilisers, plastics and dyes.

4.2 Natural Indicators Around Us

- Acids and bases can be distinguished from each other with the help of some special types of substances called as indicators. These indicators may be either natural or synthetic. Natural indicators comprise of litmus, china rose indicator, turmeric and red cabbage whereas synthetic indicators include phenolphthalein and methyl orange.
- Natural indicators are natural dyes which are extracted from plants and their chemical compounds. The different natural indicators and their functioning can be listed as follows :
  - Litmus is extracted from lichens. It has a purple colour in distilled water. It turns red in acidic solution and blue in basic solution. It is also available in the form of litmus papers. Acids turn blue litmus paper red whereas bases turn red litmus paper blue.
  - China rose turns dark pink or magenta in acidic solution and green in basic solution.
  - Turmeric remains yellow in acidic or neutral solutions whereas turns red in basic solution.
  - Red cabbage turns red in acidic solution and green in basic solution.
- Synthetic indicators are prepared in laboratory. Some common examples of synthetic indicators are phenolphthalein and methyl orange. Phenolphthalein turns colourless in acidic solution and pink in basic solution. On the other hand, methyl orange turns red in acidic solution and yellow in basic solution.
- Colour of some common indicators in acidic and basic solutions:

Nature of substance	Indicators						
	Blue litmus	Red litmus	Methyl orange	Phenol-phthalein	Turmeric	China rose	Red cabbage
Acidic	Red	No change	Red	Colourless	No change	Magenta	Red
Basic	No change	Blue	Yellow	Pink	Red	Green	Green

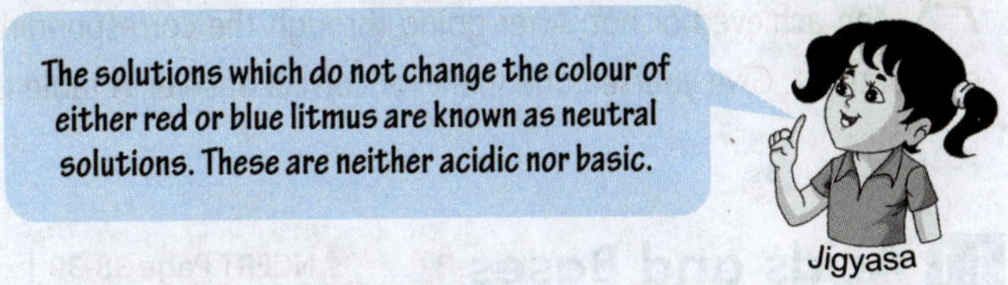

- The strength of an acid and a base is measured by a scale called **pH scale**. **pH value** of the solution indicates the concentration of hydrogen ions in the solution. The pH values range from 1 to 14. **pH paper** is used to find out the pH of a solution by matching the change in colour with a universal indicator paper. A **universal indicator** is a combination of dyes that shows a change of colour over a range of pH.

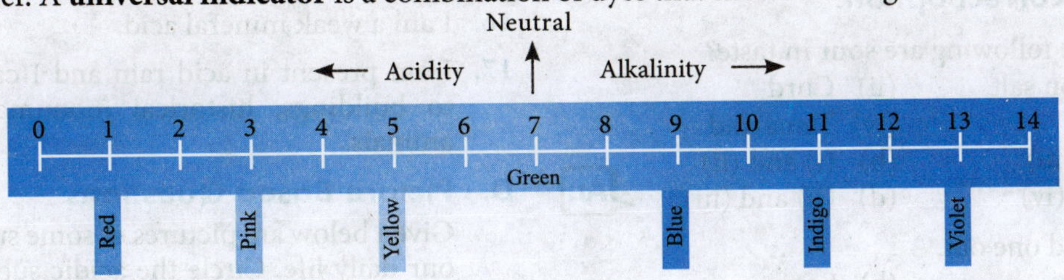

4.3 Neutralisation

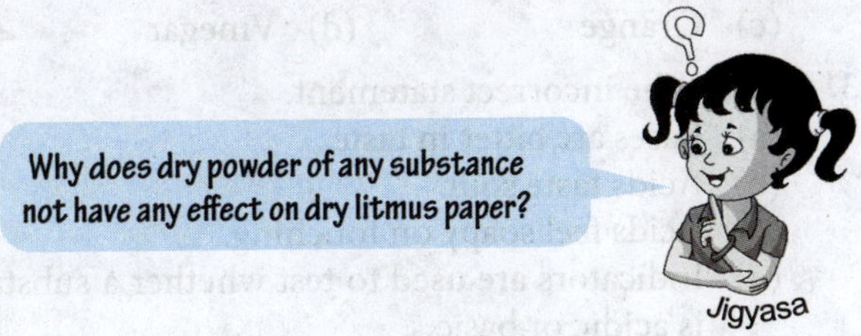

- Reaction of an acid and base is called neutralisation reaction. It results in the formation of water and salt. The salts can be classified as follows :
- **Normal salt** is a salt formed by the complete replacement of the hydrogen atoms of an acid molecule by a metal atom or a positive radical *e.g.*, NaCl, KCl, etc. A salt formed by the neutralisation of a strong acid by a strong base is **neutral**.
- **Acidic salt** is a salt formed by the partial replacement of the hydrogen atoms of a polybasic acid molecule by a metal atom or a positive radical *e.g.*, $NaHCO_3$, etc. A salt formed by the neutralisation of a strong acid by a weak base is **acidic**.
- **Basic salt** is a salt formed by the partial replacement of the hydroxyl groups or the incomplete neutralisation of a base *e.g.*, Ca(OH)Cl, Mg(OH)Cl, etc. A salt formed by the neutralisation of a weak acid by a strong base is **basic**.
- There are many applications of acids, bases, salts and neutralisation reaction in our daily life.
- The fixed number of water molecules which remain with the crystalline salt is known as **water of crystallisation**. Such water molecules give shape and colour to the crystals. Salts with water of crystallisation are called **hydrated salts**. On heating, hydrated salts lose their shape and colour and change into a powdery substance. These salts are called **anhydrous salts**.

\+ Common salt (NaCl) is used as a preservative and in the preparation of soap. Blue vitriol ($CuSO_4$) is used as fungicide and in electroplating.

4.4 Neutralisation in Everyday Life

Few important applications of neutralisation reactions are listed as follows :

- Neutralisation of excessive acid in stomach by antacid helps to relieve indigestion.
- Ant bites containing acids are neutralised by rubbing moist baking soda or calamine solution.
- Neutralisation of the acidic or basic content in soil helps in controlling the fertility of soil.
- Neutralisation reaction helps in treatment of factory waste and prevention of tooth decay.

Practice Corner

Extracted from NCERT

Assessment is complementary part of the learning process. It gives you a total insight whether the learning outcomes have been achieved or not. After going through the corresponding NCERT Textbook chapter, attempt these questions in exam like environment. Give yourself one mark for correct answer. A table is given at the end, that will help you plan your next step.

All the Best!

4.1 Acids and Bases

NCERT Page 38-39

A. Select the correct option.

1. Which of the following are sour in taste?
   (i) Common salt (ii) Curd
   (iii) Sugar (iv) Tamarind
   (a) (i) and (iii) (b) (i) and (ii)
   (c) (ii) and (iv) (d) (ii) and (iii) An

2. Select the odd one out.
   (a) *Amla* (b) Soap
   (c) Orange (d) Vinegar An

3. Select the incorrect statement.
   (a) Bases are bitter in taste.
   (b) Acids taste sour.
   (c) Acids feel soapy on touching.
   (d) Indicators are used to test whether a substance is acidic or basic. U

4. Window cleaner contains
   (a) ammonium hydroxide (b) sodium hydroxide
   (c) tartaric acid (d) calcium hydroxide. R

5. Ascorbic acid is more commonly known as
   (a) mineral (b) potassium hydroxide
   (c) vitamin K (d) vitamin C. R

B. State True (T) or False (F) for the given statements.

6. Sodium hydroxide is used in the manufacture of soap.
7. Tamarind contains oxalic acid.
8. The sting of ants and bees contains formic acid.
9. Curd contains calcium hydroxide.
10. Grapes contain ascorbic acid.
11. Bases which are insoluble in water are called alkalies.
12. Potassium hydroxide is a weak base.

C. Identify the following :

13. I am found in the sting of an ant. ______
14. I am the main component of proteins. ______
15. I am responsible to pass characters from one generation to another. ______
16. I am a weak mineral acid. ______
17. I am present in acid rain and I can cause damage to buildings, historical monuments, plants and animals. ______

D. Picture Based Questions

Given below are pictures of some substances used in our daily life. Circle the acidic substances with red colour, basic substances with blue colour and the substances which are neither acidic nor basic with green colour.

18. 

19. 

20. 

21. 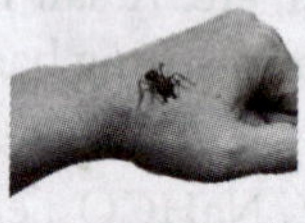

22. 

23. 

24. 

25. 

26. 

27. 

28. 

29. 

30. 

31. 

32. 

4.2 Natural Indicators Around Us

NCERT Page 39-43

A. Fill in the blanks.

33. Curd changes China rose indicator to ______ in colour.
34. Turmeric shows no effect on ______ and ______ solutions.

35. ______ can cause damage to buildings, historical monuments, plants and animals.

36. Window cleaner turns ______ litmus paper to ______ in colour.

37. Turmeric stain turns ______ after washing with soap solution.

38. Dry powder of baking soda has ______ effect on dry litmus paper.

39. Baking soda solution turns turmeric to ______.

B. Select the correct option.

40. When few drops of phenolphthalein are added to a solution of common salt, the solution
(a) becomes pink in colour
(b) remains colourless
(c) turns orange in colour
(d) turns green in colour. **An**

41. Red cabbage juice is ______ in colour, turns ______ in a basic medium and ______ in an acidic medium.
(a) purple, red, green (b) red, green, purple
(c) purple, green, red (d) red, purple, green **Ap**

42. Phenolphthalein gives ______ colour with soap solution.
(a) pink (b) colourless
(c) orange (d) green **R**

43. Methyl orange turns ______ in acidic solutions and ______ in basic solutions.
(a) yellow, red (b) red, yellow
(c) pink, blue (d) red, pink **An**

44. China rose indicator turns ______ with aerated soft drink.
(a) green (b) magenta
(c) blue (d) black **U**

45. Which of the following groups of samples will not show any change in colour with China rose indicator?
(a) Lemon juice, curd and sugar solution
(b) Distilled water, sodium chloride solution and sugar solution
(c) Distilled water, window cleaner and lime water
(d) Lime water, soap solution and lemon juice **An**

C. State True (T) or False (F) for the given statements.

46. Litmus is a naturally occurring indicator. ☐

47. Phenolphthalein gives pink colour with acidic solutions. ☐

48. Phenolphthalein is a natural acid-base indicator. ☐

49. Sodium hydroxide remains colourless with phenolphthalein. ☐

50. Neutral substances do not change the colour of red cabbage indicator. ☐

D. Note down the observations and Inferences.

S.No.	Solution	Effect on turmeric solution	Effect on China rose indicator	Inference
51.	Milk of magnesia			
52.	Orange juice			
53.	Vinegar			
54.	Soda water			
55.	Salt solution			

E. Record your observations in the given table after performing the prescribed tests.

S.No.	Solution	Effect on red litmus paper	Effect on blue litmus paper	Inference
56.	Lemon juice			
57.	Soap solution			
58.	Apple juice			
59.	Vinegar			
60.	Baking soda solution			
61.	Sugar solution			
62.	Distilled water			
63.	Common salt solution			

F. Identify the following :

64. I show pink colour with basic solution. ______

65. I have no effect on acidic and neutral solutions but my colour changes to red with basic solution. ______

66. I am not affected by indicators. ______

67. I show magenta colour with acidic solution. ______

68. I show red colour in acidic solution. ______ **Ev**

4.3 Neutralisation

NCERT Page 43-44

A. Fill in the blanks.

69. ______ is a process in which an ______ reacts with a ______ to produce ______ and ______ which may be acidic, basic or neutral in nature. In this reaction, ______ is always evolved which raises the ______ of the reaction mixture.

B. Identify the following :

70. I am the salt formed when sulphuric acid reacts with lime water. ______

71. I am formed by the reaction of an acid with a base. ______

72. I am a salt formed when NaOH reacts with HCl. ______

73. I am a salt formed when HBr reacts with KOH. ______

74. I am a salt formed when HNO_3 reacts with NaOH. ______

C. State True (T) or False (F) for the given statements.

75. Heat is always absorbed in a neutralisation reaction. ☐

76. The reaction mixture becomes cool when dilute sulphuric acid is added to lime water. ☐

77. When right amount of hydrochloric acid is mixed with sodium hydroxide, the resulting solution is neither acidic nor basic. ☐

78. The salt formed after a neutralisation reaction can be acidic, basic or neutral in nature. ☐

79. NaCl is formed when a strong acid reacts with a strong base. ☐

D. Select the correct option.

80. Sodium hydroxide is not used for neutralising the hydrochloric acid present in the stomach during acidity because

(a) it is a weak base and cannot neutralise acid
(b) it is a strong base and it will burn the mouth and walls of stomach
(c) it is not soluble in water hence cannot be swallowed
(d) the acid present in stomach does not react with sodium hydroxide. U

81. When an acid reacts with a base, a salt (*P*) and another product (*Q*) are formed. The product (*Q*) is

(a) carbon dioxide (b) nitrogen
(c) hydrogen (d) water. U

82. Sodium chloride solution is neutral in nature because

(a) it is formed by the complete neutralisation of a strong acid and a strong base
(b) it is formed by the complete neutralisation of a weak acid and a weak base
(c) it is formed by the incomplete neutralisation of a strong acid and a strong base
(d) it is formed by the incomplete neutralisation of a weak acid and a weak base. U

83. Ammonium chloride is a/an ______ salt.

(a) basic (b) acidic
(c) neutral (d) none of these An

84. Select the incorrect statement.

(a) Heat is evolved during a neutralisation reaction.
(b) NaOH reacts with HCl to produce NaCl and H_2O.
(c) Phenolphthalein remains colourless in an acidic solution.
(d) A neutralisation reaction is reversible in nature. Ev

4.4 Neutralisation in Everyday Life

A. Match the following :

85.

	Column I		Column II
(i)	Indigestion	(P)	Slaked lime
(ii)	Ant bite	(Q)	Basic substances
(iii)	Factory wastes	(R)	Organic matter
(iv)	Acidic soil	(S)	Calamine solution
(v)	Basic soil	(T)	Antacid

B. Write the chemical names of the following substances :

86. Milk of magnesia : ______

87. Baking soda : ______

88. Calamine solution : ______

89. Quick lime : ______

90. Slaked lime : ______

PROGRESS CHECK

Check your score! If your score is

> 95%	EXCELLENT !	Move on to the next chapter. You have mastered this chapter. Concepts are certainly on your fingertips.
95-85%	VERY GOOD !	Revise once more thoroughly. Recognise your mistakes and work on them. You will master this chapter.
84-75%	GOOD!	Work on your weak areas, master them and come back to this chapter in a few days.
74-65%	MEDIOCRE!	Understand your weak areas and work on strengthening your concepts. Devote more time to master this chapter.
< 65%	NOT SATISFACTORY!	This is where you fall behind from scoring well. Give special attention to this chapter. Work on clearing concepts and common errors.

NCERT Exemplar Problems

This section contains MCQs of **'NCERT Exemplar Problems'** Book.

1. The correct way of making a solution of acid in water is to
(a) add water to acid
(b) add acid to water
(c) mix acid and water simultaneously
(d) add water to acid in a shallow container.

2. Products of a neutralisation reaction are always
(a) an acid and a base
(b) an acid and a salt
(c) a salt and water
(d) a salt and a base.

3. Turmeric is a natural indicator. On adding its paste to acid and base separately, which colours would be observed?
(a) Yellow in both acid and base
(b) Yellow in acid and red in base
(c) Pink in acid and yellow in base
(d) Red in acid and blue in base

4. Phenolphthalein is a synthetic indicator and its colours in acidic and basic solutions, respectively are
(a) red and blue
(b) blue and red
(c) pink and colourless
(d) colourless and pink.

5. When the soil is too basic, plants do not grow well in it. To improve its quality what must be added to the soil?
(a) Organic matter
(b) Quick lime
(c) Slaked lime
(d) Calamine solution

6. 'Litmus', a natural dye is an extract of which of the following?
(a) China rose (*Gudhal*)
(b) Beetroot
(c) Lichen
(d) Blue berries (*Jamun*)

7. Neutralisation reaction is a
(a) physical and reversible change
(b) physical change that cannot be reversed
(c) chemical and reversible change
(d) chemical change that cannot be reversed.

8. A solution changes the colour of turmeric indicator from yellow to red. The solution is
(a) basic
(b) acidic
(c) neutral
(d) either neutral or acidic.

9. Which of the following set of substances contain acids?
(a) Grapes, lime water
(b) Vinegar, soap
(c) Curd, milk of magnesia
(d) Curd, vinegar

10. On adding phenolphthalein indicator to colourless solution, no change is observed. What is the nature of this solution?
(a) Basic
(b) Either acidic or basic
(c) Either acidic or neutral
(d) Either basic or neutral

11. Which of the following is an acid-base indicator?
(a) Vinegar
(b) Lime water
(c) Turmeric
(d) Baking soda

A&R Corner

Directions : In the following questions, a statement of assertion is followed by a statement of reason. Mark the correct choice as :
(a) If both assertion and reason are true and reason is the correct explanation of assertion.
(b) If both assertion and reason are true but reason is not the correct explanation of assertion.
(c) If assertion is true but reason is false.
(d) If both assertion and reason are false.

1. **Assertion :** Tamarind contains tartaric acid.
Reason : Lemon and orange contain acetic acid. R

2. **Assertion :** Acetic acid is a weak acid.
Reason : Acetic acid partially dissociates when dissolved in water. U

3. **Assertion :** Milk of magnesia is used as an antacid.
Reason : Milk of magnesia neutralises the excessive amount of HCl released in stomach and relieves acidity.

4. **Assertion :** Curd turns blue litmus paper red.
Reason : Curd contains lactic acid.

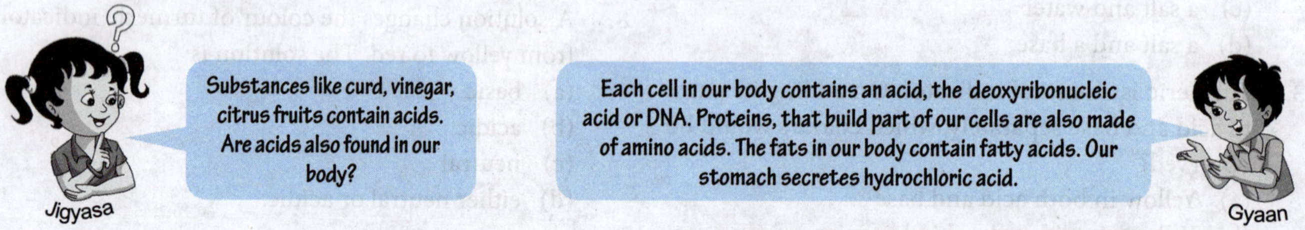

5. **Assertion :** When an acid is dissolved in water, heat is given out.
Reason : Acids are diluted by adding water to acids.

6. **Assertion :** Acids are not stored in metal containers.
Reason : All alkalis are bases but all bases are not alkalis. An

7. **Assertion :** Bases give pink colour in china rose indicator.
Reason : Base remain colourless in phenolphthalein solution.

8. **Assertion :** NaCl is a neutral salt.
Reason : Sodium acetate is a basic salt. An

9. **Assertion :** A farmer adds quick lime to basic soil.
Reason : Quick lime neutralises the excess of base present in soil.

10. **Assertion :** Distilled water does not change the colour of blue or red litmus paper.
Reason : Distilled water is neutral in nature. U

Exam Corner

This section comprises of different types of questions:

- **Objective Type Questions :** These are **one mark** questions.
- **Very Short Answer Type Questions (VSA) :** These are **one mark** questions.
- **Short Answer Type Questions-I (SA-I) :** These are **two marks** questions.
- **Short Answer Type Questions-II (SA-II) :** These are **three marks** questions.
- **Long Answer Type Questions (LA) :** These are **five marks** questions.
- **Case Based Questions (CBQs) :** These are case study / passage based questions.

OBJECTIVE TYPE QUESTIONS

A. Select the correct option.

1. Raghav was given two test tubes one containing water and other containing sodium hydroxide solution. To identify the solutions, which of the following indicators can be used by him?

(i) Blue litmus (ii) Turmeric indicator
(iii) Phenolphthalein (iv) Red litmus
(a) (i) and (iv) (b) (ii), (iii) and (iv)
(c) Only (iv) (d) Only (iii)

2. Which of the following show no change with red litmus paper?

(i) Sugar solution (ii) Soap solution
(iii) Vinegar (iv) Lime water
(v) Distilled water (vi) Soda water
(a) (ii) and (iv) (b) (i), (iii) and (iv)
(c) (iv), (v) and (vi) (d) (i), (iii), (v) and (vi)

An

3. Which of the following turn China rose indicator green?

(i) Window cleaner (ii) Salt solution
(iii) Distilled water (iv) Lime water
(v) Lemon juice (vi) Sour milk
(a) (i) and (iv) (b) (ii) and (iii)
(c) (v) and (vi) (d) (ii) and (v)

An

4. Identify the correct statements.

(i) With acidic and neutral substances, turmeric paper remains yellow.
(ii) Phenolphthalein shows pink colour with distilled water.
(iii) Blue litmus paper has no effect with lime water.
(iv) Red litmus paper turns blue in glucose solution.
(v) Turmeric paper changes to red colour in basic solutions.

(a) (i), (ii) and (v) (b) (iii) and (iv)
(c) (iii), (iv) and (v) (d) (i), (iii) and (v)

5. Identify the incorrect statements.

(a) Soda water turns green with red cabbage indicator.
(b) Window cleaner turns red with red cabbage indicator.
(c) Salt solution has no effect with red cabbage indicator.
(d) Both (a) and (b).

U

6. Citric acid is a/an ______ acid.

(a) organic (b) strong
(c) mineral (d) both (a) and (b)

R

7. ______ is used as a preservative.

(a) Sodium chloride (b) Calcium hydroxide
(c) Lime water (d) Hydrochloric acid

8. ______ is used in making batteries for vehicles.

(a) Hydrochloric acid
(b) Nitric acid
(c) Ammonium hydroxide
(d) Sulphuric acid

R

9. Select the odd one out.

(a) Formic acid (b) Nitric acid
(c) Sulphuric acid (d) Hydrochloric acid

U

B. Fill in the blanks.

10. Amino acids are the building blocks of ______.

11. Salt formed by the neutralisation of a weak acid and a strong base is a ______.

12. Curd contains ______ acid. R

13. Our stomach contains ______ acid which helps in digestion.

14. ______ acids are weak acids present in plant and animal products.

15. Soda water is ______ in nature.

C. State True (T) or False (F) for the given statements.

16. Carbon dioxide is dissolved in water to make sulphuric acid. ☐

17. Acids react with metals to form salt and hydrogen gas. ☐

18. Acids react with carbonates to produce salt, water and carbon dioxide. ☐

19. Neutralisation is an endothermic process. ☐

20. When an ant bites, it injects a basic liquid into the skin. ☐

VERY SHORT ANSWER TYPE QUESTIONS (VSA)

A. Circle the odd one out. Give reason for your choice.

21. Distilled water, Glucose, Common salt, Lime water

22. Sodium hydroxide, Potassium hydroxide, Magnesium hydroxide

23. Nitric acid, Formic acid, Acetic acid, Tartaric acid

24. Carbonic acid, Hydrochloric acid, Nitric acid, Sulphuric acid

SHORT ANSWER TYPE QUESTIONS-I (SA-I)

25. State at least four differences between acids and bases.

26. Blue litmus paper is dipped in aerated soft drink. What will happen? What is the nature of the solution?

27. Define an indicator. Give two examples of natural and synthetic indicators each.

28. Why does a turmeric stain on white dress turn red when it is washed with soap?

29. Define neutralisation with the help of an example.

30. The given table shows the pH of five substances.

Substances	pH values
I	13.9
II	9.8
III	2.5
IV	4.7
V	7.0

(a) Classify the substances as acids, bases and neutral substances.

(b) Arrange these substances in increasing order of acidity.

31. Four solutions *W*, *X*, *Y* and *Z* were taken in four test tubes and tested with four indicators—methyl orange, phenolphthalein, China rose and blue litmus. The observations are recorded in the given table. Classify *W*, *X*, *Y* and *Z* as acids, bases or neutral substances.

Soln.	Methyl orange	Phenolphthalein	China rose	Blue litmus
W	Yellow	Pink	Green	Blue
X	Orange	Colourless	Pink	Blue
Y	Yellow	Pink	Green	Blue
Z	Red	Colourless	Magenta	Red

32. Four different mixtures are taken in four test tubes and each of them is tested with indicators as shown below:

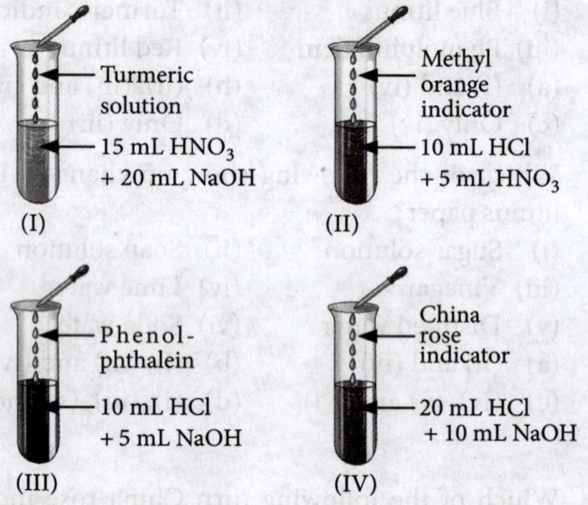

Identify the change in colour of the given solutions and give reasons also.

33. With the help of the given figures fill in the blanks in the given passage.

I am a natural dye. I am extracted from ______. I am ______ in colour in distilled water. When added to an ______ solution, I turn ______ and when a ______ solution is added, I turn ______. I am available in the form of a solution, or in the form of strips of paper, known as ______. Who am I? I am ______.

34. Observe the given figure and answer the questions that follow:

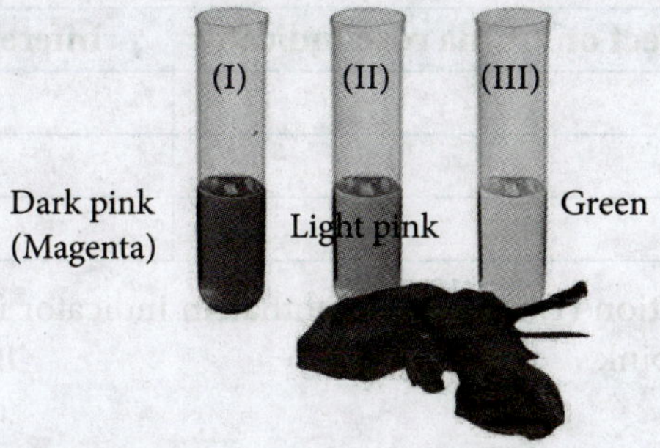

(a) Fill in the blanks in the given passage.
China rose indicator turns ______ solutions to ______ and ______ solutions to ______.

(b) If you add China rose indicator to solutions of lime water, acetic acid and common salt then which of the given test tubes represents the correct colour change observed.

Lime water : ______
Acetic acid : ______
Common salt : ______

SHORT ANSWER TYPE QUESTIONS-II (SA-II)

35. Give three examples of neutralisation reaction from our day-to-day life.

36. Define acidity of a base. Give one example each of monoacidic, diacidic and triacidic bases.

37. Define basicity of an acid. Give one example each of monobasic, dibasic and tribasic acids.

38. Shobit has two test tubes in which he has taken sodium hydroxide solution and hydrochloric acid. He has forgotten to label the test tubes. How would you help him to identify the solutions? You are provided with methyl orange indicator, phenolphthalein and China rose indicator. Ap

39. Three solutions of different pH values are given in the table. Identify the nature of these solutions by filling the correct colour changes of the given indicators.

S. No.	pH values	China rose indicator	Phenolphthalein indicator	Red litmus paper	Nature
1.	3.7				
2.	9.5				
3.	7.0				

An

40. Ravi was provided with two samples *A* and *B* containing toothpaste and curd respectively. He was told to identify the nature of these samples with the help of phenolphthalein and China rose indicators and record his observations in the given format. Help him to complete the table.

Sample	Phenolphthalein indicator	China rose indicator	Nature
A			
B			

Ap

41. You are given five samples *A*, *B*, *C*, *D* and *E*. Out of these, two are acidic, two are basic and one is neutral. (*D*) is a stronger acid than (*C*). (*B*) is neutral while (*E*) is a weaker base than (*A*). Match these samples with the given pH values: 7.0, 12.8, 2.1, 9.4 and 5.5? What is the significance of pH scale?

42. Complete the given table.

S.No.	Sample	Colour of China rose	Colour of methyl orange	Nature
(i)	Orange juice		Red	
(ii)	Lime water	Green		
(iii)	Sugar solution	Pink	Orange	
(iv)	Curd	Magenta		
(v)	Soap solution		Yellow	

43. Test the solutions enlisted in the given table with turmeric solution and China rose indicator and note down the observations and inferences.

S. No.	Solution	Effect on turmeric solution	Effect on China rose indicator	Inference
(i)	Glucose solution			
(ii)	Nitric acid			
(iii)	Sodium hydroxide			

44. In the activity shown in the figure, a colourless mixture of solution (I) and phenolphthalein indicator is taken. Excess of solution (II) is added to it until its colour changes to pink.

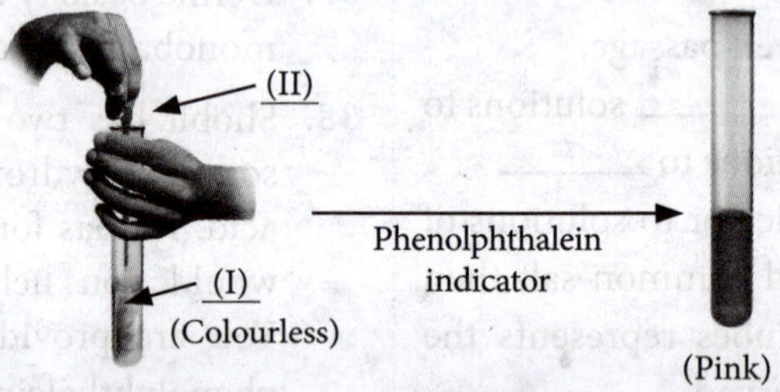

(a) What could be solutions (I) and (II)?

(b) If excess of solution (I) is added again, what could be the colour change and if excess of solution (II) is added again, what could be the colour change?

(c) What is the process called?

45. Complete the following table:

S. No.	Indicator	Colour in acidic medium	Colour in basic medium	Colour in neutral medium
(a)	Blue litmus			
(b)	Red litmus			
(c)	China rose			
(d)	Turmeric			
(e)	Methyl orange			
(f)	Phenolphthalein			

LONG ANSWER TYPE QUESTIONS (LA)

46. You are provided with three test tubes (I), (II) and (III) with three different liquids as shown in the following figures:

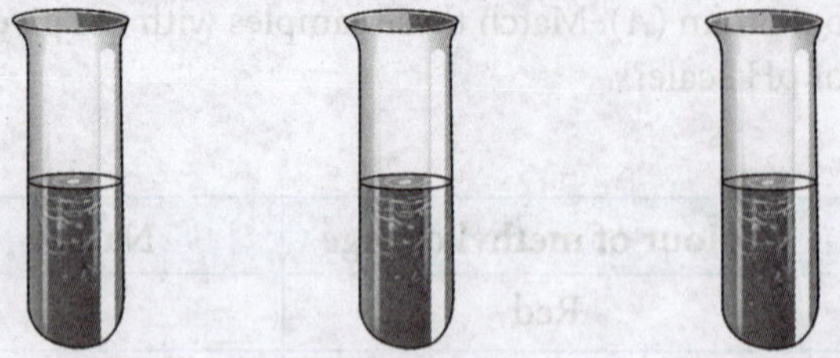

(I) Soda water | (II) Glucose solution | (III) Lime water

What will you observe when you put

(a) red and blue litmus papers in each test tube

(b) a few drops of methyl orange indicator in each test tube

(c) a piece of turmeric paper in each test tube

(d) a few drops of phenolphthalein solution in each test tube

(e) a few drops of China rose indicator in each test tube?

Make a table for your record.

47. Give reasons for the following :

(a) Sour substances should not be kept in metallic containers.

(b) Doctors advise us to brush teeth after every meal.

(c) Baking soda is used to treat a bee sting while vinegar is used to treat a wasp sting.

48. You are given three salts: potassium sulphate, sodium carbonate and ammonium sulphate. What will be the effect of aqueous solutions of these salts on

(i) Red litmus paper

(ii) Blue litmus paper
(iii) Phenolphthalein indicator
(iv) Methyl orange indicator
(v) China rose indicator
(vi) Turmeric solution
(vii) Red cabbage solution

49. Few samples are given. Fill the correct colour changes with the given indicators.

S. No.	Sample	Methyl orange	China rose	Phenolphthalein
(i)	Washing soda			
(ii)	Shampoo			
(iii)	Distilled water			
(iv)	Milk of magnesia			
(v)	Sulphuric acid			

Categorise the given samples into
(a) Acidic substances : ______________________
(b) Basic substances : ______________________
(c) Neutral substances : ______________________

50. Take some water in a plastic cup. Add a few drops of lemon juice to it. Now, with the help of a dropper, put a drop of this solution on the strips of red and blue litmus papers. Record your observation in the given table. Perform the same activity with other substances enlisted in the table.

S. No.	Solution	Effect on red litmus paper	Effect on blue litmus paper	Inference
(i)	Lime water			
(ii)	Detergent solution			
(iii)	Milk of magnesia			
(iv)	Aerated drink			
(v)	Shampoo			
(vi)	Washing soda solution			
(vii)	Window cleaner			

51. Write the importance of neutralisation reactions in treating
(a) Indigestion : ______________________
(b) Ant bite : ______________________
(c) Acidic soil : ______________________
(d) Basic soil : ______________________
(e) Factory wastes : ______________________

CASE BASED QUESTIONS (CBQs)

Case I : Read the given passage and answer the following questions :

The reaction between an acid and a base is known as neutralisation. Salt and water are produced in this process with the evolution of heat. The salt may be acidic, basic or neutral in nature. The following reaction is an example of neutralisation reaction :

$$\underset{\text{Hydrochloric acid}}{HCl} + \underset{\text{Sodium hydroxide}}{NaOH} \longrightarrow \underset{\text{Sodium chloride}}{NaCl} + \underset{\text{Water}}{H_2O}$$

52. Neutralisation is used in the treatment of
(a) ant bite
(b) indigestion
(c) factory wastes
(d) all of these.

53. Aqueous solution of sodium hydroxide turns
(a) turns red litmus blue
(b) turns blue litmus red
(c) turns red litmus yellow
(d) does not change the colour of either red or blue litmus.

54. Select the correct statement.
(a) Sodium hydroxide is used in the treatment of indigestion.
(b) Neutralisation is an endothermic process.
(c) When an ant bites, it injects hydrochloric acid into the skin.
(d) The salt formed after neutralisation can be acidic, basic or neutral in nature.

55. Which of the following is formed when sulphuric acid reacts with lime water?
(a) $CaCl_2$ (b) CaO (c) H_2 (d) $CaSO_4$

56. If a few drops of a concentrated acid accidentally falls over the hand of a person, what should be done?
(a) Wash the hand with a dilute acid.
(b) Wash the hand immediately with plenty of water and apply a paste of sodium hydrogencarbonate.
(c) After washing with plenty of water apply solution of potassium hydroxide on the hand.
(d) Neutralise the acid with a strong alkali.

Case II : Read the given passage and answer the following questions :

Special types of substances are used to test whether a substance is acidic or basic. These substances are known as indicators. The indicators change their colour when added to a solution containing an acidic or basic substance. Turmeric, litmus, China rose petals etc. are some naturally occurring indicators. While, phenolphthalein and methyl orange are some synthetic indicators.

57. What would happen to a pink coloured solution formed by adding phenolphthalein and NaOH when sulphuric acid is added to it?

58. What would happen when few drops of sour milk are put on the blue litmus paper?

59. What change is observed when blue litmus paper is added to NaCl solution?

60. How will you explain that milk of magnesia is an acid or a base by using china rose indicator?

ANSWER KEY

Practice Corner

1. (c) 2. (b) 3. (c) 4. (a) 5. (d) 6. True 7. False 8. True
9. False 10. False 11. False 12. False
13. Formic acid 14. Amino acid 15. DNA 16. Carbonic acid 17. Sulphuric acid
18. Acidic 19. Basic 20. Acidic 21. Acidic
22. Basic 23. Neutral 24. Acidic 25. Basic
26. Acidic 27. Acidic 28. Basic 29. Acidic
30. Acidic 31. Basic 32. Neutral 33. magenta
34. acidic, neutral 35. Acid rain 36. red, blue 37. red 38. no
39. red 40. (b) 41. (c) 42. (a) 43. (b) 44. (b) 45. (b) 46. True
47. False 48. False 49. False 50. True
64. Phenolphthalein 65. Turmeric solution 66. Neutral substance 67. China rose solution
68. Red cabbage indicator 69. Neutralisation, acid, base, water, salt, heat, temperature
70. Calcium sulphate 71. salt 72. NaCl 73. KBr 74. $NaNO_3$
75. False 76. False 77. True 78. True 79. True 80. (b) 81. (d) 82. (a) 83. (b) 84. (d)
85. (i) – (T), (ii) – (S), (iii) – (Q), (iv) – (P), (v) – (R) 86. Magnesium hydroxide
87. Sodium bicarbonate 88. Zinc carbonate 89. Calcium oxide 90. Calcium hydroxide

NCERT Exemplar Problems

1. (b) 2. (c) 3. (b) 4. (d) 5. (a) 6. (c) 7. (d) 8. (a) 9. (d) 10. (c)
11. (c)

A & R Corner

1. (c) 2. (a) 3. (a) 4. (a) 5. (c) 6. (b) 7. (d) 8. (b) 9. (d) 10. (a)

Exam Corner

1. (b) 2. (d) 3. (a) 4. (d) 5. (d) 6. (a) 7. (a) 8. (d) 9. (a)
10. proteins 11. basic salt 12. Lactic 13. hydrochloric
14. organic 15. acidic 16. False 17. True 18. True
19. False 20. False 52. (d) 53. (a) 54. (d) 55. (d) 56. (b)

5 Physical and Chemical Changes

NCERT Notes

Changes take place around us all the time. The changes can be divided into different types depending upon the nature of the change taking place. The changes differ in terms of appearance, colour, composition, formation of new products or any other change. Changes can be slow or fast, desirable or undesirable, periodic or non-periodic. Broadly, these changes are of two types – physical and chemical.

5.1 Physical Changes

- Change in which a substance undergoes a change in its physical properties is called a **physical change.** Properties such as shape, size, colour and state of a substance are called **physical properties.**
- Characteristics of a physical change:
  - A change where no new substances are formed.
  - Properties of the substance remain same even if the physical state changes.
  - There may or may not be evolution of heat.
  - Properties like appearance, texture, size, shape, colour, smell, state, etc. change.
  - Chemical properties of the substance do not change.
  - A physical change is generally reversible and temporary.
  - Some of the physical changes are permanent and irreversible.
- Physical changes can be reversible or irreversible. For example, shredding of paper into many small pieces is an example of irreversible physical change. The original piece of paper cannot be obtained back by joining different pieces. On the other hand, boiling of water is an example of a reversible physical change. The droplets of water can be recovered from the steam by holding an inverted glass over the steam.

5.2 Chemical Change

- Change in which a substance undergoes a change in its chemical properties is called a **chemical change.**
- Characteristics of a chemical change:
  - One or more new substances are formed during the change.
  - New substances have different properties from the original substance.
  - Heat or light or both may be produced or absorbed during the change.

- Chemical changes are usually irreversible and permanent.
- During a chemical reaction sound may be produced. A gas can be formed. A change in colour or smell may also take place.

- A chemical change is the result of a chemical reaction between two or more substances. Chemical change is also called a **chemical reaction.**

  For example : Burning of magnesium ribbon is a chemical change. The magnesium ribbon burns with a dazzling flame and forms a powdery ash known as magnesium oxide. This chemical change or chemical reaction can be represented as follows :

$$\underset{\text{Magnesium}}{2Mg} + \underset{\text{Oxygen}}{O_2} \longrightarrow \underset{\text{Magnesium oxide}}{2MgO}$$

- In addition to new products, the following may accompany a chemical change :
  - Sound may be produced.
  - Heat, light or any other radiation (ultraviolet, for instance) may be released or absorbed.
  - A change in smell can take place or a new smell may be given off.
  - A colour change may occur.
  - Formation of a gas can take place.
- The mass of the substances taken together before and after a chemical change remains the same.
- **Types of chemical reactions :**
  - In a **combination** or **synthesis reaction,** two or more reactants combine to form a product.
  - In a **decomposition reaction,** single reactant breaks down into two or more simpler products.
  - In a **displacement reaction,** one element displaces another element from a compound and takes its place. A more reactive element displaces a less reactive element from a compound in solution form.
  - In a **double displacement reaction,** two compounds react by exchanging their ions to form two new compounds.

    In a precipitation reaction, two compounds react in their aqueous state to form an insoluble product, which appears in the form of a precipitate.
- In **neutralisation reaction,** an acid reacts with a base and the radicals are exchanged to form salt and water.
- **Oxidation reaction** involves addition of oxygen or removal of hydrogen from a substance.
- **Reduction reaction** involves addition of hydrogen or removal of oxygen from a substance.
- An **oxidizing agent** oxidizes other substance by providing oxygen to them or by removing hydrogen from them.
- A **reducing agent** reduces other substance by providing hydrogen to them or by removing oxygen from them

> + Some fruits and vegetables develop a brown layer when they are out and kept in open. Certain compounds present in them react with oxygen in air and get oxidised.

- The chemical reactions can be represented in written in the form of chemical equations.
- A **chemical equation** is the representation of a chemical reaction through symbols and chemical formulae.
- Balancing of the chemical equation :
  - Write down the symbols and formulae of the reactants on the left hand side and those of the products on the right hand side of an arrow.
  - Count the atoms of each kind on both sides of the arrow.
  - Make the number of atoms of each kind, equal on both sides by using proper coefficients.

5.3 Rusting of Iron

- Rusting is a chemical change which takes place in presence of air and moisture only. It is a reddish-brown powder which is formed on the surface of iron and goes into the deeper layers.

$$\underset{\text{Iron}}{Fe} + \underset{\text{Oxygen}}{O_2} + \underset{\text{Water}}{H_2O} \rightarrow \underset{\text{Hydrated iron oxide (Rust)}}{Fe_2O_3 \cdot xH_2O}$$

Rusting is very harmful since the objects made of iron like gates, pillars, chains, bridges, etc. get rusted which results eating away the metal and slowly destroys them, the monetary loss due to rusting is huge.

Prevention of Rusting

The most important methods to prevent rusting are :

- By painting the surface of iron objects
- By greasing or oiling the surface of iron objects
- By galvanisation : Galvanisation is a process of coating the surface of iron with zinc to prevent rusting of iron.
- By alloying : Alloying is a process in which two or more metals or a metal and a non-metal are mixed in a molten state to improve the properties of metals. Iron gets rusted in moist air, iron is mixed with a small amount of carbon and metals like chromium or manganese to make stainless steel. Stainless steel does not get rusted.

5.4 Crystallisation

- It is a process of separation of pure crystals of a substance from its solution.
- Crystallisation is an example of a physical change.
- This method is used to prepare pure crystals of many compounds like sugar, copper sulphate, alum (*phitkari*).
- This method is also used to prepare pure salt from sea water.
- Large crystals of alum can be prepared by adding a small crystal of an alum in its saturated solution.
- The process of crystallisation plays an important role in the purification of an impure salt obtained from sea water. The salt is added to a mixture of boiling water and dilute acid (generally dilute sulphuric acid). The salt is dissolved and the solution is stirred continuously. After sometime, the solution is filtered and allowed to cool. Crystals of salt become visible after sometime.

Practice Corner

Extracted from NCERT

Assessment is complementary part of the learning process. It gives you a total insight whether the learning outcomes have been achieved or not. After going through the corresponding NCERT Textbook chapter, attempt these questions in exam like environment. Give yourself one mark for correct answer. A table is given at the end, that will help you plan your next step.

All the Best!

5.1 Physical Changes

NCERT Page 47-48

A. Select the correct option.

1. Which of the following are physical changes?
   (i) Souring of milk
   (ii) Dissolving salt in water
   (iii) Setting curd from milk
   (iv) Stretching of a rubber band
   (a) (i) and (iii) (b) (i) and (ii)
   (c) (iii) and (iv) (d) (ii) and (iv) An

2. Select the incorrect statement.
   (a) A change in which substance undergoes a change in its physical properties is called a physical change.
   (b) A physical change is generally irreversible.
   (c) In physical change, no new substance is formed.
   (d) Both (a) and (c) U

3. Select the odd one out.
   (a) Evaporation (b) Cutting of paper
   (c) Burning of paper (d) Condensation U

4. Identify the physical-reversible changes.
   (i) Melting of wax (ii) Slaking of lime
   (iii) Plucking of leaves
   (iv) Condensation of steam
   (a) (i) and (iii) (b) (ii) and (iv)
   (c) (i) and (iv) (d) (ii) and (iii) An

5. Identify the physical change that cannot be reversed.
   (a) Making of sugar solution
   (b) Inflating a balloon (c) Drying of clothes
   (d) Breaking of flower vase An

B. Observe the diagrams. Mark (P) for the activities which show a physical change and (C) for the activities which do not show a physical change.

6. 

7. 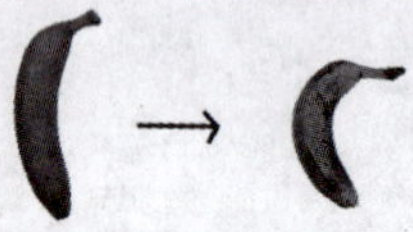

8. 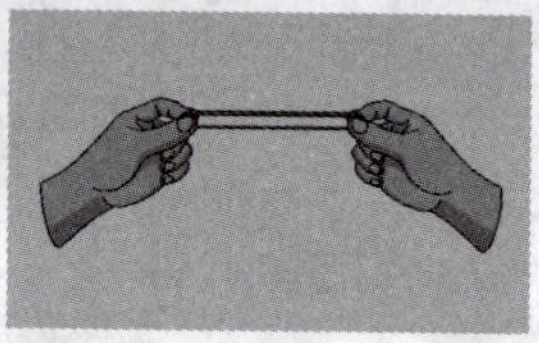

9. 

10. 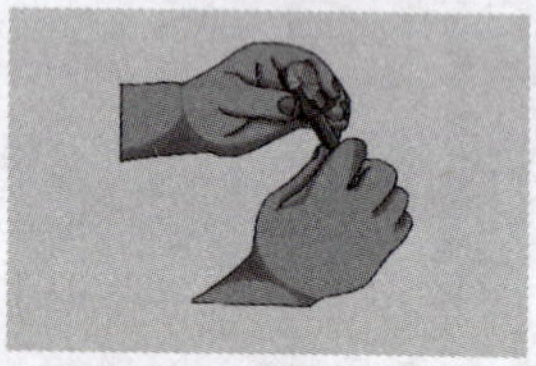

11. 

12. 

13. 

14. 

15. 

16. 

C. Some changes are enlisted in the following table. Write the property of the substance which undergoes a change during the process (shape, size, colour or state).

S.No.	Changes	Property of the substance which undergoes a change
17.	Folding a paper to make paper boat	
18.	Heating an iron nail	
19.	Making toys from clay	
20.	Cutting a log of wood	
21.	Melting of ice-cream	

D. State True (T) or False (F) for the given statements.

22. Burning of a substance is a physical change. [ ]
23. Extraction of metal from an ore is a physical change. [ ]
24. Explosion of a firework is a physical change. [ ]
25. Spoilage of food is a physical change. [ ]

E. Give an example of each of the following:

26. Physical-reversible change ______
27. Physical change in size ______
28. Physical-irreversible change ______
29. Physical change in shape ______
30. Physical change in state ______
31. Physical change in which heat is evolved ______
32. Physical change in which heat is absorbed ______

5.2 Chemical Change

NCERT Page 48-52

A. Select the correct option.

33. Select the correct statements.
    (i) During a chemical change, no new substance is formed.
    (ii) Chemical changes are generally reversible.
    (iii) Most of the chemical changes are irreversible and permanent.
    (iv) During a chemical change, chemical composition of a substance is changed.
    (a) (i) and (iii) (b) (iii) and (iv)
    (c) (ii) and (iv) (d) (i) and (ii) U
34. Which of the following are chemical changes?
    (i) Heating an iron blade
    (ii) Mixing baking soda with vinegar
    (iii) Making of a salt solution
    (iv) Burning of a magnesium ribbon
    (a) (i) and (iii) (b) (i) and (iv)
    (c) (ii) and (iv) (d) (ii) and (iii) An
35. On passing carbon dioxide gas, lime water turns milky due to the formation of
    (a) calcium oxide (b) calcium carbonate
    (c) calcium hydroxide (d) calcium. An
36. Observe the following reaction and tick the correct statement.
    Iron sulphate solution + Copper ⟶ Copper sulphate solution + Iron
    (a) Green colour of the solution changes to blue colour.
    (b) Iron is less reactive than copper.
    (c) Reaction will not take place.
    (d) None of these An
37. Curdling of milk is a ______ change.
    (a) chemical (b) reversible
    (c) physical (d) all of these U
38. Which of the following is a chemical change?
    (a) Photosynthesis (b) Transpiration
    (c) Digestion (d) Both (a) and (c) An
39. ______ gas is evolved when zinc reacts with dilute sulphuric acid.
    (a) Carbon dioxide (b) Hydrogen
    (c) Ammonia (d) Oxygen U

B. Fill in the blanks.

40. When carbon dioxide is passed through lime water, it turns milky due to the formation of ______. U
41. Bubbles of ______ gas with hissing sound are evolved on reaction between baking soda and vinegar.
42. When an iron blade is dipped in copper sulphate solution, the colour of solution changes from ______ to ______ due to the formation of ______ and the surface of iron nail gets a brown coloured deposit of ______. Ev
43. The air we breathe out is rich in ______.
44. A new product ______ is formed, by the action of water and oxygen on iron.
45. Blue colour of the copper sulphate solution changes to green due to the formation of ______.

C. Give an example of each of the following:

46. Chemical change ______
47. Chemical change in which heat is evolved ______
48. Chemical change in which light is produced ______
49. Chemical change in which sound is produced ______

D. State True (T) or False (F) for the given statements.

50. Medicines, plastics and detergents are the results of many chemical reactions. [ ]

51. No sound is produced during a chemical change.

52. Change in smell may occur during a chemical change.

53. Change in colour may take place during a chemical change.

54. A chemical change is always accompanied with the evolution of gas.

55. Explosion of a firework is a physical change.

56. Breaking down of ozone is a chemical change.

E. Identify the following :

57. Reaction between an acid and a base ______

58. Reaction involving addition of oxygen ______

59. Permanent, irreversible change in which one or more new substances are formed ______

60. Reaction involving addition of hydrogen ______

61. Formation of an insoluble product when two compounds react in their aqueous states ______

5.3 Rusting of Iron

NCERT Page 52-53

A. Select the correct option.

62. Chemically, rust is
(a) iron (b) ferrous sulphate
(c) iron oxide (d) none of these R

63. Galvanisation is a process in which
(a) iron is coated on zinc metal
(b) zinc and iron are mixed in molten state
(c) zinc is coated as a layer on iron
(d) carbon is mixed with iron and heated. R

64. What is the chemical formula of rust?
(a) $FeCO_3$ (b) $Fe_2O_3.xH_2O$
(c) FeO (d) $FeSO_4$ R

65. Rusting of iron is a
(a) physical, irreversible change
(b) physical, reversible change
(c) chemical, reversible change
(d) chemical, irreversible change

66. Which of the following metals is not used during alloying?
(a) Chromium (b) Nickel
(c) Manganese (d) Sodium

B. Fill in the blanks in the given passage.

67. ______ is a ______ change that affects iron articles and slowly destroys them. For this, the presence of both ______ and ______ is essential. It becomes faster, if the content of ______ in ______ is ______.

68. We can prevent iron articles from rusting by different ways. One simple way is to apply a coat of ______ or ______. Another way is to deposit a layer of a ______ on iron. The process of depositing a layer of ______ on iron is called ______. ______ water makes this process faster.

5.4 Crystallisation

NCERT Page 53

A. Select the correct option.

69. Crystallisation is the process in which
(a) crystals of pure substance are obtained
(b) crystals of impure substance are obtained
(c) colourless crystals of a coloured substance are obtained
(d) coloured crystals of a colourless substance are obtained.

70. Pure salt from the sea water can be obtained by
(a) neutralisation (b) boiling
(c) evaporation
(d) evaporation and crystallisation.

71. Mark the incorrect statement.
(a) A crystal is a solid in its pure form.
(b) Galvanisation is zinc coating on iron.
(c) Rusting is a chemical reversible change.
(d) Reaction of iron and copper sulphate is a displacement reaction.

B. Fill in the blanks.

72. Salt is obtained from sea water by the process of ______.

73. Copper sulphate solution is ______ in colour.

C. State True (T) or False (F) for the given statements.

74. Crystallisation is a reversible, physical change.

75. Crystallisation is used to prepare crystals of sugar.

PROGRESS CHECK

Check your score! If your score is

> 95%	EXCELLENT !	- Move on to the next chapter. You have mastered this chapter. Concepts are certainly on your fingertips.
95-85%	VERY GOOD !	- Revise once more thoroughly. Recognise your mistakes and work on them. You will master this chapter.
84-75%	GOOD!	- Work on your weak areas, master them and come back to this chapter in a few days.
74-65%	MEDIOCRE!	- Understand your weak areas and work on strengthening your concepts. Devote more time to master this chapter.
< 65%	NOT SATISFACTORY!	- This is where you fall behind from scoring well. Give special attention to this chapter. Work on clearing concepts and common errors.

NCERT Exemplar Problems

This section contains MCQs of **'NCERT Exemplar Problems'** Book.

1. Which of the following is a physical change?
   (a) Rusting of iron
   (b) Combustion of magnesium ribbon
   (c) Burning of candle
   (d) Melting of wax

2. Which of the following is a chemical change?
   (a) Twinkling of stars
   (b) Cooking of vegetables
   (c) Cutting of fruits (d) Boiling of water

3. A chemical change may involve
   (a) change in colour only
   (b) change in temperature only
   (c) evolution of gas only
   (d) any or all of the above

4. Which of the following are true when milk changes into curd?
   (i) Its state is changed from liquid to semi solid.
   (ii) It changes colour.
   (iii) It changes taste.
   (iv) The change cannot be reversed.
   Choose the correct option from below:
   (a) (i) and (ii) are correct.
   (b) (ii) and (iii) are correct.
   (c) (i), (iii) and (iv) are correct.
   (d) (i) to (iv) are correct.

5. A man painted his main gate made up of iron, to
   (i) prevent it from rusting
   (ii) protect it from sun
   (iii) make it look beautiful
   (iv) make it dust free.
   Which of the above statement(s) is/are correct?
   (a) (i) and (ii) (b) (ii) and (iii)
   (c) Only (ii) (d) (i) and (iii)

6. Iron pillar near the Qutub Minar in Delhi is famous for the following facts. Which of these facts is responsible for its long stability?
   (a) It is more than 7 metres high.
   (b) It weighs about 6000 kg.
   (c) It was built more than 1600 years ago.
   (d) It has not rusted after such a long period.

7. Galvanisation is a process used to prevent the rusting of which of the following?
   (a) Iron (b) Zinc
   (c) Aluminium (d) Copper

8. Paheli's mother made a concentrated sugar syrup by dissolving sugar in hot water. On cooling, crystals of sugar got separated. This indicates a
   (a) physical change that can be reversed
   (b) chemical change that can be reversed
   (c) physical change that cannot be reversed
   (d) chemical change that cannot be reversed.

9. Which of the following statements is incorrect for a chemical reaction?
   (a) Heat may be given out but never absorbed.
   (b) Sound may be produced.
   (c) A colour change may take place.
   (d) A gas may be evolved.

10. Two drops of dilute sulphuric acid were added to 1 g of copper sulphate powder and then small amount of hot water was added to dissolve it (step I). On cooling, beautiful blue coloured crystals got separated (step II). Step I and Step II are
    (a) physical and chemical changes respectively
    (b) chemical and physical changes respectively
    (c) both physical change
    (d) both chemical change.

A&R Corner

Directions : In the following questions, a statement of assertion is followed by a statement of reason. Mark the correct choice as :
(a) If both assertion and reason are true and reason is the correct explanation of assertion.
(b) If both assertion and reason are true but reason is not the correct explanation of assertion.
(c) If assertion is true but reason is false.
(d) If both assertion and reason are false.

1. **Assertion :** Breaking of egg is a physical change.
Reason : Boiling of egg is a chemical change. U

2. **Assertion :** Colour of copper sulphate solution changes from blue to green on immersing an iron nail in it.
Reason : Iron displaces copper from the copper sulphate solution and forms a green coloured iron sulphate solution.

3. **Assertion :** Mixing of salt in water is a reversible change.
Reason : The original salt can be recovered by evaporation. U

4. **Assertion :** Presence of oxygen and water are essential for rusting.
Reason : Rusting is a reversible chemical change.

5. **Assertion :** Iron and rust are same thing.
Reason : Zinc is coated with iron to prevent rusting.

6. **Assertion :** Slaking of lime is a chemical change.
Reason : When carbon dioxide is passed through limewater, it turns milky due to the formation of a new substance, $CaCO_3$.

7. **Assertion :** Setting of curd is reversible.
Reason : When milk is set to curd, the properties of milk and curd remain same. U

8. **Assertion :** Rusting of iron is faster in coastal areas.
Reason : Percentage of moisture is higher in coastal areas. U

9. **Assertion :** Crystallisation is a process in which pure crystals of substances are separated from saturated solution.
Reason : Crystals of pure sugar separate out from saturated solution on heating. Ap

10. **Assertion :** Burning of magnesium ribbon is a chemical change.
Reason : Burning of magnesium ribbon produces magnesium oxide (a white coloured solid). U

Exam Corner

This section comprises of different types of questions:

- **Objective Type Questions :** These are **one mark** questions.
- **Very Short Answer Type Questions (VSA) :** These are **one mark** questions.
- **Short Answer Type Questions-I (SA-I) :** These are **two marks** questions.
- **Short Answer Type Questions-II (SA-II) :** These are **three marks** questions.
- **Long Answer Type Questions (LA) :** These are **five marks** questions.
- **Case Based Questions (CBQs) :** These are case study/passage based questions.

OBJECTIVE TYPE QUESTIONS

A. Select the correct option.

1. A ______ reactive element displaces a ______ reactive element from its salt solution.
(a) more, more (b) less, more
(c) more, less (d) less, less U

2. ______ is deposited as a brown coating on the iron nails kept in copper sulphate solution.
(a) Iron (b) Ferrous sulphate
(c) Copper sulphate (d) Copper

3. Which of the following represents a displacement reaction?
(a) $2Mg + O_2 \rightarrow 2MgO$
(b) $Fe + CuSO_4 \rightarrow FeSO_4 + Cu$
(c) $MgO + H_2O \rightarrow Mg(OH)_2$
(d) $2H_2 + O_2 \rightarrow 2H_2O$ An

4. Which of the following is a balanced chemical equation?
(a) $H_2 + Cl_2 \rightarrow HCl$ (b) $Mg + O_2 \rightarrow 2MgO$
(c) $2Fe + O_2 \rightarrow FeO$ (d) $2C + O_2 \rightarrow 2CO$

5. Which of the following are molecules?
(i) Ba (ii) H_2 (iii) Mg (iv) CO_2
(a) (i) and (ii) (b) (iii) and (iv)
(c) (ii) and (iv) (d) All of these

6. Which of the following are both physical and chemical changes?
(i) Burning of wood (ii) Burning of candle
(iii) Burning of LPG (iv) Burning of biogas
(a) (i) and (iv) (b) (ii) and (iv)
(c) (i) and (iii) (d) (ii) and (iii) An

7. Which of the following statements is/are true about a compound?
(i) The composition of a particular compound remains fixed.
(ii) It cannot be separated into its constituent elements by physical methods.
(iii) The properties of a compound are same as the properties of its constituent elements.
(a) (i) and (ii) (b) Only (iii)
(c) (i) and (iii) (d) All of these

8. Which of the following reactions represents a double displacement reaction?
(a) $AB + C \rightarrow AC + B$ (b) $A + B \rightarrow AB$
(c) $XY + ZW \rightarrow XZ + YW$
(d) $XY \rightarrow X + Y$ U

9. Which substance is acting as an oxidizing agent in the given reaction?
$H_2S + Cl_2 \rightarrow S + 2HCl$
(a) HCl (b) Cl_2 (c) S (d) H_2S

10. Some examples of changes are given below:
(i) Cutting a log of wood into pieces
(ii) Breaking down of ozone
(iii) Melting of glaciers
(iv) Lime water turning milky
(v) Digestion of food
(vi) Punching a hole in a paper
Classify the above changes into
(I) Irreversible, physical change
(II) Chemical change
(III) Reversible, physical change
(a) (I) - i, vi (II) - ii, iv, v (III) - iii
(b) (I) - i, ii, v (II) - iv, vi (III) - iii
(c) (I) - i (II) - ii, iv (III) - iii, v, vi
(d) (I) - vi (II) - iii, v (III) - i, ii, iv An

11. Which of the following gases turn(s) lime water milky?
(a) Carbon dioxide gas (b) Oxygen gas
(c) Sulphur dioxide gas (d) Both (a) and (c)

12. Fill in the blanks by observing the following chemical process:

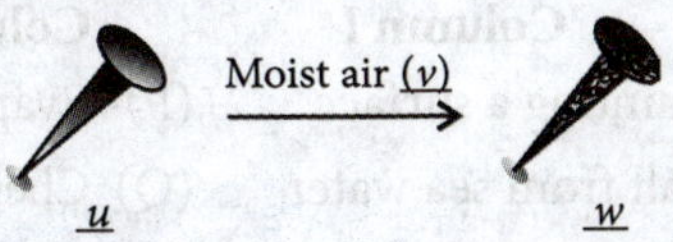

	u	*v*	*w*
(a)	Mg	O_2	MgO
(b)	Ca	CO_2	$CaCO_3$
(c)	Fe	O_2 & H_2O	$Fe_2O_3.xH_2O$
(d)	Fe	H_2O & O_2	FeO

B. State True (T) or False (F) for the given statements.

13. Rust is different from iron on which it gets deposited. ☐
14. Blue colour of copper sulphate solution changes to green when iron nail is dipped in it. ☐
15. Reaction of magnesium with oxygen gives magnesium hydroxide. ☐
16. Vinegar and baking soda when mixed together produce carbon dioxide, which turns lime water milky. ☐
17. Hydrogen gas is produced when acetic acid reacts with sodium hydrogencarbonate. ☐
18. When magnesium is burnt in air, magnesium oxide is formed. ☐
19. Copper burns with a dazzling white flame. ☐
20. Hydrogen gas turns lime water milky. ☐
21. Most of the chemical changes are reversible. ☐

C. Match the columns.

22.

Column I	Column II
(i) $Mg + O_2 \rightarrow$	(P) $CO_2 + H_2O + CH_3COONa$
(ii) $CuSO_4 + Fe \rightarrow$	(Q) $Mg(OH)_2$
(iii) $Fe + O_2 + H_2O \rightarrow$	(R) $CaCO_3 + H_2O$
(iv) $MgO + H_2O \rightarrow$	(S) $FeSO_4 + Cu$
(v) $CH_3COOH + NaHCO_3 \rightarrow$	(T) MgO
(vi) $CO_2 + Ca(OH)_2 \rightarrow$	(U) Fe_2O_3

23.

Column I	Column II
(i) Burning of paper	(P) Physical change
(ii) Crystallisation	(Q) Chemical change
(iii) Melting of ice	(R) Mixing of molten solids
(iv) Alloying	(S) Pure Solid

24.

Column I	Column II
(i) Painting a surface	(P) Evaporation
(ii) Salt from sea water	(Q) Chemical change
(iii) Cooking of food	(R) Physical irreversible change
(iv) Breaking of a flower vase	(S) Prevention of rusting

25.

Column I	Column II
(i) Making a paper boat	(P) Cut apples
(ii) Oxidation	(Q) Crystallisation
(iii) Cutting of paper into pieces	(R) Physical, reversible change
(iv) Solid in pure form	(S) Physical, irreversible change

D. Fill in the blanks.

26. When the ash formed by burning of magnesium in air is dissolved in water, ________ is formed.
27. The process of separation of crystals from a solution on cooling, is called ________. R
28. The change of state of a substance from solid to liquid and liquid to gas is a ________ change.
29. ________ gas extinguishes fire. R
30. ________ gas burns with a pop sound.

VERY SHORT ANSWER TYPE QUESTIONS (VSA)

A. Identify the following :

31. Temporary, reversible change in which no new substance is formed ________ U
32. Formation of a brown layer on an iron vessel kept in moist air ________
33. Reaction involving breaking of a single substance into two or more substances ________
34. Process of depositing a layer of zinc over iron ________
35. Formation of crystals of pure substances from their saturated solutions ________ R

B. Represent the following changes in the form of equations:

36. Burning of magnesium ribbon in air
37. Rusting of iron
38. Reaction between carbon dioxide and lime water
39. Reaction between copper sulphate solution and an iron nail
40. Reaction between zinc and dilute hydrochloric acid
41. Reaction between vinegar and baking soda
42. Reaction between ash obtained from burning of magnesium ribbon with water

43. Reaction between an acid and a base

C. Complete the given analogy.

44. Heating of calcium carbonate : Decomposition : : ______ : Combination **An**

45. Addition of hydrogen : Reduction : : ______ : Oxidation **R**

46. Dissolution : ______ : : Burning : Chemical change

47. Reaction of silver nitrate with copper : Displacement : : Heating sodium bicarbonate : ______

48. Neutralisation : Chemical change : : ______ : Physical change **An**

D. Observe the following figure and fill in the blanks in the given passage.

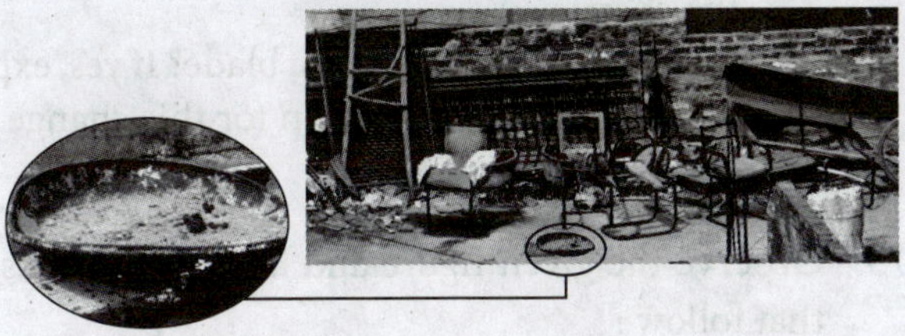

49. A change in which one or more new substances are formed is called a ______ change. These changes are very important in our lives. In addition to new products, ______, ______ or any other radiation may be given off or ______. Burning is a ______ change. Burning is always accompanied by production of ______. When a piece of iron is left open for some time, a brownish substance called ______ is formed which is different from ______. This process is called ______. **Ev**

SHORT ANSWER TYPE QUESTIONS-I (SA-I)

50. Give four differences between physical and chemical changes.

51. What will happen when a pinch of baking soda is added to vinegar? How will you test the evolution of a gas? Write the reactions involved.

52. Explain the term 'displacement reaction' and give an example.

53. (a) Why do cut vegetables and fruits turn brown when exposed to air?
    (b) What happens when a saturated solution is left for cooling?
    What types of changes are they?

54. Differentiate between alloying and galvanisation. Give an example of each. **R**

55. Justify the statement "Burning of candle is both physical and chemical change." **U**

56. Write the chemical equation for rusting of iron.

57. Explain how painting, greasing or coating with a metal prevents an iron article from rusting.

58. Explain why rusting of iron articles is faster in coastal areas than in deserts. **U**

59. Define galvanisation. Explain with example.

60. Can mixing iron with other metals prevent rusting? If yes, give an example. What is this process called?

61. Make a list of ten changes you have noticed around you and classify them as physical (P) or chemical (C) changes. **Ev**

SHORT ANSWER TYPE QUESTIONS-II (SA-II)

62. Observe the given figure and answer the questions that follow:

(a) Which process is shown in the above figure?
(b) What kind of change is it – physical or chemical? Justify your answer.
(c) Describe the process.
(d) Give one example where this process is involved in getting an important ingredient of our food. **Ev**

63. Answer the following questions.
    (a) Define the following terms:
        (i) Crystals
        (ii) Crystallisation
    (b) Describe the process of getting crystals of pure sugar from its solution.

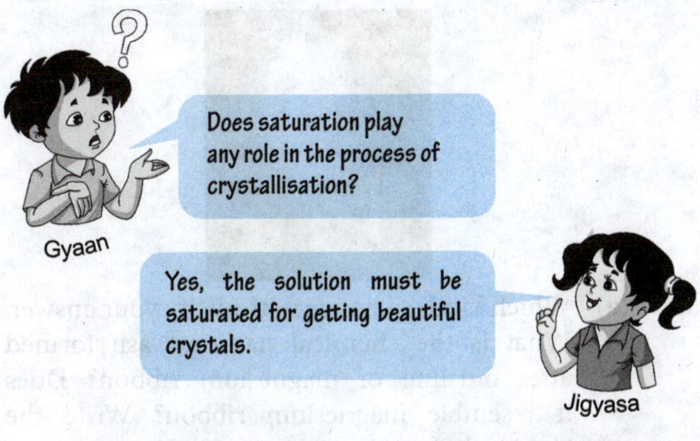

64. What is double displacement reaction? What are its two types? Explain them by giving an example of each type. **Ev**

65. Define chemical equation. Write the steps for balancing it? Explain by giving an example.

66. Which gas is evolved when dil. hydrochloric acid is added to calcium carbonate? How will you test the gas? Write the chemical equations involved.

67. Define combustion. What type of change is it? Demonstrate with an activity.

68. Define crystallisation. What type of change is it? Demonstrate with an activity.

LONG ANSWER TYPE QUESTIONS (LA)

69. Define rusting of an iron. What are the conditions necessary for rusting to take place? Write a chemical equation involved. Give any three methods by which rusting can be prevented.

70. Demonstrate an activity to show that both oxygen and water are essential for rusting to take place. Illustrate with a well-labelled diagram.

71. Define the following chemical reactions and give an example of each.
(a) Displacement reaction
(b) Oxidation reaction
(c) Combination reaction
(d) Reduction reaction
(e) Decomposition reaction

72. Give reasons for the following :
(a) A shiny copper vessel turns green after some time.
(b) Iron pipes used in homes to carry water are galvanised.
(c) Iron objects get rusted very fast in coastal areas

73. Observe the given figure which shows burning of a magnesium ribbon and answer the questions that follow:

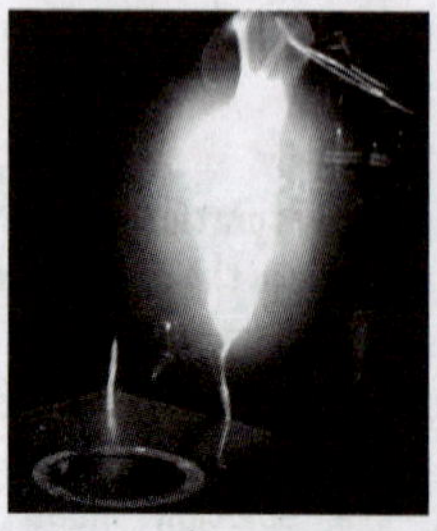

(a) Which kind of change is it? Justify your answer.
(b) What is the chemical name of ash formed after burning of magnesium ribbon? Does it resemble magnesium ribbon? Write the chemical equation.
(c) What happens when this compound is dissolved in water? Write the chemical equation. What kind of change is it? What is the nature of the compound formed – acidic or basic? How will you test?

74. Observe the given figure and answer the questions that follow:

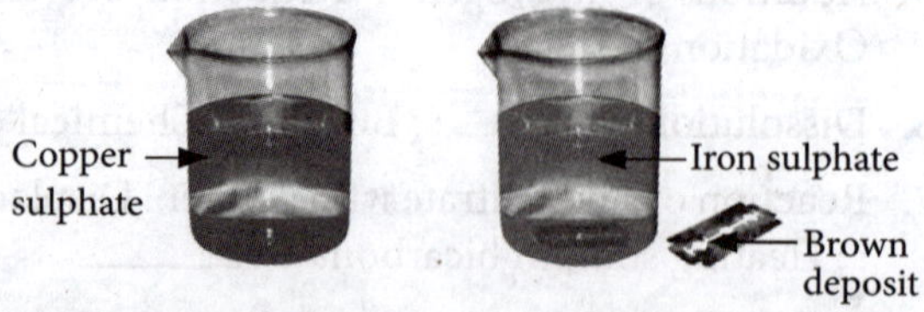

(a) What kind of change is it – physical or chemical? Justify your answer.
(b) Is there any change in colour of the solution? If yes, write the colour changes and the reason for the change.
(c) Is there any change in iron blade? If yes, explain.
(d) Write a chemical equation for this change.

Ev

75. Observe the given figure and answer the questions that follow :

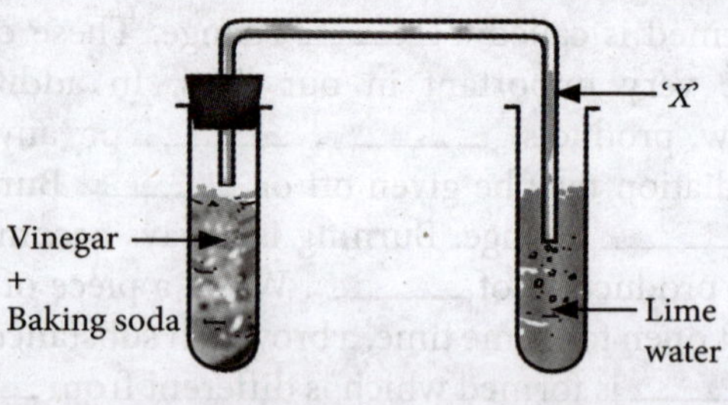

(a) What is 'X' in the given figure?
(b) What kind of change is it? Justify your answer.
(c) Write the chemical reaction taking place between vinegar and baking soda.
(d) What will happen when 'X' is passed through lime water? Give reason for your answer and write the chemical equation.
(e) What type of reaction occurs between vinegar and baking soda?

Ev

76. Look at the figures (I) and (II) given below and answer the questions that follow:

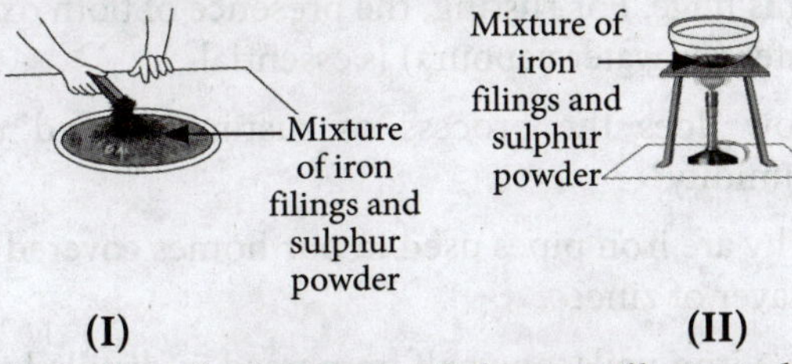

(a) Identify the types of changes illustrated by the figures (I) and (II) and justify your answer.
(b) Give four characteristics of each change.

77. Observe the following figure and answer the questions that follow:

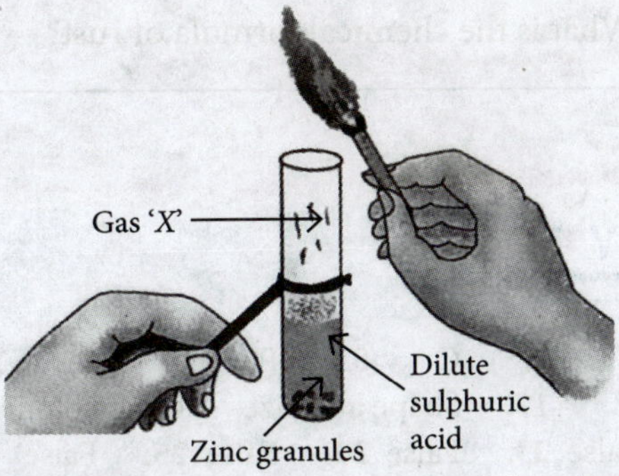

(a) What kind of change is it? Can the change be reversed?
(b) Identify the gas 'X'.
(c) Write the chemical equation involved.
(d) What will happen to the burning matchstick?
(e) Does the test tube feel warm after this change?

78. Observe the following figure and answer the questions that follow:

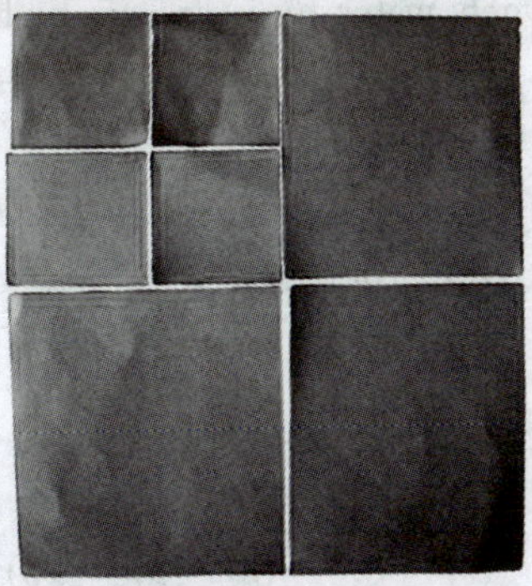

(a) Identify the type of change.
(b) Make an aeroplane or a paper boat by folding a paper. What kind of change is it?
(c) Write three characteristics of this kind of change.

79. (Do this activity in the supervision of an adult.) Take some water in a container and boil it. Hold an inverted pan by its handle over the steam at some distance from the boiling water.

(a) What do you observe?
(b) What kind of changes are these? Justify your answer.
(c) Are these changes–reversible or irreversible? Give reason.
(d) Which property of the substance changes during this activity?

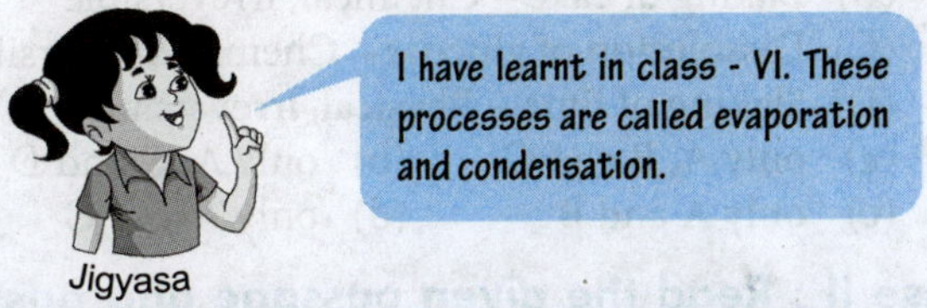

CASE BASED QUESTIONS (CBQs)

Case I : Read the given passage and answer the following questions :

A change in which one or more new substance is formed is called chemical change. A chemical change is also called a chemical reaction. Chemical changes are very important in our lives All new substances are formed as a result of chemical change.

80. Few processes have been mentioned below :
(A) Rusting of iron
(B) Melting of ice
(C) Sublimation of naphthalene
(D) Digestion of food
Which of the following is/are chemical change(s)?
(a) only A (b) only A, B and C
(c) only C (d) only A and D

81.

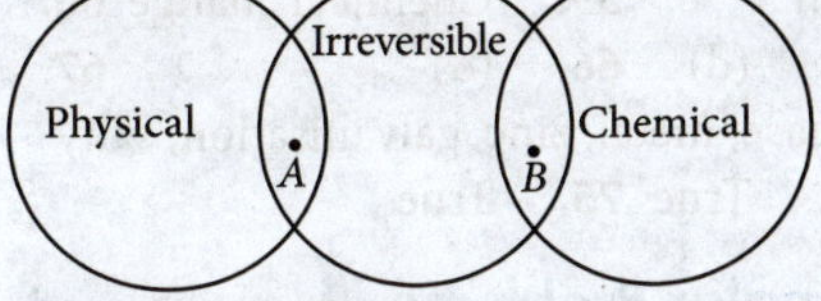

Which of the following correctly explains A and B?

	A	B
(a)	Cutting a log of of wood	Dissolving sugar in water
(b)	Melting of ice	Rusting of iron
(c)	Freezing of water	Photosynthesis
(d)	Shredding of paper	Digestion of food

82. Which of the following is an example of a displacement reaction?
(a) $Fe + O_2 + H_2O \longrightarrow Fe_2O_3$
(b) $CuSO_4 + Fe \longrightarrow FeSO_4 + Cu$
(c) $2Mg + O_2 \longrightarrow 2MgO$
(d) $Ca(OH)_2 + CO_2 \longrightarrow CaCO_3 + H_2O$

83. Which of the following chemical changes is accompanied by evolution of heat?
(A) Reaction of vinegar with baking soda

(B) Photosynthesis
(C) Respiration (D) Boiling of water
(a) only A (b) only A and B
(c) only A and C (d) only D U

84. Which of the following processes are incorrectly matched?
(A) Ripening of fruits – Chemical, reversible
(B) Baking of cake – Chemical, irreversible
(C) Dissolution of glucose – Chemical, reversible
(D) Slaking of lime – Physical, irreversible
(a) only A, B and C (b) only A, C and D
(c) only A and B (d) only A and C

Case II : Read the given passage and answer the following questions :

Rusting affects iron articles and slowly destroys them. Since iron is used in making bridges, ships, cars, truck bodies and many other articles, the monetary loss due to rusting is huge. For rusting, the presence of both oxygen and water (or water vapours) is essential.

85. How does the process of rusting depend upon humidity?
86. Why are iron pipes used in our homes covered with a layer of zinc?
87. Two iron nails, one half immersed in distilled water and the other half immersed in saline water, are taken. Which is expected to rust faster?
88. Name two methods to prevent rusting.
89. How does alloying help in prevention of rusting?
90. What is the chemical formula of rust?

ANSWER KEY

Practice Corner

1. (d) 2. (b) 3. (c) 4. (c) 5. (d) 6. P 7. C 8. P 9. P 10. P
11. P 12. C 13. P 14. P 15. C 16. P 17. Shape and size 18. colour
19. Shape 20. Shape 21. State 22. False 23. False 24. False 25. False
26. Melting of ice 27. Cutting of wood 28. Shredding of paper 29. Inflating of balloon
30. Vaporisation of water 31. Condensation 32. Evaportation
33. (b) 34. (c) 35. (b) 36. (c) 37. (a) 38. (d) 39. (b)
40. Calcium carbonate 41. carbon dioxide 42. blue, green, iron sulphate, copper
43. Carbon dioxide 44. rust (iron oxide) 45. iron sulphate 46. Burning of wood
47. Neutralisation reaction 48. Burning of candle 49. Bursting of fire crackers
50. True 51. False 52. True 53. True 54. False 55. False 56. True 57. Neutralisation
58. Oxidation 59. Chemical change 60. Reduction 61. Precipitation 62. (c) 63. (c)
64. (b) 65. (d) 66. (d) 67. Rusting, chemical, oxygen, water, moisture, air, high
68. Paint, grease, metal, zinc, galvanisation, salty 69. (a) 70. (d) 71. (c) 72. Evaporation
73. blue 74. True 75. True

NCERT Exemplar Problems

1. (d) 2. (b) 3. (d) 4. (c) 5. (d) 6. (d) 7. (a) 8. (a) 9. (a) 10. (c)

A & R Corner

1. (b) 2. (a) 3. (a) 4. (c) 5. (d) 6. (b) 7. (d) 8. (a) 9. (c) 10. (a)

Exam Corner

1. (c) 2. (d) 3. (b) 4. (d) 5. (c) 6. (d) 7. (a) 8. (c) 9. (b) 10. (a)
11. (d) 12. (c) 13. True 14. True 15. False 16. True 17. False 18. True 19. False 20. False
21. False 22. (i)-(T), (ii)-(S), (iii)-(U), (iv)-(Q), (v)-(P), (vi)-(R) 23. (i)-(Q), (ii)-(S), (iii)-(P), (iv)-(R)
24. (i)-(S), (ii)-(P), (iii)-(Q), (iv)-(R) 25. (i)-(R), (ii)-(P), (iii)-(S), (iv)-(Q)
26. magnesium hydroxide 27. saturated, crystallisation 28. physical 29. Carbon dioxide
30. Hydrogen 31. Physical 32. Rust 33. Decomposition
34. Galvanisation 35. Crystallisation 44. Burning of magnesium in air
45. Addition of oxygen 46. Physical change 47. Decomposition 48. Sublimation
49. Chemical, heat, hight, absorbed, chemical, heat, rust, iron, rusting
80. (d) 81. (d) 82. (b) 83. (c) 84. (b)

6 Respiration in Organisms

NCERT Notes

- Respiration is essential for survival of living organism. It releases energy from the food.

6.1 Why Do We Respire?

- Cells require energy to perform various functions like nutrition, transport, excretion and reproduction.
- The food we consume has stored energy, which is released during respiration.
- Respiration involves two main processes; Breathing and cellular respiration.
- The air we breathe contains oxygen which ultimately reaches the cells of the body.
- Oxygen helps in the breakdown of food (glucose) thereby releasing energy.
- This process is termed as cellular/internal respiration which takes place in the cells of the organisms.

Respiration

Aerobic respiration

Aerobic respiration is breakdown of glucose in the presence of oxygen. Its end products are carbon dioxide, water and large amount of energy. It occurs in almost all plants and animals.

$$\underset{\text{Glucose}}{C_6H_{12}O_6} + \underset{\text{Oxygen}}{6O_2} \longrightarrow \underset{\text{Carbon dioxide}}{6CO_2} + \underset{\text{Water}}{6H_2O} + \text{Energy}$$

Anaerobic respiration

Anaerobic respiration is breakdown of glucose in the absence of oxygen. Its end products are either ethyl alcohol or lactic acid, carbon dioxide and less amount of energy. This process is also known as fermentation. It occurs in yeast and some bacteria. The organisms that can survive in the absence of oxygen are called anaerobes.

$$\text{Food (glucose)} \xrightarrow{\text{In absence of oxygen}} \text{Alcohol} + \text{Carbon dioxide} + \text{Energy}$$

+ Yeast is single-celled organism. They undergo anaerobic respiration and yield alcohol. So, they are used in making beer and wine.

Anaerobic Respiration in Humans

- During heavy exercises like running, cycling and weight lifting the energy demand is high but the supply of oxygen is limited. So, muscle cells shift to anaerobic respiration for a short period of time to fulfill the demand of energy.

$$\underset{\text{(in muscle)}}{\text{Glucose}} \xrightarrow{\text{in the absence of oxygen}} \text{Lactic acid} + \text{Energy}$$

- Partial breakdown of glucose results in the formation of lactic acid in muscles which cause muscle cramps.
- Taking a hot water bath or massaging the cramped muscle improves blood circulation. This increases oxygen supply as a result of which complete breakdown of lactic acid into carbon dioxide and water occurs.

6.2 Breathing

- Breathing is a mechanical or physical process which involves inhalation (taking in) of oxygen rich air and exhalation (giving out) of carbon dioxide rich air with the help of respiratory organs. It is a continuous process that occurs throughout the life.
- Inhalation along with exhalation constitutes one breath.
- Breathing rate is defined as total number of times a person breathe per minute.
- When the energy demand increases in a body breathing becomes faster as a result of which more oxygen is available to the cells. It speeds up the process of breakdown of food and more energy is released.
- Average breathing rate of an adult human is 15-18 times per minute which increases up to 25 times per minute during heavy exercise.
- Breathing rate also increases in the case of illness.

+ When a person feels sleepy or drowsy, the lungs do not get enough oxygen. So, the brain senses it and persuade the body to take a long breath resulting in a yawn to gather a large amount of oxygen.

6.3 How Do We Breathe?

- The human respiratory system consists of the nostrils, nasal cavity, pharynx, larynx, windpipe, bronchi and lungs. Pharynx serves as common passage for both food and air.

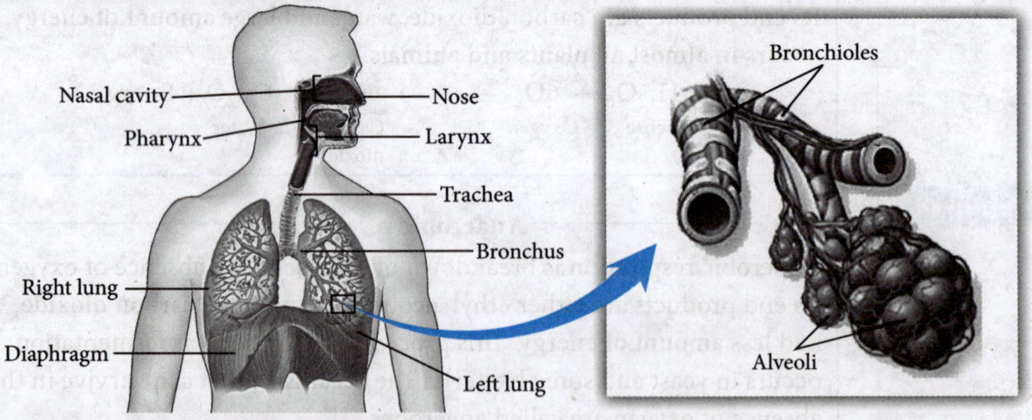

Fig.: Human respiratory system

- Air is taken up through nostrils. Then passes into the nasal cavity reaching the lungs.
- The dust, pollens and smoke particles get trapped in the hair present in the nasal cavity. Sometimes, foreign particles get past the nasal cavity and irritate the lining of nasal cavity which result in a forceful expulsion of air in the form of sneeze.
- Lungs are present in the chest cavity which is surrounded by ribs.

- Diaphragm is a large, muscular sheet which forms the floor of the chest cavity.
- Breathing involves the movement of the diaphragm and the rib cage.

Inside the lungs, the bronchus branches out into smaller tubes called bronchioles. At the ends of each bronchiole, tiny air sacs are present called **alveoli**. The actual gaseous exchange takes place in the alveoli of the lungs. Wall of alveoli are thin having rich supply of blood capillaries.

Mechanism of breathing

Inhalation

Movement of ribs is upward and outwards whereas movement of diaphragm is downwards. These movements increase space in chest cavity so that air could be rushed in the lungs.

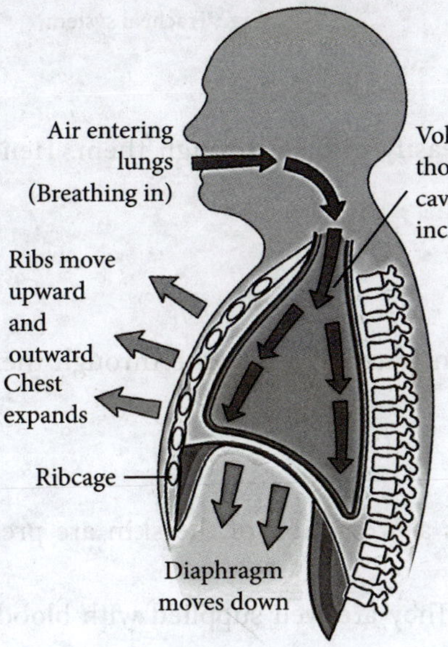

Fig.: Inhalation

Exhalation

Movement of ribs is downward and inward whereas movement of diaphragm is opposite of inhalation means returning to its previous position. These movements reduce the chest size forcing air to move out of the lungs.

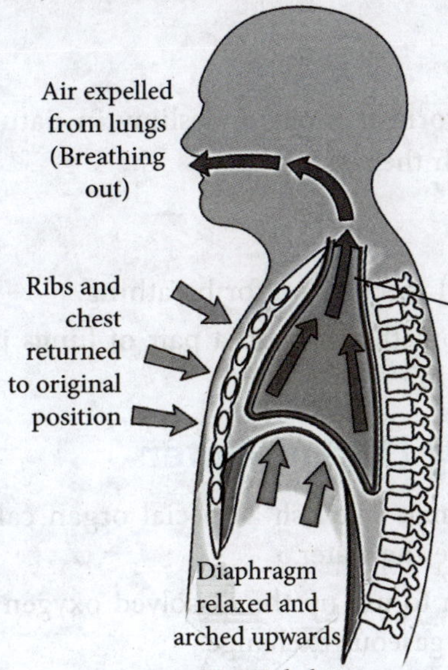

Fig.: Exhalation

Smoking is injurious to health as it reduces the area for gaseous exchange and it causes lung cancer.

6.4 What Do We Breathe Out?

To check for the presence of carbon dioxide in exhaled air.

Materials required – Test tube, freshly prepared lime water $Ca(OH)_2$ and plastic straw.

Procedure –

- Take a clean test tube.
- Put the straw in the tube such that it dips in the lime water.
- Now blow gently through the straw a few times.

Observation – The lime water turns milky.

Conclusion – In exhaled air carbon dioxide is present which reacts with the $Ca(OH)_2$ and forms $CaCO_3$, which is milky in colour.

- Air we inhale or exhale is a mixture of gases.
- Exhaled air contains - Carbon dioxide (4.4%), oxygen (16.4%) and water vapour.
- Inhaled air contains - Oxygen (21%) and carbon dioxide (0.04%).

+ Pranayama increases the lung capacity which results in more air going into lungs. Thus, more oxygen is supplied to the body.

6.5 Breathing in Other Animals

Cockroach

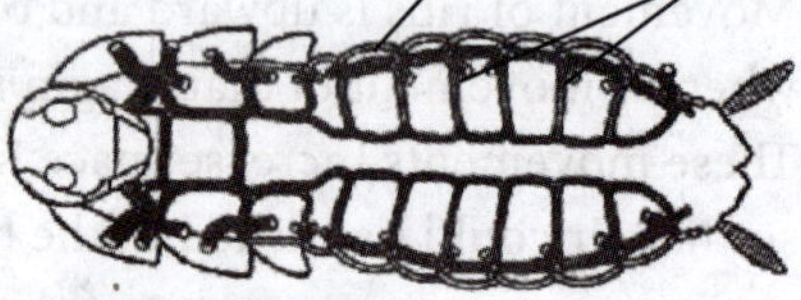

Fig.: Tracheal system

- Cockroach (insects) has small openings present on the sides of their bodies known as **spiracles**. Through these openings air rushes into tracheal tubes.
- Insects have a special network of tubes called tracheae for the purpose of gaseous exchange.
- Through these tubes air reaches to every cell of the body.

Earthworm

- Skin of earthworm is moist and slimy in nature. So, gases can easily diffuse through them. Hence, they breathe through their skins.

Frogs

- Frogs have dual mechanism for breathing.
- On land they breathe through a pair of lungs just like humans. In water they breathe through their moist and slippery skin.

6.6 Breathing Under Water

- In aquatic animals like fish a special organ called **gills,** which is a projection of the skin are present for breathing inside the water.
- Gills help them to use up the dissolved oxygen present in water. They are well supplied with blood vessels which helps in gaseous exchange.

+ Dolphins and whales often come above the surface of water to breathe.

6.7 Do Plants Also Respire?

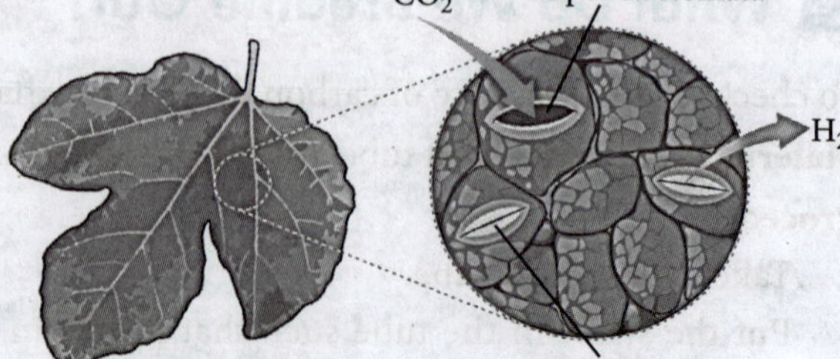

Fig.: Stomata

- In plants each part can independently take in oxygen from the air and give out carbon dioxide with the help of structures present in them.
- Stomata are tiny pores present in leaves for gaseous exchange.
- Lenticels are the pores present in the stem of woody plants which allow exchange of gases between the atmosphere and internal tissues.
- Root cells also need oxygen to generate energy. Air spaces present between the soil particles allow roots to take up air.
- Hence, the plants should not be over watered as it may block the air spaces leading to the death of the plant.

Practice Corner

Extracted from NCERT

Assessment is complementary part of the learning process. It gives you a total insight whether the learning outcomes have been achieved or not. After going through the corresponding NCERT Textbook chapter, attempt these questions in exam like environment. Give yourself one mark for correct answer. A table is given at the end, that will help you plan your next step.

All the Best!

6.1 Why Do We Respire?

NCERT Page 57-58

A. Select the correct option.

1. Select the correct statement regarding cellular respiration.
   (a) It is a biochemical process.
   (b) It involves oxidation of food into carbon dioxide and water.
   (c) It takes place within the cells.
   (d) All of these
   U

2. In human beings, muscle cramps occur after heavy exercise. It is because
   (a) partial breakdown of glucose produces lactic acid.
   (b) complete breakdown of glucose produces lactic acid.
   (c) muscle cells respire in the presence of oxygen.
   (d) supply of oxygen to muscle cells increases.
   R

3. Glucose present in our food is broken down into ________ and ________ during aerobic respiration.
   (a) alcohol, water
   (b) alcohol, carbon dioxide
   (c) carbon dioxide, water
   (d) oxygen, water
   U

4. In yeast, anaerobic break down of glucose results in the formation of
   (a) carbon dioxide (b) alcohol
   (c) oxygen (d) both (a) and (b).
   R

5. Read the given statements. Select the incorrect ones.
   (i) Cellular respiration takes place in the cells of all organisms.
   (ii) We breathe out air which is rich in lactic acid and carbon dioxide.
   (iii) Anaerobic respiration takes place in the muscle cells to fulfill the demand of energy.
   (iv) In aerobic respiration, food is broken down into alcohol and carbon dioxide in the presence of oxygen.
   (v) We get relief from cramps from hot water bath, as it increases oxygen supply which results complete breakdown of lactic acid into carbon dioxide and water.
   (a) (i), (iv) and (v) (b) (ii) and (iv)
   (c) (i), (iii) and (v) (d) (iii) and (iv)
   U

6. Sometimes during heavy physical exercise, your body cannot get enough ___(i)___ to produce the required energy. To get the additional energy, ___(ii)___ respiration occurs in your muscle cells, during which partial breakdown of glucose occurs.
   Select the correct answer for (i) and (ii).

	(i)	(ii)
(a)	Oxygen	Aerobic
(b)	Oxygen	Anaerobic
(c)	Carbon dioxide	Anaerobic
(d)	Carbon dioxide	Aerobic

R

7. Which of the following is incorrect about cellular respiration?
   (a) It occurs in all living cells.
   (b) It releases energy.
   (c) It utilises oxygen and releases carbon dioxide.
   (d) It occurs only during day.
   U

8. Which of the following options represents the correct equation for aerobic respiration?
   (a) $C_6H_{12}O_6 + 6O_2 \rightarrow CO_2 + C_2H_5OH + \text{Energy}$
   (b) $C_6H_{12}O_6 + 6O_2 \rightarrow 6CO_2 + 6H_2O + \text{Energy}$
   (c) $CO_2 + H_2O \rightarrow C_6H_{12}O_6 + 6O_2 + \text{Energy}$
   (d) $C_6H_{12}O_6 + 6O_2 \rightarrow H_2O + 6O_2 + \text{Energy}$
   U

B. Passage based questions.

9. Food that we eat has stored ________ which is released during ________. During this process, food is broken down into ________ and ________ using ________. It takes place in our cells. And this process of breaking down of food in the cells with the release of energy is called ________.

10. Respiration is of two types; ________ and ________ respiration. The first one takes place in the ________ of oxygen and the second one takes place in the ________ of oxygen.

C. State True (T) or False (F) for the given statements.

11. Cellular respiration takes place only in the cells of the lungs. ☐
12. Yeast breakdown glucose into lactic acid. ☐
13. During heavy exercise, fast running, etc., glucose is broken down into lactic acid. ☐
14. Complete breakdown of glucose takes place only in the presence of oxygen. ☐
15. Inhaled air is rich in carbon dioxide. ☐
16. Our muscle cells can respire anaerobically for a short time. ☐
17. Yeasts are single-celled organisms. ☐
18. Muscle cramps occur after heavy exercise due to the accumulation of acetic acid formed by partial breakdown of glucose. ☐

D. Figure based question.

19. Given is the image of a boy running very fast. He got muscle cramps after the run. Now, answer the questions that follow.

1. Which type of respiration occurred in the muscle cells of the boy?
2. Write down the products of such type of respiration.

6.2 Breathing

NCERT Page 58-60

A. Select the correct option.

20. An adult human at rest, breathes about ________ times in a minute.
(a) 18 - 20 (b) 15 - 18
(c) 10 - 15 (d) 10 - 18 R

21. Breathing rate
(i) remains always constant.
(ii) changes according to oxygen requirement.
(iii) is zero when the person is sleeping.
(a) (i) and (ii) (b) (ii) and (iii)
(c) Only (ii) (d) (i) and (iii) U

22. A person's breathing rate is faster when he/she is
(a) sleeping (b) running
(c) reading a book (d) walking. An

23. Select the correct statement out of the following.
(a) Normally we breathe 10 times per minute.
(b) Breathing rate increases during physical activity.
(c) Breathing rate remains same under all conditions.
(d) Both (a) and (b) An

24. Breathing is a ________ process and respiration is a ________ process.
(a) mechanical, mechanical
(b) physical, bio-chemical
(c) bio-chemical, physical
(d) chemical, chemical R

B. Fill in the blanks.

25. The taking in of air rich in oxygen into the body is called ________ and giving out air rich in carbon dioxide is known as ________.
26. Normal breathing rate of a healthy adult is ________ times/minute.
27. The breathing rate ________ when we need more energy, *i.e.*, while walking, running or exercising.
28. ________ is a part of the process of respiration.
29. A ________ is composed of one inhalation and one exhalation.

6.3 How Do We Breathe?

NCERT Page 60-63

A. Select the correct option.

30. Which of the following statements is correct regarding human respiratory system?
(a) Exchange of gases takes place in the alveoli which are surrounded by blood vessels.
(b) The blood takes oxygen to the cells where cellular respiration occurs.
(c) As the air we breathe in passes through the nostrils, it is moistened by the slimy mucus present in the nose.
(d) All of these U

31. What happens during inhalation?
(i) Oxygen is taken in.
(ii) Ribs move out.
(iii) Diaphragm moves up.
(iv) Space in the chest cavity decreases.
(a) (ii) and (iii) (b) (i) and (ii)
(c) (iii) and (iv) (d) Only (iv) An

32. Which of the following organs serves as the common passage for both food and air?
(a) Pharynx (b) Larynx
(c) Oesophagus (d) Trachea
R

33. The path followed by carbon dioxide to go out of the lungs is
(a) Lungs → Pharynx → Trachea → Nostrils
(b) Lungs → Trachea → Pharynx → Nostrils
(c) Nostrils → Pharynx → Trachea → Lungs
(d) Nostrils → Trachea → Pharynx → Lungs
An

34. Select the incorrect statements.
(i) We should always breathe through the nose.
(ii) During breathing, movement of diaphragm and the rib cage takes place.
(iii) Space in the chest cavity increases during exhalation.
(iv) During exhalation, diaphragm moves down.
(a) (i) and (iv) (b) Only (iii)
(c) (iii) and (iv) (d) (i) and (iii)
U

35. Fill in the blanks and select the correct option.
(i) From the nasal cavity, air reaches our lungs through the ________.
(ii) ________ are present in our nasal cavity which can trap unwanted particles in the inhaled air.
(iii) During ________, the lungs get filled with air.

	(i)	(ii)	(iii)
(a)	Windpipe	Cavities	Inhalation
(b)	Trachea	Cavities	Exhalation
(c)	Windpipe	Hair	Inhalation
(d)	Trachea	Hair	Exhalation

U

36. Refer to the given figures (P and Q) showing breathing mechanism in human beings. Select the incorrect option regarding P and Q.

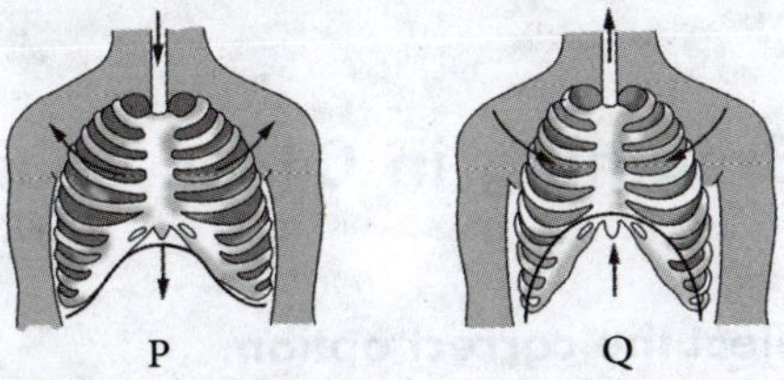

(a) During P, ribs move up and outwards and diaphragm moves down.
(b) The process Q increases the space in our chest cavity and air rushes into the lungs.
(c) During Q, ribs move down and inwards, while diaphragm moves up to its former position.
(d) The movements during P and Q can be felt easily by keeping our palm on the abdomen.
Ev

37. Study the given experimental set-up.

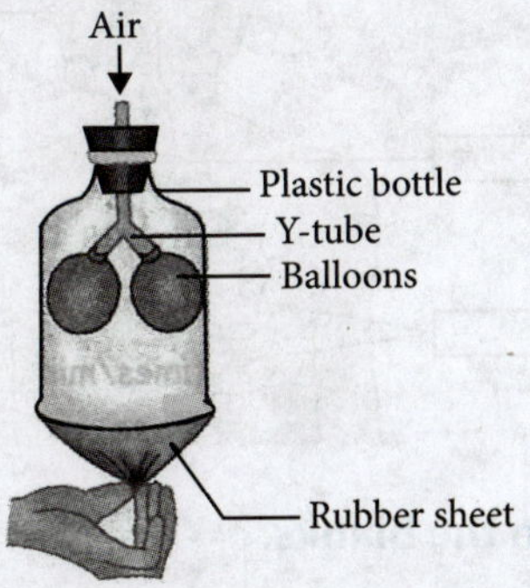

Which of the following statements holds true regarding the rubber sheet that is pulled down?
(a) Air pressure inside the bell jar decreases.
(b) The two small balloons expand.
(c) This is similar to the contraction of lungs during exhalation.
(d) Both (a) and (b)
Ev

38. In human respiratory system, the trachea is divided into two (i) , which enter into two respective lungs. Inside the lungs, (i) divide and redivide into (ii) . which further divide and finally end into (iii) . Select the correct option to complete the above paragraph.

	(i)	(ii)	(iii)
(a)	Bronchi	Bronchioles	Alveoli
(b)	Bronchioles	Bronchi	Alveoli
(c)	Bronchi	Spiracles	Bronchioles
(d)	Air sacs	Bronchi	Bronchioles

R

39. Given figure illustrates the internal structure of lungs.

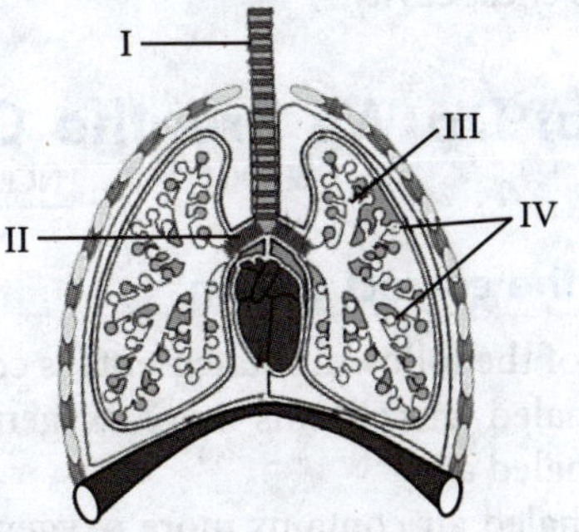

The exchange of gases takes place at which labelled structure?
(a) I (b) II
(c) III (d) IV
Ev

B. Figure based question.

40. Label the different parts of human respiratory system.

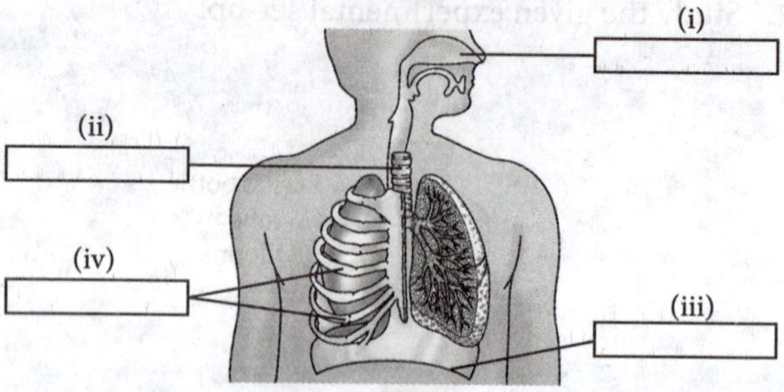

C. Fill in the blanks.

41. ________ is a large muscular sheet that forms the floor of the chest cavity.

42. ________ are the main organs of respiration present in the ________ of our body.

43. Smoking can damage your ________ and can cause ________.

44. Breathing involves the movement of the ________ and the ________.

45. ________ expels the foreign particles like dust, pollens, etc., from the inhaled air.

D. State True (T) or False (F) in the given statements.

46. During breathing, only diaphragm moves.
47. Exhalation reduces the size of the chest cavity.
48. Our lungs are surrounded by the diaphragm.
49. Our lungs expand during exhalation.
50. During exhalation, diaphragm moves up to its former position.
51. When we inhale air, it passes through our nostrils into the chest cavity.

6.4 What Do We Breathe Out?

NCERT Page 63-64

A. Select the correct option.

52. Which of the following statements is correct?
(a) Inhaled air contains more oxygen than that of exhaled air.
(b) Exhaled air contains more oxygen than that of inhaled air.
(c) Inhaled air contains equal amount of carbon dioxide and oxygen.
(d) Exhaled air contains equal amount of carbon dioxide and oxygen. U

53. The percentage of carbon dioxide in exhaled air is
(a) 0.04% (b) 4.4%
(c) 4.0% (d) 0.44%. R

54. When we blow air into a glass containing lime water, it turns milky due to
(a) oxygen (b) carbon dioxide
(c) water vapour (d) hydrogen. An

55. Which of the following correctly represents the approximate composition of exhaled air by humans?
(a) $O_2 = 21\%$ $CO_2 = 4.4\%$
(b) $O_2 = 21\%$ $CO_2 = 0.04\%$
(c) $O_2 = 16.4\%$ $CO_2 = 4.4\%$
(d) $O_2 = 16.4\%$ $CO_2 = 0.04\%$ R

B. Figure based question.

56. Refer to the given figure that illustrates the effect of exhaled air on lime water and answer the questions that follow.

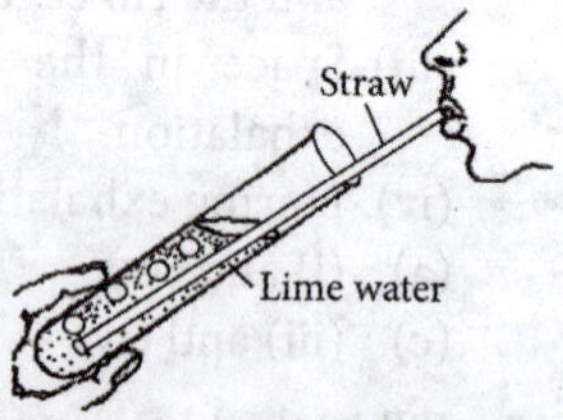

1. What is the effect of exhaled air on lime water? Explain your answer.
2. Write down the percentage of the two main gases present in both inhaled and exhaled air.

C. Passage based question.

57. Air that we inhale is a ________ of ________. It contains both ________ and ________, and their percentage in the inhaled air is ________ and ________ respectively. Their percentage in the exhaled air is ________ and ________ respectively.

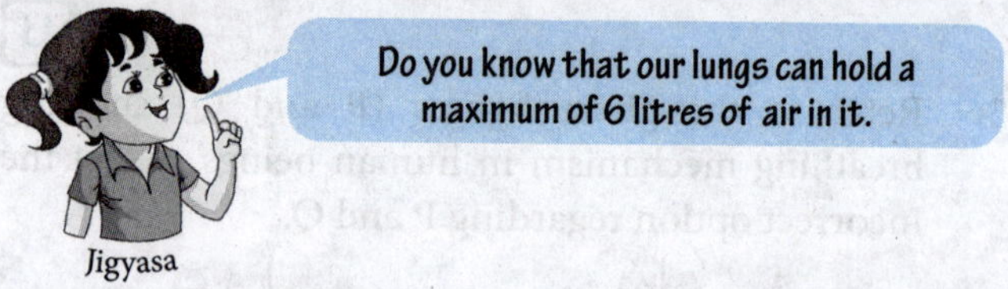

6.5 Breathing in Other Animals

NCERT Page 64-65

A. Select the correct option.

58. Match the respiratory organs in Column-I with the animals in which they are present in Column-II and select the correct option.

Column-I	Column-II
A. Gills	(i) Earthworm
B. Lungs	(ii) Fish
C. Skin	(iii) Crocodile
D. Spiracles	(iv) Grasshopper

(a) A – (iv), B – (ii), C – (iii), D – (i)
(b) A – (ii), B – (i), C – (iii), D – (iv)
(c) A – (ii), B – (iii), C – (i), D – (iv)
(d) A – (iii), B – (ii), C – (i), D – (iv) R

59. Spiracles are present in
(a) earthworms (b) snakes
(c) frogs (d) cockroaches. R

60. Frogs can breathe through their
(a) lungs (b) spiracles
(c) skin (d) both (a) and (c). R

61. Which one of the following organisms can breathe through their skin?
(a) Frogs (b) Birds
(c) Snakes (d) Lions U

62. Which of following animals possesses lungs in their chest cavities?
(a) Elephant (b) Lizard
(c) Birds (d) All of these U

63. Match Column-I with Column-II and select the correct option.

	Column-I		Column-II
A.	Process of inhalation and exhalation	(i)	Stomata
B.	Process of conversion of carbohydrate into alcohol and CO_2	(ii)	Breathing
C.	Main organs of human respiratory system	(iii)	Fermentation
D.	Plant respiration	(iv)	Lungs

(a) A – (iii), B – (ii), C – (iv), D – (i)
(b) A – (ii), B – (iii), C – (iv), D – (i)
(c) A – (iii), B – (i), C – (ii), D – (iv)
(d) A – (ii), B – (iv), C – (i), D – (iii) U

64. Select the correct analogy in the given sets.
(i) Carbon dioxide : Water : Aerobic respiration : : Oxygen : Water : Anaerobic respiration
(ii) Fish : Gills : : Plants : Stomata
(iii) Breathing : Internal respiration : : Cellular respiration : External respiration
(iv) Frog : Earthworm : Skin : : Cockroach : *Amoeba* : Spiracles
(a) Only (ii) (b) (i) and (iv)
(c) (iii) and (iv) (d) (ii) and (iii) U

B. Fill in the blanks.

65. Animals such as elephants, cows, lions, etc., have ________ for breathing.

66. ________ and ________ breathe through skin.

67. Insects such as ________ have small openings on the sides of their body called ________.

68. ________ have a pair of lungs like human beings, but they can also breathe through their ________.

69. Insects have a network of air tubes called ________ for exchange of gases.

C. State True (T) or False (F) for the given statements.

70. Snakes can breathe through their skin.

71. Small openings called spiracles are present on the sides of a frog's body.

72. Cockroaches exchange gases by the process of diffusion with the help of their skin.

73. Tracheal tubes are found only in insects.

74. Skin of earthworms is moist and slippery.

6.6 Breathing Under Water

NCERT Page 65

A. Select the correct option.

75. ________ in fish help them to use oxygen dissolved in water.
(a) Lungs (b) Gills
(c) Spiracles (d) Tracheae An

76. Exchange of gases takes place in the gills with the help of
(a) spiracles (b) blood vessels
(c) tracheae (d) muscles. U

77. Gills are the projections of the
(a) muscles (b) scales
(c) skin (d) none of these. U

B. Figure based question.

78. Observe the given image and answer the questions that follow.

1. Which respiratory organ can you see in the given image?
2. How does exchange of gases take place through this organ?

C. State True (T) or False (F) for the given statements.

79. Gills are absent in whales.

80. Gills are well-supplied with a network of tracheal tubes.

81. Fish use the dissolved oxygen present in water for breathing.

82. Whales and dolphins often come up to the water surface for breathing.

83. During breathing, the exchange of gases from the gills into the body tissues occurs through the blood vessels.

6.7 Do Plants Also Respire?

NCERT Page 65-66

A. Select the correct option.

84. Tiny pores on the leaves of plants through which exchange of gases takes place are called
(a) nostrils (b) stomata
(c) spiracles (d) lenticels. R

85. Select the correct statement regarding plant respiration.
(a) Root cells of plants need oxygen to generate energy.
(b) Stomata help in gaseous exchange in plants.
(c) Plant roots obtain oxygen from air trapped between soil particles.
(d) All of these U

86. Select the incorrect statement(s).
(i) In plants, diffusion of only oxygen takes place through the leaves.
(ii) Exchange of carbon dioxide takes place only through the roots in plants.
(iii) Root hair can absorb only oxygen.
(iv) Each part of the plant can independently take in oxygen from air and give out carbon dioxide.
(a) (i) and (ii) (b) (iii) and (iv)
(c) (i), (ii) and (iii) (d) Only (iv) Ap

87. Select the correct match(es).

	Organism		Breathing organ
(i)	Woody plant	–	Stomata
(ii)	*Paramecium*	–	Cell membrane
(iii)	Lizard	–	Spiracles
(iv)	Frog	–	Skin

(a) (ii) and (iv) (b) (ii), (iii) and (iv)
(c) (iii) and (iv) (d) Only (ii) U

88. Exchange of gases in plants take place through
(a) stomata (b) root cells
(c) lenticels (d) all of these. U

89. Select the incorrect statement regarding given structures.

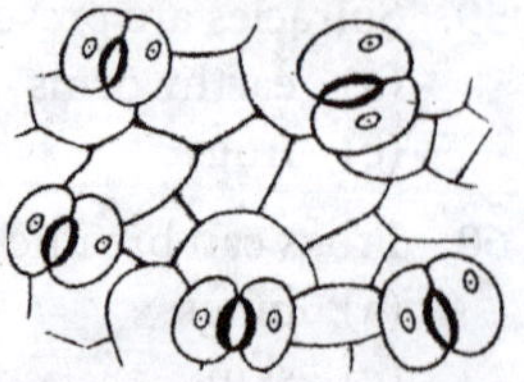

(a) These are stomata present on leaf surfaces.
(b) These structures help in gaseous exchange in plants.
(c) These open and close in response to presence and absence of water.
(d) These are present in roots also. Ev

B. State True (T) or False (F) for the given statements.

90. Unlike other living organisms, the process of respiration does not occur in plants.

91. Stomata are present on the roots and stems of plants.

92. Like all other cells, the root cells also need oxygen to generate energy.

93. Exchange of gases in plants take place only through the leaves.

94. Plants use carbon dioxide to breakdown glucose into water and oxygen with the release of energy.

C. Figure based question.

95. Refer to the given figures of plant parts.
(i) Write the names of the following plants parts.
(ii) Write roles in respiration.

Plant parts	
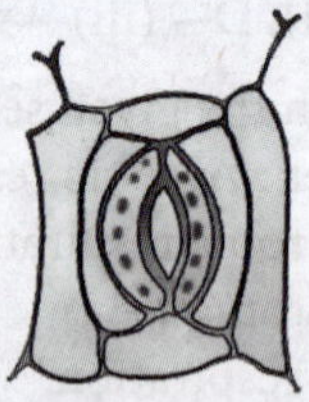	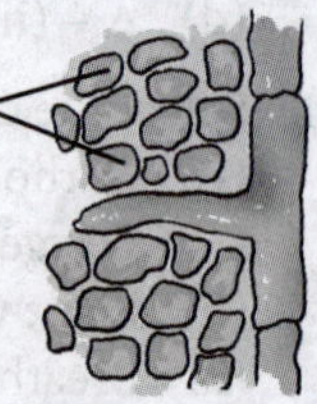
(a)	(b)

PROGRESS CHECK

Check your score! If your score is

> 95%	EXCELLENT !	Move on to the next chapter. You have mastered this chapter. Concepts are certainly on your fingertips.
95-85%	VERY GOOD !	Revise once more thoroughly. Recognise your mistakes and work on them. You will master this chapter.
84-75%	GOOD!	Work on your weak areas, master them and come back to this chapter in a few days.
74-65%	MEDIOCRE!	Understand your weak areas and work on strengthening your concepts. Devote more time to master this chapter.
< 65%	NOT SATISFACTORY!	This is where you fall behind from scoring well. Give special attention to this chapter. Work on clearing concepts and common errors.

NCERT Exemplar Problems

This section contains MCQs of **'NCERT Exemplar Problems'** Book.

1. Sometimes when we do heavy exercise, anaerobic respiration takes place in our muscle cells. What is produced during this process?
(a) Alcohol and lactic acid
(b) Alcohol and CO_2
(c) Lactic acid and CO_2
(d) Lactic acid only

2. Yeast is used in wine and beer industries because it respires
(a) aerobically producing oxygen
(b) aerobically producing alcohol
(c) anaerobically producing alcohol
(d) anaerobically producing CO_2.

3. During the process of exhalation, the ribs move
(a) down and inwards
(b) up and inwards
(c) down and outwards
(d) up and outwards.

4. Breathing is a process that
(i) provides O_2 to the body
(ii) breaks down food to release energy
(iii) helps the body to get rid of CO_2
(iv) produces water in the cells.
Which of the following gives the correct combination of functions of breathing?
(a) (i) and (ii) (b) (ii) and (iii)
(c) (i) and (iii) (d) (ii) and (iv)

5. Fish breathe with the help of gills which are richly supplied with blood vessels. The gills help the fish to
(a) take in oxygen from air
(b) take in oxygen dissolved in water
(c) absorb nutrients present in water
(d) release waste substances in water.

6. Earthworms and frogs breathe through their skin because of which the skin of both the organisms is
(a) moist and rough (b) dry and rough
(c) dry and slimy (d) moist and slimy.

A&R Corner

Directions : In the following questions, a statement of assertion is followed by a statement of reason. Mark the correct choice as :
(a) If both assertion and reason are true and reason is the correct explanation of assertion.
(b) If both assertion and reason are true but reason is not the correct explanation of assertion.
(c) If assertion is true but reason is false.
(d) If both assertion and reason are false.

1. **Assertion :** Internal respiration occurs in the body cells.
Reason : Internal respiration involves exchange of gases between the blood and the body cells.

2. **Assertion :** Normal breathing rate of healthy adult person is 15-18 times/minute.
Reason : Breathing rate may increases during fever, illness or other medical conditions.

3. **Assertion :** Anaerobic respiration involves complete oxidation of glucose.
Reason : The end products of anaerobic respiration are carbon dioxide and water.

4. **Assertion :** During inhalation, the ribs and diaphragm moves down and upward respectively.
Reason : The movement of ribs and diaphragm during inhalation decreases the volume of thoracic cavity. An

5. **Assertion :** Aerobic respiration occurs in the presence of oxygen.
Reason : The amount of energy produced during aerobic respiration is large.

6. **Assertion :** Earthworm possesses moist and slimy skin.
Reason : The skin of earthworm facilitates exchange of gases.

7. **Assertion :** In fishes, gills serve as the respiratory organs.
Reason : Gills are richly supplied with blood capillaries. U

8. **Assertion :** Lenticels are small pores present on the bark of the stem.
Reason : Lenticels help in gaseous exchange in plants. U

9. **Assertion :** Anaerobic respiration in humans occurs in skeletal muscles.
Reason : Lactic acid is the product of anaerobic respiration.

10. **Assertion :** Breathing rate of a person is measured when a person is at rest.
Reason : Breathing rate involves counting the number of breaths in one minute.

11. **Assertion :** Alveoli are the sites of gaseous exchange in lungs.
Reason : Alveoli have thick walls and are richly supplied with blood capillaries.

12. **Assertion :** Exhaled air consists of carbon dioxide, oxygen and water vapour.
Reason : Inhaled air consists of 0.04% oxygen. R

13. **Assertion :** Breathing is a physical process which involves exchange of gases.
Reason : Breathing occurs at cellular level.

14. **Assertion :** In insects, spiracles are small openings found on the sides of their bodies.
Reason : Insects exhibit tracheal respiration.

15. **Assertion :** Diaphragm is a large muscular sheet that forms the floor of the chest cavity.
Reason : Diaphragm plays an important role in expiration only.

Exam Corner

This section comprises of different types of questions:

- **Objective Type Questions :** These are **one mark** questions.
- **Very Short Answer Type Questions (VSA) :** These are **one mark** questions.
- **Short Answer Type Questions-I (SA-I) :** These are **two marks** questions.
- **Short Answer Type Questions-II (SA-II) :** These are **three marks** questions.
- **Long Answer Type Questions (LA) :** These are **five marks** questions.
- **Case Based Questions (CBQs) :** These are case study/passage based questions.

OBJECTIVE TYPE QUESTIONS

A. Select the correct option.

1. Lenticels are present in ________ of the woody plants.
(a) leaves (b) stem
(c) roots (d) all parts

2. ________ controls the entry and release of oxygen and carbon dioxide into/from the stomata.
(a) Lenticels (b) Alveoli
(c) Guard cells (d) Mucous

3. Cutaneous respiration occurs in
(a) *Amoeba* (b) earthworm
(c) *Paramaecium* (d) fish.

4. Gills are made up of large number of
(a) alveoli (b) spiracles
(c) filaments (d) lenticels.

5. The red coloured pigment present in blood is called (P). It combines with oxygen to form a temporary compound called (Q).
Select the correct option for P and Q.
(a) P – Haemoglobin, Q – Carboxyhaemoglobin
(b) P – Haemoglobin, Q – Oxyhaemoglobin
(c) P – RBCs, Q – Haemoglobin
(d) P – RBC, Q – Carboxyhaemoglobin U

6. Tiny air sacs present in the lungs are called
(a) lenticels (b) alveoli
(c) bronchioles (d) trachae.

7. Which of the following statements is correct for anaerobic respiration?
(a) Food is broken down in the absence of oxygen to release energy.
(b) Breakdown of food occurs in presence of oxygen.
(c) It is slow process compared to aerobic respiration.
(d) It produces large amount of energy compared to aerobic respiration.

8. When a person breathes in, what happens to the diaphragm and to the ribs?
(a) Diaphragm becomes flattened, ribs move downwards and inwards
(b) Diaphragm becomes flattened, ribs move outwards and upwards
(c) Diaphragm becomes more curved, ribs move downwards and inwards
(d) Diaphragm becomes more curved, ribs move outwards and upwards Ap

9. Identify the labels (P, Q and R) in the given figure and select the correct option.

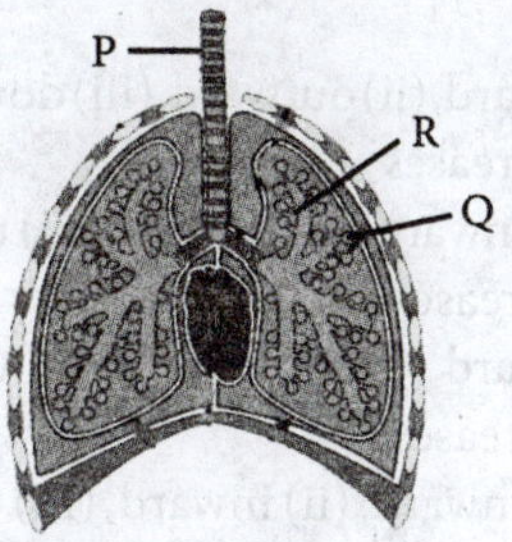

	P	Q	R
(a)	Trachea	Alveoli	Bronchiole
(b)	Bronchus	Alveoli	Lungs
(c)	Trachea	Bronchi	Alveoli
(d)	Bronchiole	Bronchi	Alveoli

10. The products of fermentation are
(a) carbon dioxide and alcohol
(b) alcohol and oxygen
(c) lactic acid and alcohol
(d) carbon dioxide and lactic acid. R

11. Select the correct statements.
(i) Inside the lungs, the windpipe divides into bronchi.
(ii) Unicellular organisms do not respire as they do not posses lungs like humans.

(iii) Oxygen is circulated in our body alongwith blood with the help of haemoglobin.
(iv) Yeasts can survive without oxygen.
(a) (i) and (iv) (b) (iii) and (iv)
(c) (i) and (iii) (d) (i) and (ii)

12. Select the correct matches.
(i) Gills – Blood capillaries
(ii) Lungs – Alveoli
(iii) Leaves – Lenticels
(iv) Roots – Stomata
(a) (ii) and (iii) (b) (i) and (iv)
(c) (i) and (ii) (d) (i), (ii) and (iii)

13. Select the incorrect statements.
(i) Mucus is a harmful component produced by the inner lining of our nose.
(ii) It is always advised to breathe in through your mouth.
(iii) Unicellular organisms like Yeast and *Amoeba* do not possess lungs.
(iv) Mangrove plants can survive in waterlogged areas.
(a) (i) and (ii) (b) (ii), (iii) and (iv)
(c) (iii) and (iv) (d) (ii) and (iv)

14. During inhalation, the ribs move (i) and (ii), and the diaphragm moves (iii). This (iv) the volume of chest cavity and the air pressure inside the lungs (v). Complete the above passage by selecting the correct option.
(a) (i) upward, (ii) outward, (iii) down, (iv) increases, (v) decreases
(b) (i) downward, (ii) inward, (iii) up, (iv) decreases, (v) increases
(c) (i) upward, (ii) outward, (iii) down, (iv) decreases, (v) increases
(d) (i) downward, (ii) inward, (iii) up, (iv) increases, (v) decreases Ap

15. Which of the following groups of organisms respire through skin?
(a) Frog and fish
(b) Earthworm and frog
(c) *Hydra* and cockroach
(d) Snake and lizard

B. Fill in the blanks.

16. In *Amoeba*, exchange of gases occurs by the process of ________ through their cell membrane.

17. Chest cavity increases in size during ________ and decreases in size during ________.

18. Insects breathe through their ________ while humans breathe through their ________.

19. ________ is the end product of anaerobic respiration in our skeletal muscles. U

20. Exchange of gases takes place in ________ of the lungs.

21. The process of ________ is also called external respiration.

22. The ________ air has more oxygen and less carbon dioxide as compared to the ________ air.

23. Respiration through skin is called ________ respiration.

24. Mangrove trees have ________ to take in air.

25. Trachea divides into two branches called ________.

26. Oxygen-rich haemoglobin is called ________.

27. ________ is an anaerobic process.

28. Increased physical activity ________ the rate of breathing.

29. The products of anaerobic respiration are ________ and ________.

30. During heavy exercise, supply of ________ to the muscle cells is insufficient and hence, ________ respiration takes place in the muscle cells.

31. The respiratory organs of woody and non-woody plants are ________ and ________ respectively. R

32. Gills are supplied with ________ for the exchange of gases.

33. Plants have root ________ that absorbs oxygen present in the air space between the soil particles.

34. Yeasts are ________ organisms which are used to make ________ and ________.

35. ________ is produced in the muscle cells when they respire anaerobically.

C. State True (T) or False (F) for the given statements.

36. Plants carry out photosynthesis only during the day and respiration only at night. ☐

37. Mucus kills the germs entering into the nose during inhalation. ☐

38. Exchange of gases is faster in plants than in animals. ☐

39. Cellular respiration is also called cutaneous respiration. ☐

40. In plants, closing and opening of stomata for gaseous exchange are controlled by guard cells. ☐

41. Internal respiration is a biochemical process.

42. Chemical reaction that occur during cellular respiration is similar to the reaction taking place during combustion.

43. Root cells take up air through spaces between the soil particles.

44. When a frog is under water, it respires through lungs whereas on land, it respires through skin.

45. The windpipe divides into two smaller tubes called bronchioles.

46. Oxidation of food during respiration releases energy.

47. Yeast respires anaerobically.

48. Earthworm respires through their skin as well as through lungs.

49. Reaction that is taking place during fermentation is similar to the reaction taking place during combustion.

50. Ribs are surrounded by diaphragm on the sides of the chest cavity.

51. Frogs can respire through their skin.

52. The number of times a person breathes in one minute is called breathing rate.

53. The size of the chest decreases during inhalation.

54. Muscle cramps are due to the accumulation of alcohol in the muscle cells as a result of anaerobic respiration.

55. Plants carry out respiration only at night.

D. Figure based questions.

56. Refer to the given figure and answer the questions that follow.

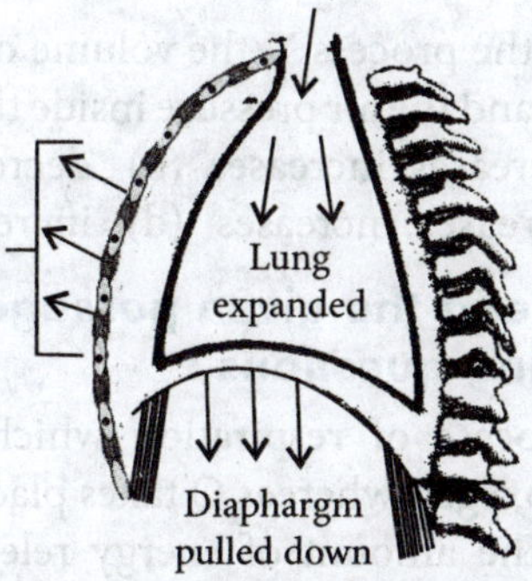

1. Which breathing process has been shown in the given figure inhalation or exhalation?
2. What changes take place during this process?

57. Study the given experimental set ups.

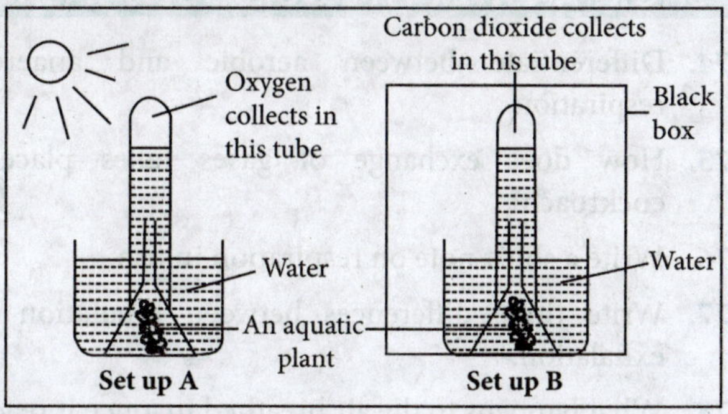

Why are different gases produced in the given set-ups A and B? Ev

VERY SHORT ANSWER TYPE QUESTIONS (VSA)

A. Answer the following questions.

58. What are the two types of respiration?

59. Write the names of two organisms that breathe through their skin.

60. Write the names of two main gases that are exchanged during breathing.

61. Write the two products that form on complete oxidation of food. R

62. Write the names of two parts of plants through which exchange of gases takes place.

63. Write the two structures that are involved in the process of breathing.

B. Find the odd one out. Give reason for your choice.

64. Earthworm, Dog, Cow, Pigeon

65. Glucose, Carbon dioxide, Alcohol, Lactic acid

66. Stomata, Root hair, Lungs, Lenticels

67. Nostrils, Ribs, Diaphragm, Skin

68. Spiracles, Gills, Lungs, Stomata

SHORT ANSWER TYPE QUESTIONS-I (SA-I)

69. What are lenticels?

70. How do the nostrils and the nasal cavity contribute to the process of breathing? U

71. Differentiate between breathing and respiration.

72. Define
(a) fermentation (b) stomata

73. How does exchange of gases takes place in earthworms?

SHORT ANSWER TYPE QUESTIONS-II (SA-II)

74. Differentiate between aerobic and anaerobic respiration.

75. How does exchange of gases takes place in cockroach? An

76. Write a short note on respiration in fish.

77. Write three differences between inhalation and exhalation.

78. What happens to the air breathed in, once it reaches the lungs?

79. Given pictures (1-6) show the various activities carried out by people. Arrange these activities in the order of increasing rate of breathing.

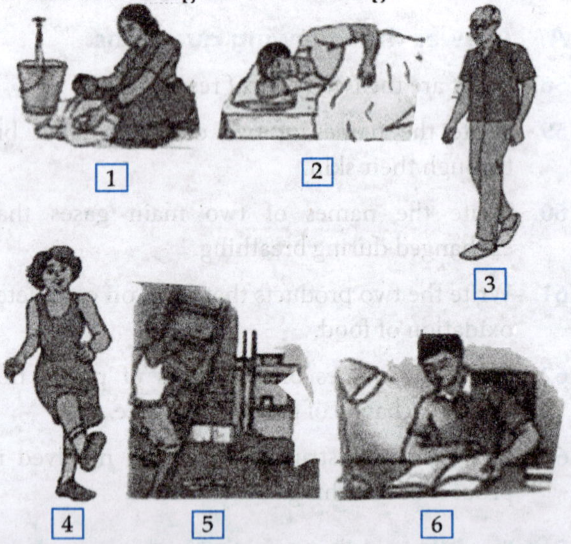

LONG ANSWER TYPE QUESTIONS (LA)

80. What is cellular respiration? Write a note on different types of cellular respiration.

81. Explain the process of breathing in humans.

82. How does respiration occur in plants?

83. How will you show that exhaled air has more carbon dioxide than inhaled air? Ev

84. Explain the different structures of human respiratory system with the help of a neat labelled diagram.

85. Give reason for the following statements:
   (a) We sneeze after inhaling air containing dust or dirt.
   (b) Yeast is used for making wine and beer.
   (c) We breathe fast during heavy exercise or running.
   (d) We should not overwater potted plants.
   (e) It is not advised to sleep under the tree at night. Ev

CASE BASED QUESTIONS (CBQs)

Case I : Read the given passage and answer the following questions :

Breathing is a part of respiration. It is a mechanical process which involves taking in of air rich in oxygen into the lungs and giving out of air rich in carbon dioxide from the lungs. The mechanism of breathing in human beings is given below.

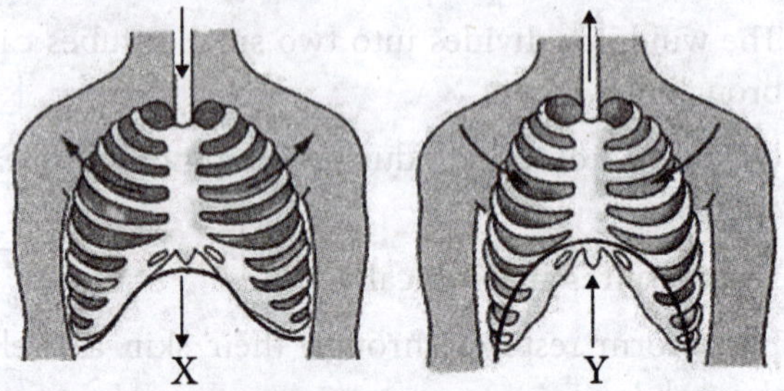

86. What does the figure X and Y represents?

	X	Y
(a)	Exhalation	Respiration
(b)	Respiration	Inhalation
(c)	Inhalation	Exhalation
(d)	Exhalation	Inhalation

U

87. During the process Y, ribs and diaphragm moves
   (a) Upward and downward respectively
   (b) Downward and upward respectively
   (c) Upward and inward respectively
   (d) Downward and outward respectively.

88. The shape of diaphragm during the process Y becomes
   (a) flat (b) dome shaped
   (c) spindle shaped (d) elliptical.

89. Which of the following events will not occur during the process X?
   (a) Decrease in air pressure inside the lungs
   (b) Increase in volume of thoracic cavity
   (c) Lungs becomes elastic and increases in size
   (d) Diaphragm return to their original position.

90. During the process Y, the volume of thoracic cavity ______ and the air pressure inside the lungs ______.
   (a) decreases, increases (b) decreases, decreases
   (c) increases, increases (d) increases, decreases

Case II : Read the given passage and answer the following questions :

P is the process of respiration which occurs in the presence of oxygen whereas Q takes place in the absence of oxygen. The amount of energy released during the process P is higher than the process Q.

91. Which of the following gives correct equation for the process P?

(a) $C_6H_6O_{12} + 6O_2 \rightarrow CO_2 + C_2H_5OH + \text{Energy}$
(b) $C_6H_{12}O_6 + 6O_2 \rightarrow 6CO_2 + 6H_2O + \text{Energy}$
(c) $CO_2 + H_2O \rightarrow C_6H_{12}O_6 + 6O_2 + \text{Energy}$
(d) $C_6H_{12}O_6 + 6CO_2 \rightarrow 6O_2 + 6H_2O + \text{Energy}$

92. The group of organisms that generally respires through the process Q is
(a) all plants and animals
(b) plants, bacteria and worms
(c) yeast, some bacteria and parasitic worms
(d) plants, bacteria and animals.

93. Which of the following equation represents the process Q?
(a) Glucose $\rightarrow$ Ethyl alcohol + CO_2 + Energy
(b) Glucose $\rightarrow$ CO_2 + H_2O + Energy
(c) Glucose $\rightarrow$ Lactic acid + Energy
(d) Both (a) and (c)

94. Explain an activity for the confirmation of product formation in process P. **Ap**

95. During heavy physical exercise shaurya got fainted as process Q occured in his muscles. Explain.

Case III : Read the given passage and answer the following questions :

Different animals ranging from microorganisms to higher animals have different organs and mechanism of breathing. Some of the organisms are given below.

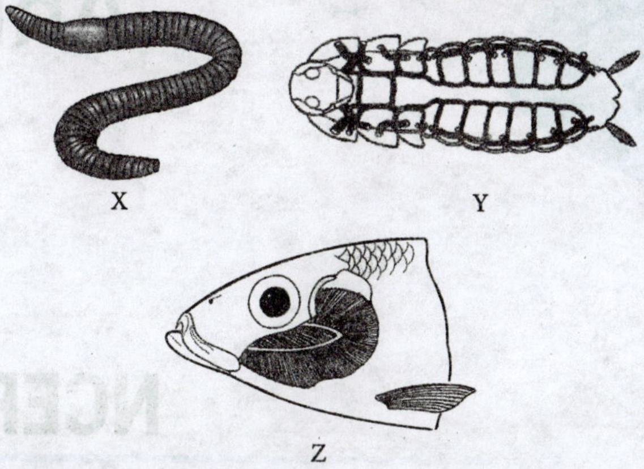

96. Which organism among the above given three organism respires through skin?

97. Which organism possess spiracles?

98. Explain briefly the type of respiration in organism Y.

99. Give one example of an organism having the similar type of respiration as X.

100. How respiration in organism Z differs from X? **An**

ANSWER KEY

Practice Corner

1. (d) 2. (a) 3. (c) 4. (d) 5. (b) 6. (b) 7. (d) 8. (b) 11. False 12. False
13. True 14. True 15. False 16. True 17. True 18. False 20. (b) 21. (c) 22. (b) 23. (b)
24. (b) 25. inhalation, exhalation 26. 15-18 27. increases 28. Breathing 29. breathe
30. (d) 31. (b) 32. (a) 33. (b) 34. (c) 35. (c) 36. (b) 37. (d) 38. (a) 39. (d)
41. Diaphragm 42. Lungs, chest cavity 43. lungs, cancer 44. diaphragm, ribcage 45. Sneeze
46. False 47. True 48. False 49. False 50. True 51. False 52. (a) 53. (b) 54. (b) 55. (c)
58. (c) 59. (d) 60. (d) 61. (a) 62. (b) 63. (b) 64. (a) 65. lungs 66. Earthworm, frog
67. Cockroach, spiracles 68. Frogs, skin 69. tracheal tubes 70. False 71. False 72. False 73. True
74. True 75. (b) 76. (b) 77. (c) 79. True 80. False 81. True 82. True 83. True 84. (b)
85. (d) 86. (a) 87. (a) 88. (d) 89. (d) 90. False 91. False 92. True 93. False 94. False

NCERT Exemplar Problems

1. (d) 2. (c) 3. (a) 4. (c) 5. (b) 6. (d)

A & R Corner

1. (a) 2. (b) 3. (d) 4. (d) 5. (b) 6. (b) 7. (b) 8. (a) 9. (b) 10. (b)
11. (c) 12. (c) 13. (c) 14. (b) 15. (c)

Exam Corner

1. (b) 2. (c) 3. (b) 4. (c) 5. (b) 6. (b) 7. (a) 8. (b) 9. (a) 10. (a)
11. (b) 12. (c) 13. (a) 14. (a) 15. (b) 16. diffusion 17. inhalation, exhalation
18. tracheae, lungs 19. Lactic acid 20. alveoli 21. breathing 22. inhaled, exhaled 23. cutaneous
24. aerial roots 25. bronchi 26. oxyhaemoglobin 27. Fermentation 28. increases
29. ethyl alcohol, carbon dioxide 30. oxygen, anaerobic 31. lenticels, stomata 32. blood vessels 33. hair
34. single-celled, beer, wine 35. Lactic acid 36. False 37. False 38. False 39. False
40. True 41. True 42. True 43. True 44. False 45. False 46. True 47. True 48. False 49. False
50. False 51. True 52. True 53. False 54. False 55. False 58. Aerobic respiration, Anaerobic respiration
59. Earthworm, Frog 60. Oxygen, Carbon dioxide 61. Carbon dioxide, Water 62. Stomata, Lenticels 86. (c)
87. (b) 88. (b) 89. (d) 90. (a) 91. (b) 92. (c) 93. (d)

7 Transportation in Animals and Plants

NCERT Notes

- Every organism requires food, water and oxygen for their survival. These substances should be transported to the various body parts for their utilisation by the organisms.
- Waste products formed during various activities like respiration, digestion, etc., by the animals should be removed from their body.
- In humans, a well-developed transport system called **circulatory system** is present. It consists of (1) blood, (2) blood vessels, and (3) heart.

7.1 Circulatory System

Blood

- Blood is a specialised fluid that flows in the blood vessels. Blood transports:
  - I. Oxygen from the lungs to the other regions of the body.
  - II. Food absorbed from small intestine during digestion to other cells of the body.
  - III. Waste for removal from the body.
- Blood consists of two components; (a) plasma and (b) blood cells.

Plasma

- Fluid part of the blood is called plasma. Plasma consists of various types of cells, that are suspended in it.

Blood cells

- In blood there are three types of blood cells :

1. **Red blood cells (RBCs):**
   - RBCs contain a red pigment called **haemoglobin**. Oxygen binds with haemoglobin and is transported to all the cells of the body.
   - Haemoglobin is crucial for effective transfer of oxygen to every cell of the body.
   - Due to the presence of haemoglobin, blood appears red in colour.
2. **White blood cells (WBCs):**
   - WBCs fight against the germs that have entered in our body.
3. **Blood platelets:**
   - Whenever there is a cut in our body, blood comes out.
   - Blood platelets prevent the bleeding by forming a dark red colour clot at the site of cut.

Blood donation can save precious lives. Blood donation can be done at hospital and authorised government places. Donated blood is stored in blood blank.

Blood Vessels

- Circulation of blood across the body is performed by blood vessels.
- Blood transports oxygen obtained from lungs during inhalation to the rest of the body parts
- Waste like carbon dioxide are also transported by blood vessels to the heart and then to the lungs.
- There are two types of blood vessels present :
  (a) **Arteries** – have thick elastic walls as the blood flows through them with high pressure. They carry oxygen rich blood from the heart to the body.
  (b) **Veins** – have thin walls and they transport carbon dioxide rich blood from every part of the body back to the heart. They have valves that allow blood to flow only in one direction towards the heart.
  – Arteries, when reach the tissues, they get further divided into smaller vessels, known as **capillaries**. These capillaries join to form the veins that empty into the heart.

- **Pulmonary artery:** It is an exception to the arteries as it carries carbon dioxide rich blood from the heart to the lungs.
- **Pulmonary vein:** It carries oxygen rich blood from the lungs to the heart.

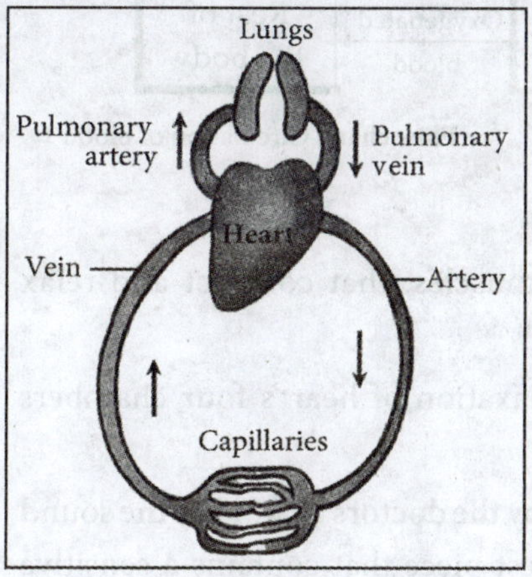

Fig.: Schematic diagram of circulation

Pulse rate

- The number of beats per minute is called the pulse rate.
- In resting person, normally pulse rate is around 70–80 beats per minute.
- Pulse is due to the blood flowing in the arteries.

Heart

- It is a muscular organ that beats continuously to pump the blood into the blood vessels.
- Human heart is about the size of a fist. The heart is located in the chest cavity with lower tip slightly tilted towards the left.
- Human heart consists of four chambers to prevent the mixing of oxygen rich blood with carbon dioxide rich blood.
- The two upper chambers are known as **atria**, while two lower chambers are called **ventricles**.

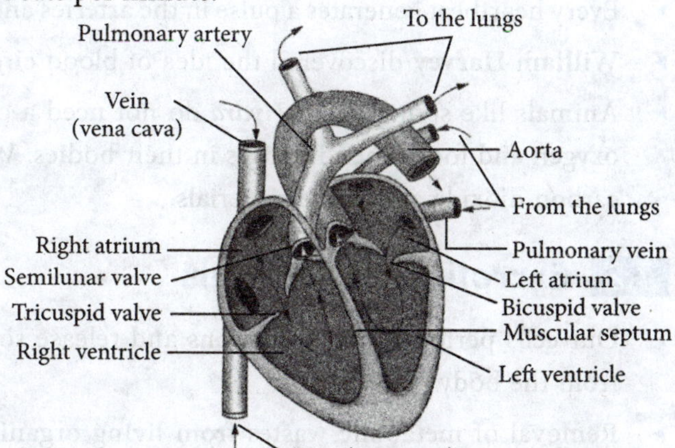

Fig.: Cross section of heart showing blood circulation (Arrows indicate the flow of blood)

- **Atria** are the receiving chambers of the heart and they have thin walls.
- **Ventricles** have thicker walls and they are the distributing chambers of the heart.

Distribution of blood in four chambers of hearts

- The vena cava (superior and inferior vena cava) transport deoxygenated blood from all body parts to right atrium. Right ventricle receives deoxygenated blood from the right atrium and transports it to lungs for oxygenation.
- Left atrium receives oxygenated blood from the lungs by pulmonary veins. Left ventricle receives oxygenated blood from left atrium and pump this blood into the aorta, from where it is transported throughout the body.

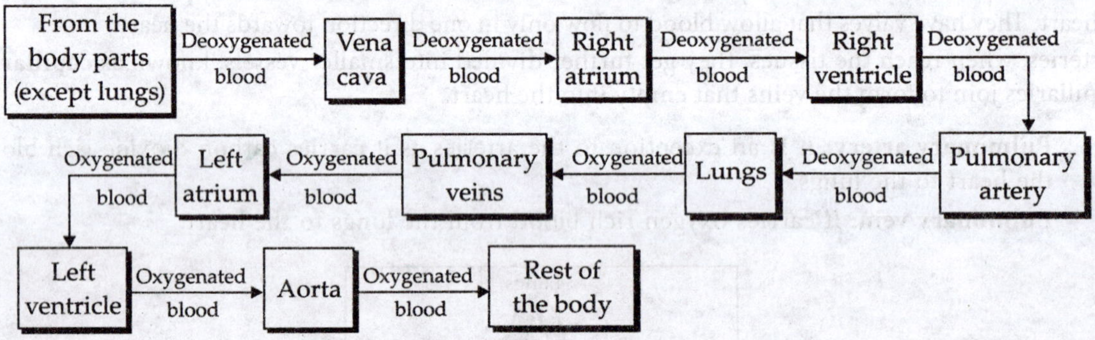

Flow chart: Circulation of blood

Heartbeat

- Heart chambers are made up of muscles, that contract and relax rhythmically to pump the blood.
- This rhythmic contraction and relaxation of heart's four chambers constitute a heartbeat.
- **Stethoscope** is an instrument used by the doctors to amplify the sound of the heart. It is made up of a chest piece that contains a sensitive diaphragm, two ear pieces and a tube that joins the other parts.
- By listening the heartbeat through stethoscope, doctors can determine the condition of your heart.

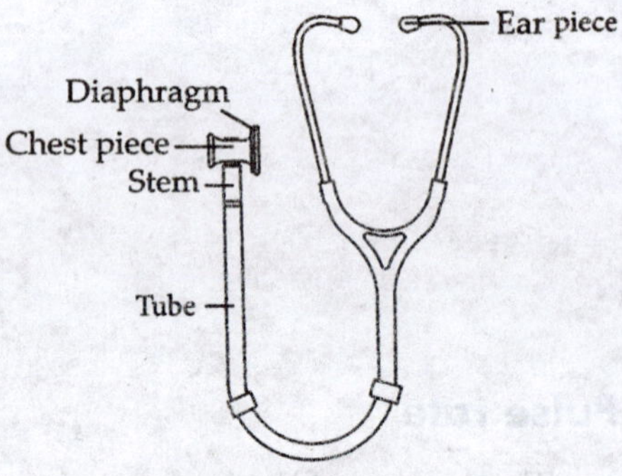

Fig.: A stethoscope

- Every heartbeat generates a pulse in the arteries and the pulse rate per minute is known as rate of the heartbeat.
- **William Harvey** discovered the idea of blood circulation.
- Animals like sponges and *Hydra* do not need a circulatory system, as the water in which they live provide oxygen and food when it enters in their bodies. When the water is removed from their bodies, it takes away carbon dioxide and waste materials.

7.2 Excretion in Animals

- Our cells perform many functions and release some waste products that are toxic and need to be removed from the body.
- Removal of metabolic wastes from living organisms is known as **excretion** and the parts involved in the excretion are called **excretory system**. For example; CO_2 is removed from body through lungs during exhalation, undigested food is removed *via* egestion.

Excretory System in Humans

- In humans, excretory system consists of a pair of kidneys, a pair of ureters, urinary bladder, urethra and urinary opening.
- Kidneys are responsible for filtering the blood from waste products. When the blood enters the two kidneys, it contains both useful and toxic materials. Useful substances are absorbed and transported back to blood.
- Wastes removed by the kidneys are in the form of liquid known as **urine**.
- Urine passes from the kidneys into urinary bladder through ureters.
- Urine is stored in the bladder until it passes out through urinary opening at the end of the urethra.
- Around 1–1.8 L of urine is passed out by an adult human being normally in 24 hours. Urine contains 95% of water, 2.5% urea and 2.5% other waste products.

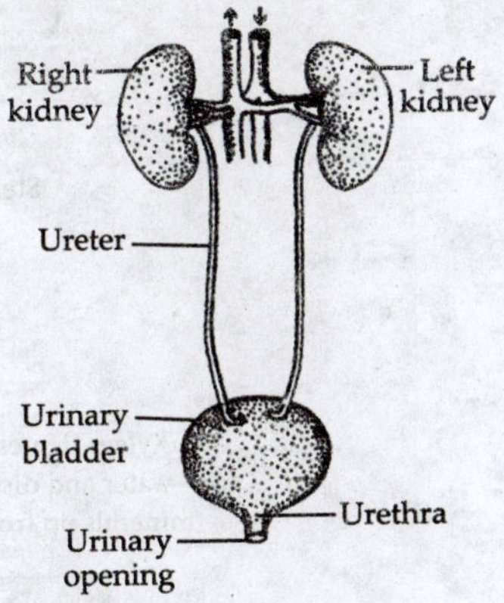

Fig.: Human excretory system

- Metabolic waste in aquatic animals like fishes is excreted out in the form of ammonia.
- Some land animals like birds, lizards, snakes excrete a semi-solid, white coloured compound (uric acid).
- Urea is a major excretory product of humans.
- **Dialysis** is the artificial method of removal of toxic substances from the blood of a patient with kidney damage or failure with the help of artificial kidneys.
- Sweating helps to cool our body. Similarly, the water kept in earthen pot (*matka*) evaporates from the pores of the pot and this makes the water inside the pot cooller.
- Salt and urea are removed along with water as **sweat**.
- **Nephrons** are tiny filtering units of the kidney. Each kidney consists of about one million nephrons.

7.3 Transport of Substances in Plants

For photosynthesis to occur, plants absorb water and minerals from soil through roots, carbon dioxide from air through leaves and solar energy is trapped by leaves.

- As food is prepared in leaves, it has to be transported to different parts of plants. For transportation of these substances, a well developed transport system, called **vascular system** is required. It comprises of xylem and phloem.

Transport of Water and Minerals

- Roots have root hair that increases the surface area for the absorption of water and minerals by the roots. The root hair is in contact with water present between soil particles.
- **Xylem** is a vascular tissue made up of specialised cells that are involved in the transport of water and nutrients from soil to entire plant.
- A continuous network of channels is formed by xylem that connects roots to the leaves through the stem and transports water to the entire plant.
- **Phloem** is a type of vascular tissue that transports food synthesised by leaves to every part of plant.

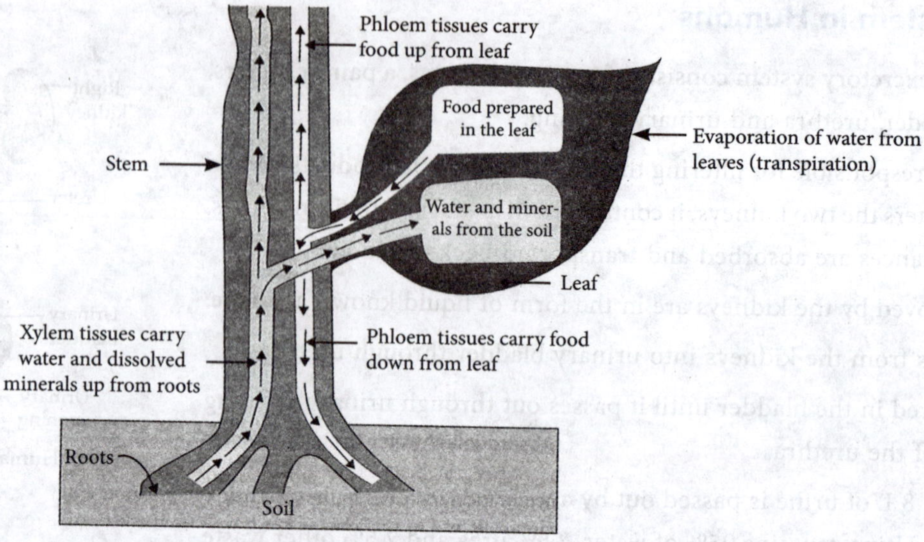

Fig.: Conduction of water and food in plants.

To observe transport of water is plants.

Materials required – Glass beaker, water, blue ink, tender herb and blade.

Procedure

- Add water to fill one-third of the beaker.
- Add few drops of blue ink to water.
- Cut the base of stem of herb and place it in glass and observe it next day.

Observation – Blue colour is seen inside the stem.

Conclusion – Stem conducts water. Just like ink, minerals dissolved in water also move up the stem along with water.

Transpiration

- Some amount of water absorbed by plant evaporates through the stomata present on the surface of leaves, this is known as **transpiration**.
- Evaporation of water creates a suction pull that enables the tall trees to pull water at great heights.
- Transpiration also cools the plants and it increases the salt concentration in the plants as well.

Stomata (singular = stoma) are tiny pores located on leaf surface from where the carbon dioxide is taken up by the leaves. Stomata is surrounded by two guard cells that control opening and closing of stomata.

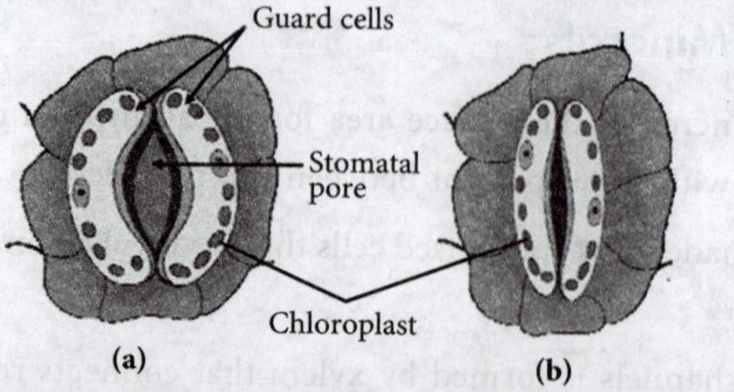

Fig.: Stomata (a) open (b) closed

Practice Corner

Extracted from NCERT

Assessment is complementary part of the learning process. It gives you a total insight whether the learning outcomes have been achieved or not. After going through the corresponding NCERT Textbook chapter, attempt these questions in exam like environment. Give yourself one mark for correct answer. A table is given at the end, that will help you plan your next step.

All the Best!

7.1 Circulatory System

NCERT Page 70-75

A. Select the correct option.

1. Haemoglobin is present in the
   (a) white blood cells (b) red blood cells
   (c) plasma (d) platelets. R

2. The pulse rate of a person at rest is between
   (a) 62 to 72 beats per minute
   (b) 72 to 80 beats per minute
   (c) 82 to 90 beats per minute
   (d) 92 to 100 beats per minute. R

3. Animals which do not posses any circulatory system are
   (a) whales and octopus (b) frogs and fishes
   (c) sponges and *Hydra* (d) whales and frogs. R

4. Human heart consists of
   (a) 2 atria and 2 ventricles
   (b) 3 atria and 1 ventricle
   (c) 2 atria and 1 ventricle
   (d) 2 atria and 3 ventricles. R

5. Pulmonary artery carries deoxygenated blood to
   (a) lungs from the heart
   (b) the heart from lungs
   (c) other organs of the body from the heart
   (d) lungs from other organs of the body. Ap

6. Transportation of blood in humans takes place through
   (a) excretory system (b) digestive system
   (c) circulatory system (d) respiratory system. R

7. ____________ form(s) the fluid part of the blood.
   (a) Haemoglobin (b) White blood cells
   (c) Platelets (d) Plasma R

8. Blood transports ____________ in our body.
   (a) waste (b) oxygen
   (c) digested food (d) all of these U

9. Device used to count the number of heartbeats is called
   (a) microscope (b) stethoscope
   (c) barometer (d) anemometer. R

10. Oxygen-rich blood is present in ____________ and ____________ of the heart.
    (a) left atrium, left ventricle
    (b) right atrium, right ventricle
    (c) right atrium, left atrium
    (d) right ventricle, left ventricle U

11. Match the columns.

	Column I (Blood component)		Column II (Function)
A.	White blood cells	1.	Helps to clot blood
B.	Red blood cells	2.	Oxygen transportation
C.	Platelets	3.	Fight against germs
D.	Plasma	4.	Contains haemoglobin
E.	Haemoglobin	5.	Fluid part of the blood

	A	B	C	D	E
(a)	1	5	2	3	4
(b)	3	4	1	5	2
(c)	3	1	5	2	4
(d)	4	2	3	1	5

R

B. Fill in the blanks.

12. ____________ carry blood throughout our body.

13. The number of heartbeats per minute is called ____________.

14. ____________ carry carbon dioxide-rich blood from all parts of the body back to the heart.

15. ____________ carries oxygen-rich blood from the lungs to the heart.

16. The heart is located in the ____________ of our body.

17. The throbbing movement felt on touching our wrist is called __________.

18. Inside the tissues, arteries divide to form __________.

19. The rhythmic contraction and relaxation of the muscles of heart constitute a __________.

20. The two lower chambers of the heart are called __________.

21. __________ carry oxygen-rich blood from the heart to all parts of our body.

C. Figure based questions.

Direction (Q.No. 22–23) : Observe the given figure and answer the questions that follow.

22. Identify the blood vessels that carry oxygen-rich blood from lungs to the heart and carbon-dioxide rich blood from heart to lungs.

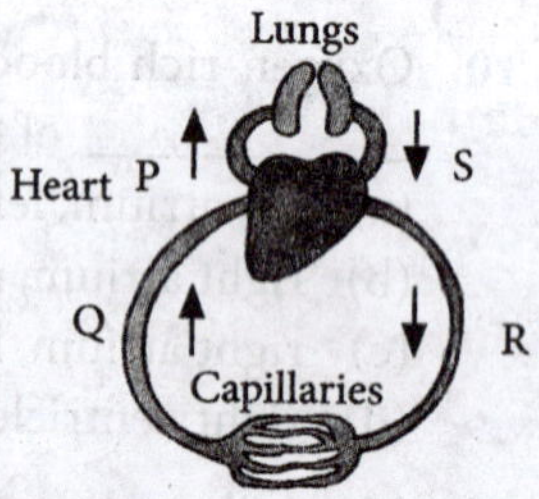

23. Which blood vessels carry carbon-dioxide rich blood from organs to the heart and oxygen rich blood from heart to the body organs.

7.2 Excretion in Animals

NCERT Page 75-77

A. Select the correct option.

24. In human excretory system, kidneys are connected to the urinary bladder through
(a) capillaries (b) ureters
(c) arteries (d) urethra. R

25. The major excretory product in humans is
(a) ammonia (b) urea
(c) uric acid (d) water. U

26. Blood containing waste products is filtered in the ______.
(a) kidneys (b) ureters
(c) urethra (d) bladder U

27. 95% of human urine consists of
(a) urea (b) water
(c) salts (d) uric acid. R

28. Excretory product of fish is
(a) ammonia (b) urea
(c) uric acid (d) nitric acid. R

B. Fill in the blanks.

29. Birds and lizards excrete a semi-solid white coloured compound __________.

30. Patients with damaged kidney can filter their blood periodically by the process of __________.

31. An adult human being passes about __________ litre(s) of urine per day.

32. The process of removal of wastes produced in the cells of living organisms is called __________.

33. Human sweat contains __________ and __________.

C. State True (T) or False (F) for the given statements.

34. The main excretory product in snakes is ammonia. ☐

35. Human urine consists of 2.5% urea. ☐

36. Sweating helps to cool our body. ☐

37. Blood reaching our kidneys contains only harmful substances which has to be removed from our body. ☐

38. The percentage of water in human urine is 25%. ☐

39. In human beings, urine is stored in the urethra. ☐

40. White patches formed on our clothes during summer is due to the salts present in our sweat. ☐

41. Wastes in our body are dissolved in water and removed as urine. ☐

42. Ureters carry urine from kidneys to urethra. ☐

D. Figure based questions.

43. Label the different parts of human excretory system in the boxes provided.

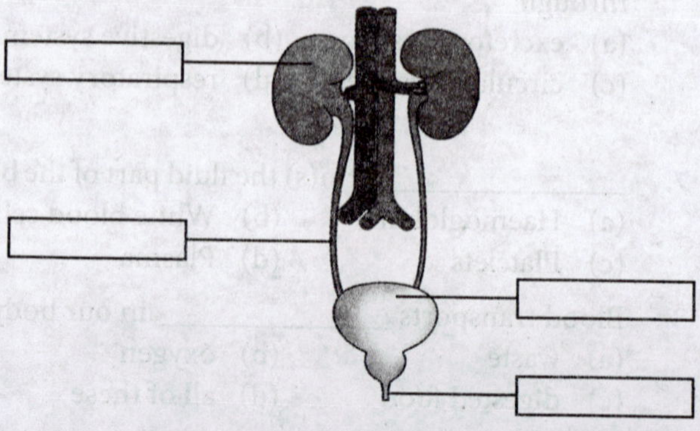

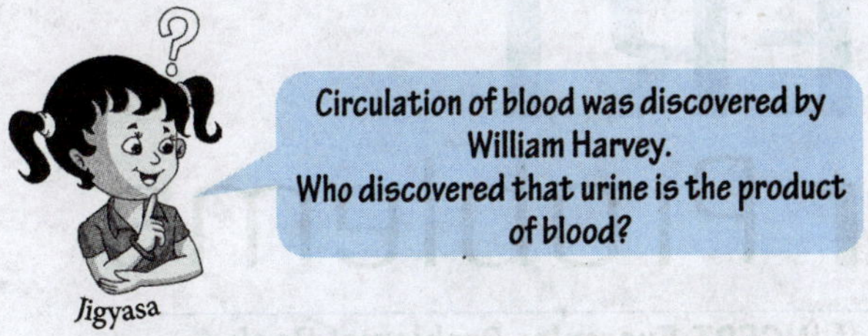

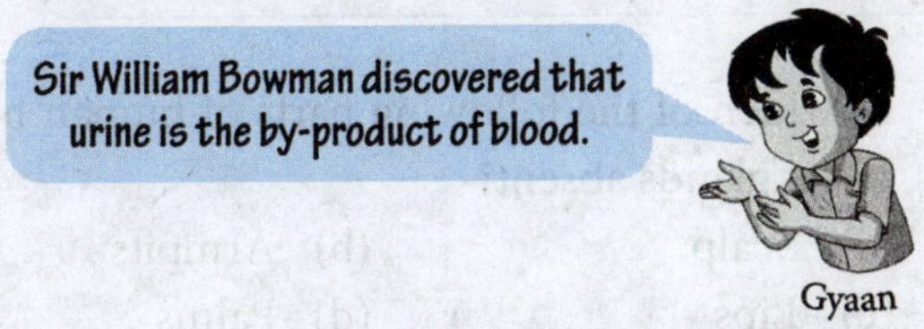

7.3 Transport of Substances in Plants

NCERT Page 77-79

A. Select the correct option.

44. Which of the following transports food to different plant parts?
(a) Xylem (b) Root
(c) Phloem (d) Leaf U

45. Water reaches great heights in the trees due to suction pull caused by
(a) evaporation (b) transpiration
(c) photosynthesis (d) respiration. R

46. In order to increase water absorption by the roots, a plant should be kept
(a) under sunlight (b) in the shade
(c) under a tubelight (d) in a dark room. U

47. The process of loss of water in plants in the form of water vapour is called
(a) circulation (b) osmosis
(c) transpiration (d) suction. R

48. Roots: ____________ : : Leaves : Photosynthesis
(a) Absorption (b) Transpiration
(c) Conduction (d) Excretion U

B. Passage based questions.

49. Fill in the blanks in the given passage.
____________ transports water from soil to different parts of a plant. The food prepared by the leaves are transported by ____________ to all other parts of the plant. They are called ____________ tissues. Not all the water absorbed by roots is utilized by the plant. Some part of it is evaporated through the ____________ present on the surface of the ____________.

C. State True (T) or False (F) for the given statements.

50. A large part of water absorbed by the plants is lost in the form of vapour. ☐

51. The root hair decreases the surface area of roots for the absorption of water. ☐

52. Phloem forms a continuous network of channels that connects roots to the leaves through the stems and branches. ☐

53. Transpiration helps in maintaining the temperature in plants. ☐

54. All the water absorbed by the plant is not utilised for photosynthesis. ☐

55. Water can move from one cell to another inside a plant. ☐

D. Figure based questions.

Direction (Q.No. 56–58) : Observe the image given below and answer the questions that follow.

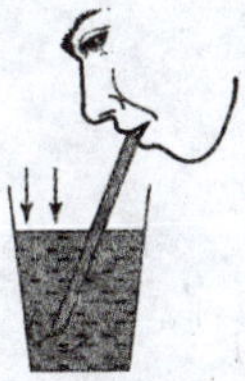

56. What happens when you suck water through a straw?

57. A similar process takes place in plants also. Write its name.

58. Write down the significance of this process in plants.

PROGRESS CHECK

Check your score! If your score is

> 95%	EXCELLENT !	- Move on to the next chapter. You have mastered this chapter. Concepts are certainly on your fingertips.
95-85%	VERY GOOD !	- Revise once more thoroughly. Recognise your mistakes and work on them. You will master this chapter.
84-75%	GOOD!	- Work on your weak areas, master them and come back to this chapter in a few days.
74-65%	MEDIOCRE!	- Understand your weak areas and work on strengthening your concepts. Devote more time to master this chapter.
< 65%	NOT SATISFACTORY!	- This is where you fall behind from scoring well. Give special attention to this chapter. Work on clearing concepts and common errors.

NCERT Exemplar Problems

This section contains MCQs of **'NCERT Exemplar Problems'** Book.

1. The muscular tube through which stored urine is passed out of the body is called
(a) kidney (b) ureter
(c) urethra (d) urinary bladder.

2. They are pipe-like, consisting of a group of specialised cells. They transport substances and form a two-way traffic in plants. Which of the following terms qualify for the features mentioned above?
(a) Xylem tissue (b) Phloem tissue
(c) Root hair (d) Both (b) and (c)

3. The absorption of nutrients and exchange of respiratory gases between blood and tissues takes place in
(a) veins (b) arteries
(c) heart (d) capillaries.

4. In which of the following parts of human body are sweat glands absent?
(a) Scalp (b) Armpits
(c) Lips (d) Palms

5. In a tall tree, which force is responsible for pulling water and minerals from the soil?
(a) Gravitational force
(b) Transportation force
(c) Suction force
(d) Conduction force

6. Aquatic animals like fish excrete their wastes in gaseous form as
(a) oxygen (b) hydrogen
(c) ammonia (d) nitrogen.

A&R Corner

Directions : In the following questions, a statement of assertion is followed by a statement of reason. Mark the correct choice as :
(a) If both assertion and reason are true and reason is the correct explanation of assertion.
(b) If both assertion and reason are true but reason is not the correct explanation of assertion.
(c) If assertion is true but reason is false.
(d) If both assertion and reason are false.

1. **Assertion :** Blood is a fluid connective tissue which flows in blood vessels.
Reason : Blood carries oxygen from the lungs to the cells of the body.

2. **Assertion :** Arteries carry oxygen-rich blood from the heart to all parts of body and have thick and elastic walls.
Reason : The blood flow in arteries is rapid and at a high pressure.

3. **Assertion :** Wound get plugged by dark red clot immediately after an injury.
Reason : Platelets help in the clotting of blood due to which further bleeding stops after injury.

4. **Assertion :** Pulse is the throbbing due to the blood flowing in the arteries.
Reason : The throbbing movements correspond to the blood being pumped by the heart into the veins. U

5. **Assertion :** Stethoscope is used to amplify the sound of the heart.
Reason : Doctors can get clues about the condition of your heart by listening through a stethoscope.

6. **Assertion :** Animals like sponges and *Hydra* which are found in water possess a well-developed circulatory system.
Reason : The blood flowing through vessels in sponges and *Hydra* transports food and oxygen in their bodies.

7. **Assertion :** Oxygen rich blood and carbon dioxide rich blood are never mixed in human heart.
Reason : Partition between the chambers of heart avoid mixing up of blood rich in oxygen with the blood rich in carbon dioxide. R

8. **Assertion :** The way in which the waste chemicals are removed from the body of the animals depends on the availability of water.
Reason : Aquatic animals like fishes, excrete cell waste as urea which directly dissolves in water.

9. **Assertion :** Transportation is the process of distribution of food, oxygen, water, enzymes and hormones inside the body of an organism.
Reason : Plants need to transport the food, water and minerals from stems to all other parts of the plant. U

10. **Assertion :** Food is the only source of energy and must be available to every cell of an organism.
Reason : In an organism, every cell gets energy by the breakdown of glucose.

11. **Assertion :** The water kept in an earthen pot (*Matka*) is cooler than normal tap water.
Reason : In earthen pot, the water evaporates from the pores present in it which causes cooling of water.

12. **Assertion :** A tissue is a group of cells that perform specialised function in an organism.
Reason : Phloem is the vascular tissue which is meant for the transport of water and nutrients in the plant. An

13. **Assertion :** The walls of ventricles are thicker than the auricles.
Reason : The thickness of wall of ventricles helps in preventing the backflow of the blood.

14. **Assertion :** Transpiration increases the concentration of mineral salts in the plant.
Reason : Transpiration lowers down the plant temperature.

15. **Assertion :** White patches are formed on our clothes especially in areas like underarms.
Reason : The sweat contains water and salts. R

Exam Corner

This section comprises of different types of questions:

- **Objective Type Questions** : These are **one mark** questions.
- **Very Short Answer Type Questions (VSA)** : These are **one mark** questions.
- **Short Answer Type Questions-I (SA-I)** : These are **two marks** questions.
- **Short Answer Type Questions-II (SA-II)** : These are **three marks** questions.
- **Long Answer Type Questions (LA)** : These are **five marks** questions.
- **Case Based Questions (CBQs)** : These are case study/passage based questions.

OBJECTIVE TYPE QUESTIONS

A. Select the correct option.

1. Fluid component of blood that contains 90% of water is
(a) enzyme (b) plasma
(c) red blood cell (d) white blood cell.

2. Vascular system of plants consists of
(a) xylem (b) phloem
(c) veins (d) both (a) and (b).
U

3. ___(i)___ transports ___(ii)___ in both upward and downward directions.
Which of the following options completes the given statement?
(a) (i) – Xylem; (ii) – water
(b) (i) – Phloem; (ii) – water
(c) (i) – Xylem; (ii) – food
(d) (i) – Phloem; (ii) – food

4. The given figure illustrates human heart with four chambers.

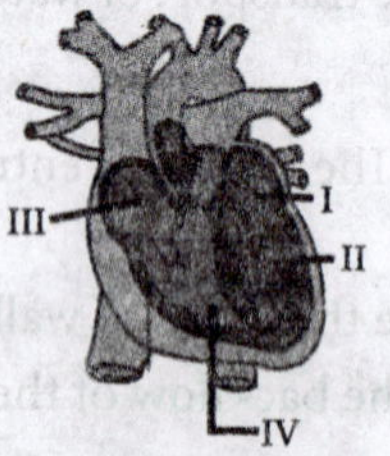

Which labelled structure receives carbon dioxide-rich blood from the body?
(a) I and II (b) I and III
(c) III and IV (d) II and IV
An

5. Select the incorrect statement(s) regarding veins.
(i) Carries oxygen-rich blood from the heart to all parts of the body.
(ii) Valves are absent.
(iii) Have thin walls.
(a) Only (i) (b) (i) and (iii)
(c) (i) and (ii) (d) (ii) and (iii)

6. Which of the following is not a part of the human excretory system?
(a) Aorta (b) Nephrons
(c) Urinary bladder (d) Ureter

7. Thinnest blood vessels are
(a) veins (b) capillaries
(c) pulmonary arteries (d) pulmonary veins.

8. Select the incorrect match(es).

	Organ		Function
(i)	Kidney	–	Urine formation
(ii)	Skin	–	Sweat formation
(iii)	Heart	–	Blood formation
(iv)	Urethra	–	Stores urine

(a) Only (iii) (b) Only (iv)
(c) (iii) and (iv) (d) (i) and (ii)

9. Select the incorrect statement(s).
(i) Sponges do not posses any circulatory system.
(ii) Fish excretes uric acid as excretory product.
(iii) Sweat contains water and salts.
(iv) Sweating helps in maintaining the body temperature.
(v) Urea is filtered in the blood by villi.
(a) Only (iii) (b) (ii) and (iv)
(c) (i), (ii) and (iii) (d) (ii) and (v)

10. Select the correct order of flow of blood inside our body.
(a) Lungs $\xrightarrow[\text{blood}]{\text{Oxygenated}}$ Pulmonary vein → Heart → Artery → Capillaries
(b) Pulmonary artery $\xrightarrow[\text{blood}]{\text{Deoxygenated}}$ Heart → Veins → Lungs
(c) Capillaries $\xrightarrow[\text{blood}]{\text{Deoxygenated}}$ Pulmonary artery → Lungs → Pulmonary vein → Heart
(d) Heart $\xrightarrow[\text{blood}]{\text{Oxygenated}}$ Capillaries → Lungs → Pulmonary Veins → Heart
An

11. Select the correct statements regarding the functions of blood.
(i) Transports food from small intestine to all other parts of the body.
(ii) Transports waste to the kidney.
(iii) Transports oxygen from lungs to tissues.
(iv) Transports carbon-dioxide from cells to lungs.
(a) (i) and (ii) (b) (iv) and (iii)
(c) (i), (iii) and (iv) (d) (i), (ii), (iii) and (iv)

12. Complete the given analogy by selecting the correct option.
Vascular bundles : Plants :: ________ : Animals
(a) Blood (b) Haemoglobin
(c) Blood vessels (d) Kidneys An

13. Select the correct match(es).

Blood component	Function
(i) Plasma	– Contains haemoglobin
(ii) WBC	– Fight against germs
(iii) RBC	– Transport other components of blood
(iv) Platelet	– Clotting of blood

(a) Only (ii) (b) (ii) and (iii)
(c) Only (iv) (d) (ii) and (iv)

14. Select the incorrect statement(s).
(i) Plasma is the fluid part of the blood.
(ii) Like humans, sponges also possess kidneys for the process of excretion.
(iii) Capillaries are present inside tissues of our body.
(iv) Our skin possess sweat glands.
(a) Only (ii) (b) (i) and (iv)
(c) Only (iii) (d) (ii) and (iii)

15. Select the correct matches.

Body fluids	Components
(i) Blood	– Plasma, blood cells
(ii) Sweat	– Water, salt
(iii) Urine	– Water, uric acid, waste products
(iv) Plasma	– Water, haemoglobin, food

(a) (i) and (iii) (b) (i) and (ii)
(c) (ii) and (iii) (d) (i) and (iv)

16. Which of the following statements are correct about figure A?
(i) The blood in X is rich in oxygen and is going to the lungs.
(ii) The blood in X is rich in carbon dioxide and is going to the body parts.
(iii) The blood in Y is rich in carbon dioxide and is coming from the heart.
(iv) The blood in Z is rich in oxygen and is coming from the lungs.

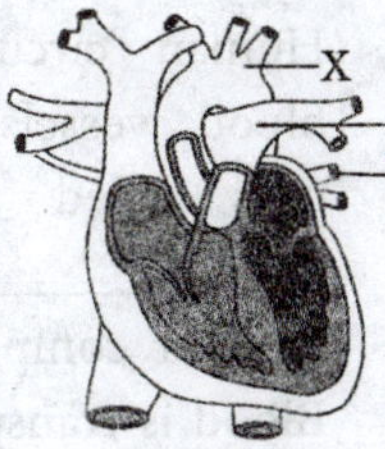

Fig.: A

(a) (i) and (ii) (b) (i) and (iv)
(c) (ii) and (iii) (d) (iii) and (iv) Ap

17. Select the correct option for labels P, Q and R in the given figure.

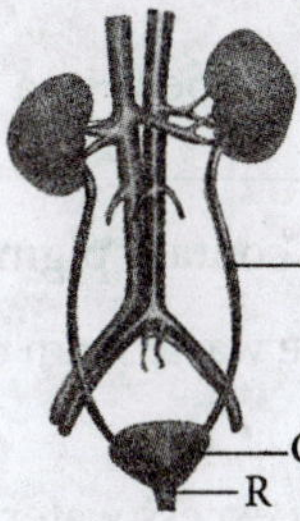

	P	Q	R
(a)	Urinary bladder	Ureter	Urethra
(b)	Ureter	Urinary bladder	Urethra
(c)	Urethra	Urinary bladder	Ureter
(d)	Urinary bladder	Urethra	Ureter

18. Which one of the following is not a function of transpiration?
(a) It causes the movement of water from roots to the leaves.
(b) It causes minerals to travel up from the roots to the leaves.
(c) It gives leaves their green colour.
(d) It is responsible for keeping the plant cool.

19. ________ increases the surface area for absorption of water and minerals in plants.
(a) Xylem (b) Phloem
(c) Roots hair (d) Leaf R

20. ________ have thick elastic walls.
(a) Arteries (b) Veins
(c) Capillaries (d) Pulmonary veins

21. Which of the following is not a part of the stethoscope?
(a) Tube (b) Septum
(c) Chest piece (d) Ear piece

22. The pressure of blood flow is higher inside
(a) veins (b) arteries
(c) capillaries (d) tissues.

23. ________ carries only oxygen-rich blood.
(a) Vein (b) Artery
(c) Pulmonary artery (d) Capillary

24. Valves are present in
(a) arteries (b) veins
(c) pulmonary artery (d) capillaries.

B. Fill in the blanks.

25. ________ help in blood clothing.

26. ________ combines with oxygen molecule and transports it to all parts of body.

27. Each heartbeat generates one ________ in the arteries.

28. The xylem and phloem in a plant make up a tissue called ________.

29. ________ contain pigment haemoglobin.

30. Kidneys remove waste from our body in the form of ________.

31. Plants get rid of excess water by ________.

C. State True (T) or False (F) for the given statements.

32. White blood cells are smaller in size than red blood cells and can move on their own. ☐

33. Auricles have comparatively thicker walls than ventricles. ☐

34. Pulse is the throbbing movement felt at our wrist which is caused due to expansion of veins. ☐

35. Ventricles are the two upper chambers of the heart with thick muscular walls. ☐

36. Transpiration of water from leaves creates a suction pull. ☐

37. *Amoeba* does not posses excretory organs. ☐

38. Septum separates the right chambers of the heart from its left chambers. ☐

39. Haemoglobin can combine with oxygen molecules. ☐

40. Food synthesised by the leaves is transported to other plant parts by phloem. ☐

41. Pulse rate is the rate of heartbeat. ☐

42. All animals possess well developed circulatory and excretory system. ☐

43. Pulmonary artery is the only artery that carries oxygen-rich blood from lungs to the heart. ☐

44. Heart acts as a pump for transport of blood inside the body. ☐

45. Human blood contains 2.5% of urea. ☐

D. Figure based questions.

Direction (Q.No. 46 and 47) : Observe the given figure regarding transport of water and minerals in a section of root and answer the questions that follow.

46. Identify labelled part A and B.

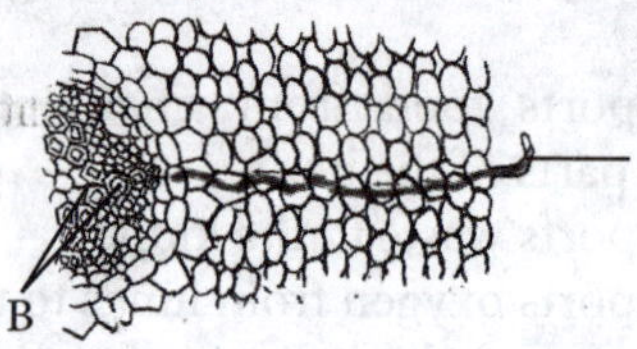

47. Name one of the process responsible for transport of water and minerals.

E. Match the columns.

48.

Column I	Column II
1. Prevents backflow of blood in the heart	A. Pulse
2. Rhythmic throbbing of arteries during blood flow	B. Heartbeat
3. Rhythmic contraction and relaxation of heart chambers	C. Septum
4. Muscular wall that prevents mixing of blood in the heart	D. Valve

(a) 1–B, 2–A, 3–C, 4–D
(b) 1–C, 2–B, 3–D, 4–A
(c) 1–A, 2–C, 3–B, 4–D
(d) 1–D, 2–A, 3–B, 4–C

49.

Column I		Column II
1. Stomata	A	Transpiration
2. Urethra	B	Collects and stores urine
3. Uric acid	C	Duct through which urine passes out
4. Urinary bladder	D	Waste product of lizard
5. Urea	E	Waste product of human

(a) 1–B, 2–C, 3–A, 4–D, 5–E
(b) 1–A, 2–C, 3–D, 4–B, 5–E
(c) 1–C, 2–B, 3–D, 4–E, 5–A
(d) 1–B, 2–E, 3–D, 4–C, 5–A

F. Passage based questions.

50. Fill in the blanks in the given passage.

Human circulatory system consists of blood, blood vessels and the heart. Blood contains cells called ________, ________ and ________, which are suspended in another component of it called ________. Blood is transported to different parts of the body through ________. They are of two types;

________ and ________. First one carries ________ blood from the heart to all parts of the body, and the later one carries ________ blood from all parts of the body back to the heart. They divide further into extremely thin tubes called ________ inside the tissues. The heart acts as a ________ for the transport of blood to all parts of the body.

VERY SHORT ANSWER TYPE QUESTIONS (VSA)

A. Answer the following in one or two words.

51. Name the two tissues that help in the transportation of food and water respectively, in plants.

52. Name the main organ of human excretory system.

53. Name the upper two chambers of the heart.

54. Name the blood vessels which carry carbon dioxide-rich blood to the lungs and oxygen-rich blood to the heart, respectively in human beings.

55. Name the two parts of human heart, one of which helps to prevent backflow of blood and the other which prevents mixing of blood in the heart.

B. Complete the given analogy.

56. Heart : Circulation : : Kidneys : ________

57. ________ : Deoxygenated blood : : Left ventricle : Oxygenated blood

58. Xylem : Connects roots to other parts of a plant : : ________ : Connects leaves to other parts of a plant

59. Leaves : ________ : : Roots : Absorb water

60. Human : Kidneys : : *Amoeba* : ________

SHORT ANSWER TYPE QUESTIONS-I (SA-I)

61. Define: (a) Heartbeat (b) Pulse rate. R

62. Differentiate between arteries and veins.

63. What are the different excretory products in land animals and aquatic animals?

64. What happens when a person's kidneys stop working? Under what conditions such a person can survive? An

65. What is the difference between xylem and phloem?

SHORT ANSWER TYPE QUESTIONS-II (SA-II)

66. Why is the colour of blood red? Write the role of the component of blood that makes it red in colour.

67. What causes a heartbeat and a pulse?

68. Briefly describe the structure and function of human heart. U

69. How circulation and excretion take place in sponges and *Hydra*?

70. Write down the importance of transpiration in plants.

71. Given image shows the internal structure of human heart. Label each part of the heart in the empty boxes provided.

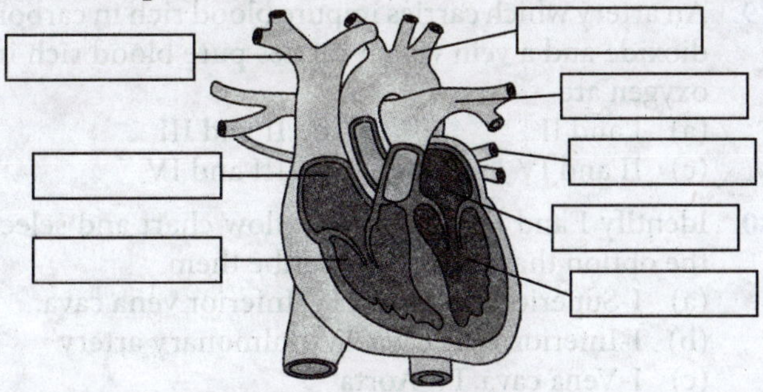

72. What is blood composed of? Why are the components of blood so important for us? An

LONG ANSWER TYPE QUESTIONS (LA)

73. What are the different blood vessels present in our body? Write down the function of each one of them.

74. Explain the process of circulation in human beings.

75. How excretion takes place in humans?

76. Explain the process of transportation in plants.

77. Give reason for the following statements.
- (a) Oxygen-rich blood and carbon dioxide-rich blood are never mixed up in human heart.
- (b) Blood in the heart flows only in one direction.
- (c) Contents of xylem move only in upward direction whereas contents in phloem move in both upward and downward direction.

CASE BASED QUESTIONS (CBQs)

Case I : Read the given passage and answer the following questions :

Heart is an organ which beats continuously to act as a pump for the transport of blood, which carries other substances with it. The heart has number of valves, that prevent the back flow of blood and allows the blood to flow in one direction only.

Analyse carefully the given flow chart of circulation of blood :

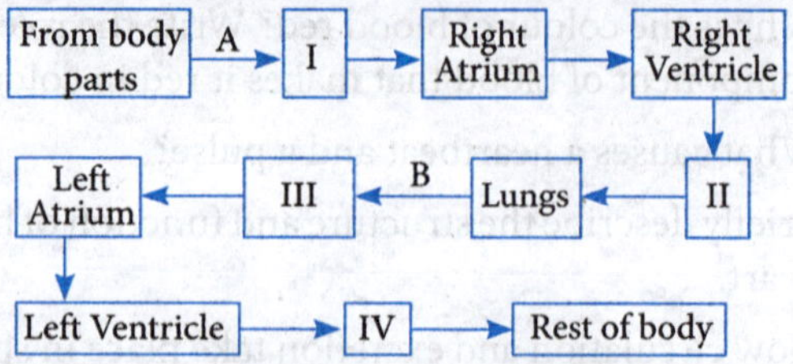

78. Select the correct option regarding A and B.

	A	B
(a)	Oxygenated	Deoxygenated
(b)	Deoxygenated	Oxygenated
(c)	Oxygen rich	Oxygen rich
(d)	Carbon rich	Carbon rich

79. An artery which carries impure blood rich in carbon dioxide and a vein which carries pure blood rich in oxygen are
(a) I and II (b) II and III
(c) II and IV (d) III and IV

80. Identify I and IV in the given flow chart and select the option that correctly describe them.
(a) I-Superior vena cava, IV-Inferior vena cava.
(b) I-Inferior vena cava, IV-pulmonary artery
(c) I-Vena cava, IV-Aorta
(d) I-Aorta, IV-Vena cava

81. Select the mismatched pair.
(a) II – Carries CO_2 rich blood
(b) III – Carries O_2 rich blood
(c) A – Oxygenated blood
(d) B – Oxygen rich blood

82. ________ carries oxygen-rich blood from the lungs to the heart.
(a) B (b) I
(c) II (d) III

Case II : Read the given passage and answer the following questions :

The given figure '*X*' is the tiny pore present on the surface of the leaves. It is surrounded by two bean shaped cells. The water evaporates through '*X*' by the process of transpiration.

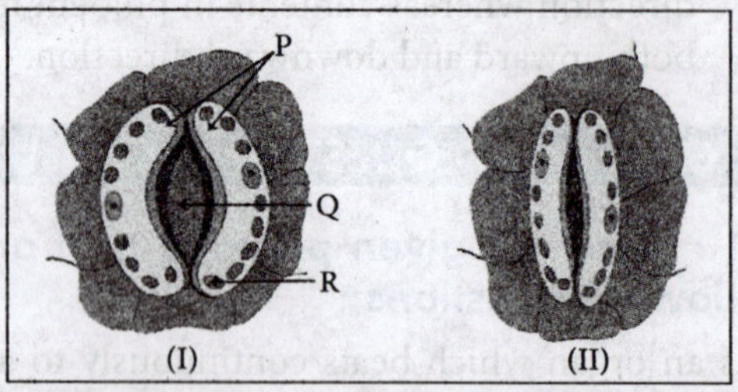

X

83. Identify '*X*'.
(a) Guard cells (b) Stomata
(c) Lenticels (d) Chloroplast

84. Select the correct option *w.r.t.* I and II.

	I	II
(a)	Open	Open
(b)	Closed	Open
(c)	Open	Closed
(d)	Closed	Closed

85. Identify P, Q and R from the given figure and select the correct option.

	P	Q	R
(a)	Guard cells	Stomatal pore	Chloroplast
(b)	Chloroplast	Stomatal pore	Guard cells
(c)	Chloroplast	Guard cells	Stomatal pore
(d)	Guard cells	Chloroplast	Stomatal pore

86. Write two functions of X?

87. The process in which the loss of water mostly occurs through X which generates suction that pulls xylem sap upward is.
(a) transpiration (b) respiration
(c) translocation (d) osmosis.

Case III : Read the given passage and answer the following questions :

P are a pair of red-coloured, bean-shaped organs, which lies in the abdominal cavity. P consist of large number of coiled tubes called Q which filter out excess water, salts and urea from the blood as it passes through them. The wastes removed by the P form a liquid called urine which passes through two tubes called R into an elastic sac called S. P must function properly to keep the body healthy by removing toxic wastes from the blood.

T is a disease in which the sugar level in the blood increases beyond the normal value, and some of the excess sugar is excreted out of the body through urine.

88. Select the correct option regarding P, Q and R in the given paragraph.

	P	Q	R
(a)	Nephrons	Kidneys	Ureters
(b)	Kidneys	Ureters	Nephrons
(c)	Nephrons	Ureters	Kidneys
(d)	Kidneys	Nephrons	Ureters

89. Main excretory organ in humans is
(a) P (b) R
(c) Q (d) S.

90. The disease is represented by T is
(a) kidney stones (b) diabetes
(c) depression (d) anxiety

91. Identify the structure R.
(a) Ureter (b) Nephron
(c) Bladder (d) Urethra

92. What is the function of S?

ANSWER KEY

Practice Corner

1. (b) **2.** (b) **3.** (c) **4.** (a) **5.** (a) **6.** (c) **7.** (d) **8.** (d) **9.** (b) **10.** (a)
11. (b) **12.** Blood vessels **13.** pulse rate **14.** Veins **15.** Pulmonary vein **16.** chest cavity
17. pulse **18.** capillaries **19.** heartbeat **20.** ventricles **21.** Arteries **24.** (b) **25.** (b) **26.** (a)
27. (b) **28.** (a) **29.** uric acid **30.** dialysis **31.** 1 – 1.8 **32.** excretion
33. water, salts **34.** False **35.** True **36.** True **37.** False **38.** False **39.** False **40.** True **41.** False
42. False **44.** (c) **45.** (b) **46.** (a) **47.** (c) **48.** (a) **50.** True **51.** False **52.** False
53. True **54.** True **55.** True **57.** Transpiration

NCERT Exemplar Problems

1. (c) **2.** (b) **3.** (d) **4.** (c) **5.** (c) **6.** (c)

A & R Corner

1. (b) **2.** (a) **3.** (a) **4.** (c) **5.** (a) **6.** (d) **7.** (a) **8.** (c) **9.** (c) **10.** (a)
11. (a) **12.** (c) **13.** (c) **14.** (b) **15.** (a)

Exam Corner

1. (b) **2.** (d) **3.** (d) **4.** (c) **5.** (c) **6.** (a) **7.** (b) **8.** (c) **9.** (d) **10.** (a)
11. (d) **12.** (c) **13.** (d) **14.** (a) **15.** (b) **16.** (d) **17.** (b) **18.** (c) **19.** (c) **20.** (a)
21. (b) **22.** (b) **23.** (b) **24.** (b) **25.** Platelets **26.** Haemoglobin **27.** pulse
28. vascular tissue **29.** RBCs **30.** urine **31.** transpiration **32.** False **33.** False **34.** False **35.** False
36. True **37.** True **38.** True **39.** True **40.** True **41.** True **42.** False **43.** False **44.** True
45. False **48.** (d) **49.** (b) **52.** Kidneys **56.** Excretion **57.** Right ventricle **58.** Phloem
59. Prepare food **60.** Cell membrane **78.** (b) **79.** (b) **80.** (c) **81.** (c) **82.** (d)
83. (b) **84.** (c) **85.** (a) **87.** (a) **88.** (d) **89.** (a) **90.** (b) **91.** (a)

8 Reproduction in Plants

NCERT Notes

- The biological process of production of new individuals from their parents is known as **reproduction**. It is one of the most important characteristics of all living organisms, *i.e.*, to produce individuals of their own kind. It is the basic process for the perpetuation of living organisms and helps to maintain the continuity of life.

8.1 Modes of Reproduction

- A flowering plant bears two types of organs - **vegetative organs** and **reproductive organs.**
- Roots, stem and leaves are vegetative organs that take part in nutrition, growth and maintenance of plant body.
- After a certain period of growth, most plants bear flowers. Flowers change into fruits, which have seeds in them. Seeds germinate to produce new plants. Thus, flowers are the reproductive parts of a flowering plant.

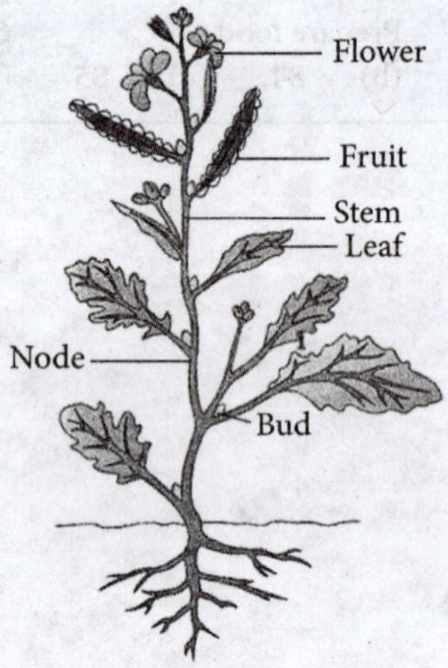

Fig.: Parts of a flowering plant

Modes of Reproduction

- **Asexual**: In this type of reproduction, only single parent is involved.
  - Vegetative propagation
  - Budding
  - Fragmentation
  - Spore formation
- **Sexual**: In this type, two parents, one male and one female are required.

Asexual Reproduction

- Asexual reproduction involves the production of a new organism by a single parent. In this type of reproduction, plants can give rise to new plants without seeds. There are many methods of asexual reproduction in plants. These include vegetative propagation, budding, fragmentation, spore formation, etc.

Vegetative Propagation

- It is a type of asexual reproduction in which new plants are produced from the **vegetative parts** of the mother plant like roots, stems, leaves and buds.
- Node is a part of the stem/branch at which a leaf arises.
- **Axil** is the point of attachment of the leaf at the node. Axil possess buds which develop into shoots. These buds are called vegetative buds. A bud consists of a short stem around which immature overlapping leaves are present. Vegetative buds can also give rise to new plants.
- Rose, *champa*, money plant produce new plants by piece of branch called **cutting**. Cutting possess nodes which are buried in the soil.
- Potato is an underground stem tuber and possess scars or depressions called eyes. Each eye represents a bud which can develop into a new plant.

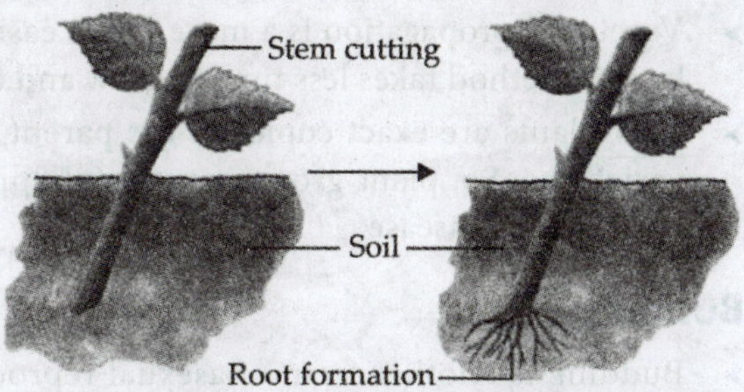

Fig.: Vegetative propagation in rose by stem cutting

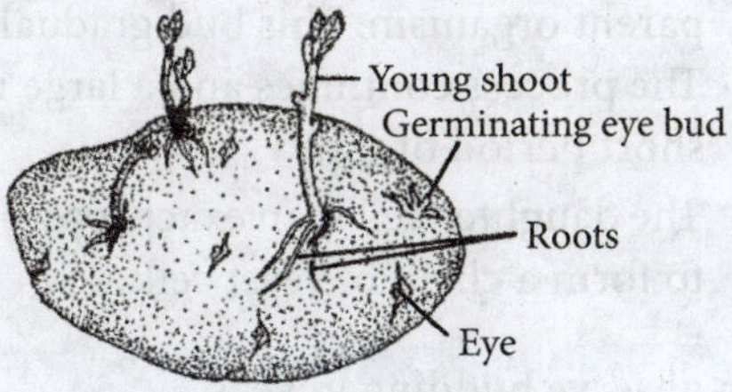

Fig.: Potato tuber

- Tuber, bulb, corm, rhizome are the different modifications of an underground stem.
- Ginger and turmeric possess rhizomes which are the main underground stems that bear buds and these buds grow to give rise to new plants. Roots develop from the lower surface of the underground stems.

Fig.: Rhizome of ginger

- The fleshy leaves of *Bryophyllum* (sprout leaf plant) has many buds on its margin. When such a leaf falls on the moist soil, each bud grows into a new independent plant.
- Tuberous roots of *Dahlia* and sweet potato become swollen due to food stored in them. In the next season new plants are produced from these roots.
- Plants such as cacti produce new plants when their parts get detached from the main plant body. Each detached part can grow into a new plant.

Fig.: Leaf buds of *Bryophyllum*

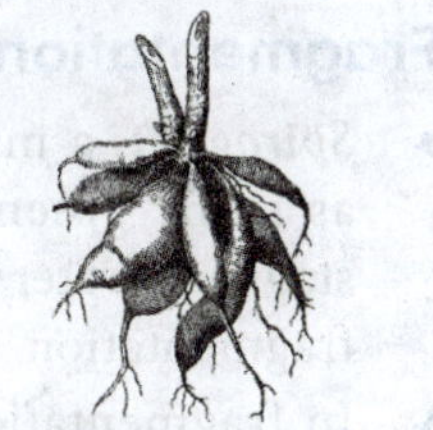
Fig.: Tuberous roots of *Dahlia*

- Several artificial methods have been developed for vegetative propagation by horticulturists to quickly multiply derived varieties of plants from parts of their somatic body.
- Vegetative propagation in plants like jasmine, vines, cherry, strawberry, etc., is done by the method of layering, in which a stem is made to produce roots while still attached to the parent plants.
- Ornamental plants, *e.g.*, rubber plant and fruit trees, *e.g.*, apple, guava, mango, etc., can be produced by the method **grafting** in which stem cutting with buds of one plant, *i.e.*, scion is joined to cut stem of another plant, *i.e.*, stock to form one plant. The stock supplies the essential nutrients to the scion. By grafting, features of two plants are combined.
- *Chrysanthemum*, *Asparagus*, orchids are developed by tissue culture method also known as micro propagation. In this method, cells of a small piece of tissue (called explant) are grown in sterile conditions which divides rapidly and form an unorganised cell mass called callus which then differentiate into roots and shoot in the nutrient medium containing plant hormones.

Advantages of vegetative propagation

- Vegetative propagation is a more rapid, easier and cheaper method of plant propagation. So, plants produced by this method takes less time to grow and bear flowers and fruits earlier than produced from seeds.
- New plants are exact copies of the parent plant; as they are produced from a single parent. They have no variations. So, plant growers can easily produce exact copies of a plant with required characteristic, like resistance to disease.

Budding

- Budding is another form of asexual reproduction which occur in unicellular organisms such as yeast and multicellular organisms such as *Hydra*.
- In budding small bulb-like projection coming out from the yeast cell called bud occurs on the body of the parent organism. This bud gradually grows and gets detached from the parent cell and forms a new yeast cell. The process continues and a large number of new yeast cell grows, matures and produces more yeast cells in a short period of time.
- The daughter cell is an exact copy of the parent cell. Under favourable conditions, bud formation occurs rapidly to form a chain of yeast cells.

To observe budding in yeast

Take some dry baker's yeast (yeast powder) in a beaker and mix it in warm water. Dissolve a spoonful of sugar into it. Keep the beaker in a warm place. After an hour, put a drop of this liquid on a glass slide and observe under the microscope. You will observe the bud formation and formation of new yeast cells. Draw simple diagrams of what you see in the slide.

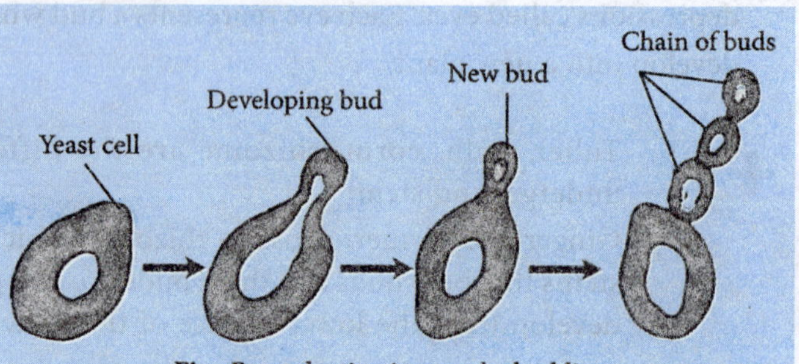

Fig.: Reproduction in yeast by budding

Fragmentation

- *Spirogyra*, a multicellular green alga which occurs as slimy green patches in ponds or are found in stagnant water bodies grow and multiply rapidly by fragmentation.
- In fragmentation, the body of the parent organism breaks up into two or more distinct fragments (pieces) after maturation, each of which can develop into a new organism. This process continues and cover a large area in a short period of time.

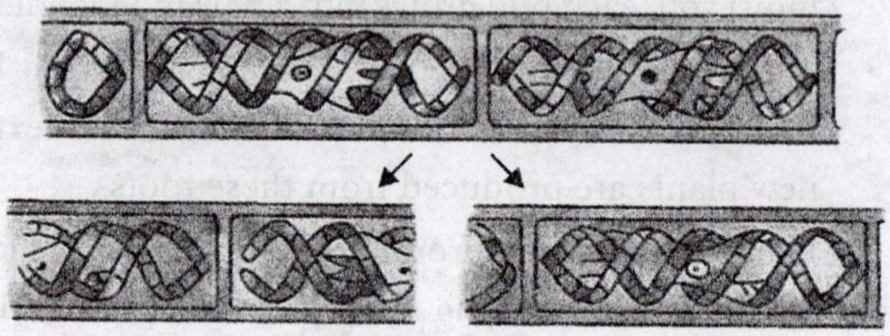

Fig. : Fragmentation in *Spirogyra* (an alga)

Spore Formation

- Each spore is a tiny, spherical reproductive body covered by a hard protective coat to withstand unfavourable conditions such as high temperature and low humidity, so that it can survive for a long time.
- Under favourable conditions, a spore germinates and develops into a new individual.
- When spores are released, they keep floating in the air. Since they are tiny and are very light, they can cover long distances and remain suspended in the air for a long time.

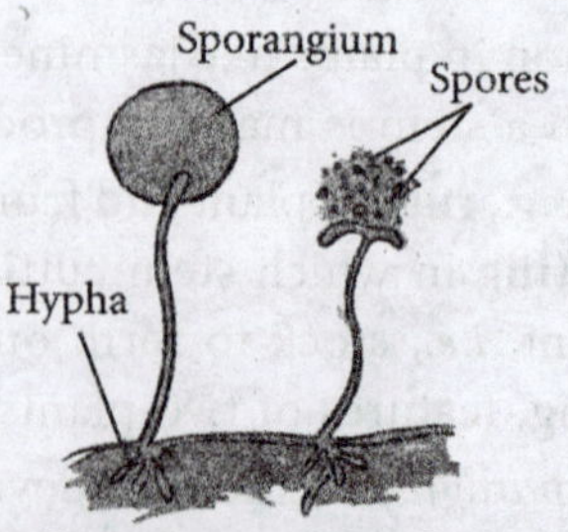

Fig.: Reproduction through spore formation in fungus

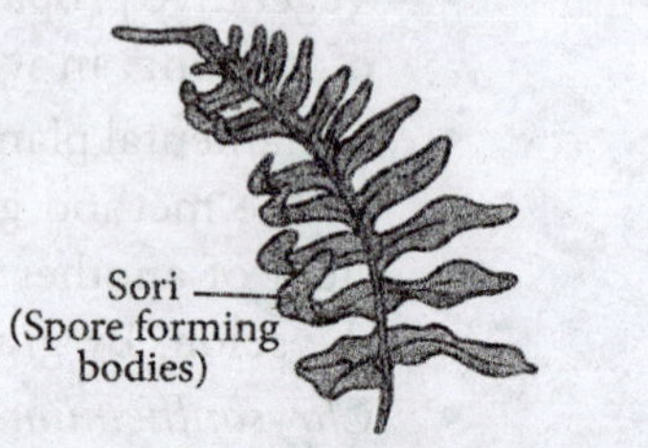

Fig.: Reproduction through spore formation in ferns

- Bread mould that can often be seen growing on moist, stale bread, grows when spores settle on the bread.
- Plants such as moss and ferns also reproduce by means of spores. Ferns have special leaves that have spore bearing structures called **sori**.

8.2 Sexual Reproduction

- Most plants reproduce sexually. In this process two reproductive cells called gametes are produced from the reproductive organs present in a flower.
- Some flowers like mustard, rose, *Petunia* contain both stamens as well as pistils are called **bisexual flowers.** Some flowers like papaya, cucumber, maize, date palm contain either only the stamen or only the pistil, are called **unisexual flowers.**

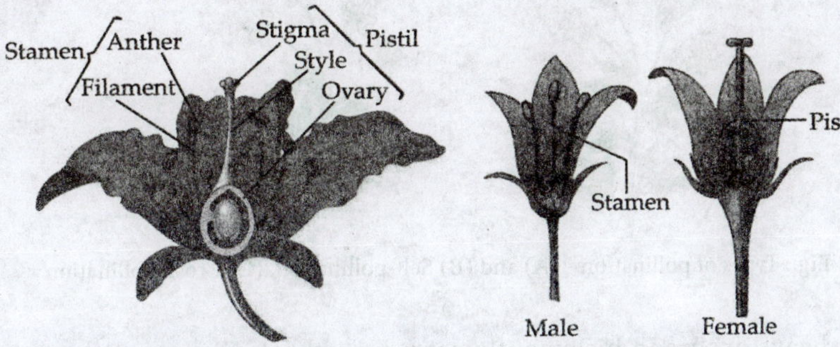

Fig.: Types of flowers

- A typical flower has a broad base or thalamus (receptacle) over which are borne four whorls of floral leaves - **sepals, petals, androecium** or **stamens** and **carpels** or **pistils** (gynoecium).

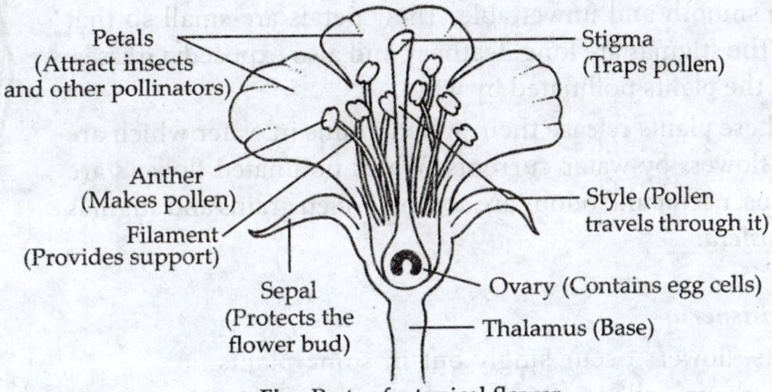

Fig.: Parts of a typical flower

- Stamens and carpels (or pistils) are the male and female reproductive parts of a flower respectively.
- Male reproductive organ, *i.e.*, stamen mainly consists of two parts: (i) the long narrow stalk-like filament and (ii) the upper, broader knob-like anther. The anther lobes consist of pollen sacs that contain millions of pollen grains. Male gametes are produced inside the pollen grains.
- A pistils is centrally located, typically consists of a swollen base, the **ovary**, which contains ovules, a stalk or style, arising from the ovary and a pollen receptive tip, the stigma, often sticky. Female gamete or the egg is formed in an ovule.

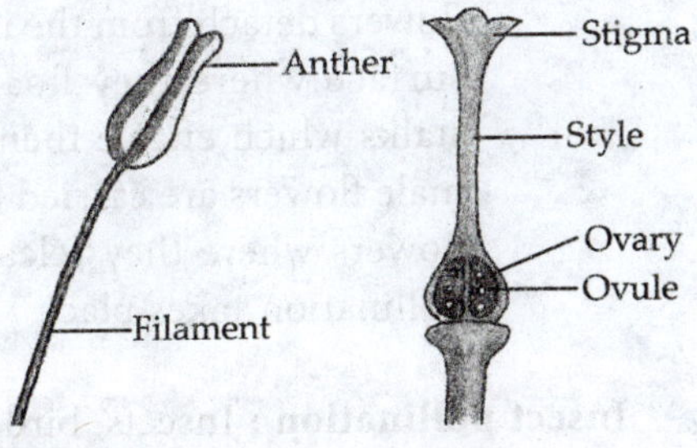

Fig.: **(A)** Parts of a stamen **(B)** Parts of a pistil

Pollination

- The process of transfer of pollen grains from the anther to the stigma of a flower is known as pollination.

Types of pollination

- There are two types of pollination: (i) self pollination and (ii) cross-pollination.
  (i) **Self pollination :** When pollen grains are transferred from the anther to the stigma of the same flower, it is called self pollination.
  (ii) **Cross-pollination :** When pollen grains are transferred between the flowers of different plants of the same species or very closely related species, it is called cross-pollination.

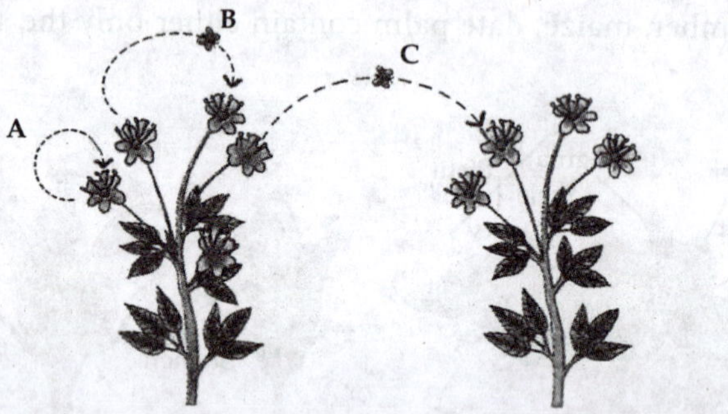

Fig.: Types of pollination - **(A)** and **(B)** Self-pollination, **(C)** Cross-pollination

> Self pollination always occurs in bisexual flowers, *e.g.*, wheat, rice, etc. Whereas cross pollination can occur in bisexual as well as in unisexual flowers.

- Pollination takes place with the help of agents such as wind, water and insects.
- **Wind pollination :** Wind pollinated flowers are small, dull, colourless and nectarless. This happens mostly in plants in which the pollen grains are small, light, dry, non-sticky, smooth and unwettable. Their petals are small so that stamens are exposed. The stigmas are long, feathery and also exposed. Grasses, maize, wheat, etc., are the plants pollinated by wind.

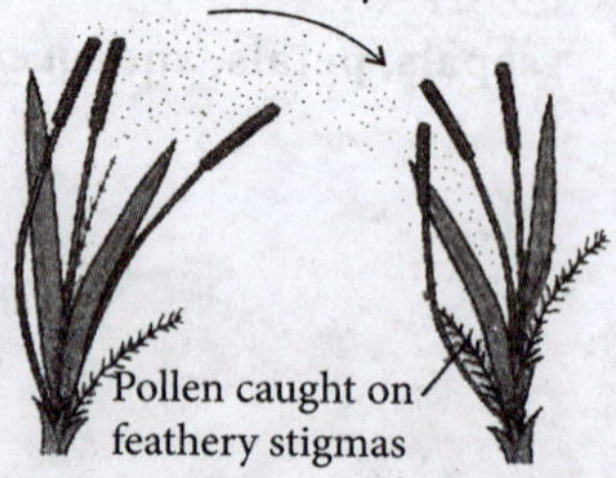

Fig.: Wind pollination

- **Water pollination :** These plants release their pollen grains in water which are carried to the female flowers by water currents. Water pollinated flowers are small and inconspicuous, nectar and odour are absent. Pollen grains and stigmas are unwettable, *e.g.*, *Zostera*.

> **Pollination in *Vallisneria***
> - In most plants, flowers occur singly but in some plants they occur in group called inflorescence. In *Vallisneria*, pollination takes place by the agency of water. The male flowers detach from the inflorescence and rise to the water surface where they float. The female flowers have long stalks which enable them to reach the water surface. The male flowers are carried by water currents towards female flowers where they release their pollens and in this way pollination takes place.

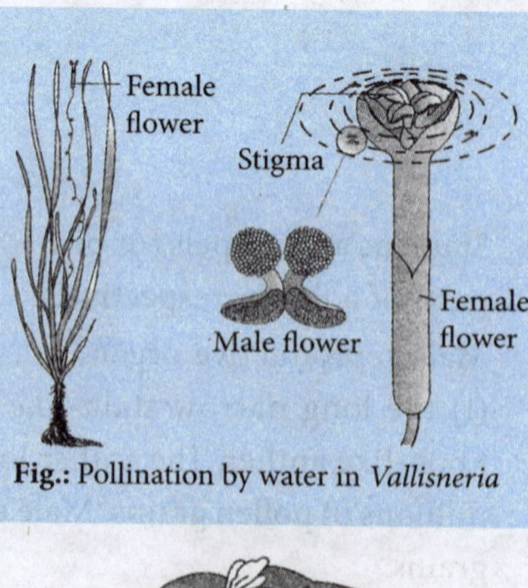

Fig.: Pollination by water in *Vallisneria*

- **Insect pollination :** Insects, birds and other animals help in cross pollination of flowers. Insect pollinated flowers are big and brightly coloured. They usually have nectaries that produce plenty of nectar. They have sticky stigma and pollen grains. *E.g.*, orchids, sunflower, *Rafflesia*, etc.

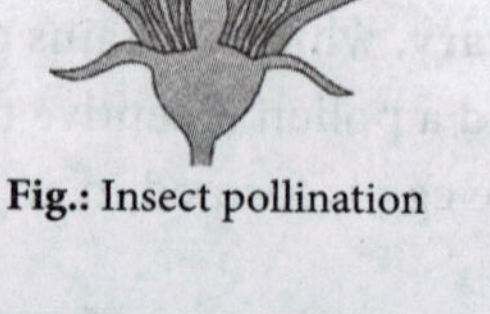
Fig.: Insect pollination

Fertilisation

- Fertilisation is the process of fusion of a male and a female gamete. Fertilisation process involves following steps : (i) On reaching the stigma, pollen grain germinates and produces a thin pollen tube. (ii) The pollen tube extends through the style. (iii) The male gamete present in the pollen tube reaches the ovary and enters the ovule.
- The whole process is called fertilisation. The cell resulting after the fusion of gametes is called **zygote**.
- The zygote is single celled which divides many times to form an embryo.

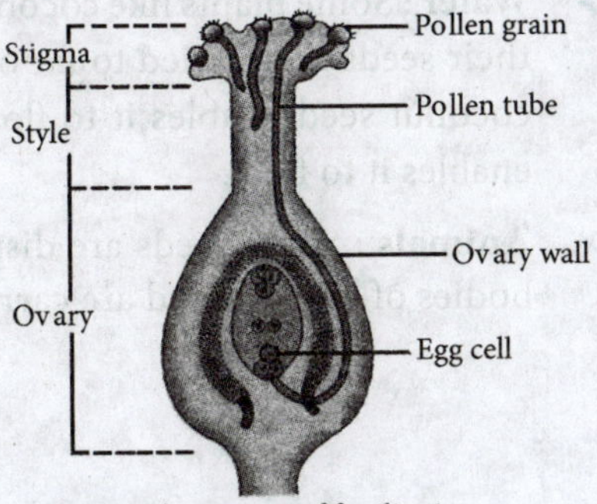

Fig.: The process of fertilisation

> The pollen tube contains two male gametes in which one of the male gametes fuses with female gamete while the second male gamete fuses with another cell in the ovule to form the endosperm which provides nourishment to the growing embryo.

8.3 Fruits and Seed Formation

- After fertilisation, the ovary grows into a fruit. So except ovary all other parts of the flower fall off.
- The ovules in the ovary develops into **seeds**. The seeds contains an embryo enclosed in a protective seed coat which protects the embryo and has stored food.
- Meanwhile, the fruit formed from ripened ovary can be as hard as almonds and walnuts or as juicy or fleshy as oranges and mangoes.

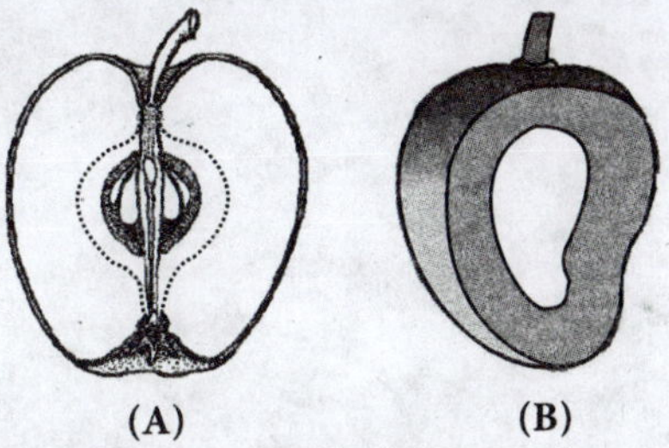

Fig.: (A) Fruit of apple (B) Fruit of mango

> - Dry fruit and fleshy fruit are two types of fruit.
> - A fruit can have one or more seeds inside it.

8.4 Seed Dispersal

- A plant produces a large number of seeds which grow into new plants under favourable conditions, it is important to ensure the continuation of that plant species. If these seeds fall at the same place, they will not be able to grow or develop into healthy plant since each of them will compete for space, sunlight and minerals.
- Nature has specified some agents of dispersal, by which the seeds of a plant get scattered over a large area. This is known as dispersal of seeds. Seed dispersal prevents competition between the plant and its own seedlings for sunlight, water and minerals. It also enables the plants to invade new habitats for wider distribution.
- Seeds and fruits may be carried away to distant places by the agency of (i) wind, (ii) water, (iii) animals and (iv) self explosion.
- **Wind :** Winged seeds of drumstick and maple, light seeds of grasses or hairy seeds of aak (*Madar*) and hairy fruit of sunflower get blown off with the wind to far away places.

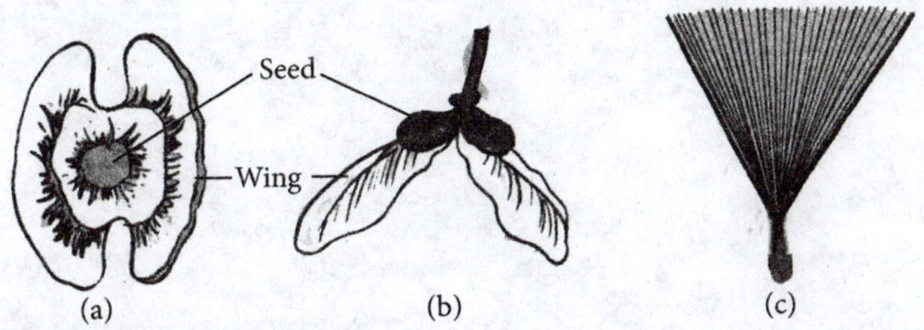

Fig.: (a) Seeds of drumstick, (b) Seeds of maple, (c) Hairy seed of *Madar* (aak)

- **Water :** Some plants like coconut and lotus grow on lakes or sea shores and their seeds are carried to far off places by water. The thick fibrous coat of coconut seed enables it to float in water, while the spongy part of lotus enables it to float.

Fig.: Fruit of coconut

- **Animals :** Some seeds are dispersed by animals, especially spiny seeds with hooks which get attached to the bodies of animals and are carried to distant places. *E.g., Xanthium* and *Urena*.

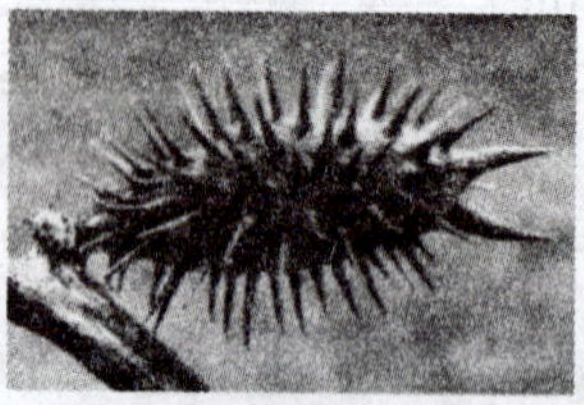

Fig.: Spiny seeds of *Xanthium*

- **Self explosion :** Some plants have fruits that burst with sudden jerks after drying. This results into scattering of seeds far away from the parent plant. This happens in the case of balsam, pea, castor, etc.

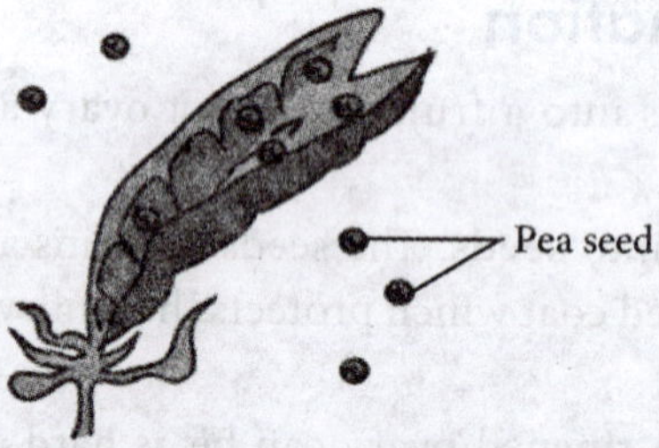

Fig.: Seed dispersal by explosion in pea

Table : Differences between asexual and sexual reproduction

S.No.	Asexual reproduction	Sexual reproduction
(i)	Only single parent is involved.	Two parents are involved.
(ii)	Offspring produced are genetically identical to the parent.	Offspring produced are different from the parents as well as from each other.
(iii)	It occurs without the formation of seed.	It occurs through seed formation.
(iv)	Vegetative plant parts such as roots, stems, leaves, etc, take part in asexual reproduction.	Flowers are the main organs of sexual reproduction in plants.

Practice Corner

Extracted from NCERT

Assessment is complementary part of the learning process. It gives you a total insight whether the learning outcomes have been achieved or not. After going through the corresponding NCERT Textbook chapter, attempt these questions in exam like environment. Give yourself one mark for correct answer. A table is given at the end, that will help you plan your next step.

All the Best!

8.1 Modes of Reproduction

NCERT Page 82-85

A. Select the correct option.

1. A ____________ plant can reproduce through the cutting of its branch.
(a) rose (b) ginger
(c) *Dahlia* (d) potato R

2. Which of the following reproduces through spores?
(a) Moss (b) *Bryophyllum*
(c) Yeast (d) *Spirogyra* U

3. ____________ is a method of vegetative propagation of asexual reproduction.
(a) Fragmentation (b) Cutting
(c) Budding (d) Spore formation R

4. Which of the following reproduces through vegetative buds?
(a) Fern (b) Moss
(c) *Bryophyllum* (d) *Dahlia* An

5. The scars on the potato are also called
(a) buds (b) eyes
(c) spores (d) fruits. R

6. Spore forming bodies present in plants are called
(a) eyes (b) buds
(c) sori (d) sporangium. R

7. *Spirogyra* reproduces asexually by the process of
(a) budding (b) fragmentation
(c) binary fission (d) regeneration. R

8. Read the following statements.
(i) *Bryophyllum* has buds in the margins of leaves.
(ii) 'Eye' of potato tuber represents a node which contains buds.
(iii) New plants cannot be grown from roots.
(iv) Plants produced by vegetative propagation take more time to grow than those produced from seeds.

Which of the above statements are true?
(a) (i) and (ii) (b) (iii) and (iv)
(c) (i) and (iii) (d) (i), (ii) and (iv) Ev

9. In which of the following, new plants cannot grow from eyes/buds?
(a) Turmeric (b) Ginger
(c) Potato (d) Sweet potato R

10. ____________ plant can reproduce asexually with the help of its roots.
(a) Rose (b) *Dahlia*
(c) *Bryophyllum* (d) Turmeric R

11. Select the correct match.

	Type of reproduction	Method	Examples
(a)	Asexual reproduction	Bud	Ginger
(b)	Vegetative propagation	Grafting	Mango
(c)	Artificial propagation	Fragmentation	*Spirogyra*
(d)	Sexual reproduction	Spore formation	Fungus

U

12. Select the incorrect analogy for the given sets.
(a) Yeast : Budding :: *Bryophyllum* : Leaf bud
(b) Flower : Vegetative part :: Spore : Reproductive part
(c) Sori : Fern :: Sporangium : Fungus
(d) *Chrysanthemum* : Tissue culture :: Sugarcane : Cutting An

13. Given figure represents the method of reproduction in bread mould.
Select the correct option for X, Y and Z.

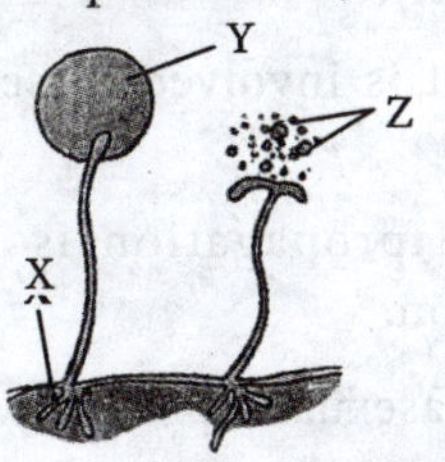

R

	X	Y	Z
(a)	Hypha	Spores	Sporangium
(b)	Hypha	Sporangium	Spores
(c)	Sporangium	Hypha	Spores
(d)	Sporangium	Spores	Hypha

14. __________ is a type of asexual reproduction in which new plants are produced from roots, stems, leaves etc.
(a) Vegetative propagation
(b) Spore formation
(c) Seed formation
(d) Budding U

B. Fill in the blanks.

15. Stems, leaves and roots of a plant are called its __________ parts.
16. A __________ is a part of the stem or branch at which a leaf arises.
17. Yeast cells reproduces through __________.
18. In asexual reproduction, new plants are obtained without production of __________.
19. __________ and __________ buds are the vegetative buds that can give rise to new plants.
20. *Spirogyra* is a/an __________.
21. Production of new individuals from their parents is called __________.
22. __________ is a single-celled organisms which can reproduce by budding.
23. __________ are called the reproductive part of a plant.

C. State True (T) or False (F) for the given statements.

24. During asexual reproduction, new individuals are produced from a single parent.
25. In vegetative propagation, some of the parental characteristics are absent in the new plants.
26. Plants produced by vegetative propagation do not bear flowers and fruits.
27. Reproduction in plants take place both sexually and asexually.
28. One parent is involved in sexual reproduction.
29. Vegetative propagation is a type of asexual reproduction.
30. Spores are asexual reproductive bodies.
31. In *Dahlia*, reproduction takes place through leaf buds.
32. Buds in the axil of leaves can give rise to new plants.

D. Figure based questions.

Direction (Q.No. 33–34) : Observe the given diagram carefully and answer the following questions.

(i)
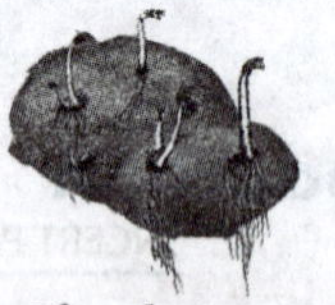
(ii)
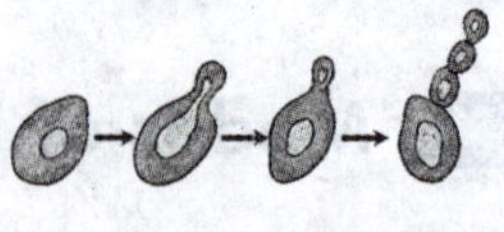

33. Identify the name of reproduction shown in figure (i).
34. Give an example of other organism showing the type of reproduction in figure (ii).

Direction (Q.No. 35–36) : Observe the given diagram carefully and answer the following questions.

(i)

(ii)

35. Identify the name of reproduction shown in figure (i).
36. In figure (ii) which type of reproduction is shown-asexual or sexual?

E. Match the columns.

37.

	Column I		Column II
I.	Production of new individuals from the vegetative part of a plant	(p)	Bud
II.	Production of new plants from seeds	(q)	Spores
III.	Bulb-like projections in yeast cells	(r)	Fragmentation
IV.	Asexual reproductive bodies in fungi	(s)	Vegetative propagation
V.	Body of plant breaks into distinct pieces to produce new offsprings	(t)	Sexual reproduction

(a) I–s, II–t, III–p, IV–q, V–r
(b) I–t, II–s, III–p, IV–r, V–q
(c) I–s, II–q, III–r, IV–p, V–t
(d) I–t, II–p, III–r, IV–q, V–s An

8.2 Sexual Reproduction

NCERT Page 85-87

A. Select the correct option.

38. Which of the following do not produce unisexual flowers?
(a) Maize (b) Mustard
(c) Papaya (d) Cucumber Ap

39. Female reproductive part of a flower is called a/an
(a) stamen (b) pistil
(c) style (d) anther. R

40. Which of the following flowers do not have both stamen and pistil?
(a) Rose (b) *Petunia*
(c) Cucumber (d) Mustard Ev

41. Which is not a part of pistil?
(a) Stigma (b) Anther
(c) Style (d) Ovary R

42. Ovules are present in
(a) anther (b) stigma
(c) style (d) ovary. R

43. Pollen grains reach the female gamete through the
(a) style (b) stigma
(c) pollen tube (d) filament. U

44. ________ is the process of fusion of male and female gametes.
(a) Fertilisation (b) Reproduction
(c) Pollination (d) Budding R

45. Observe the image given below and select the correct option for A and B.

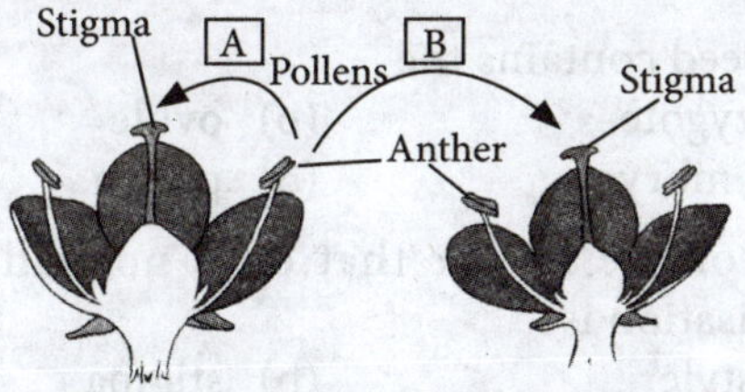

(a) A – Cross-pollination, B – Cross-pollination
(b) A – Self-pollination, B – Cross-pollination
(c) A – Cross-pollination, B – Self-pollination
(d) A – Self-pollination, B – Self-pollination Ap

46. Fertilisation occurs in plant when
(a) pollen grain leaves the anther
(b) pollen grain lands on stigma
(c) an insect sits on a plant
(d) male gamete fuses with the female gamete. U

47. Self-pollination is the transfer of pollen grains from anthers
(a) to stigma of a flower of different plants.
(b) to stigma of same flower.
(c) to stigma of a flower of a different plant of same kind.
(d) both (b) and (c) R

48. Identify the labels P, Q and R and select the correct option.

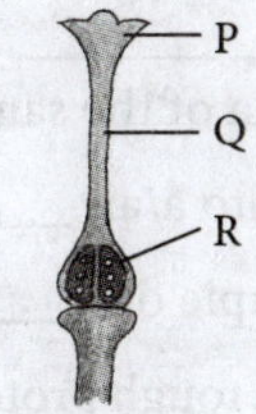

	P	Q	R
(a)	Stigma	Style	Ovary
(b)	Stigma	Ovary	Style
(c)	Ovary	Style	Stigma
(d)	Ovary	Stigma	Style

R

49. In which of the following parts, sexual reproduction takes place in plants?
(a) Leaf (b) Flower
(c) Stem (d) Fruit U

50. Fusion of male and female gametes result in the formation of
(a) embryo (b) zygote
(c) fruit (d) pollen tube. R

51. ________ : Bisexual flower :: Corn : Unisexual flower
(a) Papaya (b) Cucumber
(c) *Petunia* (d) Watermelon An

52. Select the incorrect statement(s).
(i) Pollen grains have tough protective coats.
(ii) Cross-pollination occurs with the help of wind, water and insects.
(iii) In self pollination, anther of a flower lands on the stigma of another flower of the different plant of same kind. Ap
(a) Only (ii) (b) Only (iii)
(c) (ii) and (iii) (d) (i), (ii) and (iii)

53. Study the given figure and select the incorrect statement regarding it.

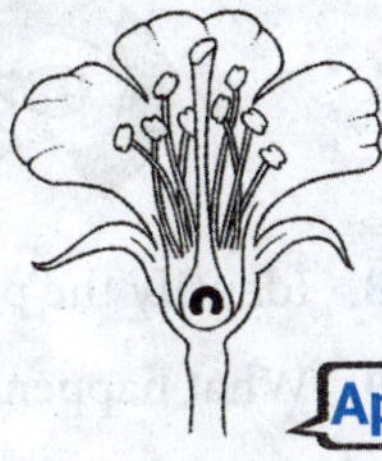

(a) It is a bisexual flower.
(b) This flower contains eight stamens.
(c) This flower contains a single pistil.
(d) It is an incomplete flower. Ap

B. Fill in the blanks.

54. Fusion of male and female gametes result into the formation of ________.

55. The female gamete is also known as ________.

56. ________ can be carried away by wind, water and animals.

57. During self ________, pollens of a flower lands on the stigma of the same flower.

58. Zygote develops into a/an ________.

59. *Petunia* is an example of ________ flower.

60. Pollen grain have a tough protective ________ which prevents them from drying up.

61. The flowers which have either the pistil or the stamen are called ________ flowers.

C. State True (T) or False (F) for the given statements.

62. In cross pollination, pollen grains are transferred from anther of one flower to the stigma of the same flower. ☐

63. Fertilisation leads to formation of the zygote. ☐

64. The pistil of a flower consists of anther and filament. ☐

65. The male gametes are produced inside pollen grains and the female gametes are produced inside the ovule. ☐

66. Anther is the part of a flower that attracts insects. ☐

67. Insects help during the process of self-pollination only. ☐

D. Figure based questions.

Direction (Q.No. 68 and 69) : Observe the given diagram carefully and answer the following questions.

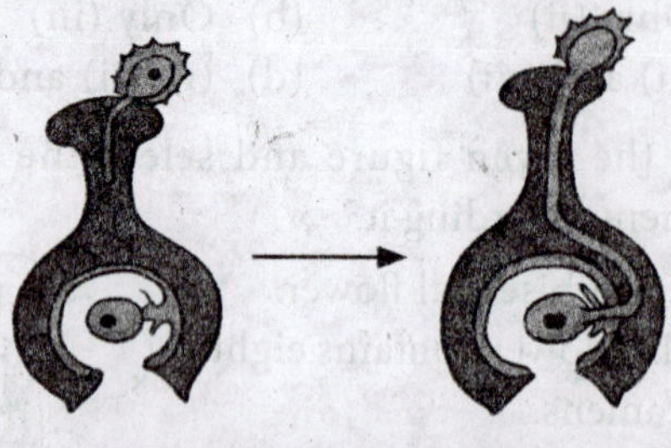

68. Identify the process shown in the given image.

69. What happens during this process?

E. Match the columns.

70.

	Column I		Column II
I.	Female or male reproductive cells	(p)	Pollen tube
II.	Contain the female gamete in flowers	(q)	Pollens
III.	Formed by fusion of male and female gametes	(r)	Ovules
IV.	Hollow tube through which male gamete reaches the ovary in plants	(s)	Gametes
V.	Contain the male gamete in flowers	(t)	Zygote

(a) I–s, II–t, III–p, IV–q, V–r
(b) I–t, II–r, III–p, IV–q, V–s
(c) I–q, II–p, III–t, IV–s, V–r
(d) I–s, II–r, III–t, IV–p, V–q [An]

8.3 Fruits and Seed Formation

NCERT Page 87

A. Select the correct option.

71. Which of the following changes into a fruit after fertilisation?
(a) Pollen (b) Ovules
(c) Ovary (d) Anther [R]

72. ________ are hard fruits.
(a) Mango and apple (b) Almond and walnut
(c) Mango and orange (d) Almond and apple [U]

73. The seed contains the
(a) zygote (b) ovule
(c) embryo (d) pollen. [R]

74. Part of the flower that does not fall off after fertilisation is
(a) style (b) stigma
(c) ovary (d) petals. [U]

B. Fill in the blanks.

75. The ________ is the ripened ovary.

76. Fruits such as ________ and ________ are fleshy and juicy.

77. The seeds develop from the ________.

C. State True (T) or False (F) for the given statements.

78. Almonds have hard seed coat. ☐

79. After fertilisation, all parts of the flower including the ovary falls off. ☐

80. Orange do not have seeds with seed coat. ☐

81. Embryo is protected inside the seed by a hard seed coat. ☐

8.4 Seed Dispersal

NCERT Page 87-88

A. Select the correct option.

82. Seeds of ______________ plant disperse through water
(a) maple (b) coconut
(c) *Xanthium* (d) castor.

83. Seeds and fruits of plants are carried away to different places by
(a) wind (b) water
(c) animals (d) all of these.

84. Winged seeds are found in
(a) *Xanthium* (b) castor
(c) sunflower (d) maple.

85. Seeds of ______________ have fibrous outer coat that help them to float in water.
(a) coconut (b) castor
(c) mango (d) pineapple.

86. A plant was found to have seeds with hooks. By which method is it most likely to be dispersed?
(a) Wind (b) Water
(c) Animals (d) Explosion of fruit

87. Seed dispersal helps the plants to
(a) prevent overcrowding.
(b) avoid competition for food.
(c) invade new habitats.
(d) all of these

88. Which of the following plants seeds are dispersed when their fruits burst?
(a) Balsam (b) Maple
(c) Sunflower (d) *Urena*

89. Select the incorrect statements.
(i) Stamen consists of stigma, style and ovary.
(ii) Growth of a new plant does not depend on seed dispersal.
(iii) Fertilised ovule is called ovary.
(iv) Bisexual flowers are incomplete.
(v) Seeds of *Urena* are dispersed by water.
(a) (i) and (iv) (b) (i), (ii), and (v)
(c) (ii), (iii) and (v) (d) All of these

B. Fill in the blanks.

90. Seeds of *Urena* plants are dispersed by ______________.

91. Fruits of sunflower are ______________, so easily blown off with the wind.

92. Castor seeds are dispersed by ______________.

93. Drumsticks have ______________ seeds which help in their dispersal.

94. Seeds of *Xanthium* have ______________ that get attached to the body of animals.

C. State True (T) or False (F) for the given statements.

95. Seed dispersal causes the growth of same kind of plants at different places. ☐

96. Coconuts are hairy seeds of coconut trees. ☐

97. Seed dispersal prevents competition between the plant and its seedlings for sunlight, water and air. ☐

98. *Xanthium* and balsam seeds are scattered far from the parent plant when their fruits burst with sudden jerks. ☐

99. Plants like *Urena* and *Xanthium* have spiny seeds with hooks. ☐

D. Figure based questions.

100. Given below are the images of seeds of different plants. Observe them carefully and answer the following question.

1. 
2. 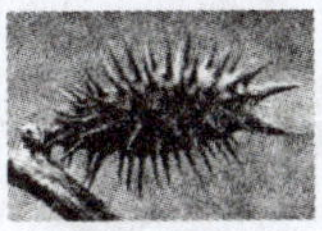
3. 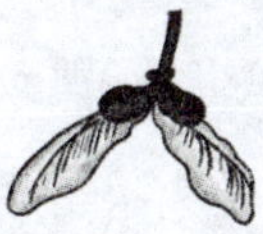

(a) Identify the seeds.
(b) How they get dispersed?

PROGRESS CHECK

Check your score! If your score is

> 95%	EXCELLENT !	- Move on to the next chapter. You have mastered this chapter. Concepts are certainly on your fingertips.
95-85%	VERY GOOD !	- Revise once more thoroughly. Recognise your mistakes and work on them. You will master this chapter.
84-75%	GOOD!	- Work on your weak areas, master them and come back to this chapter in a few days.
74-65%	MEDIOCRE!	- Understand your weak areas and work on strengthening your concepts. Devote more time to master this chapter.
< 65%	NOT SATISFACTORY!	- This is where you fall behind from scoring well. Give special attention to this chapter. Work on clearing concepts and common errors.

NCERT Exemplar Problems

This section contains MCQs of **'NCERT Exemplar Problems'** Book.

1. Which of the following parts of a plant take part in sexual reproduction?

(i) Flower (ii) Seed
(iii) Fruit (iv) Branch

Choose the correct answer from below.

(a) (i) and (ii) (b) (i), (ii) and (iii)
(c) (iii) and (iv) (d) (ii), (iii) and (iv)

2. Lila observed that a pond with clear water was covered up with green algae within a week. By which method of reproduction did the algae spread so rapidly?

(a) Budding
(b) Sexual reproduction
(c) Fragmentation
(d) Pollination

3. Seeds of drumstick and maple are carried to long distances by wind because they possess

(a) winged seeds
(b) large and hairy seeds
(c) long and ridged fruits
(d) spiny seeds.

4. The 'eye' of the potato plant is what

(a) the root is to any plant
(b) the bud is to a flower
(c) the bud is to *Bryophyllum* leaf
(d) the anther is to stamen.

5. The ovaries of different flowers may contain

(a) only one ovule
(b) many ovules
(c) one to many ovules
(d) only two ovules.

6. Which of the following statements is/are true for sexual reproduction in plants?

(i) Plants are obtained from seeds.
(ii) Two plants are always essential.
(iii) Fertilisation can occur only after pollination.
(iv) Only insects are agents of pollination.

Choose from the options given below.

(a) (i) and (iii) (b) (i) only
(c) (ii) and (iii) (d) (i) and (iv)

7. Pollination refers to the

(a) transfer of pollen from anther to ovary
(b) transfer of male gametes from anther to stigma
(c) transfer of pollen from anther to stigma
(d) transfer of pollen from anther to ovule.

A&R Corner

Directions : In the following questions, a statement of assertion is followed by a statement of reason. Mark the correct choice as :
(a) If both assertion and reason are true and reason is the correct explanation of assertion.
(b) If both assertion and reason are true but reason is not the correct explanation of assertion.
(c) If assertion is true but reason is false.
(d) If both assertion and reason are false.

1. **Assertion :** Asexual reproduction is the most common method of reproduction in plants.
Reason : Asexual reproduction involves two parents. R

2. **Assertion :** Insect pollinated flowers have nectaries to produce plenty of nectar.
Reason : Insect visit flowers for nectar.

3. **Assertion :** In *Vallisneria* pollination takes place by the agency of air.
Reason : Male flowers in *Vallisneria* lacks inflorescence.

4. **Assertion :** Vegetative propagation produces large number of plants in a shorter time.
Reason : The crops that do not produce viable seed can be grown vegetatively.

5. **Assertion :** *Oxalis* possess tuberous roots.
Reason : Tuberous roots become swollen to facilitate movement.

6. **Assertion :** *Spirogyra* reproduces by the process of fragmentation.
Reason : *Spirogyra* breaks their body into two or more fragments. R

7. **Assertion :** Bulbs are very short underground stems that have one or more buds.
Reason : Bulbs are surrounded by fleshy scale leaves.

8. **Assertion :** Stamen is the female reproductive organ of flower.
Reason : Stamen consists of stigma and style.

9. **Assertion :** Roots develop from the lower surface of the underground stems.
Reason : Rhizomes are the main underground stem that bear buds. Ap

10. **Assertion :** Callus is an unorganised mass of rapidly dividing cells of a tissue.
Reason : Callus can produce new plants *via* tissue culture.

11. **Assertion :** Stock and scion join together to from one plant.
Reason : Scion supplies the essential nutrients to the stock.

12. **Assertion :** Fertilisation is the fusion of male gamete with female gamete.
Reason : Fertilisation leads to formation of zygote. U

13. **Assertion :** Spore formation is the common method of reproduction in fungi.
Reason : Under favourable conditions of moisture and temperature spores germinate to form new individuals.

14. **Assertion :** Maize and papaya are unisexual flowers.
Reason : Flowers which contain both stamens as well as pistils are unisexual flowers.

15. **Assertion :** Roots, stem and leaves are vegetative organs.
Reason : Vegetative organs take part in formation of new plants. U

Exam Corner

This section comprises of different types of questions:
- **Objective Type Questions :** These are **one mark** questions.
- **Very Short Answer Type Questions (VSA) :** These are **one mark** questions.
- **Short Answer Type Questions-I (SA-I) :** These are **two marks** questions.
- **Short Answer Type Questions-II (SA-II) :** These are **three marks** questions.
- **Long Answer Type Questions (LA) :** These are **five marks** questions.
- **Case Based Questions (CBQs) :** These are case study/passage based questions.

OBJECTIVE TYPE QUESTIONS

A. Select the correct option.

1. The individuals produced by __(i)__ reproduction are exact copies of their parent whereas __(ii)__ reproduction helps in producing variations.
Which of the following options correctly completes the given statement?
(a) (i) asexual, (ii) sexual
(b) (i) asexual, (ii) vegetative
(c) (i) sexual, (ii) asexual
(d) (i) sexual, (ii) vegetative

2. Some pupil wanted to find out if overcrowding affected the growth of plants. They set-up two experiments as shown below in the garden.

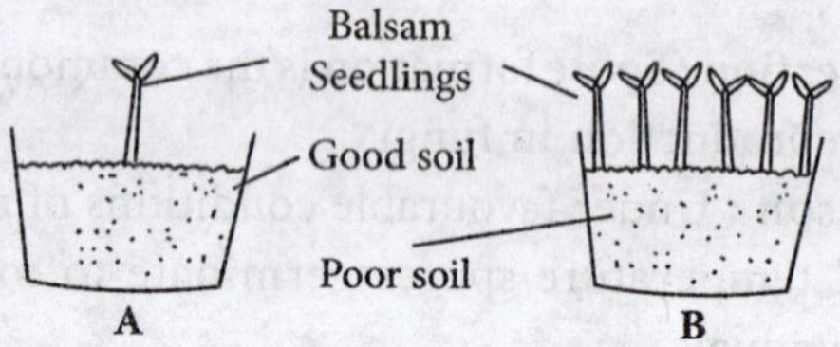

They did not conduct a fair test because
(a) the number of plants in both the pots should be the same
(b) the type of soil used in both the pots should be the same
(c) the size of the pots used should be different
(d) the place where the pots were placed should be different. **Ap**

3. Pollination by insects take place in flowers which
(a) are brightly coloured.
(b) have sweet fragrance.
(c) lack pollen grains.
(d) both (a) and (b)

4. The cut stem with roots used for grafting is called
(a) scion (b) stock
(c) corm (d) bulb.

5. The given figure illustrates a stage during sexual reproduction in flowering plants.
What is structure X?

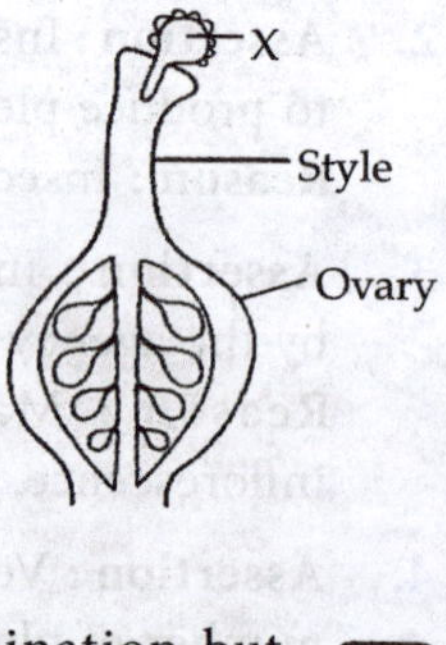

(a) An ovule before pollination, but after fertilisation.
(b) An ovule before fertilisation, but after pollination.
(c) A pollen grain before pollination, but after fertilisation.
(d) A pollen grain after pollination but before fertilisation. **U**

6. Which of the following is the correct sequence of events in the sexual reproduction of a plant from the flowers?
(a) Pollination, seed, fertilisation, germination
(b) Pollination, fertilisation, seed, germination
(c) Pollination, seed, germination, fertilisation
(d) Pollination, fertilisation, germination, seed

7. Artificial propagation of plants from a small plant tissue kept in nutrient medium is called
(a) grafting (b) cutting
(c) tissue culture (d) budding.

8. An example of bisexual flower is
(a) rose (b) corn
(c) papaya (d) cucumber. **R**

9. The method shown in the given figure belongs to

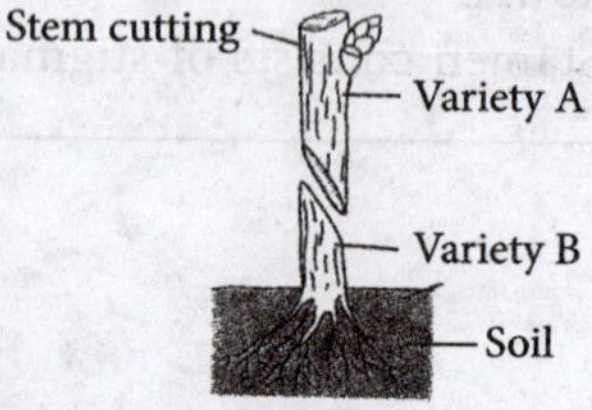

(a) sexual reproduction.
(b) asexual reproduction.
(c) vegetative propagation.
(d) both (b) and (c) **Ev**

10. Which of the following is not an artificial method of vegetative propagation?
(a) Layering (b) Budding
(c) Grafting (d) Tissue culture

11. New varieties of plants can be developed by
(i) cross pollination (ii) grafting
(iii) self-pollination.
(a) Only (i) (b) (i) and (ii)
(c) (ii) and (iii) (d) Only (iii)

12. Which of the following events in the reproduction in flowering plants can be carried out by a butterfly?
(a) Germination (b) Fertilisation
(c) Pollination (d) Seed formation

U

13. Match Column - I with Column - II and select the correct option.

	Column - I	Column - II
A.	Wind pollination	(i) Sunflower
B.	Water pollination	(ii) Grasses
C.	Insect pollination	(iii) *Vallisneria*

(a) A - (ii), B - (iii), C - (i)
(b) A - (iii), B - (ii), C - (i)
(c) A - (i), B - (iii), C - (ii)
(d) A - (ii), B - (i), C - (iii)

R

14. Select the correct sequence of words to fill in the blanks.
(i) Inside the seed, the embryo remains in a __________ stage.
(ii) Ovules grow into __________ after fertilisation.
(iii) Pollen tube grows till it reaches the __________.
(iv) __________ technique helps to develop new varieties of plants.

	(i)	(ii)	(iii)	(iv)
(a)	Resting	Seeds	Ovules	Grafting
(b)	Resting	Fruits	Ovary	Budding
(c)	Active	Fruits	Ovules	Self-pollination
(d)	Resting	Seeds	Ovary	Cross-pollination

15. Select the correct statement(s).
(i) Cross-pollination aids in the process of sexual reproduction in bisexual flowers.
(ii) Tissue culture method is also called as micro-propagation.
(iii) Spores are asexual reproductive cells found in ferns and moss.
(iv) *Bryophyllum* and yeast reproduces by vegetative buds.
(v) Seed coat protects the embryo from external harsh conditions.
(a) Only (iii) (b) (i) and (v)
(c) (ii), (iii) and (v) (d) (i), (iii) and (v)

An

16. Select the correct events that occur during sexual reproduction in flowering plants.
(a) Pollination → Pollen tube → Fertilisation → Zygote → Fruit
(b) Pollen tube → Pollination → Fertilisation → Zygote → Seeds
(c) Pollination → Fertilisation → Zygote → Embryo → Seeds
(d) Pollen tube → Fertilisation → Zygote → Pollination → Fruits

B Fill in the blanks.

17. The method of reproduction that involves only one parent is called __________.
18. Formation of seeds occurs in __________ reproduction in plants.
19. In grafting, the __________ is placed over the __________.
20. __________ is a more rapid, easier and cheaper method of plant propagation.
21. Growth in plants occur only at those places where __________ are present.
22. __________ is a sweet liquid produced by flowers that attract insects.
23. Date palm is a __________ flower.

C. State True (T) or False (F) for the given statements.

24. Pollination in *Zostera* is carried out by water. ☐
25. Brightly coloured flowers that produce nectar are mainly pollinated by wind. ☐
26. Bisexual flowers have both pistil and stamen. ☐

U

27. Mango and apple are fleshy and juicy fruits. ☐

R

28. Sexually produced offsprings have a mixture of parental genes. ☐
29. Embryo remains in the resting stage inside the seed until germination. ☐
30. Embryo inside the seed can grow only in the presence of moisture, oxygen and warmth. ☐

U

31. Ovules grow into seeds and ovary grows into the fleshy seed coat in plants like mango. ☐

32. Stigma produces the pollen tube that connects pollen in anther with the ovules present inside the ovary. ☐

33. Layering is an artificial method of vegetative propagation where a twig of one plant is placed over the cut stem of another plant and tied together. ☐

34. Plants like moss and ferns reproduce by means of spore formation. ☐

35. Pollen grains that are light weight and can be carried away easily by wind. ☐

36. Stamens are the female reproductive parts and pistil are the male reproductive parts of a flower respectively. ☐

37. Pollens are present in the anther of flowers. ☐

38. An ovule contains the female gamete or egg. ☐

39. Yeast is a multicellular organism that reproduces by budding. ☐

40. Vegetative buds can give rise to new plants. ☐

41. In asexual reproduction, new plants are obtained from seeds and spores. ☐

42. In plants like *Dahlia*, each detached body part can give rise to new plants. ☐

43. Leaf margins of some plants like rose and *Petunia* have buds that can grow into new plants. ☐

D. Match the columns.

44.

Columns I	Column II
(i) Bud of a plant cut for grafting	(p) Orchids
(ii) Helps to develop new varieties of plants	(q) Stock
(iii) Artificially propagated by tissue culture	(r) Grafting
(iv) Cut stem with roots for grafting	(s) Seed
(v) Contains stored food used for the growth of embryo	(t) Scion

(a) (i) – (t), (ii) – (r), (iii) – (p), (iv) – (q), (v) – (s)
(b) (i) – (t), (ii) – (r), (iii) – (p), (iv) – (s), (v) – (q)
(c) (i) – (s), (ii) – (r), (iii) – (t), (iv) – (p), (v) – (q)
(d) (i) – (s), (ii) – (q), (iii) – (r), (iv) – (t), (v) – (p)

An

VERY SHORT ANSWER TYPE QUESTIONS (VSA)

A. Write two examples for each of the following.

45. Forms of asexual reproduction in plants ________, ________.

46. Plants that reproduce through spore formation ________, ________.

47. Plants whose seeds are dispersed by animals ________, ________.

48. Examples of bisexual flowers ________, ________.

49. Vegetables which have buds in the form of eyes________, ________.

B. Find the odd one out. Give reason for your choice.

50. Ginger, Turmeric, *Bryophyllum*, Potato

51. Mango, Apple, Walnut, Orange

52. Buds, Stems, Leaves, Flowers

53. Mustard, Rose, Corn, *Hibiscus*

54. Moss, Fern, *Spirogyra*, Fungus

SHORT ANSWER TYPE QUESTIONS-I (SA-I)

55. Define the terms:
(a) Fertilisation (b) Pollination
(c) Germination R

56. What do you mean by tissue culture?

57. Differentiate between self-pollination and cross-pollination.

58. Write differences between asexual reproduction and sexual reproduction. U

59. Why are flowers so colourful?

60. What is the difference between cutting and grafting?

SHORT ANSWER TYPE QUESTIONS-II (SA-II)

61. Explain the process of fertilisation in plants.

62. How is the process of spore formation differs from budding? U

63. What is germination of seed? What happens to the seed during germination?

64. How is the pollen tube formed in flowering plants?

65. How are potato plants reproduced asexually?

LONG ANSWER TYPE QUESTIONS (LA)

66. Write down the importance of seed dispersal. How the seeds are dispersed?

67. What is artificial propagation? Briefly explain the different types of artificial propagation with example.

68. How is the technique of grafting done? Draw a simple diagram. Write its advantages.

69. What is pollination? How does it lead to fertilisation? Explain the process of fertilisation with the help of a diagram.

70. With the help of a diagram, describe the structure of a flower.

71. Give reason for the following
(i) Insect pollinated flowers are colourful and scented.
(ii) Pollen grains have tough protective coat.
(iii) Same kind of plants grow in different places.
(iv) Seeds of drumstick are dispersed by wind.

CASE BASED QUESTIONS (CBQs)

Case I : Read the given passage and answer the following questions :

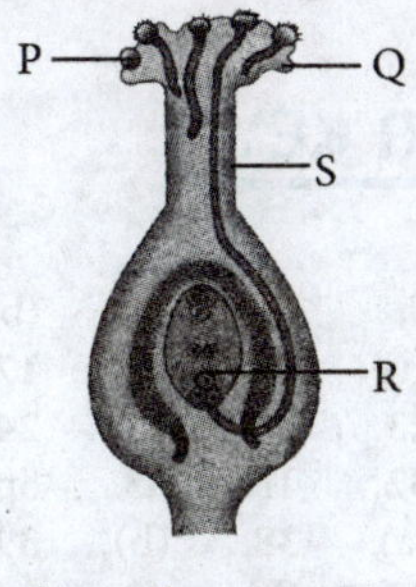

In plants, sexual reproduction takes place in flowers. A typical flower has a broad base over which are borne four whorls. The given figure shows the fourth or innermost floral whorl in which female gamete or egg cell is formed.

72. Identify the labelled parts and select the correct statement.
(a) Q is a site of pollen germination.
(b) Q, R and S form the male reproductive part of flower.
(c) On maturation R develops into fruit.
(d) S possess a tough protective coat which prevents them from drying up.

73. Match column I with column II and select the correct option.

	Column I	Column II
1.	P	(i) Connects stigma to the ovary
2.	Q	(ii) Landing platform for pollen grains
3.	R	(iii) Formed inside the anther
4.	S	(iv) Site where female gamete is formed

	P	Q	R	S
(a)	(i)	(ii)	(iv)	(iii)
(b)	(ii)	(iii)	(iv)	(i)
(c)	(iii)	(ii)	(iv)	(i)
(d)	(iii)	(iv)	(ii)	(i)

An

74. The process of fusion of gametes formed by P and R is called
(a) pollination
(b) germination
(c) fertilisation
(d) fragmentation.

75. In which plant P and R are parts formed in same plant?
(a) *Petunia*
(b) Castor
(c) Maize
(d) Papaya

76. Which of the following is not a characteristic of flower in which P is transferred by agency of water?
(a) Small and inconspicuous flower
(b) Absence of nectar and odour
(c) Feathery and long stigma
(d) Unwettable pollen grains R

Case II : Read the given passage and answer the following questions :

Vegetative reproduction is a type of asexual reproduction in which new plants are produced from vegetative parts of the plant such as roots, underground stems, leaves, bud etc. Some of the plants which can be propagate vegetatively are given below.

W X Y Z

77. Which of the following propagates through roots?
(a) W (b) X
(c) Y (d) Z

78. What does the figure Y represents?
(a) Potato tuber
(b) Rhizome of ginger
(c) Offset in water hyacinth
(d) Tuberous roots of *Dahlia*

79. Which of the following plants propagates similarly as Y?
(a) Potato (b) Dahlia
(c) *Chrysanthemum* (d) Turmeric

80. Give two examples of plants in which vegetative propagation occurs through W. R

81. Mention the vegetative propagule of Z.

Case III : Read the given passage and answer the following questions :

Cross pollination is the transfer of pollen grains from anther of a flower of one plant to the stigma of flower of another plant of same kind. It commonly occurs with the help of wind, water and insects. Given below are the plants pollinated by different agencies.

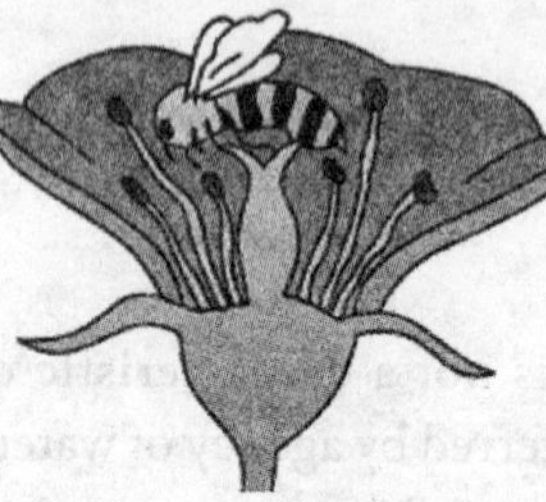

A

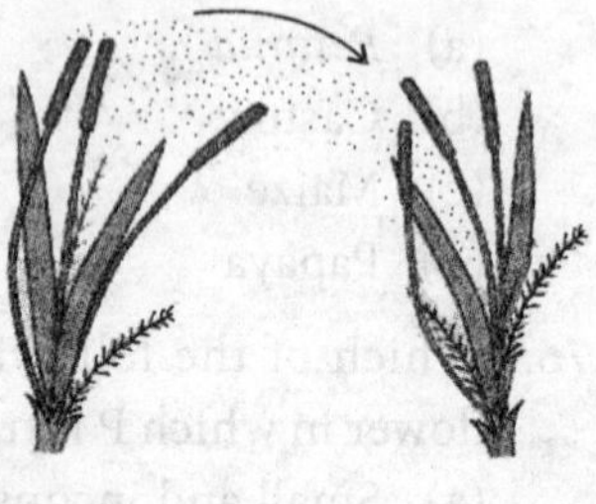

B

C

82. Give one example of plant pollinated with the help of agents A, B and C. U
83. Write down the features of plants pollinated with agency A. R
84. How does pollination occurs with the help of agency C?
85. How does the small petal size in plants pollinated with B help them in pollination?

ANSWER KEY

Practice Corner

1. (a) 2. (a) 3. (b) 4. (c) 5. (b) 6. (c) 7. (b) 8. (a) 9. (d) 10. (b)
11. (b) 12. (b) 13. (b) 14. (a) 15. vegetative 16. node 17. budding 18. seeds
19. flower, leaf 20. algae 21. reproduction 22. Yeast 23. Flowers 24. True 25. False 26. False
27. True 28. False 29. True 30. True 31. False 32. True 33. Sprouting from an 'eye' 34. *Hydra*
35. Spore formation 36. Asexual reproduction 37. (a) 38. (b) 39. (b) 40. (c) 41. (b)
42. (d) 43. (c) 44. (a) 45. (b) 46. (d) 47. (b) 48. (a) 49. (b) 50. (b) 51. (c)
52. (b) 53. (d) 54. zygote 55. egg 56. Pollen grains 57. pollination 58. embryo
59. bisexual 60. coat 61. unisexual 62. False 63. True 64. False 65. True 66. False 67. False
70. (d) 71. (c) 72. (b) 73. (c) 74. (c) 75. fruit 76. mango, orange 77. ovules
78. True 79. False 80. False 81. False 82. (b) 83. (d) 84. (d) 85. (a) 86. (c) 87. (d)
88. (a) 89. (d) 90. animals 91. hairy 92. explosion or sudden jerk 93. winged 94. hooks
95. True 96. False 97. True 98. False 99. True

NCERT Exemplar Problems

1. (b) 2. (c) 3. (a) 4. (c) 5. (c) 6. (a) 7. (c)

A & R Corner

1. (d) 2. (b) 3. (d) 4. (b) 5. (d) 6. (b) 7. (b) 8. (d) 9. (b) 10. (b)
11. (c) 12. (a) 13. (b) 14. (c) 15. (c)

Exam Corner

1. (a) 2. (b) 3. (d) 4. (b) 5. (d) 6. (b) 7. (c) 8. (a) 9. (d) 10. (b)
11. (b) 12. (c) 13. (a) 14. (d) 15. (c) 16. (a) 17. asexual reproduction 18. sexual
19. scion, stock 20. Vegetative propagation 21. buds 22. Nectar 23. unisexual 24. True 25. False
26. True 27. True 28. True 29. True 30. True 31. False 32. False 33. False 34. True 35. True
36. False 37. True 38. True 39. False 40. True 41. False 42. False 43. False 44. (a)
45. Vegetative propagation, Fragmentation 46. Moss, Ferns 47. *Xanthium, Urena* 48. Mustard, Rose
49. Potato, Ginger 50. *Bryophyllum* 51. Walnut 52. Flowers 53. Corn 54. *Spirogyra*
72. (a) 73. (c) 74. (c) 75. (a) 76. (c) 77. (b) 78. (b) 79. (d)
80. *Bryophyllum, Begonia*

9 Motion and Time

NCERT Notes

9.1 Slow or Fast

- **Motion** is defined as the change of position of an object with respect to time. Motion and rest are **relative** terms.
- An object is said to be at **rest** if the distance between the object and some reference point is not changing.
- **Types of motion :**
  - **Translatory motion :** If an object moves as a whole from one place to another, so that all its body parts move the same distance in a given time, it is said to be in a translatory motion. It is of two types :
  - **Rectilinear motion :** If an object moves in a straight line, it is said to be in a rectilinear motion.
  - **Curvilinear motion :** If an object moves along a curved path, its motion is called curvilinear motion.
- **Circular motion :** Motion of a body in a circular path around a fixed point is known as circular motion. Circular motion is of two types :
  - **Revolutionary motion :** When an object as a whole moves around a fixed centre, its motion is called revolutionary motion.
  - **Rotatory motion :** When an object moves in a circular path about its own axis, its motion is called rotatory motion.
- **Oscillatory motion :** When an object moves to and fro about a fixed point, it is said to be in an oscillatory motion.
- **Periodic motion :** The motion which repeats itself after a fixed interval of time is called a periodic motion.

9.2 Speed

- **Speed** is defined as the distance travelled by an object in a unit time.
  - Speed of objects helps us to determine which one is moving faster than the other.
  - The basic unit of speed is **metre per second (m/s)**.
  - $\text{Speed} = \dfrac{\text{distance}}{\text{time}} = \dfrac{1\text{ km}}{\text{h}}$

$$= \frac{1000\text{ m}}{3600\text{ s}} = \frac{5}{18}\text{ m/s} = \frac{250}{9}\text{ cm/s}$$

- Average speed is defined as the ratio of distance covered to the total time taken.

$$\text{Average speed} = \frac{\text{total distance covered}}{\text{total time taken}}$$

- The change in the position of a moving body in a particular direction is called its **displacement**.
  - If a body moves between two points along different paths, its displacement remains same for all the paths, though the distance covered by it may be different for the different paths.
  - If a body starts moving from a point and returns to the same point, its displacement will be **zero**.
- **Velocity** is defined as displacement per unit time. The SI unit of velocity is m/s.
  - Speed of a moving body can never be zero but velocity of a moving object will be zero if it returns to its original position.
- If an object travels equal distances in equal intervals of time, then it is said to be in **uniform motion**.
- If an object travels unequal distances in equal intervals of time, then it is said to be in **non-uniform motion**.

+ Speed requires magnitude only to define itself whereas, velocity requires both magnitude and direction to define itself.

9.3 Measurement of Time

- **Time** refers to the interval between two events taking place.
  - The SI unit of time is **second**.
  - Units of time in decreasing order:

1 millennium	10 centuries
1 century	10 decades
1 decade	10 years
1 year	365 days
1 day	24 hours
1 hour	60 minutes
1 minute	60 seconds

  - Old devices that were used for measuring time are:

1. 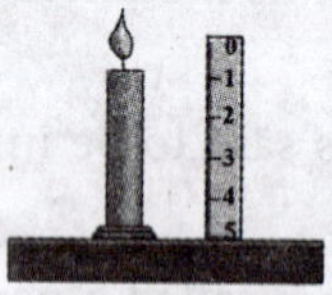

Candle clock

A candle clock is a thin candle with consistently, spaced markings, that when burned, indicates the passage of periods of time.

2. 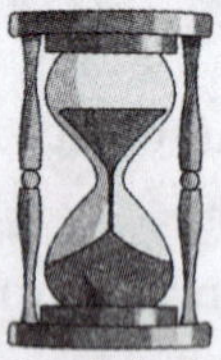

Sand clock

Sand clock is also known as the hour glass. A sand clock works on the principle that all the sand from the upper chamber fall into the lower chamber in a fixed interval of time.

3. 

Sundial

The sundial is based on the principle of shadow formation due to sunlight, the shadow of pointer varies with the position of the Sun in the sky and tells the hours of the day.

4. 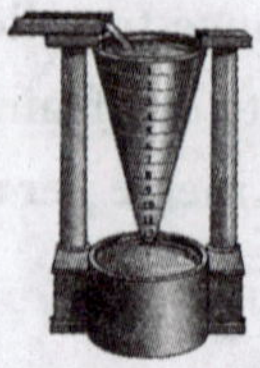

Water clock

A water clock is a time keeping device that works on the principle of inward or outward regulated flow of water.

- Though earlier clocks were not very accurate, modern watches were discovered, *e.g.*, mechanical, digital, quartz and stop watch.

- A **simple pendulum** consists of a small metal ball (or a small **mass**), known as **bob**, suspended by a light, flexible and inextensible string.
  - The bob of a pendulum executes **oscillatory motion.**
  - The **frequency** of a pendulum is the number of oscillations completed by it in one second.
  - The time taken by the bob to complete one oscillation is called the **time period** of the pendulum.

The time period of a simple pendulum depends upon its **length** and acceleration due to gravity.

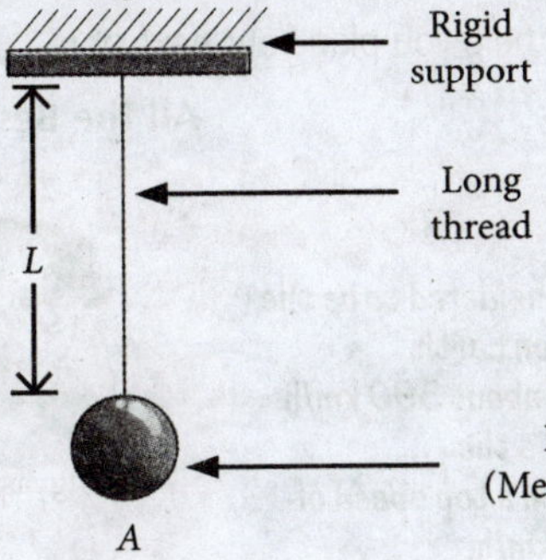

Simple pendulum

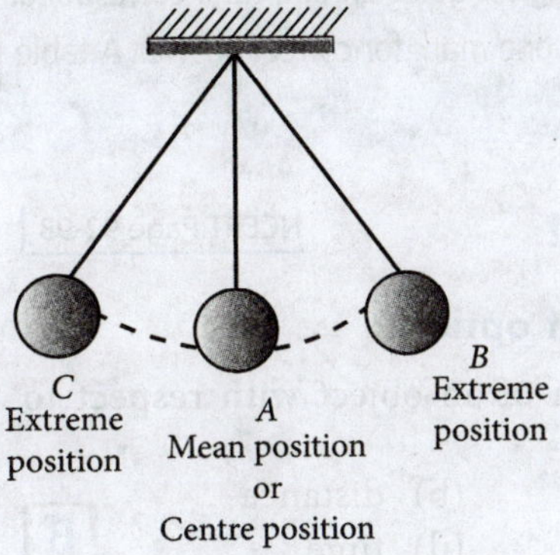

Motion of a simple pendulum

9.4 Measuring Speed

- A **speedometer** shows the speed of a vehicle with which it is moving and an **odometer** measures the distance travelled by it.

> + There are devices like speedometer for measuring speed and odometer for measuring distance travelled which reduces human effort.

9.5 Distance - Time Graph

- A **graph** is a diagrammatic representation of two interrelated quantities. It has two axes.
- The **distance-time graph** of a body moving in a **uniform motion** is represented by a straight line.
- The **distance-time graph** of a body moving in a **non-uniform motion** is represented by a curved line.
- The **distance-time graph** of a **stationary body** is represented by a straight line, parallel to the time-axis.

Practice Corner

Extracted from NCERT

Assessment is complementary part of the learning process. It gives you a total insight whether the learning outcomes have been achieved or not. After going through the corresponding NCERT Textbook chapter, attempt these questions in exam like environment. Give yourself one mark for correct answer. A table is given at the end, that will help you plan your next step.

All the Best!

9.1 Slow or Fast

NCERT Page 92-93

A. Select the correct option.

1. Change in position of an object with respect to time is known as
   (a) speed (b) distance
   (c) motion (d) time. R

2. When a body spins, the body is in
   (a) revolutionary motion
   (b) rectilinear motion
   (c) rotatory motion
   (d) periodic motion.

3. Motion of a bus on a straight path is an example of
   (a) periodic motion (b) translatory motion
   (c) rotatory motion (d) oscillatory motion. U

B. State True (T) or False (F) for the given statements.

4. Motion of Mars around the Sun is an example of periodic motion. ☐ R

5. A car moving at a constant speed shows periodic motion. ☐

6. The vehicle having higher speed than the other is said to be faster. ☐

C. Figure based questions.

Identify the slower and the faster moving vehicle in each pair.

7. 

8. 

9. 

10. 

11. 

The peregrine falcon is considered to be the fastest animal on Earth. It can achieve a speed of about 390 km/h. The cheetah is the fastest land animal with a top speed of about 120 km/h.

Jigyasa

9.2 Speed

NCERT Page 93-94

A. Select the correct option.

12. Which of the following is true?
   (i) Speed = $\frac{\text{Distance}}{\text{Time}}$
   (ii) Distance = $\frac{\text{Speed}}{\text{Time}}$
   (iii) Time = $\frac{\text{Distance}}{\text{Speed}}$
   (iv) Time × Speed = Distance
   (a) (i), (ii), (iii) and (iv)
   (b) (i), (iii), and (iv)
   (c) (ii) and (iii)
   (d) (iii) and (iv) An

13. When a body covers equal distance in equal interval of time, then it is said to be in
   (a) average speed
   (b) speed
   (c) uniform motion
   (d) non-uniform motion.

14. Which of the following is not the unit of speed?
   (a) Miles per hour
   (b) Metre per second
   (c) Pounds per square inch
   (d) Kilometre per hour

15. The speed of a moving object means
   (a) how far it goes in a certain time
   (b) how long it goes on moving
   (c) how far it goes
   (d) none of these U

16. A car covers 45 km in the first hour, 60 km in the second hour and 75 km in the third hour. The car is in
(a) uniform motion
(b) non-uniform motion
(c) cannot be explained
(d) none of these
Ap

17. The speed of a body
(a) remains constant irrespective of the distance
(b) becomes zero with the increase in distance
(c) decreases with the increase in the ratio of distance to time
(d) increases with the increase in the ratio of distance to time.

B. State True (T) or False (F) for the given statements.

18. Speed is the total distance covered divided by the total time.

19. A higher speed indicates that a given distance is covered in a shorter time.

20. If the speed of an object moving along a straight line keeps changing, its motion is said to be uniform.

21. Speed of a moving body can never be zero.

9.3 Measurement of Time

NCERT Page 94-97

A. Select the correct option.

22. Which of the following is different among these?
(a) Quartz clock (b) Water clock
(c) Sundial (d) Sand clock
U

23. Identify the correct one.
(a) 50 kms (b) 50 km
(c) 50 km. (d) 50 Km

24. The gap between two consecutive noons is
(a) an hour (b) a second
(c) a night (d) a solar day.

25. On Monday, Barnali spent 20 minutes on her science homework, 38 minutes on english homework and 25 minutes on mathematics homework. How much time did she spend on her homework?
(i) 83 minutes
(ii) 1 hour 23 minutes
iii) 4980 seconds
(iv) 4990 seconds
Ev
(a) (i), (ii) and (iii) (b) (i), (ii) and (iv)
(c) (i) and (ii) (d) none of these

26. What part of a second is called a nanosecond?
(a) One billionth (b) One hundredth
(c) One thousandth (d) One millionth

27. How many minutes are there in 6.5 hours?
(a) 390 (b) 590 (c) 490 (d) 290

28. If a simple pendulum completes 20 oscillations in 40 seconds, then the time taken by one complete oscillation is
(a) 0.2 second (b) 0.5 second
(c) 2 seconds (d) 1 second.
Ev

29. Which of the following statements is true about the time period of a pendulum?
(i) The amount of displacement has no effect on the time period.
(ii) As the length increases, time period of the simple pendulum also increases.
(iii) The mass of the bob has no effect on the time period.
(a) (i), (ii) and (iii) (b) (i) and (ii)
(c) (ii) and (iii) (d) (i) and (iii)

B. Fill in the blanks.

30. A simple pendulum works on the principle of __________.

31. Simple pendulum consists of a small metallic ball called __________ of the pendulum.

32. The to and fro motion of a simple pendulum is an example of a periodic or an __________ motion.

33. The time taken by the pendulum to complete one oscillation is called its __________.

C. State True (T) or False (F) for the given statements.

34. The resting position of the bob of a pendulum is known as mean position.

35. International standard time follows the Greenwich Mean Time.

36. A sundial works by casting a shadow in different positions at different times of a day.

37. Time period of a simple pendulum depends upon the mass of the bob.

38. The duration from one sunset to sunrise is night.

39. A water clock can be used to determine the time interval that has passed.

D. Figure based questions.

40. Observe the given figures. Which one of these pendulums has larger average time period? Give reason for your answer.

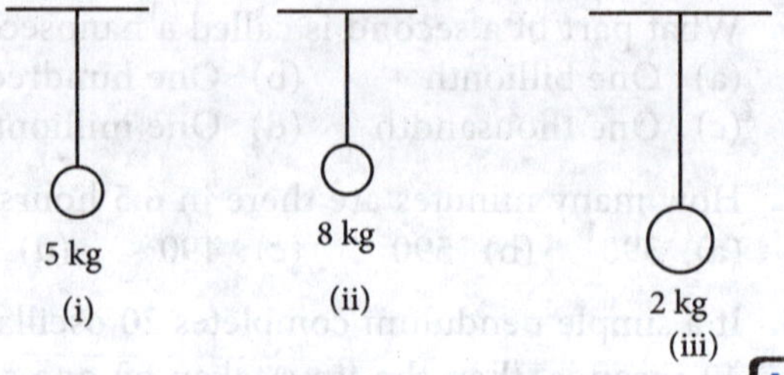

9.4 Measuring Speed

NCERT Page 97-100

A. Select the correct option.

41. A car is moving with an average speed of 50 km/h. The time taken by the car to complete its journey of 300 km is
(a) 6 h (b) 10 h (c) 5 h (d) 15 h

42. A speedometer measures the speed in
(a) km/h (b) m/h (c) m/s (d) cm/s

43. Which of the following is not matched correctly?
(a) Anemometer : Wind speed
(b) Speedometer : Speed
(c) Odometer : Odour
(d) Stopwatch : Time

44. A train leaves a station *X* at 5:00 pm and reaches to another station *Y* at midnight. Its speed is 90 km/h? What is the distance between *X* and *Y*?
(a) 480 km (b) 630 km
(c) 800 km (d) 830 km

45. A car with non-uniform motion travels 200 km in 5 hours. What can be said about the speed of the car?
(a) Its speed is 40 km/h for most of the journey.
(b) Its average speed is 40 km/h during the journey.
(c) Its speed is constant at 40 km/h during the journey.
(d) Its speed is 40 km/h at the beginning and at the end of the journey and varies in between.

46. The speed of a bus is 90 km/h whereas the speed of a car is 15 m/s. Which one of these is moving faster?
(a) Bus
(b) Car
(c) Both with same speed
(d) Data insufficient

47. Train *A* travels with a speed of 90 km/h from Hyderabad to Bangalore. Train *B* travels with a speed of 90 km/h from Bangalore to Hyderabad.
Which of the following statements is true?
(a) Both trains are travelling with the same speed and same velocity.
(b) Both trains have the same velocity.
(c) Trains *A* and *B* have the same speed but different velocities.
(d) Trains *A* and *B* have the same velocity but different speeds.

B. Fill in the blanks.

48. An instrument used to measure the speed of a vehicle is ______________.

49. An odometer measures the ______________ moved by a vehicle.

50. The basic unit of speed is ______________.

C. Figure based question.

51. Avinash is travelling by a car at an average speed of 30 km/h in the direction as shown in figure. What is the time taken by him to reach the starting point A by following the path?

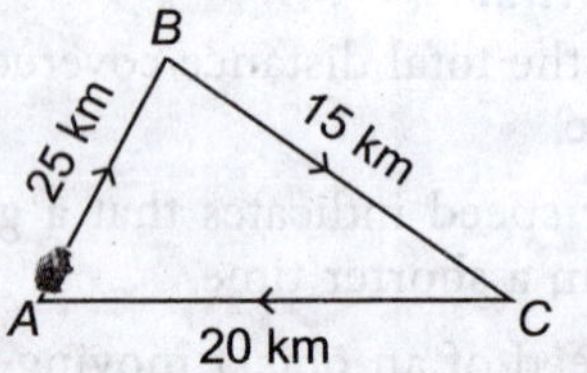

9.5 Distance - Time Graph

NCERT Page 100-104

A. Select the correct option.

52. When a body is moving with a constant speed, the distance-time graph will be a
(a) curved line (b) parabola
(c) straight line (d) none of these

53. The given graph shows that the object is

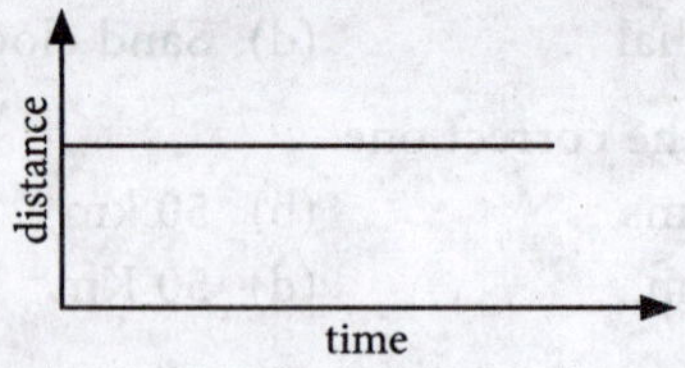

(a) in non-uniform motion
(b) in uniform motion
(c) at rest
(d) in an oscillatory motion.

54. On which axis the dependent variable is represented?
(a) Y - axis (b) X - axis
(c) Any axis (d) Depends on the data

55. The speed of an object can be determined from a ______________ graph.
(a) work-energy (b) force-distance
(c) distance-time (d) none of these

56. Look at the following graph carefully and find the velocity of the moving body.

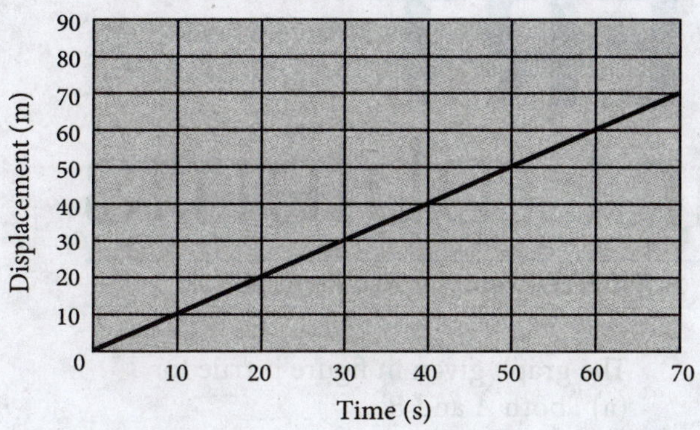

(a) 0 m/s (b) 1 m/s
(c) 2 m/s (d) 3 m/s

Ev

57. According to the following graph, what happens to the distance covered by the body from 0-10 minutes?

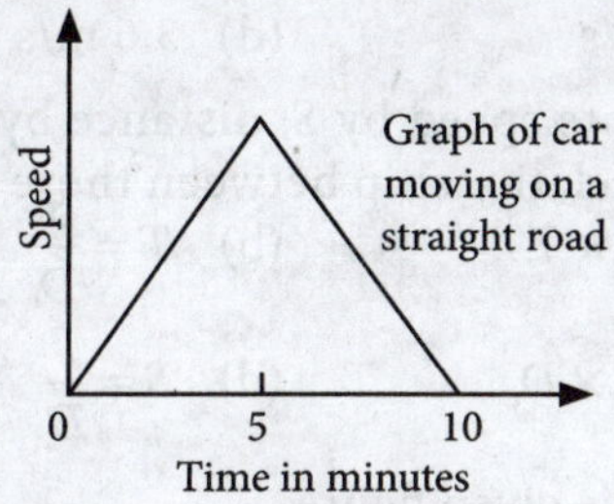

(a) It goes on increasing.
(b) It goes on decreasing.
(c) It first increases and then decreases.
(d) It first decreases and then increases.

Ap

B. State True (T) or False (F) for the given statements.

58. A non-uniform motion appears as a curved line on a distance-time graph. ☐

59. A part of distance-time graph parallel to the time axis means that the body is in rest. ☐

C. Figure based questions.

60. Interpret the distance-time graph (in terms of type of motion and average speed) that shows the journey of a scooter.

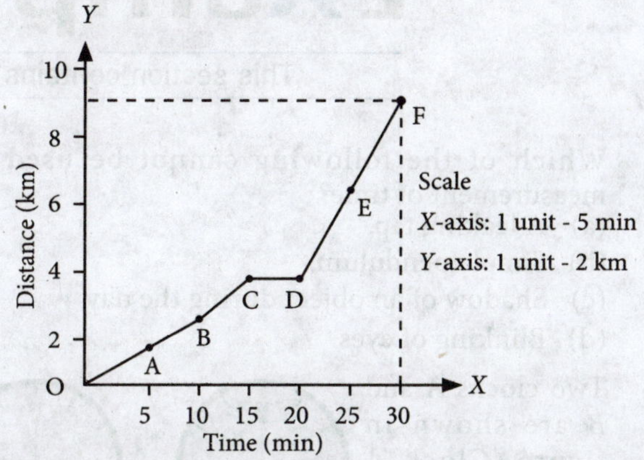

61. The given figure represents the distance-time graph for the motion of three moving bodies *X*, *Y* and *Z*. Which one of them is the fastest moving body? Give reason to support your answer.

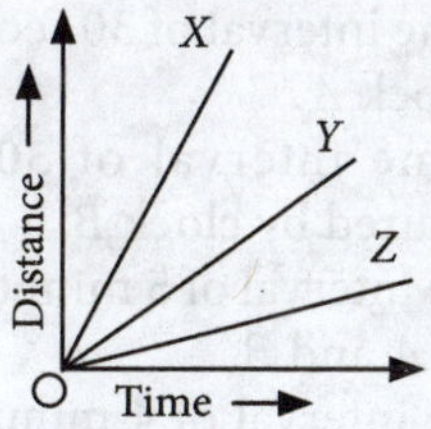

An

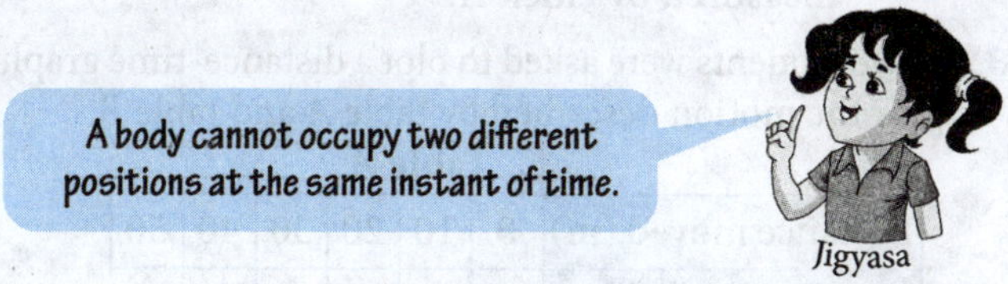

PROGRESS CHECK

Check your score! If your score is

> 95%	EXCELLENT !	- Move on to the next chapter. You have mastered this chapter. Concepts are certainly on your fingertips.
95-85%	VERY GOOD !	- Revise once more thoroughly. Recognise your mistakes and work on them. You will master this chapter.
84-75%	GOOD!	- Work on your weak areas, master them and come back to this chapter in a few days.
74-65%	MEDIOCRE!	- Understand your weak areas and work on strengthening your concepts. Devote more time to master this chapter.
< 65%	NOT SATISFACTORY!	- This is where you fall behind from scoring well. Give special attention to this chapter. Work on clearing concepts and common errors.

NCERT Exemplar Problems

This section contains MCQs of **'NCERT Exemplar Problems'** Book.

1. Which of the following cannot be used for measurement of time?
(a) A leaking tap.
(b) Simple pendulum.
(c) Shadow of an object during the day.
(d) Blinking of eyes.

2. Two clocks *A* and *B* are shown in figure. Clock *A* has an hour and a minute hand, whereas clock *B* has an hour hand, minute hand as well as a second hand. Which of the following statement is correct for these clocks?

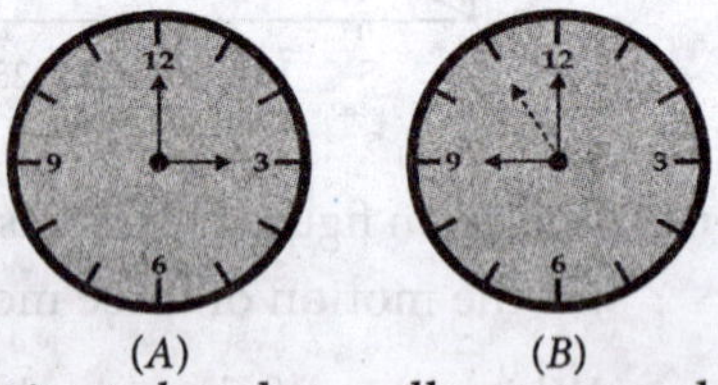

(A) (B)

(a) A time interval of 30 seconds can be measured by clock *A*.
(b) A time interval of 30 seconds cannot be measured by clock *B*.
(c) Time interval of 5 minutes can be measured by both *A* and *B*.
(d) Time interval of 4 minutes 10 seconds can be measured by clock *A*.

3. Two students were asked to plot a distance-time graph for the motion described by table *A* and table *B*.

Table A

Distance moved (m)	0	10	20	30	40	50
Time (minutes)	0	2	4	6	8	10

Table B

Distance moved (m)	0	5	10	15	20	25
Time (minutes)	0	1	2	3	4	5

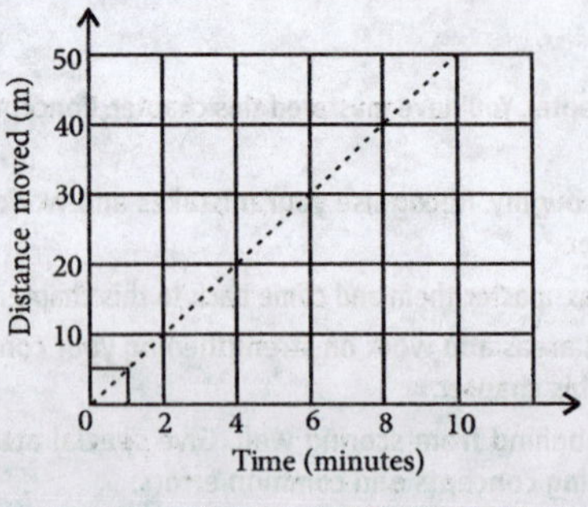

The graph given in figure is true for
(a) both *A* and *B*.
(b) *A* only.
(c) *B* only.
(d) neither *A* nor *B*.

4. A bus travels 54 km in 90 minutes. The speed of the bus is
(a) 0.6 m/s (b) 10 m/s
(c) 5.4 m/s (d) 3.6 m/s

5. If we denote speed by *S*, distance by *D* and time by *T*, the relationship between these quantities is
(a) $S = D \times T$ (b) $T = \frac{S}{D}$
(c) $S = \frac{1}{T} \times D$ (d) $S = \frac{T}{D}$

6. Observe the given figure.
The time period of a simple pendulum is the time taken by it to travel from

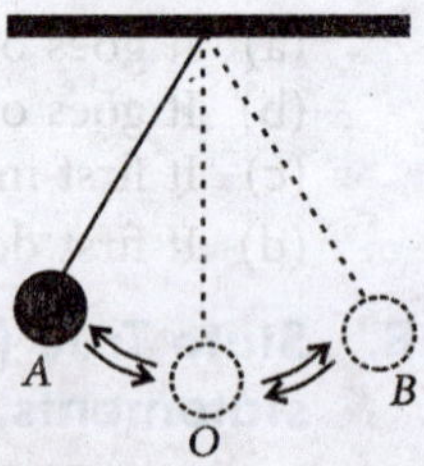

(a) *A* to *B* and back to *A*.
(b) *O* to *A*, *A* to *B* and *B* to *A*.
(c) *B* to *A*, *A* to *B* and *B* to *O*.
(d) *A* to *B*.

7. Figure shows an oscillating pendulum.
Time taken by the bob to move from *A* to *C* is t_1 and from *C* to *O* is t_2. The time period of this simple pendulum is

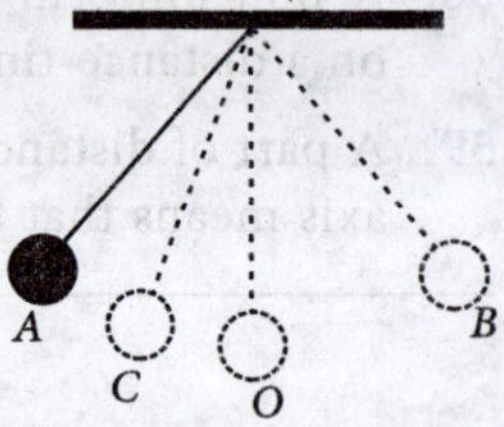

(a) $(t_1 + t_2)$ (b) $2(t_1 + t_2)$
(c) $3(t_1 + t_2)$ (d) $4(t_1 + t_2)$

8. The correct symbol to represent the speed of an object is
(a) 5 m/s (b) 5 mp
(c) 5 m/s^{-1} (d) 5 s/m

9. Boojho walks to his school which is at a distance of 3 km from his home in 30 minutes. On reaching he finds that the school is closed and comes back by a bicycle with his friend and reaches home in 20 minutes. His average speed in km/h is
(a) 8.3 (b) 7.2
(c) 5 (d) 3.6

A&R Corner

Directions : In the following questions, a statement of assertion is followed by a statement of reason. Mark the correct choice as :
(a) If both assertion and reason are true and reason is the correct explanation of assertion.
(b) If both assertion and reason are true but reason is not the correct explanation of assertion.
(c) If assertion is true but reason is false.
(d) If both assertion and reason are false.

1. **Assertion :** 1 decade is equal to 10 years.

   Reason : Every century is divided into 10 decades. R

2. **Assertion :** The time time taken by a pendulum to complete one oscillation is called its time period.

   Reason : If there is a slight change in displacement, the time period remains same.

3. **Assertion :** In uniform motion, a body covers equal distances in equal interval of time.

   Reason : Displacement is directly proportional to velocity.

4. **Assertion :** The motion of the earth around the sun is periodic but not oscillatory.

   Reason : Oscillatory motion is necessarily periodic but periodic motion is not necessarily oscillatory. U

5. **Assertion :** Speedometer records the speed of the vehicle generally in km/h.

   Reason : Odometer measures the distance moved by the vehicle in one hour.

6. **Assertion :** The distance moved by an object in unit time is called its speed.

   Reason : Faster vehicles have higher speeds. Ap

7. **Assertion :** An object is at rest when the position of object does not change with respect to time.

   Reason : The displacement time graph for an object at rest is a straight line parallel to time axis.

8. **Assertion :** Less is the steepness of graph between distance and time, lesser be the speed of object.

   Reason : The slope of the distance time graph gives the speed of object.

9. **Assertion :** The time taken by the pendulum to complete one oscillation is called time period of pendulum.

   Reason : The time period of the pendulum depends on the mass of the bob. R

10. **Assertion :** The speed of scooter read by the speedometer is 18 km/h.

    Reason : To convert the speed from km/h to m/s multiply by 5/18.

Exam Corner

This section comprises of different types of questions:

- **Objective Type Questions :** These are **one mark** questions.
- **Very Short Answer Type Questions (VSA) :** These are **one mark** questions.
- **Short Answer Type Questions-I (SA-I) :** These are **two marks** questions.
- **Short Answer Type Questions-II (SA-II) :** These are **three marks** questions.
- **Long Answer Type Questions (LA) :** These are **five marks** questions.
- **Case Based Questions (CBQs) :** These are case study/passage based questions.

OBJECTIVE TYPE QUESTIONS

A. Select the correct option.

1. ________ is used to measure the distance traveled by a moving vehicle.
(a) Speedometer
(b) Odometer
(c) Manometer
(d) Motometer
R

2. Which of the following motions are associated with the Earth?
(i) Vibratory motion
(ii) Periodic motion
(iii) Rotatory motion
(iv) Revolutionary motion
(a) (i), (ii) and (iii)
(b) (ii), (iii) and (iv)
(c) (i), (iii) and (iv)
(d) (ii) and (iii)

3. On Saturday night, Prachi spent 18 minutes on social science homework, 35 minutes on mathematics homework and 22 minutes on English homework. How much time did she spend on her homework?
(a) 1 h 75 min
(b) 2 h 15 min
(c) 2 h 75 min
(d) 1 h 15 min

4. Hunny takes 30 minutes to travel to his school with a speed of 2 m/s. How far is the school?
(a) 2.6 km
(b) 6.2 km
(c) 3.6 km
(d) 3.2 km
Ev

5. How many weeks are there in 63 days?
(a) 8 (b) 6
(c) 9 (d) 7

B. State True (T) or False (F) for the given statements.

6. Standard unit of velocity is m/s. ☐
7. Galileo Galilei proved that the motion of a pendulum is periodic. ☐
8. The time period of a pendulum can be changed by changing the bob with one of a different weight. ☐
9. The displacement is the longest distance between initial and final position. ☐
10. When the speed of a body decreases with time, the distance-time graph of the moving body gives negative slope. ☐

Ap

C. Match the columns.

11.

Column I	Column II
(i) Swinging back and forth	(P) Quartz
(ii) A crystal used in electronic watches	(Q) Time period
(iii) Movement of an object with variable speed	(R) Non-uniform motion
(iv) Time taken by a pendulum to complete one oscillation	(S) 1/100 millennium
(v) One decade	(T) Oscillation

An

VERY SHORT ANSWER TYPE QUESTIONS (VSA)

A. Write one example for each of the following:

12. Instrument used for measuring time ________
13. Oscillatory motion ________
14. Periodic motion ________
15. Rotatory motion ________

16. Uniform motion ________

B. Write one word for each of the following:

17. Maximum displacement of the pendulum on either side of its mean position ________
18. An instrument used to measure short time periods accurately ________
19. An instrument used to determine the distance traveled by a vehicle ________
20. A change in the position of an object with time ________
21. The comparison of an unknown quantity with a known quantity of the same kind ________

SHORT ANSWER TYPE QUESTIONS-I (SA-I)

22. Draw the distance-time graph for the motion in the following cases:
 (a) A person standing on a side of road.
 (b) A person running with a constant speed. **U**
23. Find the speed of an object traveling 7200 m in one minute.
24. Define average speed.
25. An object is moving with a velocity of 20 m/s. If the motion is uniform, what will be the velocity after 10 s?
26. Explain the limitations of a sundial. **U**

SHORT ANSWER TYPE QUESTIONS-II (SA-II)

27. Differentiate between uniform and non-uniform motion.
28. Find the average speed of a car which travels 50 km in the first hour, 45 km in the second hour, 65 km in the third hour, 70 km in the fourth hour and 75 km in the fifth hour.
29. Draw a distance-time graph for non-uniform motion.
30. Car *A* traveled a distance of 15,360 metre in 3 hours while car *B* traveled a distance of 56 kilometre in 7 hours. Which car was moving faster? **Ev**

LONG ANSWER TYPE QUESTIONS (LA)

31. What do you mean by a simple pendulum? Explain its working and principle.
32. Explain the sundial, sand clock and water clock with diagram.
33. Rest and motion are relative terms. Explain with example.
34. Give reason for the following.
 (i) Displacement can never be greater than the distance traveled by an object.
 (ii) Ancient methods of measuring time were abandoned.
 (iii) Accurate measurement of time became possible much after accurate measurement of length and mass.

CASE BASED QUESTIONS (CBQs)

Case I : Read the given passage and answer the following questions :

Distance is defined as the length of actual path traveled and displacement is the length of shortest distance between two points. The speed is defined as the distance covered per unit time and velocity is defined as displacement per unit time.

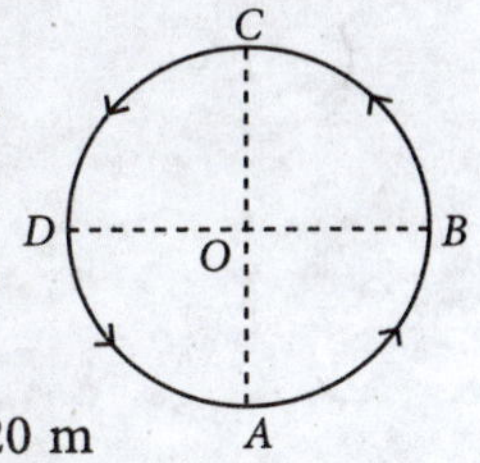

35. A man moves around a circular path of radius 70 m as shown. Find the distance traveled in one complete round.
 (a) 440 m (b) 220 m
 (c) 110 m (d) 140 m
36. What is the displacement covered if the man moves from *A* to *C*.
 (a) 70 m (b) 140 m
 (c) 35 m (d) 280 m **Ev**
37. If a man goes from $A \rightarrow B \rightarrow C \rightarrow D$ in 10 sec find his speed.
 (a) 110 m/s (b) 22 m/s
 (c) 33 m/s (d) 44 m/s
38. If man completes one round in 30 sec, find the average velocity.
 (a) 140 m/s (b) 33 m/s
 (c) 44 m/s (d) 0 m/s

Case II : Read the given passage and answer the following questions :

The graph between the distance and time gives an idea of motion of body. The slope of distance time graph gives speed for uniform motion, the body covers equal distance in equal interval of time while for non-uniform motion, the body covers unequal distances in equal interval of times.

39. Draw distance-time graph which represents non-uniform motion.

40. In the given graph, which of the following slope shows maximum speed.

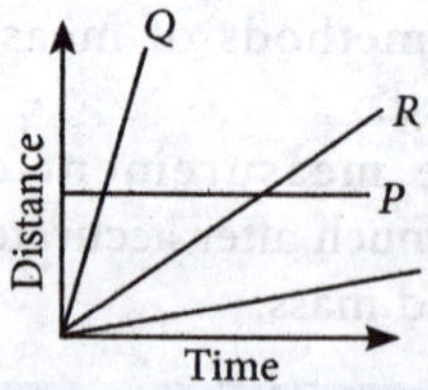

41. In the given graph find the maximum speed?

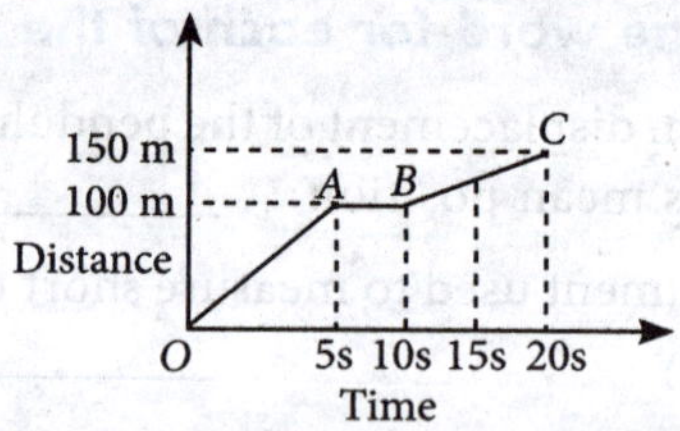

Ev

42. In the above graph find average speed in the total journey from 0 to 20 s.

ANSWER KEY

Practice Corner

1. (c) **2.** (c) **3.** (b) **4.** True **5.** False **6.** True **12.** (b) **13.** (c) **14.** (c) **15.** (a) **16.** (b) **17.** (d) **18.** True **19.** True **20.** False **21.** True **22.** (a) **23.** (b) **24.** (d) **25.** (a) **26.** (a) **27.** (a) **28.** (c) **29.** (a) **30.** periodic motion **31.** bob **32.** oscillatory **33.** time period **34.** True **35.** True **36.** True **37.** False **38.** True **39.** True **41.** (a) **42.** (a) **43.** (c) **44.** (b) **45.** (b) **46.** (a) **47.** (c) **48.** speedometer **49.** distance **50.** m/s **52.** (c) **53.** (c) **54.** (a) **55.** (c) **56.** (b) **57.** (a) **58.** True **59.** True

NCERT Exemplar Problems

1. (d) **2.** (c) **3.** (a) **4.** (b) **5.** (c) **6.** (a) **7.** (d) **8.** (a) **9.** (b)

A & R Corner

1. (a) **2.** (b) **3.** (b) **4.** (b) **5.** (c) **6.** (b) **7.** (a) **8.** (a) **9.** (c) **10.** (b)

Exam Corner

1. (b) **2.** (b) **3.** (d) **4.** (c) **5.** (c) **6.** True **7.** True **8.** False **9.** False **10.** True **11.** (i)-T; (ii)-P; (iii)-R; (iv)-Q; (v)-S **12.** Digital clock **17.** Amplitude **18.** Stopwatch **19.** Odometer **20.** Motion **21.** Measurement **35.** (a) **36.** (b) **37.** (c) **38.** (d)

10 Electric Current and its Effects

NCERT Notes

10.1 Symbols of Electric Components

- An **electric circuit** consists of electric cell or battery, electric wires, switch and bulb.
- Electric components and their symbols are :

S.No.	Electric component	Symbol	S.No.	Electric component	Symbol
1.	Electric cell 	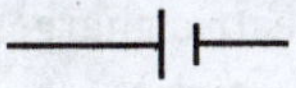	2.	Electric bulb 	
3.	Switch in ON position 	 or 	4.	Switch in OFF position 	 or 
5.	Battery 	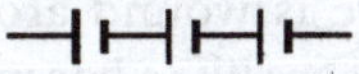	6.	Wire 	

- Symbolic representation of an electric circuit with its components is known as **circuit diagram**.
- Flow of electric charges through a closed circuit is known as **electric current**. It flows from the positive terminal to the negative terminal of a cell in the circuit. Also, it flows from a higher potential to a lower potential.
- A group of two or more cells forms a **battery**.
- Arrangement of cells:

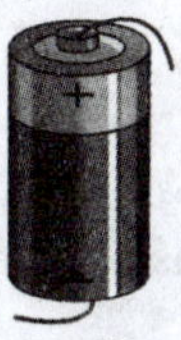

A cell

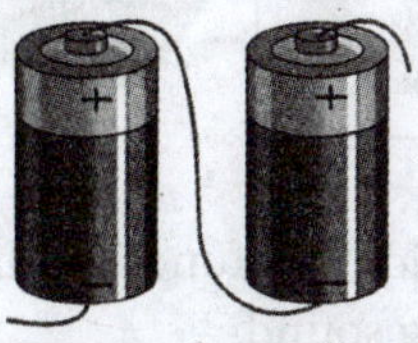

Battery of two cells

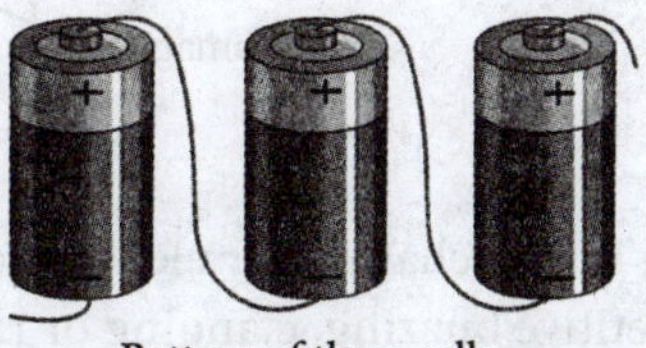

Battery of three cells

- A **switch** is used to control the flow of electricity in a circuit.
- A **bulb** glows when electric current passes through its filament. Its **filament** is made up of tungsten.

10.2 Heating Effect of Electric Current

- Current flowing in a wire can produce heat and this is known as the **heating effect of current.**
- The amount of heat produced by current depends upon the
  - nature of the material of object
  - the amount of current flow
  - the amount of time for which current flows.
- The heating effect of current is utilized in the heating devices like electric iron, kettle, geyser, toaster, etc.
- The coils of heating devices are made of **nichrome.**
- Materials like tungsten and nichrome have the ability to withstand high temperatures, without melting.
- A **fuse** is a safety device for electrical circuits and appliances, based on heating effect of current. It is a thin small wire made of tin or an alloy of tin and copper whose melting point is low.
- The function of a fuse is to break a circuit, in case there is overheating due to short-circuiting or overloading.
- **Miniature Circuit Breakers (MCBs)** are now widely used instead of fuses. These are switches which automatically turn off when current in a circuit exceeds the safe limit.

10.3 Magnetic Effect of Electric Current

- A current flowing in a wire can produce a **magnetic field** around the wire. This is known as **the magnetic effect of electric current.**

+ Magnetism is a natural force produce by moving electric charges. Magnetic field can attract or repel other magnets, and change the motion of other charged particles.

10.4 Electromagnet

- The property of electric current is used to change magnetic materials like soft iron into magnets by passing electricity through them, such magnets are called **electromagnets.**
- An electromagnet loses its magnetism as soon as the electric current is switched off. Thus, it is a **temporary magnet.**
- The strength of electromagnet is directly proportional to the amount of current flowing through coil and the number of turns of the coil. It is inversely proportional to the length of the coil.
- **Solenoid** is a device in which a long insulated wire is wound around a hollow metallic core. A current- carrying solenoid behaves like a bar magnet.

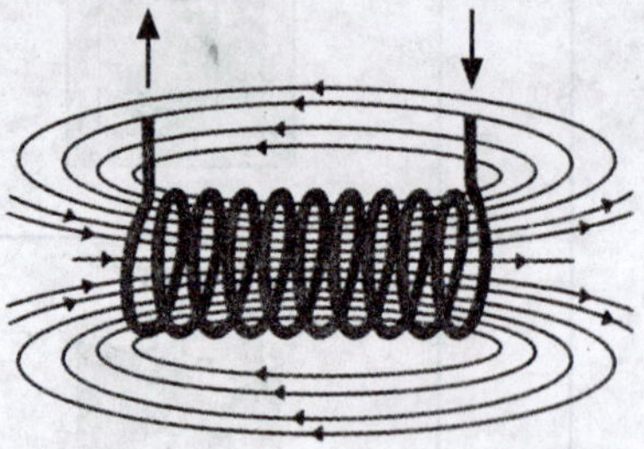

10.5 Electric Bell

- An **electric bell** uses an electromagnet.

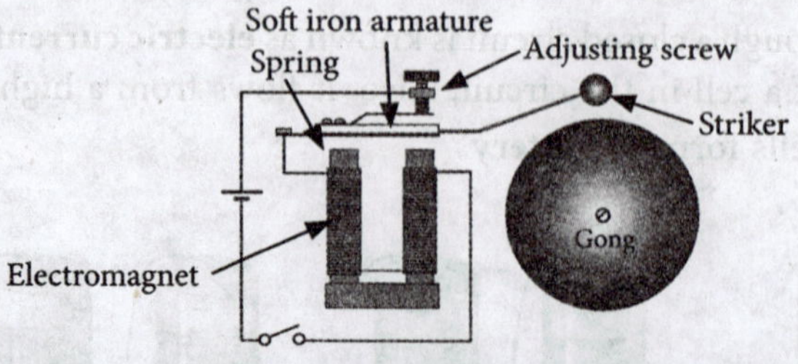

+ An electric bell is a mechanical or electronic device that functions by means of an electromagnet. It is used to produce repetitive buzzing, clanging or ringing sound.

Practice Corner

Extracted from NCERT

Assessment is complementary part of the learning process. It gives you a total insight whether the learning outcomes have been achieved or not. After going through the corresponding NCERT Textbook chapter, attempt these questions in exam like environment. Give yourself one mark for correct answer. A table is given at the end, that will help you plan your next step.

All the Best!

10.1 Symbols of Electric Components

NCERT Page 109-112

A. Select the correct option.

1. The symbol used for a switch in 'ON' condition is

(a)
(b) 
(c) 
(d) 

R

2. An electric bulb does not glow in a circuit if
(a) there is a broken circuit.
(b) there is no conducting material.
(c) there is no source of electric current.
(d) all of these

3. A switch or a key in a circuit can be placed
(a) on the right side of the battery only
(b) on the left side of the battery only
(c) near the positive terminal of the bulb only
(d) anywhere in the circuit.

4. In an electric circuit, the current starts from
(a) the positive terminals of the battery
(b) the negative terminal of the battery
(c) either of the terminals of the battery
(d) none of the terminals of the battery.

U

5. In which circuit will the bulb or bulbs glow the brightest?
(a) A simple circuit with one bulb and one cell.
(b) A simple circuit with one bulb and two cells.
(c) A simple circuit with two bulbs and one cell.
(d) A simple circuit with two bulbs and two cells.

An

6. Study the circuit shown here. Which switch if opened will cause the light bulb to stop glowing?

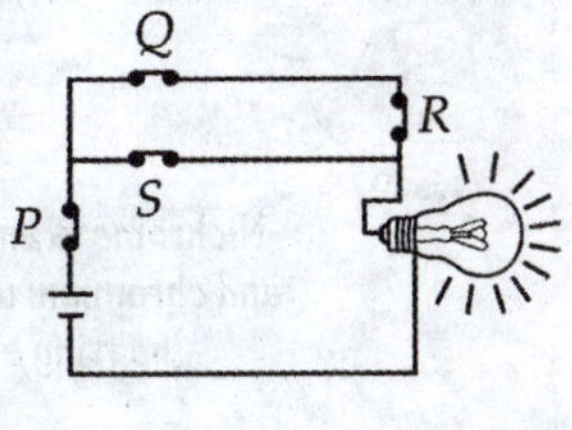

(a) P (b) Q
(c) R (d) S

7. The bulb in the circuit given here does not glow. Which labelled part is responsible for this?

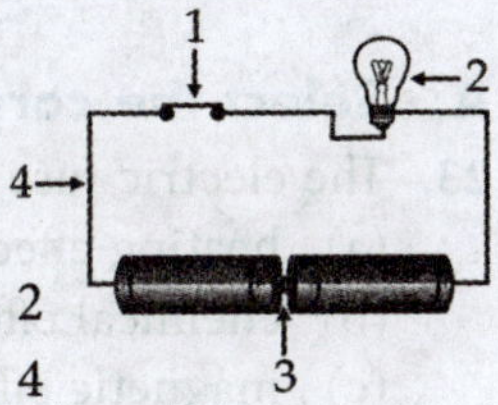

(a) 1 (b) 2
(c) 3 (d) 4

B. Fill in the blanks.

8. A battery is a combination of two or more ________.

R

9. In the symbol of an electric cell, the longer line represents the ________ terminal while the thicker and shorter line represents the ________ terminal.

10. The thin wire inside a bulb is known as ________.

11. The device that is used to prevent the flow of current in the circuit is called ________.

C. State True (T) or False (F) for the given statements.

12. A single cell is also known as battery.

13. Electric current flows from positive terminal to the negative terminal of a cell in an electric circuit.

14. 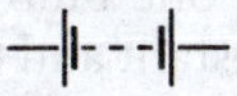 is the symbol of a battery.

15. Electric current flows in an open circuit.

16. A switch can be placed anywhere in the circuit.

D. Figure based questions.

Write the name of electric components for the following symbols in the boxes given below.

17. 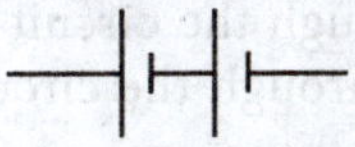

18. 

19. 

20.

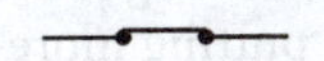

21.

22. 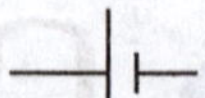

Ev

Resistance is a property that resists the flow of electrons in a conductor. It depends directly on length and material of the conductor and inversely proportional to its area of cross-section.

Jigyasa

10.2 Heating Effect of Electric Current

NCERT Page 112-116

A. Select the correct option.

23. The electric fuse works on the phenomenon of
(a) heating effect of current
(b) chemical effect of current
(c) magnetic effect of current
(d) none of these

R

24. ________ mark is necessary on electric appliances.
(a) FICC (b) ISI
(c) KSK (d) AGMARK

25. The coil of wire contained in heater or geyser is known as
(a) circuit (b) component
(c) spring (d) element.

26. Mark out the correct statement.
(a) Fuses and MCBs are safety devices.
(b) Fuses are safety devices but MCBs are not.
(c) MCBs are safety devices but fuses are not.
(d) Neither fuses nor MCBs are safety devices.

27. A fuse is always connected to the ________ wire.
(a) neutral (b) live
(c) earth (d) all of these

28. Megha makes a simple circuit with one bulb and five cells. The bulb lights up for an instant and then goes out. It happened because
(a) the wires melted in the heat.
(b) electricity could not flow through the circuit, subsequently.
(c) too much electricity passed through the filament.
(d) all of these

An

29. A short circuit occurs when
(a) a small current flows through the circuit
(b) too much current flows through the circuit
(c) the fuse blows in a circuit
(d) current does not flow in the circuit.

30. Overloading is
(a) putting more current across a wire than it can handle
(b) touching of live wire with the earth wire
(c) touching of neutral wire with the earth wire
(d) touching of live wire with the neutral wire.

B. Fill in the blanks.

31. The heating coil of an electric geyser is made up of ________.

32. The full form of MCB is ________. R

33. The amount of heat produced will be increased if the amount of current flowing is ________ in a circuit. U

C. State True (T) or False (F) for the given statements.

34. A fuse is an application of chemical effect of current.

35. The amount of heat produced does not depend on the nature of material of the wire.

36. An ISI mark is necessary for electrical appliances.

37. Heating effect of electric current is used in an electric bell.

38. A fuse wire has low melting point and high conductivity.

39. The connecting wires in an electric circuit do not get heated as these wires have low resistance.

D. Figure based questions.

List the appliances shown in the figure which convert:

40. Electrical energy into mechanical energy.

41. Electrical energy into heat energy.

(a) 

(b) 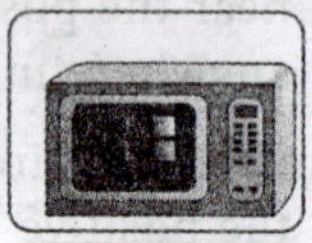

(c) 

(d) 

(e) 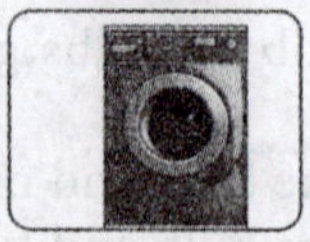

(f) 

U

What is nichrome?

Gyaan

Nichrome is an alloy of nickel and chromium used for making heating elements.

Jigyasa

10.3 Magnetic Effect of Electric Current

NCERT Page 116-117

tA. Select the correct option.

42. If same amount of electric current is passed through the following devices, then which will show the strongest magnetic strength?
(a) Coil of wire
(b) Solenoid wound on a wooden core
(c) Solenoid wound on an iron core
(d) Straight conducting wire

43. A light steel bar and a light iron bar are attracted to a magnet as shown. What will possibly happen when the magnet is removed?

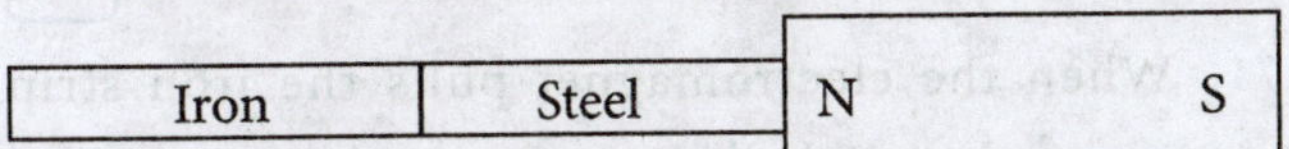

(a) The steel and iron bars repel each other.
(b) Both steel and iron bars lose their magnetism.
(c) Steel bar retains its magnetism and iron bar loses its magnetism.
(d) Iron bar retains its magnetism and steel bar loses its magnetism. An

B. Fill in the blanks.

44. Magnetic effect of current was discovered by ________. R

45. The needle of a magnetic compass shows ________ when it is brought near a current carrying wire.

46. When an electric current flows through a wire, it behaves like a ________.

47. Under normal conditions, a magnetic compass needle always rests in ________ direction.

C. State True (T) or False (F) for the given statements.

48. A compass needle shows deflection when it is brought near a bar magnet. ☐

49. A compass needle always rests in North - South direction when the current is switched off. ☐

50. A compass needle shows deflection even when electric current is not passing through the coil. ☐ U

D. Figure based question.

51. If a compass needle is brought near the given device, does it show deflection? Give reason to support your answer.

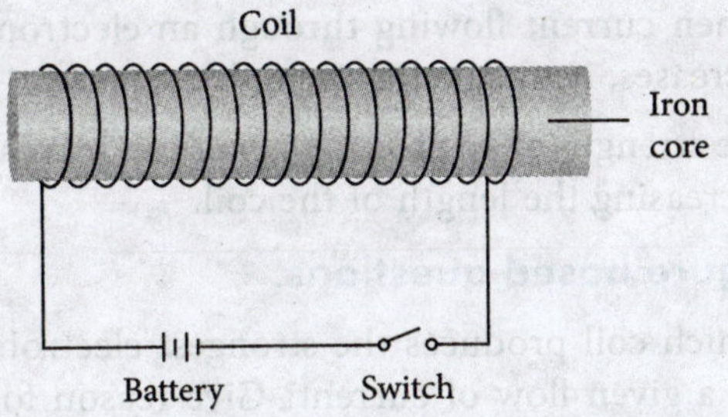

10.4 Electromagnet

NCERT Page 117-118

A. Select the correct option.

52. Temporary magnets are made of
(a) brass (b) soft iron
(c) soil (d) lead. R

53. Which of the following is a temporary magnet?
(a) Electromagnet
(b) Ring-shaped magnet
(c) Bar magnet
(d) Magnetite

54. When an iron rod is put inside a current-carrying wire, the strength of the electromagnet
(a) remains same
(b) decreases
(c) increases
(d) becomes zero. U

55. Which coil produces the strongest electromagnet for a given flow of current?
(a) A 10 cm coil with 100 turns
(b) A 5 cm coil with 200 turns
(c) A 10 cm coil with 200 turns
(d) A 20 cm coil with 200 turns

B. Fill in the blanks.

56. Doctors use very small but strong ________ to remove iron dust from a patient's eye. R

57. If the amount of current passing through the coil of an electromagnet is decreased, the strength of the electromagnet will ________.

58. A current-carrying coil of an insulated wire wrapped around a piece of iron is called an ________.

C. State True (T) or False (F) for the given statements.

59. Electromagnets are made by electrical methods. ☐

60. Electromagnet is a permanent magnet. ☐

61. Electromagnets attract iron pieces. ☐

62. When current flowing through an electromagnet increases, its magnetic strength decreases.

63. The strength of an electromagnet can increased by decreasing the length of the coil.

D. Figure based questions.

64. Which coil produces the strongest electromagnet for a given flow of current? Give reason for your choice.

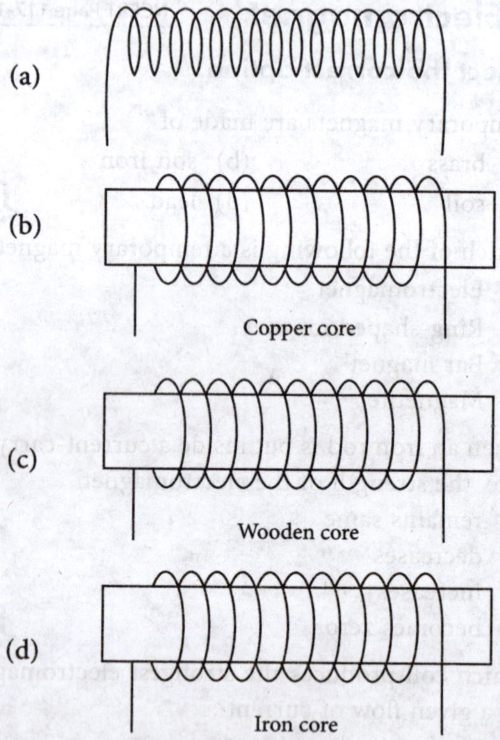

An

10.5 Electric Bell

NCERT Page 118

A. Fill in the blanks.

65. An electric bell is an application of ________.

R

66. An electric bell works on the principle of ________ effect of electricity.

67. Gong, hammer, armature and push button are the components of a/an ________.

B. State True (T) or False (F) for the given statements.

68. An electric door bell has a coil of wire wound on a soft iron core which is known as electromagnet.

69. An electric bell works on the principle of magnetic effect of electricity.

70. An electric bell works in the absence of electricity.

71. When the electromagnet pulls the iron strip in an electric bell, It connects the circuit and current flows through the coil.

U

C. Figure based questions.

Write the name of the components of an electric bell in the figure given below.

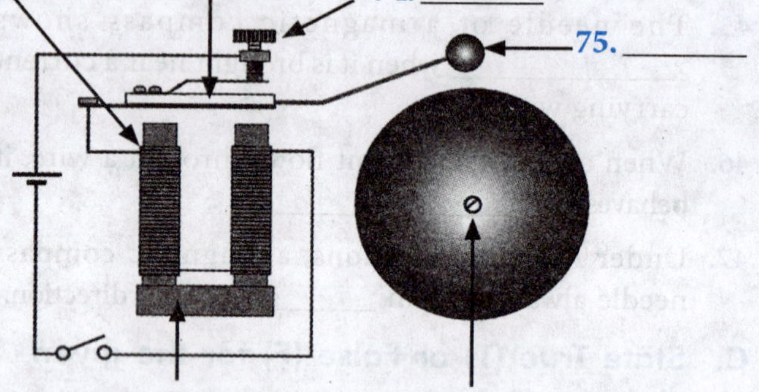

72. ________ 73. ________ 74. ________ 75. ________ 76. ________ 77. ________

PROGRESS CHECK

Check your score! If your score is

Score	Rating	Advice
> 95%	EXCELLENT !	Move on to the next chapter. You have mastered this chapter. Concepts are certainly on your fingertips.
95-85%	VERY GOOD !	Revise once more thoroughly. Recognise your mistakes and work on them. You will master this chapter.
84-75%	GOOD!	Work on your weak areas, master them and come back to this chapter in a few days.
74-65%	MEDIOCRE!	Understand your weak areas and work on strengthening your concepts. Devote more time to master this chapter.
< 65%	NOT SATISFACTORY!	This is where you fall behind from scoring well. Give special attention to this chapter. Work on clearing concepts and common errors.

NCERT Exemplar Problems

This section contains MCQs of **'NCERT Exemplar Problems'** Book.

1. When an electric current flows through a copper wire *AB* as shown in figure, the wire

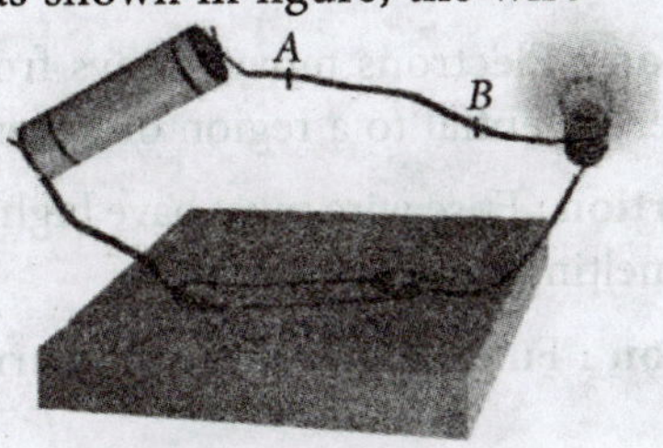

(a) deflects a magnetic needle placed near it.
(b) becomes red hot.
(c) gives electric shock.
(d) behaves like a fuse.

2. Choose the statement which is not correct in the case of an electric fuse.

(a) Fuses are inserted in electric circuits of all buildings.
(b) There is a maximum limit on the current which can safely flow through the electric circuits.
(c) There is a minimum limit on the current which can safely flow in the electric circuits.
(d) If a proper fuse is inserted in a circuit it will blow off if current exceeds the safe limit.

3. Three bulbs *A*, *B*, *C* are connected in a circuit as shown in figure. When the switch is 'ON'

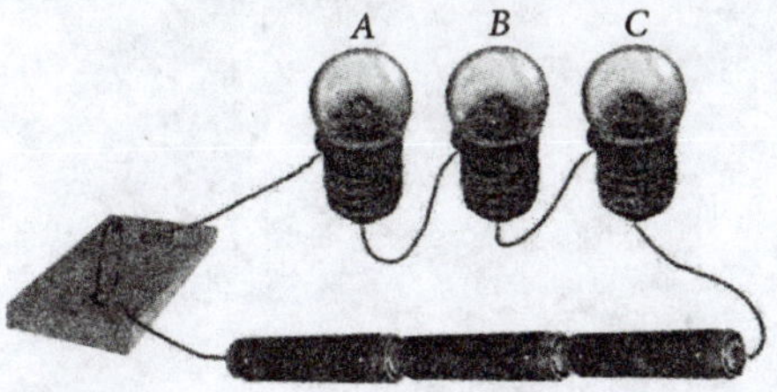

(a) bulb *C* will glow first.
(b) bulb *B* and *C* will glow simultaneously and bulb *A* will glow after some time.
(c) all the bulbs *A*, *B* and *C* will glow at the same time.
(d) the bulbs will glow in the order *A*, *B* and *C*.

4. When a switch is in OFF position,

(i) circuit starting from the positive terminal of the cell stops at the switch.
(ii) circuit is open.
(iii) no current flows through it.
(iv) current flows after some time.

Choose the combination of correct answer from the following.

(a) all are correct
(b) (ii) and (iii) are correct
(c) only (iv) is correct
(d) only (i) and (ii) are correct

5. Which of the following precautions need not be taken while using electric gadgets/appliances/circuit?

(a) We should never touch a lighted electric bulb connected to the mains.
(b) We should never experiment with the electric supply from the mains or a generator or an inverter.
(c) We should never use just any wire or strip of metal in place of a fuse.
(d) We should never turn the switch in ON position.

A&R Corner

Directions : In the following questions, a statement of assertion is followed by a statement of reason. Mark the correct choice as :
(a) If both assertion and reason are true and reason is the correct explanation of assertion.
(b) If both assertion and reason are true but reason is not the correct explanation of assertion.
(c) If assertion is true but reason is false.
(d) If both assertion and reason are false.

1. **Assertion :** Good conductors of heat are also good conductors of electricity and vice versa.
   Reason : Mainly electrons are responsible for conduction. U

2. **Assertion :** Tungsten metal is used for making filaments of incandescent lamps.
   Reason : The melting point of tungsten is very low.

3. **Assertion :** Alloys are commonly used in electrical heating devices, like electrical iron, toasters etc.
   Reason : Alloys do not oxidise (burn) readily at high temperatures. U

4. **Assertion :** A cell is a device which converts chemical energy into electrical energy.
   Reason : Cell maintains a constant potential difference between its terminals for a long time.

5. **Assertion :** A current carrying wire should be charged.
   Reason : The current in a wire is due to flow of bound electrons in a random direction.

6. **Assertion :** Electron has a negative charge.
   Reason : Electrons move always from a region of higher potential to a region of lower potential.

7. **Assertion :** Fuse wire must have high resistance and low melting point.
   Reason : Fuse is used for small current flow only. R

8. **Assertion :** The connecting wires are made of copper.
   Reason : The electrical conductivity of copper is high.

9. **Assertion :** The magnetic field around a current carrying conductor is due to the flow of electric current in the wire.
   Reason : If more current flows through the wire, more be the magnetic field created around the wire. An

10. **Assertion :** An electric cell is a device which converts chemical energy into electrical energy.
    Reason : More be the cells connected in a regular manner more be the current in the circuit.

Exam Corner

This section comprises of different types of questions:

- **Objective Type Questions :** These are **one mark** questions.
- **Very Short Answer Type Questions (VSA) :** These are **one mark** questions.
- **Short Answer Type Questions-I (SA-I) :** These are **two marks** questions.
- **Short Answer Type Questions-II (SA-II) :** These are **three marks** questions.
- **Long Answer Type Questions (LA) :** These are **five marks** questions.
- **Case Based Questions (CBQs) :** These are case study/passage based questions.

OBJECTIVE TYPE QUESTIONS

A. Select the correct option.

1. Which of the following statements explains why a bulb in a circuit may blow?

(a) Too many batteries have been connected in the circuit.
(b) Too many switches have been connected in the circuit.
(c) The dry cells are not connected properly.
(d) Too many bulbs have been connected in the circuit. An

2. Resistance of a wire depends on the

(a) thickness of the wire
(b) material of the wire
(c) length of the wire
(d) all of these U

3. Identify the odd one out.

(a) Steel spoon (b) Iron nail
(c) Cobalt strip (d) Wooden ruler R

4. The strength of a magnetic field due to solenoid can be increased by

(a) winding the solenoid around a magnetic material.
(b) increasing the current in the solenoid.
(c) increasing the number of turns in the solenoid.
(d) all of these

5. How does the magnetic strength of a current carrying coil depend on the amount of current?

(a) It increases with the decrease in the amount of current.
(b) It increases with the increase in the amount of current.
(c) It decreases with the increase in the amount of current.
(d) It remains same with the increase or decrease in the amount of current.

B. State True (T) or False (F) for the given statements.

6. Battery stores chemical energy and makes it available in electrical form. ☐

7. A 10 cm coil with 100 turns will produce a stronger electromagnet in comparison to a 10 cm coil with 200 turns. ☐ Ev

8. The direction of electric current is taken as same to that of flow of electrons. ☐

9. Resistance resists the flow of electrons in a conductor. ☐

10. An MCB turns off automatically when current in a circuit exceeds the safe limit. ☐ R

C. Match the columns.

11.

	Column I		Column II
(i)	The coil of wire used in a heater to get heat	(P)	Filament
(ii)	Heating effect of current	(Q)	CFL
(iii)	Magnetic effect of current	(R)	Element
(iv)	Made of alloy with low melting point	(S)	Electromagnet
(v)	Consumes less energy than bulb	(T)	Fuse

U

VERY SHORT ANSWER TYPE QUESTIONS (VSA)

A. Write one word for each of the following:

12. A device made of a long wire that has been wound many times into tightly packed coil ________

13. A device used to measure the potential difference between two terminals of an electric circuit ________

14. Combination of two or more cells in a circuit ________

15. A safety device used in an electrical circuit to prevent a large amount of current flowing through a circuit ________
16. Symbolic representation of an electric circuit ________

B. Draw the symbols for the following components:

17. Switch in 'ON' position
18. Battery having three cells
19. Electric bulb
20. Electric cell
21. Switch in 'OFF' position An

SHORT ANSWER TYPE QUESTIONS-I (SA-I)

22. Does the bulb glow in the circuit given below? Give reason to support your answer.

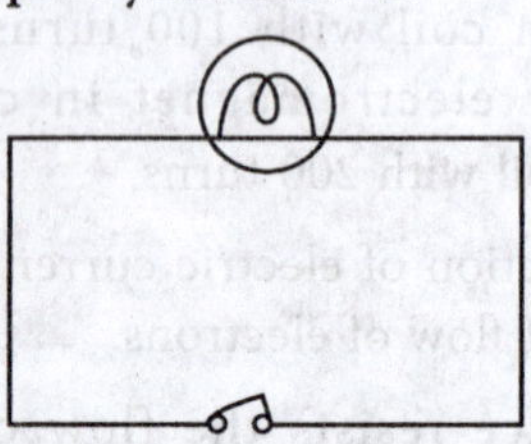

23. What are MCBs? How do they work?
24. Differentiate between a fuse wire and a heating wire.
25. What is the heating effect of the electric current?
26. Why does an electric bulb get hot if it is switched on for a while?

SHORT ANSWER TYPE QUESTIONS-II (SA-II)

27. What are the factors on which heating effect of electric current depends? U
28. Explain the construction of a battery.
29. What are electric fuses? Explain their importance.
30. How does an electric iron work?

LONG ANSWER TYPE QUESTIONS (LA)

31. Explain the working of an electric bell with diagram.
32. What are storage batteries? Write their uses. R
33. What is an electromagnet? Write its applications.
34. Give reason for the following
    (i) A thin wire of tungsten is used in the filaments of bulbs instead of copper wire.
    (ii) The heating element of heater becomes red hot but the connecting wire does not.
    (iii) We should never touch a lighted bulb. U
    (iv) Why does an electric fuse consist of wire made up of an alloy of tin and lead with a very low melting point?

CASE BASED QUESTIONS (CBQs)

Case I : Read the given passage and answer the following questions :

When the electric current pass through a conductor, the conductor becomes heated. This is called heating effect of electric current. The amount of heat produced depends on the electric current flows through the conductor, resistance of the conductor and time for which the current flows through the circuit.

35. Which of the following device does not depend on heating effect of current?
    (a) Electric fuse (b) Electric switch
    (c) Electric bulb (d) Electric geyser
36. The heating elements are made by nichrome which is an alloy of
    (a) nickel and chromium
    (b) sodium and chromium
    (c) chromium and platinum
    (d) brass and chromium. R
37. If we increase the amount of electric current passing through a conductor, the heat produced
    (a) decreases (b) increases
    (c) remains same (d) can't say
38. What are the properties of heating elements?
    (a) High resistance, high melting point.
    (b) High resistance, low melting point.
    (c) Low resistance, high melting point.
    (d) Low resistance, low melting point.

Case II : Read the given passage and answer the following questions :

When a magnetic compass is placed near a current carrying conductor, there is a deflection in magnetic compass. So, it shows that a magnetic field is generated near a current carrying conductor. This is known as magnetic effect of electric current. The strength of magnetic field depends on the amount of current passing through the coil and number of turns in the coil.

39. What is the material used to make the core of a solenoid? U

40. What is a solenoid?

41. What are the characteristics of a current carrying solenoid?

42. Give the condition for the strongest electromagnet? Give reason for your choice.

ANSWER KEY

Practice Corner

1. (d) **2.** (d) **3.** (d) **4.** (a) **5.** (b) **6.** (a) **7.** (c) **8.** cells **9.** positive, negative **10.** filament
11. switch **12.** False **13.** True **14.** False **15.** False **16.** True **17.** Battery **18.** Open key **19.** Bulb
20. Closed key **21.** Electric wire **22.** Electric cell **23.** (a) **24.** (b) **25.** (d) **26.** (a) **27.** (b)
28. (d) **29.** (b) **30.** (a) **31.** nichrome **32.** Miniature circuit breaker **33.** increased **34.** False
35. False **36.** True **37.** False **38.** True **39.** True **40.** (a), (e), (f) **41.** (b), (c), (d) **42.** (c) **43.** (c)
44. Hans Christian Oersted **45.** deflection **46.** Magnet **47.** North-South **48.** True **49.** True
50. False **52.** (b) **53.** (a) **54.** (c) **55.** (b) **56.** Electromagnet **57.** decrease **58.** Electromagnet
59. True **60.** False **61.** True **62.** False **63.** True **64.** (d) **65.** Electromagnet **66.** magnetic
67. Electric bell **68.** True **69.** True **70.** False **71.** False **72.** Spring **73.** Soft iron armature
74. Adjusting screw **75.** Striker **76.** Gong **77.** Electromagnet

NCERT Exemplar Problems

1. (a) **2.** (c) **3.** (c) **4.** (b) **5.** (d)

A & R Corner

1. (b) **2.** (c) **3.** (a) **4.** (b) **5.** (d) **6.** (c) **7.** (c) **8.** (a) **9.** (b) **10.** (b)

Exam Corner

1. (a) **2.** (d) **3.** (d) **4.** (d) **5.** (b) **6.** True **7.** False **8.** False **9.** True **10.** True
11. (i)-R; (ii)-P; (iii)-S; (iv)-T; (v)-Q **12.** Solenoid **13.** Voltmeter **14.** Battery **15.** Fuse
16. Circuit diagram **35.** (b) **36.** (a) **37.** (b) **38.** (a)

11 Light

NCERT Notes

11.1 Light Travels Along a Straight Line

- **Light** is a form of energy. It travels along a **straight line**. This property of light is known as **rectilinear propagation of light**.

> + A person will be not be able to see an object through a bent pipe as light travels in a straight line.

11.2 Reflection of Light

- When light falls on an object, some of it is absorbed and the rest is bounced back.
- The phenomenon of bouncing back of light from a surface is known as **reflection** of light. **Reflection** of light depends upon the **nature** of object through which it passes.

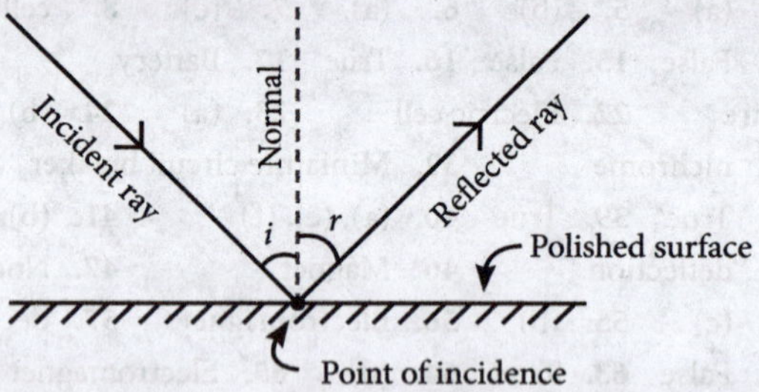

- Light passes through glass, absorbed by unpolished wood and reflected by a mirror.

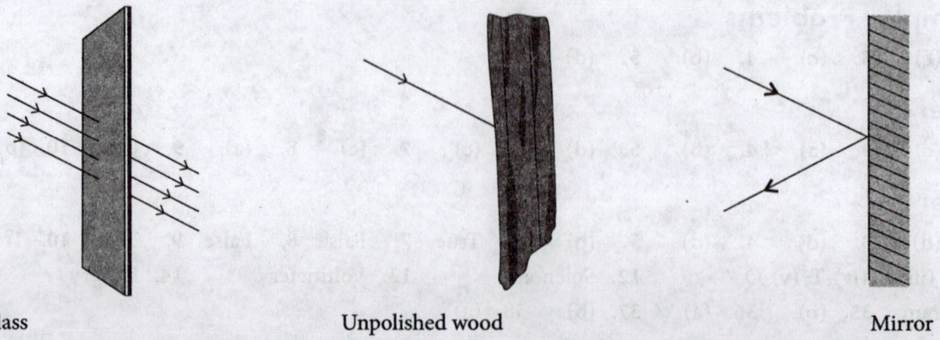

- **Regular reflection** takes place on an even surface or a shiny surface like mirror. Regular reflection results in the formation of a clear image.

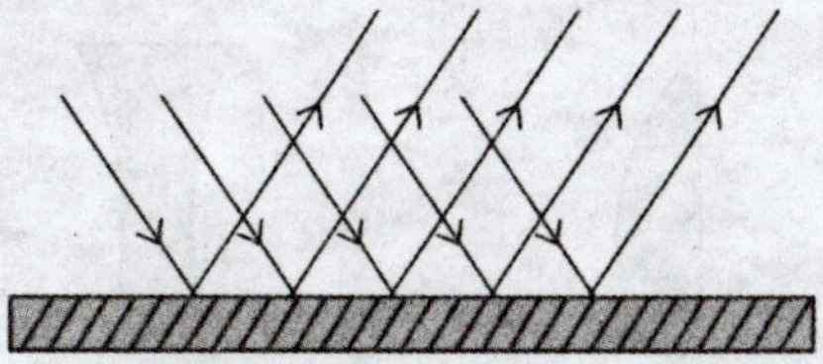

Regular reflection

- Uneven or rough surface reflects light in all directions. This reflection is known as **diffused reflection.** It does not result in the formation of an image or a blurry image is formed at most.

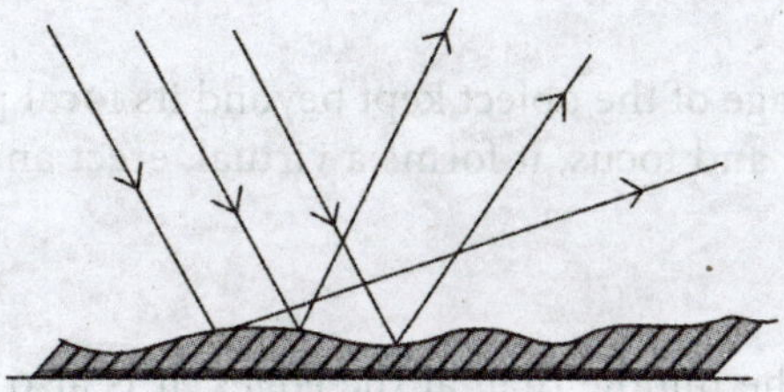

Diffused reflection

- An image that cannot be formed on a screen is called a **virtual image**. Rays of light do not actually pass through a virtual image.
- An image that can be formed on a screen is called a **real image**. The image is formed by rays of light actually meeting a point.
- Mirrors are of two types: **plane** and **spherical.**
- A **plane mirror** is a flat smooth glass surface which is polished by silver on one of its sides and the other side is used as the reflecting surface.
  - Radius of curvature and focal length of a plane mirror is infinite.
  - The image formed in a plane mirror is always virtual and erect and cannot be obtained on a screen.
  - The image is formed at the same distance from the mirror as the object is kept in front of it.

11.3 Right or Left!

- In case of a plane mirror, size of the image is equal to the size of the object and is laterally inverted.

> **+** The word 'Ambulance' is written laterally inverted so the word appears correct in the rear view mirror of the vehicles ahead.

11.4 Playing with Spherical Mirrors

- Spherical mirrors are of two types : **concave** and **convex.**

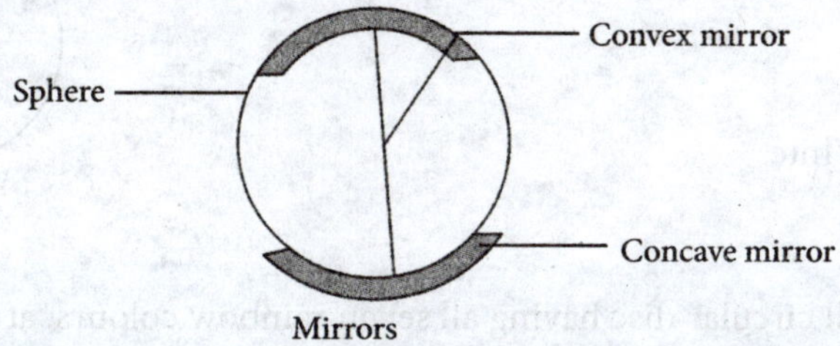

Mirrors

- A **concave mirror** can form a real as well as an inverted image. When the object is placed very close to the mirror, the image formed is virtual, erect and magnified.
- Image formed by a **convex mirror** is erect, virtual and smaller in size than the object.

11.5 Images Formed by Lenses

- **Lens** is a transparent medium bounded by two surfaces of which at least one is spherical.

- A **convex lens** is thicker in the middle than at the edges. It is also known as **converging lens** as it converges the rays of light falling on it.

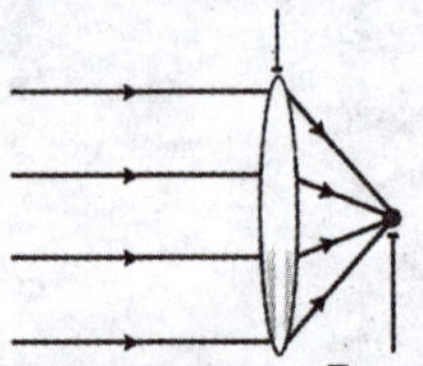

- It forms a real and inverted image of the object kept beyond its focal point. For an object kept between its optical centre and focus, it forms a virtual, erect and magnified image.

- A **concave lens** is thinner in the middle than at the edges. It is also known as **diverging lens** as it diverges the rays of light falling on it.
- It forms a virtual, erect and diminished image of all objects irrespective of their distance from the lens.

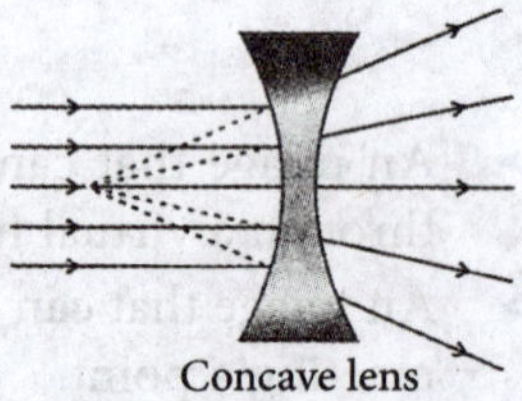

- **Refraction** is a phenomenon in which light propagates from one medium to another. It causes the change in the speed of light.

11.6 Sunlight-White or Coloured?

- When white light passes through a prism, it splits into its constituent colours. This phenomenon is known as **dispersion of light**. The colours so formed is called the **spectrum of light**.

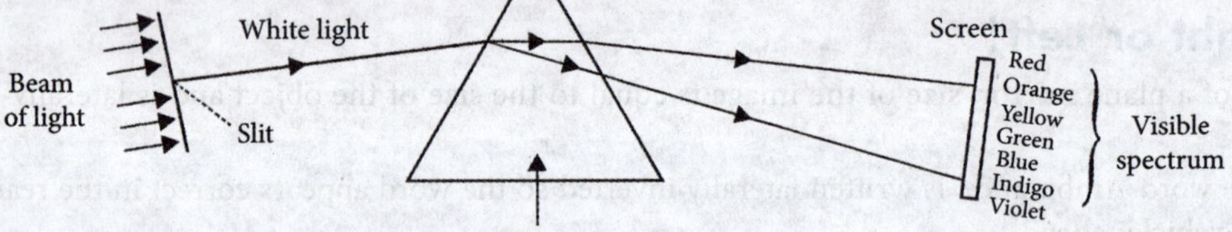

- Blue, green and red are the three **primary colours** of white light. Other colours can be obtained by mixing the primary colours.

  Red + Green = Yellow

  Red + Blue = Magenta

  Blue + Green = Cyan

  Red + Blue + Green = White

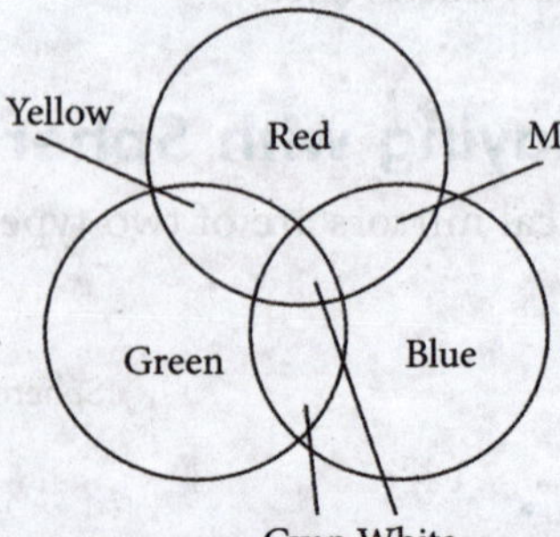

+ Rotating a top with small circular disc having all seven rainbow colours, at a rapid rate will make it appear nearly white.

Practice Corner

Extracted from NCERT

Assessment is complementary part of the learning process. It gives you a total insight whether the learning outcomes have been achieved or not. After going through the corresponding NCERT Textbook chapter, attempt these questions in exam like environment. Give yourself one mark for correct answer. A table is given at the end, that will help you plan your next step.

All the Best!

11.1 Light Travels Along a Straight Line

NCERT Page 123-124

A. Select the correct option.

1. Light always travels in a ________ path.
(a) straight
(b) curved
(c) sometimes straight, sometimes curved
(d) none of these
R

2. We cannot see a lighted candle through a bent pipe because
(a) we can only see through a transparent object
(b) bent pipe is an opaque object
(c) reflection of light does not occur due to bent pipe
(d) light travels in a straight line.

3. The property of light travelling in a straight line is known as
(a) scattering of light
(b) dispersion of light
(c) rectilinear propagation of light
(d) reflection of light.

4. The path of light can be changed
(a) by placing a mirror in its path
(b) by placing any shiny surface in its path
(c) both (a) and (b)
(d) neither (a) nor (b)
R

B. Figure based question.

5. In the given figure, a boy is able to see the light of torch through the four holes *A*, *B*, *C* and *D*. Why is he able to see the light through these holes?

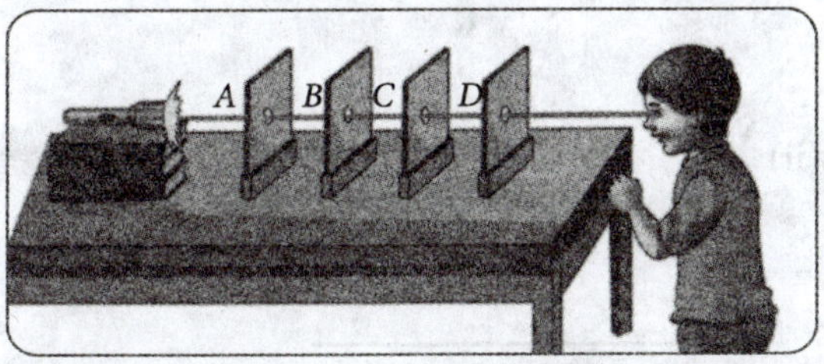

11.2 Reflection of Light

NCERT Page 124-126

A. Select the correct option.

6. A polished surface acts as a/an
(a) mirror (b) image
(c) shadow (d) screen
R

7. Which of the following shows reflection?
(a) Wood (b) Plastic
(c) Water (d) None of these

8. In the mirror image from plane mirror of word 'TRAVELLING', which alphabets appear smaller than their original size?
(a) E and L (b) R and I
(c) All of these (d) None of these

9. Why does a black coloured cloth appear black?
(a) Because it reflects light of all colours and absorb black coloured light.
(b) Because it reflects light of black colour and absorb light of all the colours.
(c) Because it reflects light of all colours.
(d) Because it does not reflect any colour to our eyes.
An

10. If a pin is placed in front of, and to the right of a plane mirror as shown in figure, then where is the image of the pin formed?

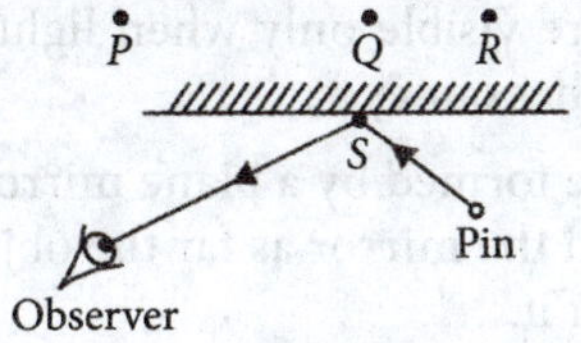

(a) *P* (b) *Q*
(c) *R* (d) *S*
U

11. When a ray of light is reflected from a surface, then ________ changes.
(a) direction of light (b) speed of light
(c) both (a) and (b) (d) colour of light

12. The angle of incidence is formed between the
(a) incident ray and the normal
(b) reflected ray and the normal
(c) incident ray and the mirror
(d) reflected ray and the mirror.

13. The given figure shows
(a) diffused reflection
(b) refraction
(c) regular reflection
(d) none of these

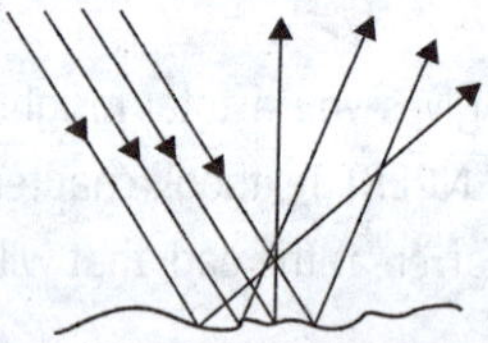

14. An object is held in front of a plane mirror. Which of the following images will be formed?

(a)  (b) 

(c) 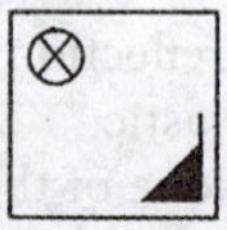 (d) 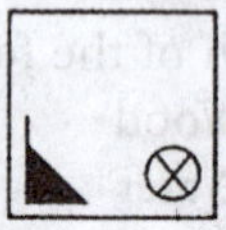

B. Fill in the blanks.

15. A/An ________________ shows the details of an object like colour, shape etc.

16. ______________ is the phenomenon of bouncing back of light into the same medium.

17. An opaque, smooth, highly polished surface, typically made of glass coated with a metal amalgam, which reflects a clear image is called ________________.

C. State True (T) or False (F) for the given statements.

18. A plane mirror forms an erect image. ☐

19. The size of the image in a plane mirror is same as the size of the object. ☐

20. A polished surface does not show reflection. ☐

21. Objects are visible only when light reflected from them reaches our eyes. ☐

22. The image formed by a plane mirror is always so far behind the mirror as far the object lie in front of it. ☐

23. The colour of the reflected light gives the object its colour. ☐

24. Our eyesight is completely dependent on light which causes the sensation of vision. ☐

25. The image formed by a plane mirror can be projected on a screen. ☐

D. Figure based question.

26. If a sharpener is kept at a distance of 10 cm in front of a mirror, then the distance between its image and the mirror will be ________________. Give reason.

11.3 Right or Left!

NCERT Page 127

A. Select the correct option.

27. The image formed in a plane mirror is always
(a) erect and laterally inverted
(b) upside down
(c) straight and blurred
(d) larger than the original size.

28. In the mirror image of word 'ELECTRIC', which alphabets are written as same?
(a) E and C (b) L and I
(c) T and I (d) C and L

B. State True (T) or False (F) for the given statements.

29. An image in a mirror shows lateral inversion. ☐

30. Changing of left side of an object to the right side of an image is known as lateral inversion. ☐

31. The correct image of the alphabet 'R' on a plane mirror placed in front of it is 'Я'. ☐

32. The image of symmetrical letters like A, H, I, M, T and U are not affected by lateral inversion. ☐

C. Figure based question.

33. Write down the words as seen in the mirror images formed in each of the given figures.

(i) SCIENCE  ________________

(ii) SCIENCE

____

11.4 Playing with Spherical Mirrors

NCERT Page 128-132

A. Select the correct option.

34. A __________ mirror is used as the rear view mirror of vehicles.
(a) concave (b) plane
(c) convex (d) none of these

35. Enlarged and virtual images are created by
(a) concave mirrors (b) plane mirrors
(c) convex mirrors (d) concave lenses.

36. In a __________ mirror, the reflecting surface is curved outwards.
(a) plane (b) concave
(c) convex (d) all of these

37. The focal length of a concave mirror is 5 cm. Find its radius of curvature.
(a) 2.5 cm (b) 5 cm
(c) 10 cm (d) None of these **Ev**

B. Fill in the blanks.

38. The mirrors used as rear view mirrors in cars and in car headlights are __________ and __________ respectively. **U**

39. __________ mirrors make things look larger when objects are placed close to them.

40. The image that can be obtained on a screen is called __________ image.

41. __________ are used in telescopes to reflect light. **R**

C. State True (T) or False (F) for the given statements.

42. Doctors use convex mirror for examining eyes, ears, nose and throat.

43. A virtual image can be obtained on a screen.

44. A concave mirror forms a real as well as an inverted image.

When the object moves towards a concave mirror, the size of the image of the object increases. Full length image of an object is formed by a concave mirror, only when the object is far away from the mirror.

11.5 Images Formed by Lenses

NCERT Page 132-134

A. Select the correct option.

45. Which of the following is true regarding convex lens?
(a) It forms a magnified image wherever the object is placed.
(b) It forms a magnified image only when the object is very close to the lens.
(c) It always forms diminished and erect images.
(d) It is not made of a transparent material.

46. Which one of the following lenses is used for getting a real and inverted image as well as a virtual and erect image?
(a) Concave lens (b) Convex lens
(c) Both (a) and (b) (d) None of these **U**

47. A concave lens forms
(a) inverted, virtual and smaller image
(b) erect, real and smaller image
(c) erect, virtual and smaller image
(d) erect, virtual and magnified image.

48. Which of the following cases is/are possible for convex lens?

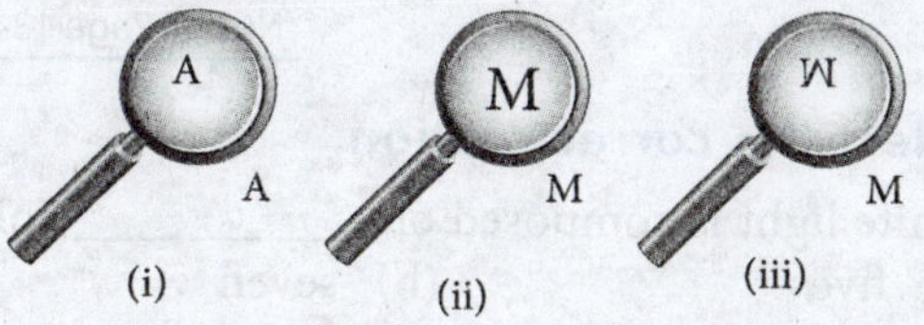

U

(a) (i) and (ii) (b) (ii) and (iii)
(c) (iii) and (i) (d) Only (i)

49. Refraction of light occurs due to
(a) the colour of the medium
(b) the absorption of light
(c) a change in the direction of light
(d) a change in the speed of light.

B. Fill in the blanks.

50. A __________ lens is used as a magnifying glass.

51. __________ lens always forms a virtual image.

52. The lenses which are thicker in the middle than at the edges are called __________ lenses.

53. A drop of water on a leaf forms a magnified image of the veins because of __________ shaped water droplets. **An**

C. State True (T) or False (F) for the given statements.

54. Concave lens forms a diminished image.

55. Convex lens can form both real and virtual images.

56. If a far away object is brought towards the focus of a convex lens, the size of the image will increase.

57. Concave lens is used in spectacles to correct far-sightedness. **U**

58. Convex lens is diverging in nature.

59. A concave lens is used by a man while shaving.

D. Figure based question.

60. In given figure, when a magnifying glass is placed close to the object, the image appears larger and when placed far from the object, the image appears inverted. What type of lens is used in this magnifying glass?

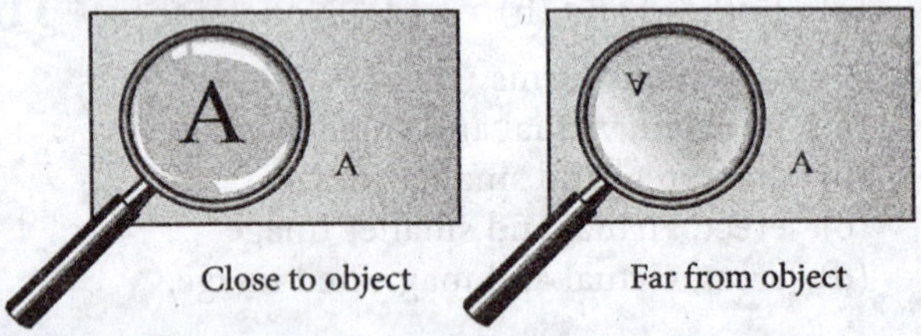

Close to object Far from object

11.6 Sunlight – White or Coloured?

NCERT Page 134-136

A. Select the correct option.

61. White light is composed of ________ colours.
(a) five (b) seven
(c) nine (d) eight

62. If Newton's colour disc is rotated rapidly, then
(a) seven colours of light look like a single colour black
(b) seven colours of light look like a single colour violet
(c) seven colours of light look like a single colour white
(d) none of these U

63. Which one of the following statements regarding a rainbow is correct?
(a) It is always seen as a circle.
(b) The order of colours is always (from top to bottom as seen from the ground) violet, indigo, blue, green, yellow, orange, red.
(c) Its order of colours is always (from top to bottom as seen from the ground) red, orange, yellow, green, blue, indigo, violet.
(d) The order of colours can be either violet to red or red to violet depending upon the time of the day.

B. Fill in the blanks.

64. If we mix the colours of rainbow, we will get ________ light. R

65. The ________ colour bends the most when white light is passed through a prism.

66. We can see a rainbow only when our ________ is towards the Sun.

67. The phenomenon of splitting of white light into its seven constituent colours is known as ________. R

68. ________ was the first to show that ordinary white light is made up of seven colours.

C. State True (T) or False (F) for the given statements.

69. We cannot get white light when we mix seven colours.

70. Black colour splits into seven colours.

71. In VIBGYOR, B stands for black.

D. Figure based question.

72. Incomplete Newton's disc is given below. Complete the disc to show the seven spectral colours in correct order.

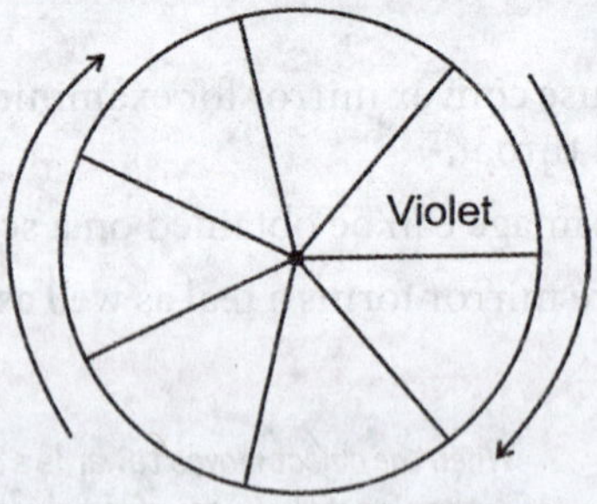

U

PROGRESS CHECK

Check your score! If your score is

> 95%	EXCELLENT !	- Move on to the next chapter. You have mastered this chapter. Concepts are certainly on your fingertips.
95-85%	VERY GOOD !	- Revise once more thoroughly. Recognise your mistakes and work on them. You will master this chapter.
84-75%	GOOD!	- Work on your weak areas, master them and come back to this chapter in a few days.
74-65%	MEDIOCRE!	- Understand your weak areas and work on strengthening your concepts. Devote more time to master this chapter.
< 65%	NOT SATISFACTORY!	- This is where you fall behind from scoring well. Give special attention to this chapter. Work on clearing concepts and common errors.

NCERT Exemplar Problems

This section contains MCQs of **'NCERT Exemplar Problems'** Book.

1. Boojho and Paheli were given one mirror each by their teacher. Boojho found his image to be erect and of the same size whereas Paheli found her image erect and smaller in size. This means that the mirrors of Boojho and Paheli are, respectively
   (a) plane mirror and concave mirror.
   (b) concave mirror and convex mirror.
   (c) plane mirror and convex mirror.
   (d) convex mirror and plane mirror.

2. Which of the following can be used to form a real image?
   (a) Concave mirror only.
   (b) Plane mirror only.
   (c) Convex mirror only.
   (d) Both concave and convex mirrors.

3. If an object is placed at a distance of 0.5 m in front of a plane mirror, the distance between the object and the image formed by the mirror will be
   (a) 2 m (b) 1 m
   (c) 0.5 m (d) 0.25 m

4. You are provided with a concave mirror, a convex mirror, a concave lens and a convex lens. To obtain an enlarged image of an object you can use either
   (a) concave mirror or convex mirror.
   (b) concave mirror or convex lens.
   (c) concave mirror or concave lens.
   (d) concave lens or convex lens.

5. A rainbow can be seen in the sky
   (a) when the sun is in front of you.
   (b) when the sun is behind you.
   (c) when the sun is overhead.
   (d) only at the time of sun rise.

6. An erect and enlarged image can be formed by
   (a) only a convex mirror.
   (b) only a concave mirror.
   (c) only a plane mirror.
   (d) both convex and concave mirrors.

7. You are provided with a convex mirror, a concave mirror, a convex lens and a concave lens. You can get an inverted image from
   (a) both concave lens and convex lens.
   (b) both concave mirror and convex mirror.
   (c) both concave mirror and convex lens.
   (d) both convex mirror and concave lens.

8. An image formed by a lens is erect. Such an image could be formed by a
   (a) convex lens provided the image is smaller than object.
   (b) concave lens provided the image is smaller than object.
   (c) concave lens provided the image is larger than object.
   (d) concave lens provided the image is of the same size.

A&R Corner

Directions : In the following questions, a statement of assertion is followed by a statement of reason. Mark the correct choice as :
(a) If both assertion and reason are true and reason is the correct explanation of assertion.
(b) If both assertion and reason are true but reason is not the correct explanation of assertion.
(c) If assertion is true but reason is false.
(d) If both assertion and reason are false.

1. **Assertion :** Light does not travel in the same direction in all the media.
   Reason : The speed of light does not change as it enters from one transparent medium to another.
2. **Assertion :** The mirrors used in search lights are concave spherical.
   Reason : In a concave spherical mirror the image formed is always virtual.
3. **Assertion :** Light travels faster in air than in glass.
   Reason : Glass is optical denser than air. U
4. **Assertion :** For observing traffic at back, the driver mirror used is convex mirror.
   Reason : A convex mirror has much larger field of view than a plane mirror.
5. **Assertion :** Mirror formula can be applied to a plane mirror.
   Reason : A plane mirror is a spherical mirror of infinite focal length. U
6. **Assertion :** It is not possible to see a virtual image by eye.
   Reason : The rays that seem to emanate from a virtual image in fact emanates from the image.
7. **Assertion :** If an object is placed at a distance of 5 cm from a plane mirror, the distance between the image and the mirror is 5 cm.
   Reason : The image formed by a plane mirror is as far behind the mirror as the object is in front of it.
8. **Assertion :** Virtual image are always erect.
   Reason : Virtual images are formed by diverging lenses only.
9. **Assertion :** When white light falls on a prism, the white light spilts into seven colours.
   Reason : The phenomenon of spiltting of white light into its seven constituent colours is called dispersion. R
10. **Assertion :** In the phenomenon of dispersion, the least deviated colour is red.
    Reason : Rainbow formation is due to the dispersion of light. U

Exam Corner

This section comprises of different types of questions:

- **Objective Type Questions :** These are **one mark** questions.
- **Very Short Answer Type Questions (VSA) :** These are **one mark** questions.
- **Short Answer Type Questions-I (SA-I) :** These are **two marks** questions.
- **Short Answer Type Questions-II (SA-II) :** These are **three marks** questions.
- **Long Answer Type Questions (LA) :** These are **five marks** questions.
- **Case Based Questions (CBQs) :** These are case study/passage based questions.

OBJECTIVE TYPE QUESTIONS

A. Select the correct option.

1. The focal length is defined as
   (a) the distance from the focal point to the centre of the lens
   (b) the distance from the image to the centre of the lens
   (c) the distance from the light source to the image
   (d) the distance from the object to the centre of the lens. **U**

2. Spherical mirrors are widely used as rear view mirrors in the automobiles. Why the word 'AMBULANCE' is differently painted in front of the hospital vans?
   (a) It is accurately readable in front of the rear view mirror of other vehicles.
   (b) It reads erratic in front of the rear view mirror of other vehicles.
   (c) Only for word art.
   (d) None of these

3. ____________ is not a luminous object.
   (a) Moon (b) Sun
   (c) Candle (d) Bulb **R**

4. The diagram given below shows magenta light shining through the prism and it splits into the colours *X* and *Y*. The two colours *X* and *Y* are ____________ respectively.

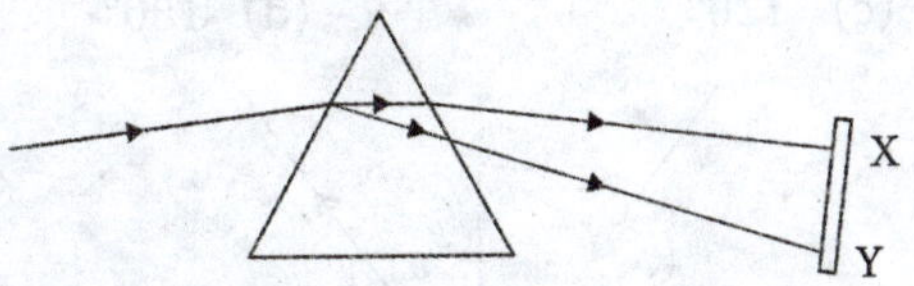

   (a) red and blue (b) blue and green
   (c) green and red (d) blue and red

5. The image of the teeth seen by a dentist while testing teeth is
   (a) erect and real
   (b) erect and virtual
   (c) inverted and virtual
   (d) inverted and real. **U**

B. State True (T) or False (F) for the given statements.

6. The three primary colours of white light are blue, green and red.
7. When the light reflects through an unpolished surface, it produces blurred image.
8. Refraction is a phenomenon in which light propagates from one point to another in the same medium.
9. A plane mirror is used in kaleidoscopes.
10. Focal length of a plane mirror is infinite.

C. Match the columns.

11.

Column I	Column II
(i) Used in street light	(P) Concave mirror
(ii) Image formed is upright and of a larger size	(Q) Convex mirror
(iii) Thicker in the middle	(R) Concave lens
(iv) Rainbow	(S) Convex lens
(v) Image formed can be virtual, smaller and in front of optical instrument	(T) Dispersion

An

VERY SHORT ANSWER TYPE QUESTIONS (VSA)

A. Write one word for each of the following:

12. Splitting of light into seven colours ____________ **R**

13. Bouncing back of light in the same medium after falling on a surface __________
14. Band of seven colours as seen in a rainbow __________
15. The part of eye that acts as a screen and is connected to the brain by the optic nerve __________ R
16. A ray of light falling on the reflecting surface __________

B. Circle the odd one out.

17. Rear view mirror, Vigilance mirror, Astronomical telescope, Side mirror of a car
18. For a plane mirror: Virtual, Always upright, Same size of image as the object, Size is different for different distances from mirror
19. Torches, Car headlights, Shaving mirror, Spectacles
20. Transparent medium, Speed of light, Direction of light, Shadow
21. Water droplets in air, Compact disc, Prism, Convex lens

SHORT ANSWER TYPE QUESTIONS-I (SA-I)

22. Why does dispersion occur?
23. *X* and *Y* are two point objects placed in front of a plane mirror.

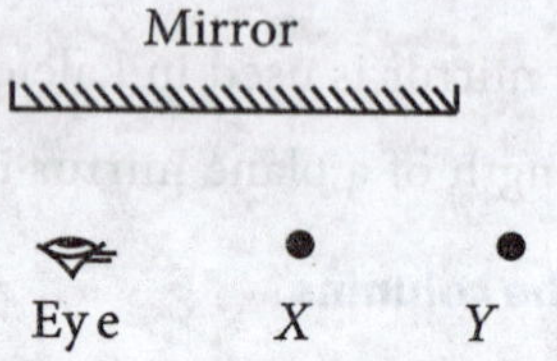

An

Find out whether the image of *X* in the plane mirror is visible to the eye or the image of *Y*?

24. Distinguish between a real image and a virtual image.
25. What is a convex mirror? What is the nature of image formed by it?
26. Why does a convex lens used as a magnifying glass? U

SHORT ANSWER TYPE QUESTIONS-II (SA-II)

27. If we see a red coloured cloth in blue light, it will appear black. Will it appear black if we see it in yellow light?
28. What is the reason behind the use of a convex rear view mirror in the car instead of a plane mirror?
29. Distinguish between regular and diffused reflection.
30. What are the characteristics of an image formed by a plane mirror?
31. What are the uses of concave and convex mirrors?

LONG ANSWER TYPE QUESTIONS (LA)

32. Explain the formation of image by a plane mirror with the help of ray diagrams.
33. Define the term "source of light" and its types.
34. Differentiate between a concave lens and a convex lens.
35. Give reason for each of the following:
    (i) A convex lens is said to have a real focus and a concave lens a virtual focus.
    (ii) Seas, lakes and rivers often appear less deeper than they actually are.
    (iii) We need a shiny surface for reflection.

CASE BASED QUESTIONS (CBQs)

Case I : Read the given passage and answer the following questions :

When light falls on a shiny smooth surface, it bounce back. This phenomenon is called reflection of light. There are two laws of reflection. First Law is, the angle incidence is equal to angle reflection. Second law is angle of incidence, angle of reflection and normal to the plane of incidence all lie in the same plane.

36. Which type of reflection takes place on the surface of newspaper?
    (a) regular reflection (b) diffused reflection
    (c) both (a) and (b) (d) none of these U
37. What is the angle of incidence and angle of reflection in the given figure?

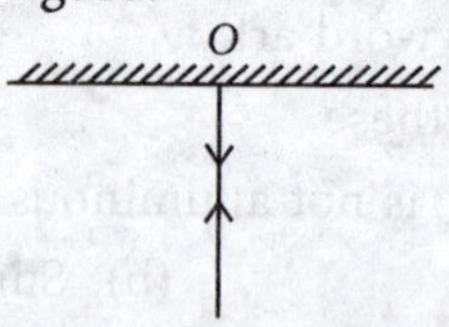

    (a) 360° (b) 180°
    (c) 90° (d) 0° U
38. If the angle of incidence is 60°, then the angle of reflection will be
    (a) 30° (b) 60°
    (c) 120° (d) 180°
39.

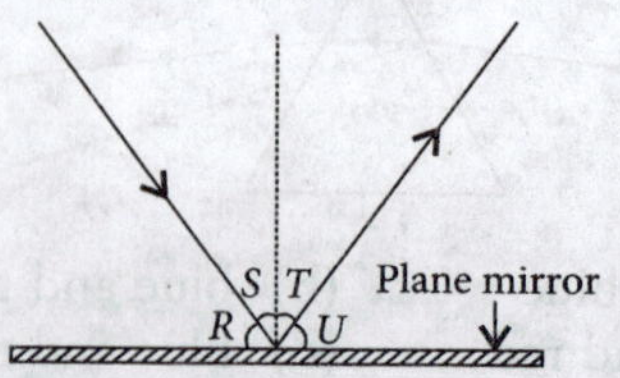

If $\angle R = 35°$, then $\angle T$ will be equal to

(a) 35° (b) 90°

(c) 55° (d) 53°. **Ap**

Case II : Read the given passage and answer the following questions :

The colour of a particular object depends on the colour of light reflected by the object when white light falling on it.

Blue, green and red are the three primary colours of white light. Other colours can be obtained by mixing the primary colours.

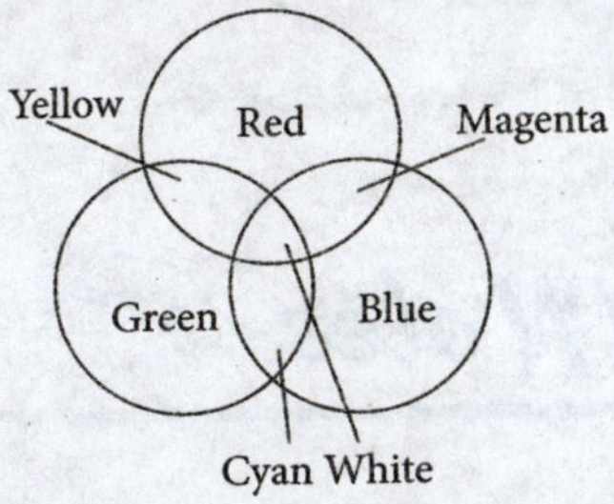

Red + Green = Yellow

Red + Blue = Magenta

Blue + Green = Cyan

Red + Blue + Green = White

40. Why rose flower appears red, when white light falls on it. What is the actual colour of the flower?

41. What colour of rose appears when blue light falls on it.

42. Out of the following: violet, red, Green and blue. Which is not a primary colour. **U**

43. What is the resultant colour when we mix red and green colour. **U**

ANSWER KEY

Practice Corner

1. (a) **2.** (d) **3.** (c) **4.** (c) **6.** (a) **7.** (c) **8.** (d) **9.** (d) **10.** (c) **11.** (a) **12.** (a)
13. (a) **14.** (b) **15.** image **16.** Reflection **17.** Mirror **18.** True **19.** True **20.** False **21.** True
22. True **23.** True **24.** True **25.** False **27.** (a) **28.** (c) **29.** True **30.** True **31.** False **32.** True **34.** (c)
35. (a) **36.** (c) **37.** (c) **38.** Convex, concave **39.** Concave **40.** real
41. Concave mirror **42.** False **43.** False **44.** True **45.** (b) **46.** (b) **47.** (c) **48.** (b) **49.** (d) **50.** Convex
51. Concave **52.** Convex **53.** Convex **54.** True **55.** True **56.** True **57.** False **58.** False **59.** False
60. Bi-convex **61.** (b) **62.** (c) **63.** (c) **64.** White **65.** Violet **66.** Back **67.** dispersion
68. Issac Newton **69.** False **70.** False **71.** False

NCERT Exemplar Problems

1. (c) **2.** (a) **3.** (b) **4.** (b) **5.** (b) **6.** (b) **7.** (c) **8.** (b)

A & R Corner

1. (c) **2.** (c) **3.** (a) **4.** (a) **5.** (a) **6.** (d) **7.** (a) **8.** (c) **9.** (b) **10.** (b)

Exam Corner

1. (a) **2.** (a) **3.** (a) **4.** (a) **5.** (b) **6.** True **7.** True **8.** False **9.** True **10.** True
11. (i)-Q; (ii)-P; (iii)-S; (iv)-T; (v)-R **12.** Dispersion **13.** Reflection **14.** Spectrum **15.** Retina
16. Incident ray **17.** Astronomical Telescope **19.** Spectacles **20.** Shadow **21.** Convex lens
36. (b) **37.** (d) **38.** (b) **39.** (c)

12 Forests : Our Lifeline

NCERT Notes

- A large area of uncultivated land completely covered with trees,shrubs and herbs , is called forest,which serves as **green lungs and purifying system** of earth.
- Every component of the forest is dependent on the other component. If we remove one component, say trees, all other components would be affected."
- **Forest is a dynamic living entity**' because it regenerates and grow and forest also have capacity to maintain itself.
- Forest provide basic necessity for living such as food , shelter, timber and medicines,etc.

> Forest provide medicinal plants such as *neem*, eucalyptus, *amla*, cassava. *Cinchona* trees provide the medicine called **Quinine** which is used for treating malaria disease.

12.1 Visit to A Forest

- Forest resources are very valuable as they form an integral part of the ecosystem.
- Destruction of forest results in increase of temperature, less precipitation, high soil erosion, flood, extinction of several species, imbalance in ecosystem, etc.

Forest Layer

- Due to variation in climate and weather different types of trees form different horizontal layer of forest. These are as follows:
  - The tallest and giant trees of forest forms a layer, called **emergent layer**. Being the uppermost layer, it receives most of the sunlight.
  - Branches of tall trees forms an umbrella like roof over the other plant in forest called **canopy**. Being the thickest layer this layer stops the much of sunlight and rain.

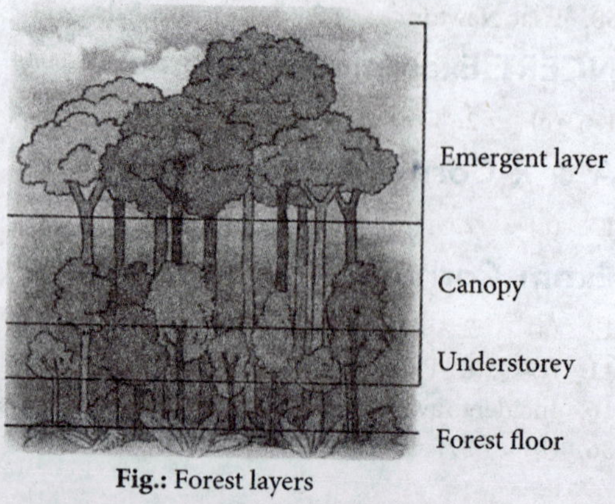

Fig.: Forest layers

- Crowns of different sizes of branches forms different horizontal layers in forest. This layer is called **understorey**. It grows under the shade of canopy. Many animals like boar, bison, jackals, porcupine, elephants live in the deeper areas of the forest.
- Dark coloured, damp layer of forest covered with dead and decaying as leaves, fruits, seeds, twigs and herbs, is called the **forest floor**. It is an moist, warm, spongy layer, helps in decomposition, seed germination, rain water absorption, etc. Numerous insects, spiders, squirrels, ants and various other small animals on the bark of the trees are present here.

Components of Forest

➤ Forest is made up of both living and non-living components. Living components includes three major groups. These are as follows:

- **Producers** – In forest organism which shows autotrophic mode of nutrition, *i.e.*, prepare their own food are known as **producers**, *e.g.*, green plants.
- **Consumers** – The living component of forest which shows heterotrophic mode of nutrition, (they depends on others for their food,) are known as **consumers** *e.g.*, herbivores,carnivores and omnivores.
- **Saprotrophs** – Saprotroph (decomposers) are consumers which breaks down the complex dead and decaying organic matter to dark coloured substance called **humus** *e.g*, fungus (tiny mushrooms) and some microorganism. This process is called decomposition.
- Presence of humus ensures that the nutrients of the dead plants and animals are released into the soil. In this way, the nutrients are cycled. So, nothing goes waste in a forest.

Producers	Consumers	Decomposers
Make their own food	Eat other organisms for food	Break down dead remains of plants and animals.

- The position that an organism occupies in a food chain is called **trophic level**.
- Producers (autotrophs) or green plants constitute the first trophic level of a food chain. Producers convert the solar energy into chemical energy of food by the process of photosynthesis.
- Decomposers operate at all trophic levels of food chain. Decomposers feed on dead remains of plants and animals. They act as recyclers and serve very useful for maintaining the balance of nutrients in the soil.
- Scavengers are animals that consume dead animals and help in keeping the environment clean. Example - crow, jackal, hyena, vulture, etc.

Food Chain

➤ **Food chain** is a simple representation of the flow of energy from producers to consumers, and to decomposers. Sometimes in a food chain predator act as a prey.

➤ It tells who eats what in the environment. **Sun is the ultimate source of energy in a food chain.**

Fig.: Food chain

Food web a network of inter-connecting food chains in a habitat.

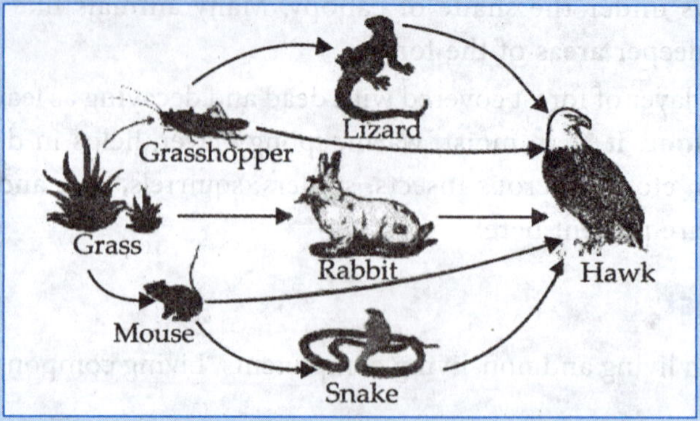

Fig.: Food web

Importance of Forest

- The dense bushes and the tall grass provide animals with the food and shelter.
- Rain water gets stored in the forest soil and seeps down by root system, which is absorbed by plant and further evaporates during transpiration as water vapours.
- Water vapours helps in cooling of surrounding, regulation of water cycle, controlling the flood and water streams maintenance.
- Green plants perform **photosynthesis**. In this process plant consume CO_2 and purifies the air, and provide oxygen for respiraton of other living organism, this creates balance of oxygen and carbon dioxide in the atmosphere. That is why forests are called **green lungs**.
- In forests roots of plants binds with the soil and provide stability, which prevent soil erosion.
- Many wooden items like plywood, fuel wood, boxes, paper, matchsticks, furniture, gum, oils, spices, fodder for animals and medicinal plants are some products that we get from the forest.
- The forest provides favourable conditions for seeds to germinate and develop into seedlings and is home to various animals.

Fig.: Timber

Fig.: Spices

Interdependence Between Animal and Plants

- Plants provide greater opportunities for fodder and shelter, while wide varieties of animal helps in seed dispersal, pollination and regeneration of forest.
- Carbon dioxide and oxygen balance is also stabilised by plants and animals.
- Tribe people depend on the forests. The forest provides them with food, shelter, water and medicines. They have traditional knowledge about many medicinal plants in the forest.
- Animal dung also provides nutrients to the seedlings for their growth.

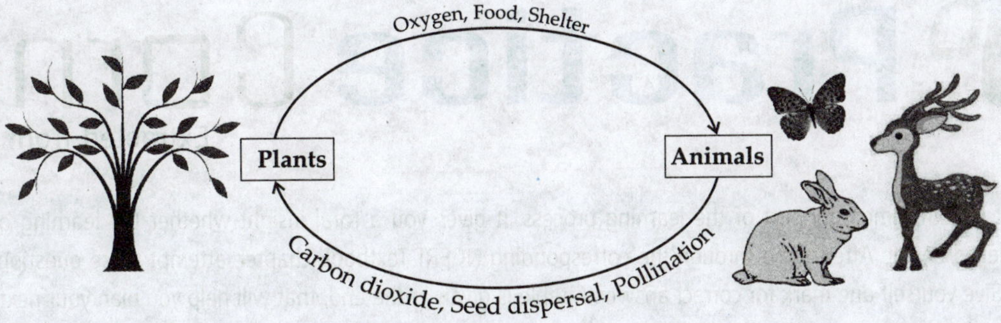

Fig.: Interdependence of plants and animals

Seeping of Rainwater in Forest

- Plants absorbs water from their roots and release water vapour into the air through transpiration, the evaporation further leads to clouds formation and rain. Rainwater water does not stagnate in the forest it seeps down in the ground.
- Forest also acts as a natural absorber of rainwater and allows it to seep. It helps in the maintaining the water table through out the year.

Deforestation: Causes, Effect and Prevention

- Permanent destruction of trees in a forest is called deforestation. Deforestation is cutting down of trees on the large-scale.
- One of the major cause for deforestation is increasing human population,which leads to increase in demand and human activities in forest area.
- Natural disasters such as volcanic eruption, storm, lightning and forest fire also leads to deforestation.
- Roots of trees normally bind the soil, but in their absence the soil is washed away or eroded by air and water.
- Forest keeps their surrounding cool by lowering the amount of carbon dioxide. If forests disappear, the amount of carbon dioxide will increase and resulting in the increase of earth's temperature. So, deforestation will endanger our life and environment.

Fig.: Deforestation

- **Greenhouse effect** is the trapping of solar radiations which enter into the earth's surface by greenhouse gases such as carbon dioxide, methane, carbon monoxide, sulphur dioxide, etc.
- On large-scale planting of trees is called **afforestation**. It helps to save the environment from the bad effect of deforestation.
- Desertification is caused due to **deforestation**. The Sahara desert once used to be a lush green forest, became a desert as a result of extensive deforestation.

Forest Conservation

We can conserve forest by following ways –

- By reducing the rate of deforestation
- By controling the forest fire.
- By utilising forest resources in a controlled manner.

Practice Corner

Extracted from NCERT

Assessment is complementary part of the learning process. It gives you a total insight whether the learning outcomes have been achieved or not. After going through the corresponding NCERT Textbook chapter, attempt these questions in exam like environment. Give yourself one mark for correct answer. A table is given at the end, that will help you plan your next step.

All the Best!

12.1 Visit to A Forest

NCERT Page 142-152

A. Select the correct option.

1. Which of the following statements are correct regarding forest?
   (i) It serves as green lungs.
   (ii) It influences climate, water cycle and air quality.
   (iii) It is a cause of soil erosion.
   (iv) It is home for plants and animals.
   (a) (i) and (iv) (b) (i), (iii) and (iv)
   (c) (i), (ii) and (iv) (d) (ii) and (iii) An

2. ________ is the branchy part of a tree above the stem.
   (a) Canopy (b) Crown
   (c) Understorey (d) Forest floor R

3. Study the food chain given below.

   Here, the population of wolf will increase due to
   (i) decrease in population of tigers.
   (ii) increase in population of squirrels.
   (iii) increase in population of plants.
   (a) Only (i) (b) Only (ii)
   (c) (i) and (ii) (d) (i), (ii) and (iii) An

4. Forests are not responsible for
   (a) providing home for many animals and plants.
   (b) providing oxygen for respiration.
   (c) providing medicinal plants.
   (d) causing floods and droughts. U

5. ________ convert dead plants and animals into a dark-coloured substance called humus.
   (a) Autotrophs (b) Heterotrophs
   (c) Saprotrophs (d) Producers R

6. Which of the following is a consequence of deforestation?
   (i) Decreased rainfall
   (ii) Decrease in carbon dioxide amount in air
   (iii) Soil erosion
   (iv) Floods and droughts
   (a) (i) and (ii)
   (b) (i), (ii) and (iv)
   (c) (i), (iii) and (iv)
   (d) (i), (ii) and (iii) An

7. Select the incorrect statements.
   (i) Plants provide food and shelter only to animals.
   (ii) Plants replenish the air with carbon dioxide.
   (iii) Animals disperse seeds of some plants.
   (iv) Plants provide us timber, honey, wax, gum, medicines, etc.
   (a) (i), (ii) and (iii) (b) (ii), (iii) and (iv)
   (c) (i) and (ii) (d) (iii) and (iv) An

8. In a forest, the vegetation that grow under shade of the tall trees is known as __I__ and the branchy part of the forest trees above the stem is known as __II__.

	I	II
(a)	understorey,	crown
(b)	canopy,	crown
(c)	forest floor,	canopy
(d)	understorey,	crown

R

9. Given below are different shapes of crown of some trees.

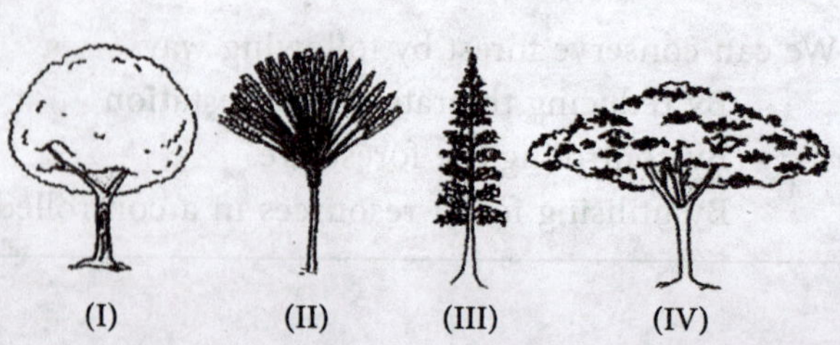

Which of the above trees would be most suitable for growing along a walkway that gets heated in the daytime due to bright sunlight.

(a) (I) (b) (II)

(c) (III) (d) (IV) An

10. Match the columns and select the correct option.

Column - I	Column - II
(i) Herbivores	A. Bacteria and fungi
(ii) Carnivores	B. Green plants
(iii) Producers	C. Wolf and lion
(iv) Decomposers	D. Deer and buffalo

(a) (i) – B, (ii) – D, (iii) – C, (iv) – A

(b) (i) – D, (ii) – C, (iii) – B, (iv) – A

(c) (i) – D, (ii) – A, (iii) – B, (iv) – C

(d) (i) – C, (ii) – D, (iii) – A, (iv) – B U

11. The branches of tall trees that look like an umbrella shaped roof over the other plants. This is known as

(a) crown (b) canopy

(c) understorey (d) forest floor. R

12. Which of the following statements is correct?

(a) The dead and decaying matter on a forest floor feels moist and warm.

(b) Producers are unable to synthesize their own food.

(c) Food chains exist independently in a forest.

(d) Cutting down of trees on Large-scale is called afforestation. An

B. State True (T) or False (F) for the given statements.

13. Many food chains independently without linking exist in forest.

14. Forests protect the soil from erosion.

15. Forests act as a natural absorber of rainwater.

16. Forests cause floods as they help in bringing heavy rainfall.

17. Vegetation that grows under the shade of tall trees is called crown.

18. Every components of the forest is dependent on each other.

19. In the absence of trees, the amount of carbon dioxide in air will decrease.

20. Noise pollution is more in the places near the forest.

21. The canopy layer of forests intercepts the flow of rain.

22. Larger number of herbivores means decreased availability of food for carnivores.

C. Fill in the blanks.

23. ____________ are microorganisms that convert dead plants and animals into humus.

24. ____________ is the branches of tall trees over the other plants in the forest.

25. ____________ form the lowest layer in understoreys.

26. Animals help in the process of seed ____________.

27. All food chains are ____________ in forest ecosystem.

28. Forests protect ____________ and provide ____________ to a large number of animals.

29. ____________ maintain the balance of oxygen and carbon dioxide in the atmosphere.

30. ____________ in the forest are enrich by decaying leaves and animal droppings.

31. Plants release oxygen during the process of ____________.

32. Decomposers, such as ____________ and ____________ help in recycling of nutrients.

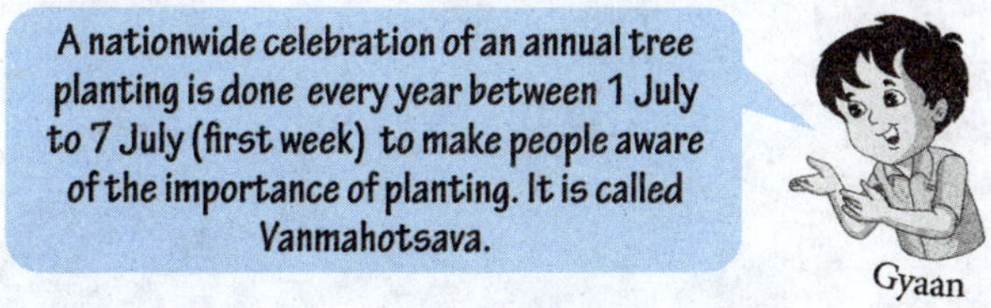

D. Passage based question.

33. Decomposers play an important role in ___(i)___ of nutrients. Bacteria and ___(ii)___ are the examples of decomposers that break down the dead remains of plants and animals. Through this process, nutrients are released into the ___(iii)___ from where they are absorbed by the ___(iv)___ of the plants.

E. Figure based question

34. Observe the image carefully. Describe the inter-relationship between the different components of a forest with the help of labellings.

35. Study the given food chain operating in a crop field and answer questions that follow.

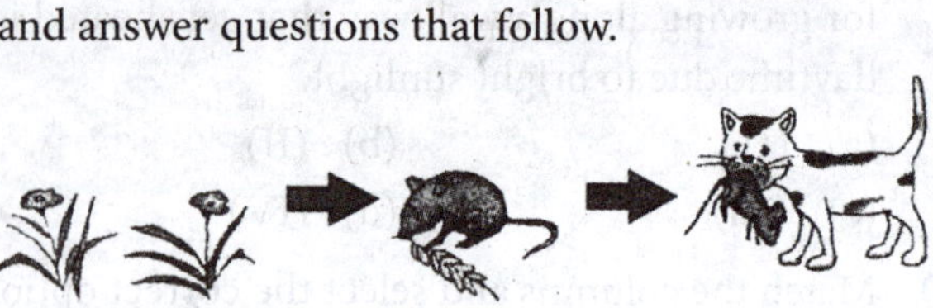

(a) How will drought affect the mice living in the region?

(b) Will it also affect the wild cats living in the region?

PROGRESS CHECK

Check your score! If your score is

> 95%	EXCELLENT !	- Move on to the next chapter. You have mastered this chapter. Concepts are certainly on your fingertips.
95-85%	VERY GOOD !	- Revise once more thoroughly. Recognise your mistakes and work on them. You will master this chapter.
84-75%	GOOD!	- Work on your weak areas, master them and come back to this chapter in a few days.
74-65%	MEDIOCRE!	- Understand your weak areas and work on strengthening your concepts. Devote more time to master this chapter.
< 65%	NOT SATISFACTORY!	- This is where you fall behind from scoring well. Give special attention to this chapter. Work on clearing concepts and common errors.

NCERT Exemplar Problems

This section contains MCQs of **'NCERT Exemplar Problems'** Book.

1. Which of the following serve as green lungs?
(a) Green pigment of the plants
(b) Forests
(c) Kitchen gardens
(d) Greenhouse gases

2. Boojho visited a forest near his town with his classmates and his teacher. As they were entering the forest, their class teacher told them not to make noise in the forest as noise could disturb
(a) birds
(b) animals
(c) both birds and animals
(d) plants.

3. Which among the following forest animals is the smallest?
(a) Fox (b) Boar
(c) Bison (d) Porcupine

4. Which of the following has the strongest stem?
(a) A tree (b) A creeper
(c) A climber (d) A bush

5. Which of the following is not prepared from the wood obtained from forest?
(a) Paper (b) Thermocol
(c) Matchsticks (d) Plywood

6. Which of the following is not the name of a tree?
(a) Teak (b) Sal
(c) Porcupine (d) *Kachnar*

7. Pick the option which gives the names of a tree and an animal, respectively from the following.
(a) *Semal*, hornbill
(b) Sal, *khair*
(c) *Chinkara*, blue bull
(d) *Neem*, *palash*

8. Which of the following products is not obtained from a forest?
(a) Honey (b) Catechu
(c) Gum (d) Ginger

9. The branchy part of a tree above the stem is known as
(a) crown (b) canopy
(c) sapling (d) humus.

10. Forests are not responsible for
(a) providing medicinal plants
(b) maintaining the flow of water into the streams
(c) creating flood conditions
(d) absorbing rainwater and maintaining water table.

A&R Corner

Directions : In the following questions, a statement of assertion is followed by a statement of reason. Mark the correct choice as :
(a) If both assertion and reason are true and reason is the correct explanation of assertion.
(b) If both assertion and reason are true but reason is not the correct explanation of assertion.
(c) If assertion is true but reason is false.
(d) If both assertion and reason are false.

1. **Assertion :** Many food chains of the forest are linked together and form a food web.
Reason : Disturbance in one food chain can affects the other food chain in a food web.

2. **Assertion :** If the forests disappear, the earth's temperature will increase.
Reason : In the absence of trees the amount of carbon dioxide will increase that will eventually increase the temperature. An

3. **Assertion :** Plants take up carbon dioxide for respiration.
Reason : Oxygen is required by plants for photosynthesis.

4. **Assertion :** Humus is a product of decomposition of dead plant and animal tissues.
Reason : Fungi are the only responsible for production of humus.

5. **Assertion :** Deforestation promotes soil erosion.
Reason : Without trees, the soil get exposed to the surface water and wind, so gets eroded.

6. **Assertion :** Trees check air pollution.
Reason : Trees absorb CO_2 which is a chief air pollutant. U

7. **Assertion :** The branchy part of a tree above stem is known as crown.
Reason : The closed canopy and many layers of vegetation slow down the speed of raindrops.

8. **Assertion :** Tribals living in forests have traditional knowledge about many medicinal plants.
Reason : Forests provide home to tribals who use forests as a source of medicinal plants. U

9. **Assertion :** The canopy is the thickest layer of forest.
Reason : Canopy has thick foliage of trees.

10. **Assertion :** The animals can disperse the seeds of certain plants.
Reason : Animals have limited role in the growth and regeneration of forest.

11. **Assertion :** Greater the variety of plants in a forest the more will be the population of herbivores.
Reason : Greater variety of plants in a forest provides greater opportunities for food and habitat for organisms. Ap

12. **Assertion :** Forests play a great role in reduction of noise pollution.
Reason : Trees in the forests absorb sound of the nearby areas.

13. **Assertion :** Forests are called as green lungs.
Reason : Forests help to maintain a balance between O_2 and CO_2 in the atmosphere.

14. **Assertion :** Forests floor receives minimal levels of sunlight.
Reason : The forest floor consist of only decaying matter which are wet and cool.

15. **Assertion :** Plants in the forests absorb water from the soil and release excess water which gets evaporated into the air by the process of transpiration.
Reason : The transpired water in the air has no role in cloud formation and rainfall. An

Exam Corner

This section comprises of different types of questions:

- **Objective Type Questions :** These are **one mark** questions.
- **Very Short Answer Type Questions (VSA) :** These are **one mark** questions.
- **Short Answer Type Questions-I (SA-I) :** These are **two marks** questions.
- **Short Answer Type Questions-II (SA-II) :** These are **three marks** questions.
- **Long Answer Type Questions (LA) :** These are **five marks** questions.
- **Case Based Questions (CBQs) :** These are case study/passage based questions.

OBJECTIVE TYPE QUESTIONS

A. Select the correct option.

1. Which of the following represents a correct food chain?
(a) Grass → Mice → Insect → Rabbit
(b) Mice → Owl → Insect → Grain
(c) Grain → Insect → Frog → Snake
(d) Owl → Mice → Insect → Grain
An

2. Select the incorrect statement(s).
(i) Only bacteria can help in the recycling of nutrients and are called as decomposers.
(ii) Decomposers can convert dead matter and wastes into nutrient rich humus.
(iii) Fungi can only decay food but cannot decompose dead matter.
(iv) Snails, termites and millipedes are decomposers.
(a) Only (iii)
(b) (i) and (iii)
(c) (i) and (iv)
(d) (i), (iii) and (iv)

3. ________ is not a way of conservation of forests.
(a) Deforestation
(b) Planned cultivation
(c) Afforestation
(d) Minimising overgrazing
R

4. Even after heavy rains, forests are not flooded because
(a) forests act as natural absorbers of rainwater
(b) raindrops do not hit the forest floor directly
(c) trees breathe in oxygen from atmosphere
(d) both (a) and (b)

5. Study the given flow chart.

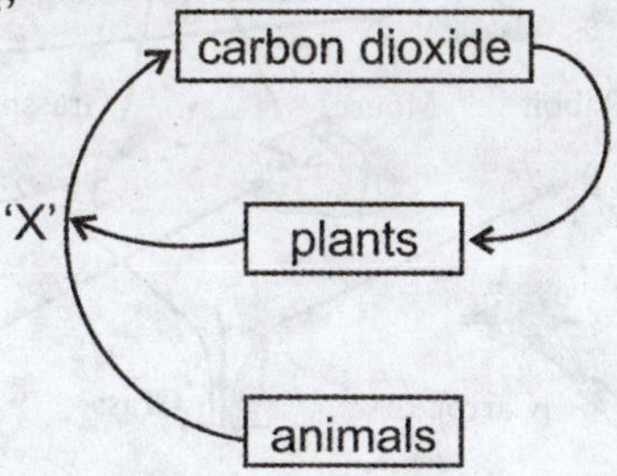

What is the name of process 'X' in the figure?
(a) Respiration
(b) Digestion
(c) Feeding
(d) Photosynthesis
U

6. Forest can prevent
(i) floods
(ii) soil erosion
(iii) decrease in the level of water table
(iv) deforestation.
(a) (i) and (ii) (b) (ii) and (iv)
(c) (i) and (iv) (d) (i), (ii) and (iii)

7. The understorey is formed by
(a) palms (b) shrubs
(c) grasses (d) Both (a) and (b)

8. One of these is not a forest product. Identify it.
(a) Latex (b) Timber
(c) Fuel (d) Plastics
U

9. Select the incorrect match.
(a) Crown – Branchy part of a tree
(b) Afforestation – Plantation of trees
(c) Soil erosion – Consequence of deforestation
(d) Producers – Second trophic level in a food chain.

10. In the following food chain, decomposers are represented by

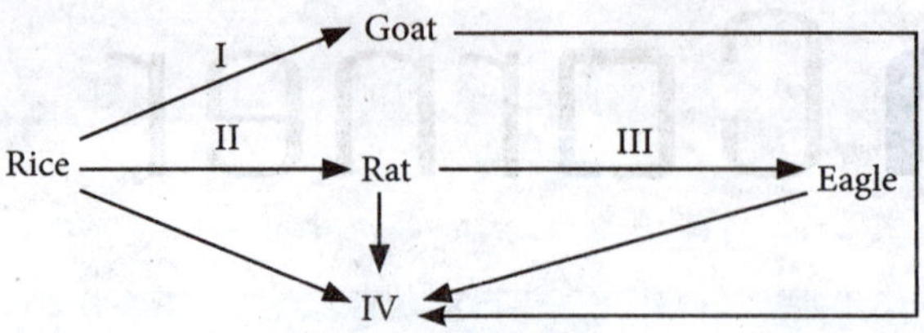

(a) I (b) II
(c) III (d) IV

Direction: (Question number 11 to 14). Study the given food web and answer the following questions

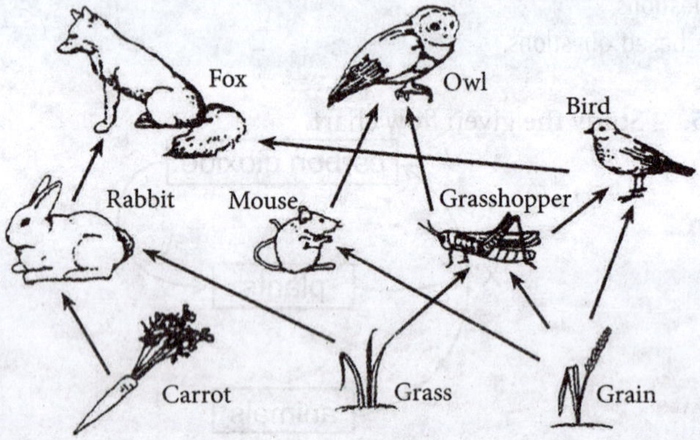

11. How many food chains are there in the given food web?
(a) 7 (b) 5
(c) 8 (d) 6 Ev

12. Owl and fox in the given food web represents
(a) primary consumers
(b) producers
(c) secondary consumers
(d) top consumers.

13. Rabbit and grasshopper represent ________ in the given food web.
(a) producers
(b) top consumers
(c) primary consumers
(d) secondary consumers

14. Grasshopper is a part of ________ food chains in the given food web.
(a) 4 (b) 5
(c) 3 (d) 2 Ev

15. Read the following statements.
- The tallest trees of the rainforest are present in this layer.
- Some of the trees grow as tall as 200 feet.
- These trees get lot of sunlight.

The above statements correspond to which of the following layers of forest?
(a) Emergent layer (b) Understorey
(c) Canopy (d) Forest floor

16. Forests are called nature's lungs because they
(a) release oxygen during photosynthesis
(b) take in carbon dioxide during photosynthesis
(c) produce food during photosynthesis
(d) both (a) and (b)

17. Select the correct match(es).
(i) Crown – Branching part of the tree above the trunk
(ii) Canopy – Covered with a layer of dead and decaying leaves
(iii) Forest floor – Looks like an umbrella from top
(iv) Understorey – Vegetation that grows under the shade of tall trees
(a) Only (iv) (b) (i) and (iv)
(c) (ii) and (iii) (d) (ii), (iii) and (iv)

18. Study the food chain given below.
Grass → Insects → Frog → Snake → Eagle
The population of frog will increase if,
(i) the population of snake decreases.
(ii) the population of eagle decreases.
(iii) the population of insects increases.
(a) (i) and (iii)
(b) (ii) and (iii)
(c) (i) and (ii)
(d) (i), (ii) and (iii) An

19. Select the correct statement.
(i) The emergent layer of tall trees get a lot of sunlight.
(ii) Canopy is the thickest forest layer which prevents most of the sunlight to enter into the forest.
(iii) Animals found in understorey include frogs, lizards, snakes, monkeys, butterflies etc.
(iv) If one animal is removed from the forest it does not affect others.
(a) (i) and (ii) (b) (ii) and (iii)
(c) (i), (ii) and (iii) (d) (i), (ii) and (iv)

20. In which forest layers shrubs and herbs grow?
(a) Emergent (b) Canopy
(c) Understorey (d) Forest floor

21. In the absence of forests, the amount of (i) in air will increase, resulting in an (ii) of earth's temperature.
Select the correct option for (i) and (ii).
(a) (i) oxygen (ii) increase
(b) (i) oxygen (ii) decrease
(c) (i) carbon dioxide (ii) increase
(d) (i) carbon dioxide (ii) decrease

22. A food chain consists of
(a) producers (b) consumers
(c) decomposers (d) all of these.

23. Which of the following is not a decomposer?
(a) Fungi (b) Bacteria
(c) Earthworm (d) Vulture

24. Which of the following statements is not correct?
(a) Forests protect the soil erosion.
(b) Plants and animals in a forest are not dependent on one another.
(c) Forests influence the climate and water cycle.
(d) Soil helps forests to grow and regenerate.

25. Select the incorrect match out of the following.
(a) Decomposers – Consumers that feed on dead remains of plants and animals
(b) Canopy – Vegetation that grows under the shade of tall trees
(c) Forest floor – Covered with a layer of dead and decaying leaves
(d) Afforestation – Practice of renewing a forest by planting trees

26. Which of the following is representing a correct food chain?
(a) Rabbit → Grass → Fox → Lion
(b) Grass → Rabbit → Fox → Lion
(c) Lion → Fox → Rabbit → Grass
(d) Rabbit → Lion → Fox → Grass

27. Forests are called as 'lungs of nature' because
(a) they increase carbon dioxide concentration in the atmosphere.
(b) they decrease oxygen level in the atmosphere.
(c) they maintain the balance of oxygen and carbon dioxide in the atmosphere.
(d) they increase the level of methane in the atmosphere.

28. The ultimate source of energy in nature is
(a) oxygen (b) carbon dioxide
(c) fossil fuel (d) sun.

29. Select the incorrect statements.
(i) Plants and animals do not depend on each other.
(ii) Humans are the only primary consumers in any food chain.
(iii) Climate is influenced by forests.
(iv) Plants do not obtain nutrients directly from animals.
(a) (i) and (ii)
(b) (ii) and (iv)
(c) (i), (ii) and (iii)
(d) (i), (ii) and (iv)

30. Select the correct match.
(a) Medicinal plant – Teak
(b) Primary consumer – Fox
(c) Deforestation – Flood
(d) Decomposer – Eagle

31. Which of the following combinations is the correct order according to the layers of a forest starting from the top?
(a) Canopy, understorey, emergent, forest floor
(b) Forest floor, canopy, emergent, understorey
(c) Emergent, canopy, understorey, forest floor
(d) Understorey, canopy, forest floor, emergent

32. Which of the following groups consists of a decomposer, a producer and a predator?
(a) Grass, goat, eagle
(b) Mushroom, sugarcane, lizard
(c) Papaya plant, caterpillar, bird
(d) Mushroom, deer, earthworm

B. Match the columns.

33.

	Column I		Column I
1.	Large scale plantation of trees	A.	Crown
2.	Represents the flow of energy in nature	B.	Food chain
3.	Indiscriminate cutting down of trees	C.	Deforestation
4.	The branchy part of a tree above the stem	D.	Canopy
5.	Dense roof of trees formed by the branches	E	Understorey
6.	Layer of vegetation that grows under canopy	F	Afforestation

	1	2	3	4	5	6
(a)	A	C	B	F	D	E
(b)	F	B	C	A	D	E
(c)	B	A	D	C	E	F
(d)	A	C	B	F	D	E

C. Figure based question.

34. Three soil samples were taken in three different vessels A, B and C. In all the vessels, plantlets were grown (maximum number in A and least in C). All the vessels were kept in a tilted position as shown in the figure. Water was slowly poured at the top in each vessel. The flowing water was then collected from the other end of each vessel.

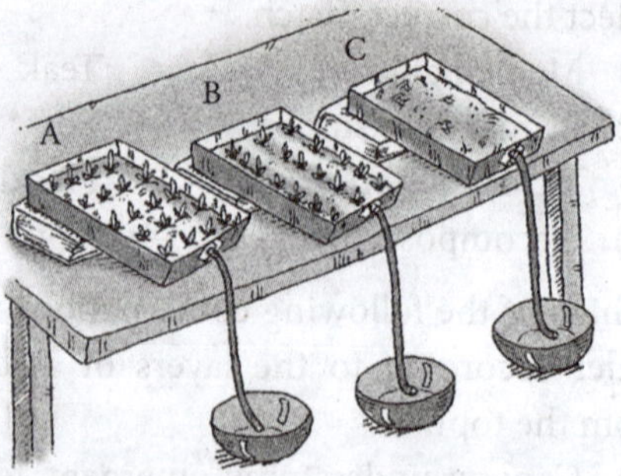

(a) From which vessel the removal of top layer of soil by the flowing water is the most? Give reason for your answer. An
(b) Which process is demonstrated with this experiment? Describe the process.
(c) What does this experiment tells you about the importance of forests?

D. Fill in the blanks.

35. A ________ shows the type of food eaten by an organism and the interrelationship between different plants and animals for food in a certain habitat.
36. ________ are animals that eat only plants.
37. ________ is the layer of forest which stops sunlight and rain by its thick foliage.
38. Crow, jackal and hyena are examples of ________. U
39. ________ can lead to an increase in the level of ________ in the atmosphere which results in an increase in global temperature.
40. Forests also act as natural absorber of ________ and allow it to seep into the ground.
41. Carbon dioxide, ________ and ________ are some greenhouse gases.
42. Herbivores are ________ consumers and carnivores are ________ consumers.
43. The position that an organism occupies in a food chain is called ________.
44. Removal of top fertile layer of soil by wind or rain is called ________.
45. ________ are animals that eat both plants and animals.
46. ________ are called ________ as they can produce their own food. R
47. ________ prevents soil erosion.
48. ________ is a dark layer of dead and decayed plant and animal remains that forms a part of the soil.
49. A ________ is made up of many interconnected food chains.
50. The various components of the forest are ________ on each other.
51. ________ are primary consumers while ________ are secondary consumers.
52. In a forest, trees form the uppermost layer, followed by ________, and the ________ form the lowest layer of vegetation.
53. ________ is the process by which seeds get scattered over a wide area.
54. Forests influence ________, ________ and air quality.

VERY SHORT ANSWER TYPE QUESTIONS (VSA)

A. Write two examples for each of the following:

55. Medicinal plants
________, ________ U
56. Products obtained from forests
________, ________
57. Decomposers ________, ________
58. Carnivores found in forest
________, ________
59. Herbivores found in forest
________, ________

B. Arrange the following organisms in the correct order to form food chain.

60. Grains, Hen, Cat : ________ → ________ → ________
61. Mouse, Grains, Owl : ________ → ________ → ________
62. Snake, Hawk, Rabbit, Carrot : → ________ → ________ → ________
63. Tiger, Deer, Grass, Vulture : → ________ → ________ → ________

SHORT ANSWER TYPE QUESTIONS-I (SA-I)

64. Write the difference between canopy and understorey. U
65. What are decomposers?
66. Write the difference between afforestation and deforestation.

67. What do you understand by the terms food chain and food web?

68. Define trophic level. R

SHORT ANSWER TYPE QUESTIONS-II (SA-II)

69. How forest maintains the water table and also prevents flood?

70. Differentiate between producers and consumers.

71. A forest is a 'dynamic living entity'. Justify this statement. An

72. How animals help to regenerate forests?

LONG ANSWER TYPE QUESTIONS (LA)

73. Write down the consequences of deforestation.

74. Describe the forest layers in a rainforest.

75. Why forests are important for us? An

76. Give reason for the following statements
(a) Plants are called producers.
(b) Forests are called green lungs.
(c) Carbon dioxide is called greenhouse gas.

CASE BASED QUESTIONS (CBQS)

Case I : Read the given passage and answer the following questions :

Due to the requirement of land for housing and industrial development many forests have been cleared till now. Massive clearing of forests have disastrous effects.

77. What has caused the transformation of A to B?
(a) Afforestation (b) Deforestation
(c) Regeneration (d) Soil erosion

78. The population of animals in B as compared to A will
(a) increases
(b) decreases
(c) remain unchanged
(d) initially increase then decrease.

79. Soil in figure B will be prone to ________.
(a) erosion (b) regeneration
(c) mineralisation (d) humification U

80. Figure C is indicating ________.
(a) cyclone (b) flood
(c) landslide (d) drought

81. What will happen to carbon dioxide concentration in the atmosphere from A to B?
(a) Increases
(b) Decreases
(c) It will initially decrease then increase
(d) Neither increases nor decreases

Case II : Read the given passage and answer the following questions :

In a biology class, students were taught about how different organisms are related to each other. A sequence of transfer of energy occurs when one organism is consumed by another organism.

82. Figure 'X' represents ________.
(a) food chain (b) transpiration
(c) food web (d) photosynthesis

83. Which of the following is/are autotrophs in 'X'?
(a) Grass (b) Grasshopper
(c) Frog and Snake (d) Eagle An

84. What will happen when frog is removed from the given situation?
(a) Population of grasshopper will increase
(b) Population of snake will decrease
(c) Population of grass will increase
(d) Both (a) and (b)

85. Which of the following are primary and secondary consumers respectively?
(a) Grass and frog
(b) Frog and snake
(c) Snake and eagle
(d) Grasshopper and frog U

86. Name the organism(s) which is/are predator as well as prey.

Case III : Read the given passage and answer the following questions :

A forest is a large uncultivated land area densely covered with various types of trees, herbs, shrubs, climbers, creepers, etc. Students were taken for a forest trip so that they can learn about different layers of forest. As a class assignment they were asked to identify different forest layers depending upon their features/description.

87. Identify layers A, B, C and D.
(a) A-Emergent, B-Canopy, C-Understorey, D-Forest Floor
(b) A-Canopy, B-Emergent, C-Understorey, D-Forest Floor
(c) A-Forest Floor, B-Emergent, C-Understorey, D-Canopy
(d) A-Canopy, B-Emergent, C-Understorey, D-Forest Floor

88. In which of the following layers maximum photosynthesis occurs?
(a) A (b) B
(c) C (d) D

89. Choose the incorrect option.
(a) Layer D receives minimum sunlight.
(b) Layer C comprise of growth of shrubs, young trees, palms and woody plants.
(c) Layer B is the thickest forest layer due to thick foliage.
(d) Only birds can be found in layer A.

90. Describe the characteristic feature of layer D. Name two insects present in layer D.

ANSWER KEY

Practice Corner

1. (c) **2.** (b) **3.** (d) **4.** (d) **5.** (c) **6.** (c) **7.** (c) **8.** (a) **9.** (d) **10.** (b)
11. (b) **12.** (a) **13.** False **14.** True **15** True **16.** False **17.** False **18.** True **19.** False **20.** False
21. True **22.** False **23.** Decomposers **24.** Canopy **25.** Herbs **26.** dispersal **27.** linked
28. soil, shelter **29.** Forests **30.** Soil **31.** photosynthesis **32.** bacteria, fungi
33. (i) recycling (ii) fungi (iii) soil (iv) roots

NCERT Exemplar Problems

1. (b) **2.** (c) **3.** (d) **4.** (a) **5.** (b) **6.** (c) **7.** (a) **8.** (d) **9.** (a) **10.** (c)

A & R Corner

1. (a) **2.** (a) **3.** (d) **4.** (c) **5.** (a) **6.** (a) **7.** (b) **8.** (a) **9.** (a) **10.** (c)
11. (a) **12.** (a) **13.** (a) **14.** (c) **15.** (c)

Exam Corner

1. (c) **2.** (d) **3.** (a) **4.** (d) **5.** (a) **6.** (d) **7.** (d) **8.** (d) **9.** (d) **10.** (d)
11. (c) **12.** (d) **13.** (c) **14.** (a) **15.** (a) **16.** (d) **17.** (b) **18.** (a) **19.** (c) **20.** (c)
21. (c) **22.** (d) **23.** (d) **24.** (b) **25.** (b) **26.** (b) **27.** (c) **28.** (d) **29.** (d) **30.** (c)
31. (c) **32.** (b) **33.** (b) **35.** food chain **36.** Herbivores **37.** Canopy **38.** Scavengers
39. Deforestation, carbon dioxide **40.** rainwater **41.** methane, nitrous oxide **42.** primary, secondary
43. trophic level **44.** soil erosion **45.** Omnivores **46.** Green plants, producers **47.** Forest **48.** Humus
49. food web **50.** dependent **51.** Herbivores, carnivores **52.** shrubs, herbs **53.** Seed dispersal
54. climate, watercycle **55.** Neem, Tulsi **56.** Timber, Latex **57.** Bacteria, Fungi **58.** Lion, Wolf
59. Deer, Goat **60.** Grains → Hen → Cat **61.** Grains → Mouse → Owl **62.** Carrot → Rabbit → Snake → Hawk
63. Grass → Deer → Tiger → Vulture **77.** (b) **78.** (b) **79.** (a) **80.** (b) **81.** (a) **82.** (a)
83. (a) **84.** (d) **85.** (d) **87.** (a) **88.** (a) **89.** (d)

13 Wastewater Story

NCERT Notes

- The water that appears foamy, black-brown in colour or mixed with oil is called **wastewater**.
- Main sources of wastewater at home are washing, brushing teeth, bathing, flushing toilet, etc.
- This wastewater should be reused by removing pollutants from it.

13.1 Water, Our Lifeline

- One of the basic needs of a human being is the availability of clean water.
- Although clean water is not available for everyone, billions of people around the world are forced to consume water unsafe for drinking due to no access of clean drinking water.
- Consumption of dirty water causes large number of water related diseases and, in some cases, even death.
- Releasing wastewater directly into the water bodies without treatment causes pollution.
- Women walk for several kilometres just to collect clean water.
- Requirement of fresh water is increasing due to industrial development, population growth, pollution, etc.
- On 22nd march 2005, the general assembly of United Nations declared 2005-2015 as the international decade for action on "Water for life".
- During this decade, lot of effort were made with aim to reduce the number of people who drink unsafe water to half.
- Process of removing the pollutants before it can be reused or enters a water body is known as cleaning of water.
- Generally, treatment of wastewater is known as "**Sewage Treatment**".

13.2 What is Sewage?

- Wastewater released by homes, industries, hospitals, etc. and rainwater that washes of roads and street is known as sewage.
- Sewage is mostly water that has dissolved and suspended impurities in it.

+ Sewage contains many impurities called contaminants. Many disease-causing microorganisms such as *Entamoeba histolytica* which causes dysentery, is present in sewage.

Table : Contaminants of sewage

S.No.	Type of contaminants	Examples
(i)	Organic impurities	Human faeces, urea (urine), animal waste, kitchen waste, etc.
(ii)	Inorganic impurities	Nitrates, phosphates and metals
(iii)	Pathogenic microorganisms	*Vibrio cholera* that causes cholera, *Salmonella paratyphi* causes typhoid and protozoans which cause dysentery
(iv)	Nutrients	Compounds of phosphorous and nitrogen

13.3 Water Freshens Up-An Eventful Journey

- At most houses and buildings there are two types of pipes. One which brings clean water, while another that takes away the sewage.
- This network of pipes is called sewers, that transports the sewage from source, *i.e.*, houses and offices etc., to treatment plant.
- Sewers are linked to each other to form a network called **sewerage system**.
- Manholes are openings on the road surface located at every 50 m to 60 m in the sewerage that are covered with heavy cemented or metallic lids, which help to reach the underground sewerage for cleaning and maintenance.

\+ Sewers are of two types :

- **Sanitary sewers** which carry only domestic sewage. It can overflow during floods and there is also a risk of flood water contaminating drinking water supplies that can cause waterborne diseases.
- **Storm water sewers** which help in carrying run-offs from rain and melted snow.

Treatment of Polluted Water

To understand the process of wastewater treatment.

Materials required - A glass jar, orange peels or grass pieces, detergent, few drops of ink, water, test tubes, chlorine tablet, funnel, filter paper, beakers, sand and gravel.

Method -

- Fill the 3/4 of glass jar with water and add orange peels or grass pieces, detergent and few drops of ink.
- Cover the jar and shake it well and put the mixture in sun for at least two days.
- After two days, shake the jar and pour the mixture into the test tube. Label the tube as Sample 1.
- Use a mechanical stirrer or a mixer to stir the sample several times.
- Next day after aeration transfer the mixture into another test tube and label it as Sample 2.
- Take a piece of filter paper and fold it to form cone and place it in a funnel.
- Wet the filter paper with tap water.
- Put sand and fine gravel and medium gravel to form layers.
- Pour the sample 2 through the filter into beakers. Filter the liquid few times to get a clear water.
- Pour this liquid in another tube and label it as Sample 3.
- Pour the liquid in sample 3 in fourth test tube and add a chlorine tablet and mix the solution till it become clear and label the tube as Sample 4.

Observations - Sample 1 has bad odour whereas sample 2 has clear and odourless water. In sample 3 heavy objects like sand and grit are removed due to filtering. In sample 4, disinfected water is obtained.

13.4 Wastewater Treatment Plant (WWTP)

- Wastewater treatment involves three processes (i) **physical** process that removes physical objects, (ii) **chemical** process removes chemical matter and (iii) **biological** process removes organic matter from the wastewater.

- Treatment of wastewater in a WWTP involves the following stages:
- The first step of wastewater treatment is to pass the wastewater through bar screens, by which large solid materials such as cans, plastic bags, etc., are removed.
- Water then goes to a grit and sand removal tank where the speed of the incoming wastewater is decreased so that solid objects like sand, grit and stones settle down.
- Then water is allowed to settle in a large sedimentation tank that is sloped towards the middle, where faeces settle at bottom and are removed by a scrapper.
- The waste material which settles down at the bottom is known as sludge. Floatable solids like grease and oil are removed by skimmer.
- Water after treatment by skimmer emerging from sedimentation tank is called clarified water.
- Collected sludge is then transferred to a tank where it will be decomposed by the anaerobic bacteria and biogas is released.

Fig.: (A) Bar screens, (B) Grit and sand removal tank, (C) Sedimentation tank, (D) Aeration tank

- Aerobic bacteria are allowed to grow by pumping air into the clarified water.
- Aerobic bacteria consume organic matter, soaps, detergents, etc. from the clarified water.
- After few hours, the microbes settle at the bottom of the tank as activated sludge. Water is then removed from the top.
- Activated sludge contains around 97% water which is removed by sand drying beds or machines. Dried sludge is useful as manure.
- Treated water contains very low level of organic matter, and now it can be discharged into a sea, river or in the ground.
- Treated water is sometimes disinfected with chlorine and ozone before releasing into the nature.
- Water in river is cleaned by natural processes similar to that of wastewater treatment plant.

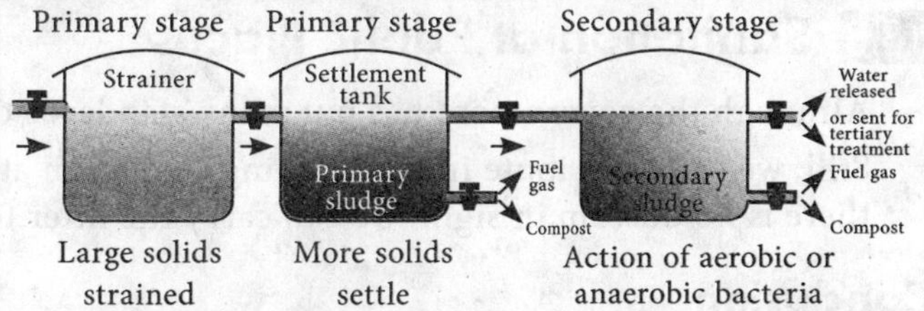

Sewage may go through two to three stages of treatment

- Eucalyptus trees can absorb excess wastewater rapidly and release pure water vapour into the atmosphere when grown alongside sewage ponds.

Become An Active Citizen

- Human activities generate a lot of waste, that affects us in several ways.
- Flies, mosquitoes and other insects breed on the open drains, during the rainy seasons the drain start to overflow, mud pools are also formed due to this.
- We should approach the gram panchayat or the municipality and enlighten them, to cover the open drains.
- If anyone is making the neighbourhood dirty, we can request them to think about other's health.

13.5 Better Housekeeping Practices

- One way to minimise the waste generation at the source is to manage what we release in the drain.
- Cooking oil and fats should be thrown in the dustbin and not in the drain as they can harden and block the pipes. Also, fats clog the soil pores and reduce their effectiveness in filtering water.
- Chemicals like medicines, paints, insecticides should not be thrown in the drain as they can kill the microbes involved in purifying the water.
- Sanitary towels, food remains, used tea-leaves, cotton, etc., can choke the drains. They prevent the oxygen flow which restrict the degradation process.
- Government of India initiated "Swachh Bharat" mission in the year 2016 under which providing toilets for everyone and proper sewage disposal mechanisms have been adopted.

13.6 Sanitation and Disease

- Large number of diseases are caused by contaminated water.
- Still majority of people in our country are without the sewerage facilities.
- Untreated human excreta is a health hazard causing water pollution as well as soil pollution.
- As the water gets polluted it becomes the major source of water born diseases such as polio, cholera, hepatitis *etc.*

13.7 Alternate Arrangement for Sewage Disposal

- On site sewage disposal systems such as septic tanks, composting toilets, chemical toilets, can be used to improve the sanitation. At those places where there are no sewerage system, septic tanks are available.
- Human waste can be disposed on-site by some toilets. Excreta from these toilet seats flow directly into biogas plant.
- Biogas produced can act as source of energy.
- In vermi-processing toilet, human excreta is treated by earthworms, using less water.
- Human excreta in vermi-processing toilets is converted to vermi cake that can act as much needed resource by soil.

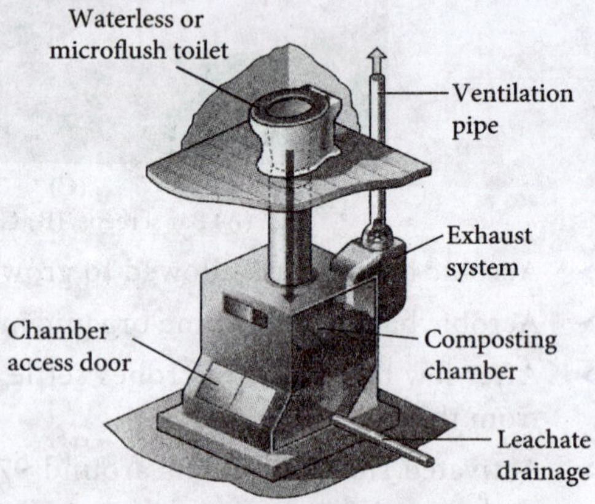

Fig.: Composting toilet-Internal structure

13.8 Sanitation at Public Places

- Although the government has put many standards of sanitation but they are not strictly enforced.
- Still, we can contribute in maintaining sanitation at public places, by not throwing waste anywhere, when there is no dustbin in sight, we can carry the litter to our home and throw it in the dustbin at home.

Conclusion

- We must realise our responsibilities in keeping our water resources clean.
- We should adopt good sanitation and encourage others to do the same.
- When people work together a lot can be done.

Practice Corner

Extracted from NCERT

Assessment is complementary part of the learning process. It gives you a total insight whether the learning outcomes have been achieved or not. After going through the corresponding NCERT Textbook chapter, attempt these questions in exam like environment. Give yourself one mark for correct answer. A table is given at the end, that will help you plan your next step.

All the Best!

13.1 Water, Our Lifeline

NCERT Page 156-157

A. Select the correct option.

1. On March 22, 2005, the General Assembly of the United Nations proclaimed the period ________ as the International Decade for action on 'Water for life'.
   (a) 2010 – 2015 (b) 2005 – 2015
   (c) 2014 – 2020 (d) 2015 – 2020 R

2. Select the correct statement(s).
   (i) Cleaning of water is a process of removing pollutants before it enters a water body or is reused.
   (ii) The process of wastewater treatment is known as 'Sewage Treatment'.
   (iii) Wastewater is the dirty, black-brown water that flows down the drains from sinks, showers, toilets, etc., from our homes.
   (iv) Every human being has equal access to safe drinking water on earth.
   (a) (i) and (ii) (b) (i), (ii) and (iii)
   (c) Only (iv) (d) (iii) and (iv) An

3. Increasing scarcity of freshwater is due to
   (i) population growth
   (ii) pollution
   (iii) industrial development
   (iv) mismanagement.
   (a) (i) and (ii) (b) (i), (ii) and (iii)
   (c) (ii) and (iii) (d) All of these An

B. Figure based questions.

4. Identify the given logo and write down its importance.

C. State True (T) or False (F) for the given statements.

5. We must clean wastewater by removing pollutants in it and then reuse it.
6. Wastewater is rich in lather, mixed with oil and black-brown in colour
7. The main aim of the action of 'Water for life' is to reduce by half the number of people who do not have access to safe drinking water.
8. "Sewage Treatment" takes place in only one stage.
9. A large number of water-related diseases and even deaths are due to drinking contaminated and dirty water.

13.2 What is Sewage?

NCERT Page 157

A. Select the correct option.

10. An inorganic impurity present in sewage is
    (a) oil (b) urea
    (c) nitrate (d) bacteria. R

11. Contamination of drinking water with sewage water can cause diseases like ________ in people consuming it.
    (a) dysentery (b) typhoid
    (c) cholera (d) all of these U

12. Organic impurities present in sewage are
    (a) bacteria (b) metals
    (c) pesticides (d) nutrients. An

B. Match the columns.

13.

Column I (Components of wastewater)	Column II (Examples)
1. Organic impurities	A. Causative agents of typhoid and cholera

2.	Inorganic impurities	B.	Pesticides and herbicides
3.	Nutrients	C.	Nitrogen and phosphorus
4.	Disease causing bacteria	D.	Metals and phosphates

	1	2	3	4
(a)	A	C	D	B
(b)	B	D	C	A
(c)	B	A	C	D
(d)	C	B	D	A

C. Fill in the blanks.

14. Sewage is a ____________. It is ____________ released by homes, industries, offices, etc. It also includes ____________ that has run down the street during a storm or heavy rain. It contains many dissolved and suspended impurities called as ____________. Thus, sewage is a complex mixture containing suspended solids, ____________ and ____________ impurities, ____________, saprotrophic and disease causing bacteria and other microbes.

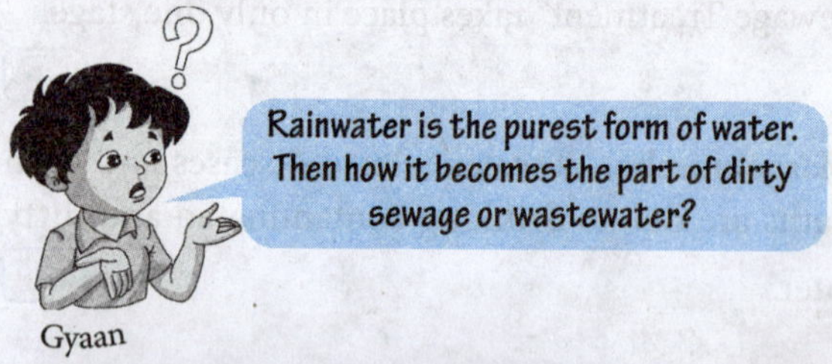

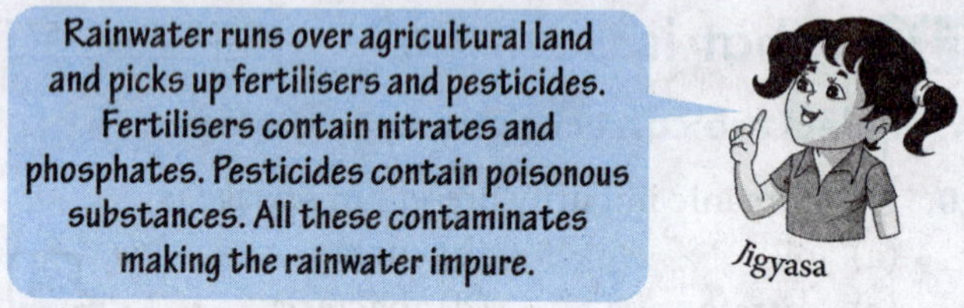

13.3 Water Freshens Up – An Eventful Journey

NCERT Page 157-159

A. Select the correct option.

15. ____________ is/are a network of underground pipes that carries sewage from the point of being produced to the point of disposal.
(a) Sewers (b) Sewerage
(c) Treatment plant (d) Manholes **R**

16. Manholes are located at every ____________ in the sewerage, at the junction of two or more sewers and at points where there is a change in direction.
(a) 50 m to 60 m
(b) 100 m to 150 m
(c) 10 m to 50 m
(d) 1000 m to 1500 m **U**

17. Which chemical is added to the wastewater to treat it?
(a) Sulphur (b) Chlorine
(c) Nitrate (d) Pesticide **R**

18. Select the correct sequence of steps involved to treat polluted water.
(a) Sewage → Aeration → Filtration → Chlorination
(b) Sewage → Filtration → Aeration → Chlorination
(c) Sewage → Chlorination → Filtration → Aeration
(d) Sewage → Aeration → Chlorination → Filtration **An**

19. Select the incorrect statement(s).
(i) Manholes are located only at the junction of two or more sewers.
(ii) During the process of filtration, filter papers are used to filter liquid impurities of wastewater in a treatment plant.
(iii) During the treatment of polluted water, we get clear water after adding chlorine tablets into the wastewater.
(a) (i) and (iii) (b) (i) and (ii)
(c) Only (ii) (d) (ii) and (iii) **U**

B. Figure based questions

Direction (Q.No. 20-21) : Observe the given figure and answer the questions that follow.

20. Which step of wastewater treatment is being shown in the above image?

21. What is the purpose of this step during sewage treatment?

13.4 Wastewater Treatment Plant (WWTP)

NCERT Page 159-161

A. Select the correct option.

22. Treatment of wastewater involves ____________ processes which remove physical, chemical and biological matter that contaminates the wastewater.
(a) biological (b) chemical
(c) physical (d) all of these **U**

23. The activated sludge is about ____________ water.
(a) 97% (b) 60%
(c) 87% (d) 50% **R**

24. Given image represents a part of the Wastewater Treatment Plant. Which of the following does not take place here?

(i) Solids like faeces are removed with the help of a scraper.
(ii) Large objects like rags, sticks, napkins are removed.
(iii) Floatable solids like oil and grease are removed.
(iv) Air is pumped for growing aerobic bacteria.
(a) (i), (iii) and (iv) (b) Only (ii)
(c) (i) and (ii) (d) (iii) and (iv)

25. Why clarified water is aerated in a Wastewater Treatment Plant?
(a) To help anaerobic bacteria to grow.
(b) To help aerobic bacteria to grow.
(c) To remove the suspended particles floating on the surface of clarified water.
(d) To mix the anaerobic bacteria well with the clarified water.

26. Select the incorrect statement(s).
In a grit and sand removal tank,
(i) the speed of the incoming wastewater is decreased.
(ii) sludge is removed from the wastewater.
(iii) biogas is produced.
(iv) sand, grit and pebbles present in the sewage are settled down.
(a) (i), (ii) and (iii) (b) (ii) and (iii)
(c) (i) and (ii) (d) (i), (iii) and (iv)

B. Fill in the blanks.

27. In a treatment plant, wastewater is first passed through ____________ to remove large objects .

28. Solids like faeces which settle at the bottom of the sedimentation tank is called____________.

29. Wastewater which is free from large objects, sludge and floatable solids like oil and grease, is called ____________ .

30. A ____________ is used to remove floatable oil and grease from wastewater.

31. Sludge is decomposed with the help of____________ bacteria to produce ____________.

32. In the aeration tank, the growing ____________ bacteria can consume human and animal waste, soaps and other unwanted matter in the clarified water.

33. The water from the activated sludge is removed by ____________ or machines.

34. ____________ is used as manure, returning organic matter and nutrients to the soil.

35. Disinfectants such as ____________ and ____________ are added to the treated water before releasing it into the distribution system.

36. The low quantity of organic material and suspended matter still remaining in the treated water is cleaned up by ____________ when discharged into the water bodies.

C. State True (T) False (F) for the given statements.

37. Sludge and floatable solids are removed from wastewater with the help of a scraper.

38. The water coming from the sedimentation tank is very clear and free from suspended solids.

39. Solids like faeces, food waste, etc., which get settled down in the aeration tank is called activated sludge.

40. Biogas is used only as a fuel.

41. Waste generation is accelerated as human population increased.

42. We can limit the type of waste and quantity of waste produced.

43. Dried sludge is used as a fuel and to produce electricity.

D. Figure based questions

Direction (Q.No. 44–46) : Observe the given figure and answer the questions that follow.
Identify the given images and write down the role of each one of them during wastewater treatment process in the given table.

44.

Name and role ____________________

45.

Name and role ____________________

46.

Name and role ____________________

13.5 Better House Keeping Practices

NCERT Page 161-162

A. Select the correct option.

47. Which of the following should not be thrown into the sink?
(a) Oils and fats (b) Used tea leaves
(c) Paints and solvents (d) All of these Ap

48. Cooking oil and fats should not be thrown into the drain because
(i) they can harden and block the pipes.
(ii) they can kill microbes that help to purify water.
(iii) they can clog soil pores and reduce filtering of water.
(a) (i) and (ii) (b) (i) and (iii)
(c) (ii) and (iii) (d) Only (i) An

49. Select the correct statements.
(i) We should throw oil and fats in the dustbin.
(ii) Used tea leaves can be thrown into the drains as it is biodegradable waste.
(iii) Chemical solvents can kill microbes that help to purify water.
(iv) Only solid food remains can be thrown into the sink.
(a) (i), (ii) and (iii) (b) (i), (ii) and (iv)
(c) (i), (iii) and (iv) (d) (i) and (iii) An

B. Figure based questions

Direction (Q.No. 50–52) : Observe the given sets of images carefully. In each set tick (✓) the one which you think is a better house keeping practice and cross (×) the one which you think is not a better house keeping practice. First one is done for you.

50.

51.

52.

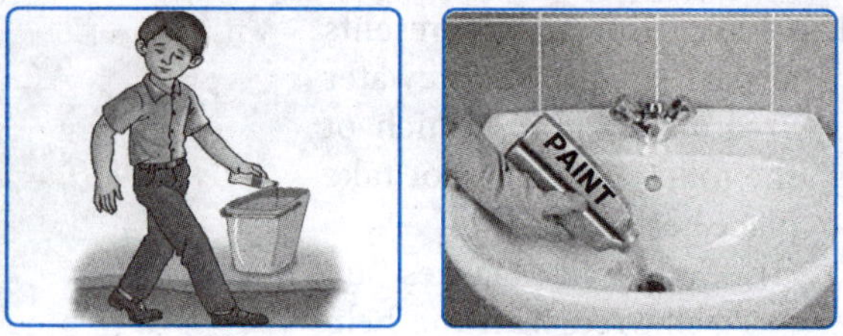

13.6 Sanitation and Disease

NCERT Page 162

A. Select the correct option.

53. Which of the following is cause of a large number of diseases?
(a) Poor sanitation
(b) Contaminated drinking water
(c) Untreated human excreta
(d) All of these.

54. Which of the following is not a water-borne disease?
(a) Cholera (b) Malaria
(c) Typhoid (d) Hepatitis R

55. Untreated human excreta is a health hazard. It results in
(a) pollution of soil and water
(b) spread of water-borne diseases
(c) contamination of ground water and surface water
(d) all of these. An

56. Seema was suffering from dysentery. What could be the cause?
(a) She drank contaminated water.
(b) She did not eat a balanced diet.
(c) She drank filtered water.
(d) She got bitten by mosquito causing dysentery. An

C. Fill in the blanks.

57. Poor _______ and contaminated drinking water is the cause of many diseases.

58. Both groundwater and _______ get polluted due to defecation in the open.

59. _______ forms the common route for water-borne diseases.

60. Like cholera and dysentery, some other water-borne diseases are _______, _______ and _______.

13.7 Alternative Arrangement For Sewage Disposal

NCERT Page 162

A. Select the correct option.

61. Which of the following is not a low cost onsite sewage disposal system?
(a) Chemical toilets
(b) Composting toilets

(c) Septic tanks
(d) None of these **U**

62. What is true about a vermi-processing toilet?
(a) It is a novel, low water-use toilet.
(b) Human excreta is treated by earthworms.
(c) Human excreta is treated with no water or small volume of flush water.
(d) All of these **An**

63. Which of the following methods should not be adopted if no sewage system is available?
(a) Allowing untreated sewage to flow into the rivers.
(b) Making septic tanks for sewage disposal.
(c) Allowing sewage to flow into a biogas plant.
(d) Using a vermicomposting toilet. **An**

B. Fill in the blanks.

64. ____________ are the low cost onsite sewage disposal system which are suitable for places where there is no sewerage system, for hospitals and isolated buildings. Nowadays, a new type of toilet is used for hygienic on-site disposal of human waste. This type of toilet does not require ____________. Here, excreta from the toilet seat flows through covered drains into a ____________, where it is decomposed to produce ____________ which acts as a source of energy.

13.8 Sanitation At Public Places

NCERT Page 162-163

A. Select the correct option.

65. Which of the following places can generate a large volume of waste?
(a) Railway stations (b) Hospitals
(c) Airports (d) All of these **U**

66. We can help in waste management by
(i) not littering anywhere
(ii) reducing the amount of garbage produced
(iii) throwing litter only in the dustbin
(iv) disposing litter in plastic bags.
(a) (i) and (ii) (b) (i) and (iii)
(c) (i), (ii) and (iv) (d) (i), (ii) and (iii) **An**

67. Select the correct statements.
(i) If there is no dustbin in any public place, we should take the litter home and throw it in the dustbin.
(ii) Adopting good sanitation practices should be our way of life.
(iii) The government has laid down certain standards of sanitation which are strictly being enforced in our country.
(iv) We should create awareness among people about waste management.
(a) (ii) and (iv) (b) (ii), (iii) and (iv)
(c) (i), (ii) and (iv) (d) (iii) and (iv) **An**

B. Figure based questions

Direction (Q.No. 68–70) : Observe the given figure and answer the questions that follow.

A B

68. Which one of the following images show a good sanitation practice?

69. Give an advantage for the good sanitation practice.

70. List some good sanitation practices other than those given in the images.

PROGRESS CHECK

Check your score! If your score is

> 95%	EXCELLENT !	- Move on to the next chapter. You have mastered this chapter. Concepts are certainly on your fingertips.
95-85%	VERY GOOD !	- Revise once more thoroughly. Recognise your mistakes and work on them. You will master this chapter.
84-75%	GOOD!	- Work on your weak areas, master them and come back to this chapter in a few days.
74-65%	MEDIOCRE!	- Understand your weak areas and work on strengthening your concepts. Devote more time to master this chapter.
< 65%	NOT SATISFACTORY!	- This is where you fall behind from scoring well. Give special attention to this chapter. Work on clearing concepts and common errors.

NCERT Exemplar Problems

This section contains MCQs of **'NCERT Exemplar Problems'** Book.

1. Which of the following is wastewater?
(a) Water trickling from a damaged tap
(b) Water coming out of a shower
(c) Water flowing in a river
(d) Water coming out of a laundry

2. Sewage is mainly a
(a) liquid waste
(b) solid waste
(c) gaseous waste
(d) mixture of solid and gas.

3. Which of the following is/are product(s) of wastewater treatment?
(a) Biogas
(b) Sludge
(c) Both biogas and sludge
(d) Aerator

4. Open drain system is a breeding place for which of the following?
(a) Flies
(b) Mosquitoes
(c) Micro-organisms which cause diseases
(d) All of these

5. Water polluted by various human activities causes a number of water borne diseases. Which of the following is not a water borne disease?
(a) Cholera (b) Typhoid
(c) Asthma (d) Dysentry

6. Pick from the following one chemical used to disinfect water.
(a) Chlorine (b) Washing soda
(c) Silica (d) Coal

7. The system of a network of pipes used for taking away wastewater from homes or public buildings to the treatment plant is known as
(a) sewers (b) sewerage
(c) transport system (d) treatment plant.

8. Which of the following is a part of inorganic impurities of the sewage?
(a) Pesticides (b) Urea
(c) Phosphates (d) Vegetable waste

9. In a filtration plant water is filtered using layers of
(a) sand and clay
(b) clay and fine gravel
(c) sand and fine gravel
(d) sand, fine gravel and medium gravel.

10. Which of the following is not a source of waste water?
(a) Sewers (b) Homes
(c) Industries (d) Hospitals

A&R Corner

Directions : In the following questions, a statement of assertion is followed by a statement of reason. Mark the correct choice as :
(a) If both assertion and reason are true and reason is the correct explanation of assertion.
(b) If both assertion and reason are true but reason is not the correct explanation of assertion.
(c) If assertion is true but reason is false.
(d) If both assertion and reason are false.

1. Assertion : Eucalyptus trees should be grown on the bank of the sewage ponds.
Reason : Eucalyptus trees absorb all surplus waste water rapidly and release pure water vapour into the atmosphere. Ap

2. Assertion : The biogas is produced while transferring of sludge into separate tank called digesters.
Reason : The biogas is used as a fuel or can be used to produce electricity.

3. Assertion : Sewage treatment is the process of removing pollutants from the waste water.
Reason : Sewage treatment involves either physical or chemical processes to remove the contaminants. U

4. Assertion : Wastewater is passed through bar screens to remove small objects.
Reason : The speed of the incoming wastewater is increased to allow sand, grit and pebbles to settle down in grit and sand removal tank.

5. Assertion : In septic tank, the sewage is allowed to flow into a tank in which aerobic bacteria decompose the waste.
Reason : The septic tank acts as filtration cum-digestion tank.

6. Assertion : Unhygienic and unsanitary conditions are major causes for the bad health of human beings.
Reason : Flies, mosquitoes and other insects breed in contaminated water.

7. Assertion : Sewage is a complex mixture containing disease causing bacteria and other microbes.
Reason : Chemicals like chlorine and ozone are used to disinfect water.

8. Assertion : Sewage is a liquid waste released by homes, industries, hospitals and offices.
Reason : Pesticides are inorganic impurities used to kill insects of sewage.

9. Assertion : Air is pumped into the clarified water to help anaerobic bacteria to grow.
Reason : During aeration of water, carbon dioxide is circulated throughout to remove the foul odour. An

10. Assertion : Sludge is decomposed by anaerobic bacteria.
Reason : The treated water has a very low level of organic material.

11. Assertion : Untreated human excreta is a health hazard.
Reason : Cholera, typhoid and polio are water borne diseases.

12. Assertion : Lot of people around the globe have no access to clean drinking water.
Reason : Consuming contaminated water results in diseases like polio, meningitis etc.

13. Assertion : The materials that cause pollution are known as pollutants.
Reason : The presence of desirable materials in water bodies is known as pollution.

14. Assertion : Clean water is a basic need of human being.
Reason : Untreated water is the major cause of ground and surface water pollution. U

15. Assertion : To prevent water pollution, wastewater should be treated properly.
Reason : Useful chemicals need to be eliminated before water enters the rivers.

Exam Corner

This section comprises of different types of questions:

- **Objective Type Questions** : These are **one mark** questions.
- **Very Short Answer Type Questions (VSA)** : These are **one mark** questions.
- **Short Answer Type Questions-I (SA-I)** : These are **two marks** questions.
- **Short Answer Type Questions-II (SA-II)** : These are **three marks** questions.
- **Long Answer Type Questions (LA)** : These are **five marks** questions.
- **Case Based Questions (CBQs)** : These are case study/passage based questions.

OBJECTIVE TYPE QUESTIONS

A. Select the correct option.

1. Which of the following is not a step involved in wastewater treatment?
   (a) Chlorination
   (b) Vermi-composting
   (c) Aeration
   (d) Sedimentation R

2. Which of the following helps in the purification of water in nature?
   (a) Neem tree
   (b) Tulsi plant
   (c) Eucalyptus tree
   (d) All of these

3. The stream of sewage which enters the treatment plant is called
   (a) influent (b) effluent
   (c) incoming stream (d) inflow.

4. Which kind of problem(s) is/are encountered in open drains?
   (a) May cause breeding of mosquitoes and flies
   (b) Foul smell
   (c) Rainwater starts overflowing due to blockages by plastic bags
   (d) All of these

5. Scrapers are used to remove ______ from sewage.
   (a) large solid wastes such as rags and napkins
   (b) oil and grease
   (c) faeces
   (d) solid objects like sand and grit

6. In a composting toilet, decomposition of excreta takes place through
   (a) aerobic process
   (b) anaerobic process
   (c) chemicals
   (d) aerobic process with the use of chemicals.

7. Which of the following statements is wrong about dried sludge?
   (a) It contains 97% of water.
   (b) It has high amount of soil nutrients.
   (c) It is rich in organic matter.
   (d) It is used as a manure.

8. Select the incorrect match.
   (a) Aerobic bacteria – Cannot survive in the absence of oxygen
   (b) Bar screens – Remove the larger solid particles from sewage
   (c) Composting toilet – Uses chemicals to decompose human excreta
   (d) Activated sludge – Suspended microbes that settle down at the bottom of aeration tanks. U

9. Which of the following options includes organic impurities present in the sewage?
   (a) Nitrates, phosphates and nitrogen
   (b) Disease causing bacteria and microbes
   (c) Phosphorus and metals
   (d) Urea, pesticides, herbicides, etc. R

10. Select the incorrect statements.
(i) Wastewater can never be reused.
(ii) Sewage is a liquid waste.
(iii) Wastewater is generated only in public places.
(iv) Rainwater is not a part of wastewater.
(a) (i) and (iii) only (b) (ii) and (iv) only
(c) (ii) and (iii) only (d) (i), (iii) and (iv)

11. Aeration is done during the wastewater treatment to
(i) remove foul smell from the sewage.
(ii) enhance the growth of anaerobic bacteria.
(iii) enhance the growth of aerobic bacteria.
(a) (i) and (iii) (b) (i) and (ii)
(c) Only (i) (d) Only (ii)

12. Given figure represents a part of the Wastewater Treatment Plant. Which of the following steps takes place here?

(a) Solids like faeces are removed with a scraper.
(b) Water is treated with chlorine.
(c) Solids like large pieces of plastics, cans, etc. are removed.
(d) Sand, grit and pebbles are removed from wastewater.

13. Select the incorrect statement(s).
(i) Vermi-cakes are a rich source of nutrients needed for soil.
(ii) Activated sludge contains human excreta.
(iii) Sludge obtained in the sedimentation tank is rich in soil nutrients.
(iv) Biogas is used as a fuel.
(a) (i) and (ii) (b) (ii) and (iii)
(c) Only (ii) (d) (i), (iii) and (iv)

An

14. Match the columns and select the correct option.

	Column I		Column II
A.	Bar screens	(i)	Sludge is removed
B.	Clarifiers	(ii)	Removes foul smell from sewage
C.	Aerators	(iii)	First step in WWTP
D.	Digesters	(iv)	Contains anaerobic bacteria

(a) A – (i), B – (ii), C – (iv), D – (iii)
(b) A – (iii), B – (i), C – (ii), D – (iv)
(c) A – (iii), B – (i), C – (iv), D – (ii)
(d) A – (ii), B – (iii), C – (i), D – (iv)

15. Select the incorrect statement(s) about biogas.
(i) It is released by deomposition of sludge in digesters.
(ii) It is a methane rich gas.
(iii) It is also called as gobar gas.
(iv) It is one of the major cause of pollution.
(a) (i) and (ii) (b) (i) and (iv)
(c) (ii) and (iii) (d) Only (iv)

U

16. Which of the following is the quality of wastewater?
(a) Dirty look (b) Foul smell
(c) Bad taste (d) All of these

17. Which of the following is used in vermi-composting toilets?
(a) Cockroach
(b) Earthworm
(c) Aerobic bacteria
(d) Anaerobic bacteria

18. Sludge is decomposed to form biogas with the help of
(a) yeasts (b) earthworms
(c) aerobic bacteria (d) anaerobic bacteria.

19. Organic impurities : ____________ :: Inorganic impurities : Metals
(a) Urine
(b) Phosphates
(c) Nitrogen
(d) Microbes

20. Which of the following is not an onsite sewage disposal system?
(a) Biogas plant
(b) Vermi-composting toilet
(c) Chemical toilet
(d) Composting pits

21. Which of the following is the first step of wastewater treatment?
(a) Chlorination (b) Aeration
(c) Sedimentation (d) Filtration

22. The full form of WWTP is
(a) world wide treatment plant.
(b) wastewater treatment plant.
(c) wastewater treatment process.
(d) world waste treatment programme.

23. Select the incorrect statement regarding septic tanks.
(a) Aerobic decomposition takes place in septic tanks.
(b) It is a low cost onsite sewage disposal system.
(c) It is done in areas where water table is very low.
(d) Septic tanks are suitable for places where there is no sewerage system.

24. Which of the following statements is incorrect?
(a) Rainwater is also a constituent of sewage.
(b) Sewers that carry only domestic sewage are called storm sewers.
(c) The dissolved and suspended impurities present in sewage are called contaminants.
(d) Sewage contamination may cause soil and water pollution.

25. Match the columns and select the correct option.

	Column I		Column II
A.	Filtration	(i)	Heavy matter settles at the bottom to form sludge
B.	Disinfection	(ii)	Addition of chlorine in water to kill pathogens
C.	Sedimentation	(iii)	Water percolates through layers of sand and gravel
D.	Aeration	(iv)	Exposure of wastewater to circulating air

(a) A – (iii), B – (ii), C – (i), D – (iv)
(b) A – (iii), B – (i), C – (iv), D – (ii)
(c) A – (ii), B – (iii), C – (i), D – (iv)
(d) A – (i), B – (iv), C – (ii), D – (iii)

26. A simple diagrammatic representation of the processes that take place at the wastewater treatment plant is shown below.

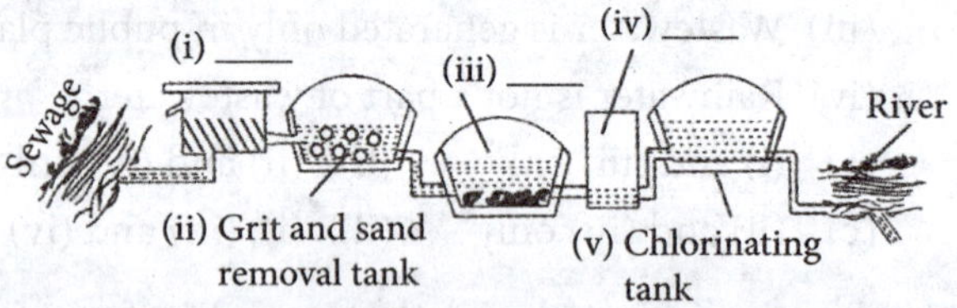

Select the correct option to fill the blanks.

	(i)	(iii)	(iv)
(a)	Sedimentation	Filtration	Aeration
(b)	Filtration	Sedimentation	Aeration
(c)	Aeration	Filtration	Sedimentation
(d)	Sedimentation	Aeration	Filtration

27. What is the function of the structure shown in given figure?

(a) It removes the suspended impurities from wastewater.
(b) It removes the floatable materials such as oil and grease.
(c) It removes sludge from the wastewater.
(d) It removes large objects like plastic bags, sticks, cans, rags etc.

28. Match the columns and select the correct option.

	Column I		Column II
1.	Sewer	A.	Interconnected pipes that carry sewage to a WWTP
2.	Contaminants	B.	Solid wastes that settle at the bottom of aeration tank
3.	Activated sludge	C.	Impurities present in sewage

4.	Cholera epidemics	D.	A consequence of groundwater pollution
5.	Sewerage	E.	Removes oils and grease from wastewater
6.	Skimmer	F.	Pipes that carry sewage

	1	2	3	4	5	6
(a)	B	C	E	F	A	D
(b)	A	B	D	C	F	E
(c)	F	C	B	D	A	E
(d)	F	B	C	D	E	A

B. Fill in the blanks.

29. __________ are openings on the road surface that are covered with heavy cemented lids that help to reach the underground sewerage for cleaning.

30. Sedimentation tanks of wastewater treatment are also called as __________.

31. Sludge is decomposed in a __________ with the help of __________ bacteria.

32. In a sewage treatment plant, clarified water is fed into a __________ tank and treated with aerobic bacteria.

33. Biogas is a fuel mainly rich in __________ gas.

34. Activated sludge comprises of 97% __________ and remaining 3% consists of __________ that settle down at the base of the aeration tank.

35. __________ bacteria do not require oxygen for their survival.

36. Untreated sewage is a major source of __________ and __________ pollution.

37. In a septic tank, sewage is acted upon by __________ bacteria to decompose the waste.

38. Human excreta is completely converted into vermi-cakes with the help of __________ in a vermi-composting toilet.

C. Figure based questions.

Direction (Q.No. 39–41) : Observe the given diagram and answer the questions that follow.

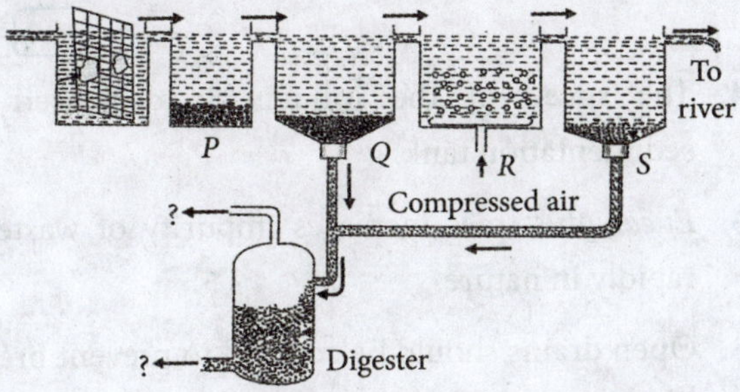

39. Which process is being depicted by the above image?

40. Label each step marked as P, Q, R and S involved in this process.

41. What are the products obtained from the digester after this process?

D. State True (T) or False (F) for the given statements.

42. Domestic waste does not contain microorganisms.

43. Aeration tanks contain anaerobic bacteria.

44. Oils and fats can clog the soil pores and reduce water seepage through it.

45. The treated water has high level of organic material and suspended matter.

46. Gobar gas is used only as a fuel while biogas can be used as a fuel as well as to generate electricity.

47. Faeces that settle down in the sedimentation tank can be removed by using a scraper.

48. Cholera, typhoid and jaundice are water-borne diseases.

49. In vermi-composting toilets, microorganisms are used to break down organic matter into inorganic substances.

50. Pesticides and herbicides are inorganic impurities present in sewage.

51. Cleaning of water is a process of removing pollutants before it enters water body or is reused.

52. Biogas is obtained by the action of anaerobic bacteria on organic wastes. ☐

53. Sewerage is a network of pipes that carry sewage. ☐ R

54. The speed of the influent is decreased in a sedimentation tank. ☐

55. *Eucalyptus* trees increases impurity of wastewater rapidly in nature. ☐

56. Open drains should be covered to prevent breeding of mosquitoes and flies. ☐

57. Chemicals like paints and medicines should not be thrown into the sink while insecticides can be poured into it as it helps to kill the disease causing microbes present in the sink. ☐

58. Blocking of drains do not allow free flow of oxygen which, ultimately, slow down the process of degradation of wastes present in it. ☐

59. Clarified water is free from disease causing bacteria and faeces but contains small volumes of suspended particles like plastics and oils. ☐

VERY SHORT ANSWER TYPE QUESTIONS (VSA)

A. Give one word for the following statements.

60. Name any two sources of wastewater.

61. Name any two objects that are removed by bar screens in a Wastewater Treatment Plant. U

62. Name two diseases that are caused by drinking contaminated water.

63. Name two alternative methods of sewage disposal system.

64. Name two nutrients present in sewage.

B. Circle the odd one out. Give reason for your choice.

65. Nitrates, Herbicides, Phosphates, Metals

66. Scraper, Grit and sand removal tank, Aeration tank, Skimmer

67. Composting pits, Septic tanks, Sewage treatment plants, Chemical toilets

68. Pesticides, Herbicides, Nitrogen, Urea

69. Cholera, Typhoid, Heart attack, Dysentery

SHORT ANSWER TYPE QUESTIONS-I (SA-I)

70. Write down the functions of skimmer and scraper in a sewage treatment plant. R

71. How is sludge decomposed?

72. Write one use of the following :
    (a) Dried sludge
    (b) Biogas

73. Why is it advised to grow *Eucalyptus* trees all along a sewage pond?

74. Why are chemicals like chlorine and ozone added to treated water?

SHORT ANSWER TYPE QUESTIONS-II (SA-II)

75. What is sewage? What will happen if untreated sewage is released into rivers or lakes? An

76. 'Untreated excreta is a health hazard.' Explain the given statement.

77. How do kitchen wastes block the drains?

78. What is the relation between sanitation and disease?

79. What is sludge? How it is treated?

LONG ANSWER TYPE QUESTIONS (LA)

80. Describe any two types of low cost onsite sewage disposal systems.

81. List out the better house keeping practices.

82. Describe the steps involved during the treatment of sewage in a treatment plant.

83. Outline your role as an active citizen in relation to sanitation. Ev

84. Give Reason:
    (a) Oils and fats should not be thrown into the drain.
    (b) Air is pumped into clarified water in a sewage treatment plant.
    (c) Speed of the influent is slowed down in a grit and sand removal tank.

CASE BASED QUESTIONS (CBQs)

Case I : Read the given passage and answer the following questions :

A teacher demonstrates the working of wastewater treatment plant through pictures A, B, C and D in classroom. Treatment of wastewater involves physical, chemical and biological processes, which remove physical, chemical and biological matter that contaminates the wastewater.

A

B

C

D

85. Match the columns I with II and select the correct option.

Column I		Column I	
I.	A	p.	Aerator
II.	B	q.	Sedimentation tank
III.	C	r.	Bar screen
IV.	D	s.	Grit and sand removal tank

(a) I-p, II-q, III-r, IV-s
(b) I-s, II-r, III-q, IV-p
(c) I-q, II-r, III-p, IV-s
(d) I-r, II-s, III-q, IV-p

An

86. Identify the correct order of wastewater treatment plant.

(a) $B \rightarrow C \rightarrow D \rightarrow A$ (b) $D \rightarrow A \rightarrow C \rightarrow B$
(c) $A \rightarrow B \rightarrow C \rightarrow D$ (d) $C \rightarrow B \rightarrow D \rightarrow A$

R

87. In which stage large objects like plastic packets are removed?

(a) A (b) B
(c) C (d) D

88. Identify the stage where speed of incoming waste water is decreased.

(a) A (b) B
(c) C (d) D

89. Biogas is produced by the action of which type microorganisms in picture C?

(a) Aerobic bacteria (b) Anaerobic bacteria
(c) Aerobic microbes (d) None of these

Case II : Read the given passage and answer the following questions :

Sewages like sullage water, foul waste and trade waste originating from our kitchen, toilets and industries are rich in organic impurities (A), inorganic impurities (B), nutrients (C) and diseases causing microbes (D) and (E) which are responsible for diseases like typhoid and dysentery respectively. We would see a network of big and small pipes, called sewers, forming the F.

90. Select the option which correctly identifies the organic and inorganic impurities A and B respectively.

(a) Nitrates and fruits
(b) Phosphates and urea
(c) Nitrates and phosphates
(d) Oil and metal

91. Select the correct statement about D and E.

(a) The disease causing microbe D is *Vibrio cholera*.
(b) The disease causing microbe E is *Salmonella typhi*.
(c) The disease causing microbe D and E are *Salmonella typhi* and Protozoan (*Entamoeba histolytica*) respectively.
(d) The disease causing microbe D and E are *Vibrio cholerae* and *Salmonella typhi*.

92. The network of big and small pipes called sewers forms F which is known as ________.
(a) sewers (b) sewerage
(c) manhole (d) treatment plant

93. Match the columns and select the correct option.

Column I		Column I	
1.	A	p	Phosphate
2.	B	q	Pesticides
3.	C	r	*Salmonella typhi*
4.	D	s	Nitrogen

(a) 1-q, 2-p, 3-s, 4-r
(b) 1-q, 2-r, 3-s, 4-p
(c) 1-p, 2-s, 3-r, 4-q
(d) 1-s, 2-p, 3-r, 4-q

94. Name any two nutrients labelled as 'C'.

ANSWER KEY

Practice Corner

1. (b) **2.** (b) **3.** (d) **4.** Logo shows 'Water for life' (2005-2015)
5. True **6.** False **7.** True **8.** False **9.** True **10.** (c) **11.** (d) **12.** (c) **13.** (b)
14. liquid, wastewater, rainwater, contaminants, organic, inorganic, nutrients. **15.** (b) **16.** (a)
17. (b) **18.** (b) **19.** (b) **20.** Filtration process **22.** (d) **23.** (a) **24.** (a) **25.** (b) **26.** (b)
27. bar screens **28.** sludge **29.** clarified water **30.** skimmer **31.** anaerobic, biogas **32.** aerobic
33. sand drying beds **34.** dried sludge **35.** chlorine, ozone **36.** nature **37.** False **38.** True
39. True **40.** False **41.** True **42.** True **43.** False **47.** (d) **48.** (b) **49.** (d) **54.** (b) **55.** (d)
56. (a) **57.** sanitation **58.** surface water **59.** untreated human excreta
60. typhoid, polio, meningitis, hepatitis **61.** (d) **62.** (d) **63.** (a)
64. Septic tanks, scavenging, biogas plant, electricity **65.** (d) **66.** (d) **67.** (c)

NCERT Exemplar Problems

1. (d) **2.** (a) **3.** (c) **4.** (d) **5.** (c) **6.** (a) **7.** (b) **8.** (c) **9.** (d) **10.** (a)

A & R Corner

1. (a) **2.** (b) **3.** (c) **4.** (d) **5.** (c) **6.** (a) **7.** (b) **8.** (c) **9.** (d) **10.** (b)
11 (b) **12.** (b) **13.** (c) **14.** (b) **15.** (c)

Exam Corner

1. (b) **2.** (c) **3.** (a) **4.** (d) **5.** (c) **6.** (a) **7.** (a) **8.** (c) **9.** (d) **10.** (d)
11. (a) **12.** (a) **13.** (b) **14.** (b) **15.** (d) **16.** (d) **17.** (b) **18.** (d) **19.** (a) **20.** (a)
21. (d) **22.** (b) **23.** (a) **24.** (b) **25.** (a) **26.** (b) **27.** (d) **28.** (c) **29.** Manholes
30. clarifiers **31.** digester, anaerobic **32.** aeration **33.** methane
34. water, suspended microbes **35.** Anaerobic **36.** ground water, surface water **37.** anaerobic
38. earthworms **39.** Wastewater Treatment Plant [WWTP] or Sewage Treatment Plant (STP)
42. False **43.** False **44.** True **45.** False **46.** False **47.** True **48.** True **49.** False **50.** False **51.** True
52. True **53.** True **54.** False **55.** False **56.** True **57.** False **58.** True **59.** False
60. Hospital, factories **61.** Cans, plastic bags
62. Cholera, typhoid **63.** Septic tank, composting toilet
64. Phosphorus, nitrogen **65.** Herbicides **66.** Aeration tank **67.** Sewage treatment plant **68.** Nitrogen
69. Heat attack **85.** (d) **86.** (c) **87.** (a) **88.** (b) **89.** (b) **90.** (d) **91.** (c) **92.** (b)
93 (a) **94.** Phosphorus and nitrogen

HINTS & EXPLANATIONS

1 Nutrition in Plants

Practice Corner

1. (d) : Oxygen is released by plants during photosynthesis.

2. (c) : Plants can prepare their own food.

3. (a)

4. (b) : Oxygen is released by plants during photosynthesis.

5. Nutrition

6. Animals/Humans/Heterotrophs

7. heterotrophs

8. fats, proteins, carbohydrates, vitamins, minerals

9. plants

10. (a) : Leaves are called as food factories or kitchens of plant because the process of photosynthesis occurs in the leaves. Leaves synthesise food on which all other plant parts depend.

11. (b) 12. (c) 13. (c)

14. (c) : Plants cannot absorb atmospheric nitrogen directly. Plants can synthesise fats and proteins.

15. (d) 16. (a)

17. (b) : Stomata are tiny pores that help in exchange of gases.

18. leaves, photosynthesis

19. starch 20. chlorophyll

21. Leaves 22. water, carbohydrates

23. bacteria 24. glucose

25. False. Leaves with other colour pigments like red, brown also have chlorophyll and can carry out the process of photosynthesis.

26. False. Chlorophyll helps the leaves to capture sunlight.

27. True

28. False. Plants use carbon dioxide and water to synthesise carbohydrates.

29. True

30. False. Stomata are surrounded by the guard cells.

31. True 32. True

33. True 34. True

35. Only the part of the leaf that is exposed to the sunlight turns blue black in colour, while the part of the leaf covered with the black paper appeared non-coloured.

36. This shows the presence of starch in parts of leaf exposed to sunlight. Thus sunlight is necessary for photosynthesis.

37. (b)

38. (d) : Algae can produce their food.

39. (c)

40. (d) : *Cuscuta* obtains its nutrients from the host plant.

41. (a) 42. (b)

43. (b) : *Nepenthes* leaf is modified into pitcher.

44. (a)

45. (d) : *Rhizobium* is not an autotroph. It cannot prepare its own food and depends on the plant where it lives.

46. (d) : Insectivorous plants can carry out photosynthesis still they obtain their N_2 requirement by eating insects. Hence, they are called autotrophs.

47. (a) : Yeast is saprotroph.

48. chlorophyll, host, parasites, parasitic mode of nutrition

49. Pitcher plant

50. Both autotrophic and heterotrophic mode of nutrition.

51. False. Pitcher plant has chlorophyll and is green in colour.

52. True

53. False. The plant on which *Cuscuta* plant climbs is called host.

54. True

55. False. Amarbel is a parasite plant and derives the valuable nutrients from their host plant.

56. False. Pitcher plants form a pitcher-like structure with a lid by modifying their leaves for trapping insects.

57. True

58. (a)

59. (d) : Fungi and mushrooms are saprotrophs that obtain their food from dead and decaying matter.

60. (a) : Lichen is an example of a symbiotic relationship between an alga and fungus that live together and are mutually beneficial to each other. Alga is an autotroph and fungus is a saprotroph. Fungus provides shelter, water, and minerals to the alga. The alga, in return, prepares food for the fungus by photosynthesis.

61. (d) 62. (c)

63. (b) : Saprotrophs are the organisms that obtain their nutrition from dead and decaying organic matter, usually plant and animal matter. These organisms release digestive juices on the dead and decaying matter, convert it into soluble form and then absorb the nutrients from it. This mode of nutrition is called saprotrophic nutrition.

64. (b) 65 (a)

66. True

67. False. In symbiotic relationship, both organisms live together and benefit from each other.

68. False. Mushroom is a saprotroph.

69. False. Symbiotic relationship also exists between bacteria and root of leguminous plant.

70. True 71. True

72. hot, humid 73. digestive juices

74. rainy 75. symbiotic

76. wet, warm 77. food, water, minerals

78. These cotton-like threads spread on the piece of bread are fungi.

79. Such organisms have saprophytic mode of nutrition.

80. Mushroom

81. Saprophytic mode of nutrition

82. (a)

83 (b) : Although nitrogen is present in abundance in the atmosphere, plants cannot use this free nitrogen directly. Plants obtain nitrogen either through fertilizers added into the soil or through certain nitrogen fixing bacteria (*e.g.*, *Rhizobium* bacteria) which convert atmospheric free N_2 into soluble nitrogenous compounds and release them into the soil.

84. (b) : *Moong* is a leguminous plant.

85. (d)

86. (c) : Growing leguminous plants naturally add nitrogen into the soil.

87. (d) 88. (d)

89. Fertilisers, nitrogen, potassium, phosphorus, proteins, soluble, *Rhizobium*, leguminous plants

90. Gram, peas, groundnut, rajma, moong

NCERT Exemplar Problems

1. (b) : Autotrophs are those organisms which are able to prepare their own food by the process of photosynthesis, *e.g.*, green plants. Photosynthesis (Gk *photos* - light, *synthesis*) is an enzyme regulated anabolic process of manufacturing of organic compounds inside the chlorophyll containing cells from carbon dioxide and water with the help of sunlight as a source of energy.

2 (b) : Chlorophyll is the green photosynthetic pigment, which is present in the cells of green leaves. It traps solar energy. This energy is then used to synthesise food with the help of CO_2 and water by the process of photosynthesis.

3. (a) : Animals cannot manufacture their own food so they are heterotrophs, not autotrophs.
Carbon dioxide is a raw material for photosynthesis. In the process of photosynthesis, plants manufacture carbohydrate, inside the chlorophyll containing cells from carbon dioxide and water with the help of solar energy. So, CO_2 is essential for photosynthesis.

4. (b) : Pitcher plant (*Nepenthes*) is an insectivorous plant. It grows in the soils that are usually nitrogen-deficient. It is capable of photosynthesising and manufactures its food. But in order to obtain its nitrogen nutrition it traps and digests insects.

5. (c) : Bread mould, yeast and mushroom are all fungi that derive their food from non-living organic matter. They secrete digestive juices on organic matter which aid in its extracellular digestion and convert it into soluble form. Then they absorb this simplified soluble form of food through their body. This method of getting nutrients in the form of simple soluble form (liquid) is known as saprophytic nutrition.

6. (a) : Lamina is the green expanded part of the leaf with veins and veinlets. Midrib is middle prominent vein. Veins provide rigidity to leaf and act as channels for transport of water, minerals and food materials. Stomata are the minute pores usually located on the underside of the leaves and take part in exchange of gases (O_2 and CO_2) during photosynthesis and respiration. They are surrounded by guard cells.

7. (d) : Symbiosis is a special association where two different organisms live together and are mutually benefited. *E.g.*, lichen is a symbiotic association between algae and fungus where fungus provides water, minerals and shelter to algae and in return algae provides nutrition (food) to fungus.

8. (b) : Carbon dioxide is the raw material for photosynthesis which is present in air. Photosynthesis is an enzyme regulated anabolic process of manufacture of carbohydrate which is an organic compounds inside the chlorophyll containing cells from carbon dioxide and water with the help of sunlight as a source of energy.

$$6CO_2 + 6H_2O \xrightarrow[\text{Radiant energy}]{\text{Chlorophyll/enzyme}} C_6H_{12}O_6 + 6O_2\uparrow$$

A & R Corner

1. (d) : Photosynthesis is the process of synthesising complex organic substances, *i.e.*, carbohydrates from simple inorganic raw materials (CO_2 and water) with the help of chlorophyll in the presence of sunlight. Oxygen is released during photosynthesis.

2. (a)

3. **(a) :** Sun is the primary source of energy on the earth and the solar energy is captured by the leaves and convert it into chemical energy and stored in the plant in the form of food by the process of photosynthesis.

4. **(d) :** The leaves other than green colour also have chlorophyll, hence photosynthesis takes place in these plants. The large amount of different pigments mask the green colour.

5. **(b)**

6. **(a) :** Mushrooms (Fungi) appear suddenly during rainy season because warm and moist atmosphere provides favourable condition for fungal spores to grow.

7. **(c)**

8. **(d) :** *Cuscuta* is a parasitic plant that takes readymade food from the living host plant.

9. **(b)**

10. **(d) :** Plants use simple inorganic substances (CO_2, H_2O and minerals) for the synthesis of food, *i.e.*, carbohydrates which are complex organic substances.

11. **(a) :** The survival of almost all living organisms directly or indirectly depends upon the food made by the plants. Oxygen is essential for the survival of all organisms is produced during photosynthesis.

12. **(c) :** Carbon dioxide is needed by plants for the synthesis of food by the process of photosynthesis.

13. **(b)**

14. **(c) :** Xylem vessels conducts water.

15. **(a)**

Exam Corner

1. **(c) :** During the process of photosynthesis, solar energy of sun is converted to chemical energy.

2. **(a)** **3.** **(b)**

4. **(b) :** Food prepared by the leaves is transported to different parts of the plant by phloem.

5. **(a)** **6.** **(c)**

7. **(c) :** *Cuscuta* (*Amarbel*) is a leafless and rootless parasitic plant that cannot perform photosynthesis and derives its food from their host plant.

8. **(d)** **9.** **(b)** **10.** **(c)**

11. **(c) :** *Cuscuta* shows parasitic mode of nutrition. It lives as parasite on other plant called host. Mosquitoes are also parasites. They obtain nutrition by sucking the blood of host (human), thereby showing parasitic mode of nutrition. Yeasts lack chlorophyll. They cannot synthesise their own food. They obtain nutrition by feeding on dead and decaying organic matter. Hence, they show saprotrophic mode of nutrition.

12. **(a) :** Given picture shows mushroom which is a fungus. It is a saprotrophic organism *i.e.*, it feeds on dead and decaying organic matter. It cannot synthesise its own food as it does not contain chlorophyll. Some of the varieties of mushroom are edible and some others are poisonous.

13. **(c)** **14.** **(d)**

15. **(b) :** Given figure represents the pitcher of the pitcher plant, *Nepenthes*. *Nepenthes* is an insectivorous plant in which leaf gets modified into a pitcher to trap and digest the insects.

16. grana **17.** haustoria

18. leaf **19.** nitrogen

20. Guard cells, stomata **21.** parasitic

22. consumers **23.** *Azotobacter*

24. Chlorophyll **25.** host

26. Cell membrane **27.** autotrophic, saprotrophic

28. parasite **29.** digestive juices

30. *Cuscuta*

31. False. Some plants also have heterotrophic mode of nutrition. Example: *Cuscuta*, pitcher plant, etc.

32. True **33.** True

34. False. Mushroom grows on dead and decaying matter.

35. True **36.** True

37. True

38. False. The fluid matrix in the chloroplast is called stroma.

39. False. Saprophytes are non-green in colour as they lack chlorophyll.

40. True

41. False. Saprotrophs are non-green plants that lack chlorophyll. Hence, they cannot synthesise their own food.

42. False. Yeast and mushrooms are saprophytic organisms.

43. False. In symbiotic relationship, both the organisms are benefited.

44. True **45.** True

46. False. Leaves of desert plants are modified into spines to reduce the process of transpiration.

47. True. Mistleloe is a partial parasite or heterotroph.

48. True

49. False. *Cuscuta* plants do not have chlorophyll and so they derive nutrients from host plant.

50. True

51. Pea plant. After a crop is harvested, the soil becomes deficient in nitrogen. Farmers may grow leguminous crops (*e.g.*, peas, beans etc.) to replenish nitrogen in the soil because

Rhizobium bacteria present in roots of legume crops add soluble nitrogenous compounds in the soil to be absorbed by plants.

52. A. (v) Phloem B. (vi) Photosynthesis
C. (viii) Saprophytes D. (i) Symbiosis
E. (ii) Parasites F. (iv) Chlorophyll
G. (iii) Lichen H. (vii) Xylem

53. The two main modes of nutrition are autotrophic and heterotrophic nutrition.

54. Water and carbon dioxide along with the chlorophyll and sunlight are the raw materials required for photosynthesis.

55. Yeast and mushroom

56. Pitcher plant and Venus flytrap

57. Beans and *moong*

58.

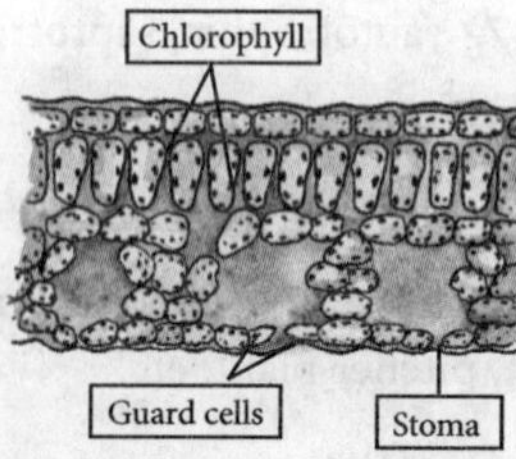

59. Leaf is known as kitchen of plant where food is synthesised.

60. Algae. It is an autotroph while others are heterotrophs.

61. Starch. It is the form of carbohydrate produced after the conversion of glucose during photosynthesis while others are raw materials of photosynthesis.

62. Lichen. It is an association of an alga and a fungus while others are examples of insectivorous plants.

63. Mango. It is a producer (autotroph) while others are consumers (heterotrophs).

64. Mushroom. It is a saprotroph while others are nitrogen fixing bacteria.

65. Photosynthesis is the synthesis of carbohydrates from CO_2 and water with the help of chlorophyll in the presence of sunlight. It takes place in leaves of plants.

66.

	Autotrophs	Heterotrophs
(i)	They are capable of synthesising their own food.	They cannot synthesise their own food.
(ii)	They form the first trophic level of any food chain.	They form the second or higher than second trophic levels in any food chain.
(iii)	They usually contain chlorophyll.	Chlorophyll is absent in them.

67. (a) Thylakoids are disc-shaped structure present in the chloroplast. They are arranged in stacks like piles of coins called grana.

(b) The organism from which a parasite derives its nutrients is called host.

(c) Mycorrhiza is symbiotic association in which certain fungi live in the roots of leguminous plant. The leguminous plant being photosynthetic provides food to the fungi and in return, fungi provides water and minerals to the leguminous plants.

(d) When two organisms live together and share shelter and nutrients, their association is called symbiosis or symbiotic relationship, and the organisms are called symbionts. They mutually help each other.

68. Fungi are useful for human beings :

(i) Some fungi, *e.g.*, mushrooms are edible and are used as vegetables. They are rich in vitamins.

(ii) Yeasts are the fungi that are used in baking and brewing industries.

(iii) Some fungi are also used in the preparation of medicines, *e.g.*, *Penicillium* is used to make an important antibiotic penicillin.

69. Leaves are called as food factories or kitchens of plant because the process of photosynthesis occurs in the leaves. Leaves synthesise food on which all other plant parts depend. Cells of green leaves contain chloroplasts. Chloroplasts contain green pigment chlorophyll which traps sunlight energy to carry out the process of photosynthesis.

70. Gardener is adding fertiliser into the soil. Fertilisers are rich in nitrogen. They provide nitrogen to the soil and increase its fertility. Plants obtain nitrogen through these fertilisers.

71.

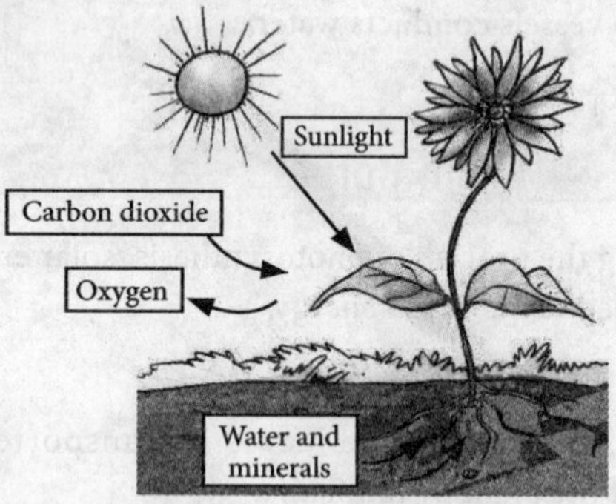

72. The given figure is stomata. These are the tiny pores present in the leaves. They allow carbon dioxide to pass in the atmosphere for photosynthesis to occur. Stomata are controlled by surrounding guard cells. The stomatal pores open only when carbon dioxide is to be taken in or oxygen is to be released, otherwise they remain closed.

73.

	Algae	Fungi
(i)	It is autotrophic organism.	It is heterotrophic organism.
(ii)	It can make their own food.	It cannot make their food.

74. Significance of photosynthesis :
(i) The survival of almost all living organisms directly or indirectly depends upon the food made by the plants.
(ii) During photosynthesis plants absorbs CO_2 and releases O_2. In this way, plants helps to maintain the balance between O_2 and CO_2 levels in the atmosphere.
(iii) Plants released oxygen during the process of photosynthesis which is used by animals for respiration.

75. Conducting tissues transport water and food to the different parts of the plant. Xylem and phloem are two types of conducting tissues present in plants.
Xylem vessels transport water and minerals absorbed by the plant through root hair, to the root, stem, branches and leaves. The food synthesised by the green leaves is transported to the other parts of the plant like stem, its branches and root system through phloem.

76. Saprotrophic bacteria and fungi are also known as decomposers as they decompose *i.e.*, break down the dead and decaying organic matter and carry out the natural process of decomposition. Decomposers play a vital role in cleaning of environment and recycling of nutrients.

77. Plants absorb mineral nutrients from the soil. So their amount in the soil keep on declining. Fertilizers and manures contain nutrients such as nitrogen, potassium, phosphorous, etc. Therefore, to overcome the deficiency of these nutrients in the soil we need to add these fertilizers and manures from time to time to enrich the soil.

78. Plants synthesize carbohydrates by the process of photosynthesis. Plants use carbohydrates to synthesize other components of the food such as proteins, fats, etc. But plants require nitrogen for protein synthesis. Certain bacteria in the soil convert atmospheric nitrogen into its soluble form which are absorbed by the plants. Plants fulfil their requirement of nitrogen also from the fertilizers added by the farmers.

79. Saprotrophs are the organisms that obtain their nutrition from non-living organic matter, usually dead and decaying plant and animal material. These organisms release digestive juices on the dead and decaying matter, convert it into soluble form and then absorb the nutrients from it. This mode of nutrition in which organisms take in nutrients in solution form, from dead and decaying matter is called saprotrophic nutrition.

80. Lichens are the organisms in which an alga and a fungus live together. The fungus provides shelter, water and minerals to the alga and in return, alga provides food to fungus which is prepared by photosynthesis. Lichen is an example of a symbiotic relationship between an alga and a fungus.

81. Leguminous plants and *Rhizobium* bacteria share symbiotic relationship with each other called mycorrhiza. *Rhizobium* can take atmospheric nitrogen and convert it into a soluble form (soluble nitrogenous compounds) in the soil that the plants can absorb. *Rhizobium*, being a heterotroph, cannot make its own food and therefore, lives in the roots of leguminous plants like beans, gram, peas and moong where it gets food and shelter. In return, it enriches the soil with soluble form of nitrogen which can easily taken by leguminous plant.

82. Insectivorous plant such as pitcher plant in which leaves are modified into pitcher-like structure. The apex of the leaf forms a lid which can open and close the mouth of the pitcher. Inside the pitcher there are hair which are downwardly directed. When an insect lands in the pitcher, it slips inside and the lid closes. The trapped insect is entangled into the hair. The insect is digested by the digestive juices secreted in the pitcher.

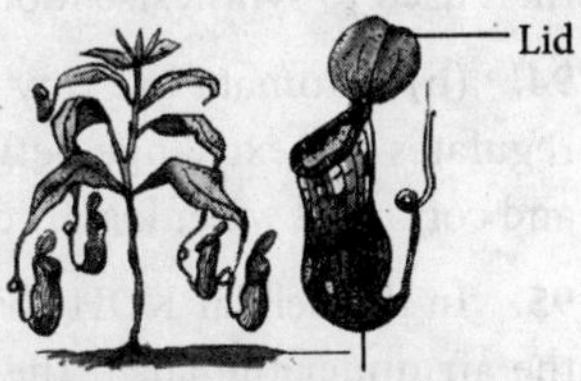

Leaf modified into pitcher

83. Manures add organic matter to the soil. Fertilizers are rich in specific nutrients such as nitrogen, phosphorus and potassium. Legume crops replenish the nitrogen content of soil because *Rhizobium* bacteria present in the roots of legume plants add soluble nitrogenous compounds in the soil. Therefore, replenishment of nutrients in the soil can be done by adding, manures, fertilizers and growing legume crops.

84. (a) The leaves can carry out the process of photosynthesis because they contain chlorophyll. The large amount of red, violet and brown pigments mask the green colour of chlorophyll.
(b) Pitcher plant is green and can carry out photosynthesis to prepare carbohydrates. Even then; to fulfil their requirement of nitrogenous compound for its growth and development, it feeds upon insects. Such plants do not get the retrieved amount of nutrients from the soil in which they grow. Such plants are also called insectivorous plants.
(c) Green plants are the autotrophs that manufacture their own food from simple inorganic raw materials by using chlorophyll and sunlight energy through the process of photosynthesis. Thus, green plants are called as producers.

85. Autotrophs - Mango, orange, sunflower, rose, *Dahlia*, banyan. Heterotrophs - Butterfly, leopard, parrot, peacock, dog, elephant, monkey

86. **(d)**

87. **(d) :** C (Autotrophs) are the organisms which synthesise their own food with the help of simple inorganic substances. All green plants, algae and some bacteria belongs to this group.

88. **(d)**

89. Nutrition (B) is the mode of taking food by an organism and its utilisation by the body.
The various types of nutrition are : autotrophic and heterotrophic nutrition.

90. Nutrition (B) is important for living organisms, as they enable them to build their bodies to grow, repair damaged parts and provide energy to carry out life process.

91. **(a)**

92. **(a) :** The green pigment (C) chlorophyll is found in chloroplast of the leaves.

93. C represents chlorophyll. It is a green pigment which helps leaves to capture the energy of sunlight. These energy is then used to synthesise food from carbon dioxide and water.

94. **(b) :** Stomata are tiny pores located on leaf surface. It regulates gas exchange between the plant and environment and control of water loss by changing the size of stomatal pore.

95. In the bell jar KOH absorbed all the CO_2 (A) present in the air under the jar. If the given plant is placed under this bell jar, it becomes deprived of CO_2. Thus, in the absence of CO_2 plant could not carry out photosynthesis and did not synthesise starch.

96. **(b) :** Amarbel (*Cuscuta*) is a parasitic (P) plant.

97. Insectivorous plants (Q) feed on insects because they grow in soil which is poor in nutrients, so they eat insects to fulfill their nutrient requirement (mainly nitrogen).

98. **(c) :** Plants need nitrogen in soluble form and the bacterium *Rhizobium* can take atmospheric nitrogen and convert it into soluble form and this soluble form of nitrogen is used by plants.

99. **(c)**

100. Q is insectivorous plant such as *Nepenthes*. It grows in nitrogen deficient soil and obtain nitrogen from insects.

2 Nutrition in Animals

Practice Corner

1. **(a)**

2. **(a) :** Mosquitoes have long tube like mouth to suck the blood of humans.

3. **(b)**

4. Photosynthesis, mode of intake, utilisation, Siphoning, sponging, sucking, chewing

5.

Name of Animals	Kind of food	Mode of feeding
Butterfly	Nectar	Siphoning
Leech	Blood	Sucking
Snake	Small animals like, rats, eggs of animals	Swallowing
Ant	Insects, fruits, vegetables, etc	Scraping

6. Given figure is of starfish. It feeds on animals covered by hard shells of calcium carbonate. After opening the shell, the starfish pops out its stomach through its mouth to eat the soft animal inside the shell. The stomach then goes back into the body and the food is slowly digested.

7. **(c)** **8.** **(b)**

9. **(c) :** The food absorbed into the blood is transported to different parts of the body. It is used to provide energy and materials for growth and repair of body tissues. This process is known as assimilation.

10. **(a)** **11.** **(b)**

12. **(c) :** Saliva is secreted by salivary glands present in buccal cavity.

13. **(a)**

14. **(c) :** Digestion of food starts in mouth and gets completed in small intestine. In large intestine, water and some salts are absorbed from the undigested food.

15. **(a) :** The waste food which is now semi-solid is stored in the last part of the large intestine called the rectum. It is then passed out of the body through the anus in the form of faeces. This is called egestion.

16. **(c)**

17. **(b) :** The inner lining of stomach secretes mucus, hydrochloric acid (HCl) and digestive juice (or gastric juice). HCl makes the medium in the stomach acidic to help the digestive enzymes to act. HCl also kills bacteria that enter into the stomach along with food.

18. starch **19.** 7.5 m

20. Windpipe, foodpipe

21. Water, salts **22.** fat

23. iodine **24.** milk teeth

25. Diarrhoea **26.** Tongue

27. villi **28.** True

29. False. Absorption is the process in which digested food pass into the blood vessels in the wall of intestine.

30. False. Egestion of faecal matter occurs through the anus.

31. True **32.** True

33. False. The pancreatic juice acts on carbohydrates, fats and proteins and changes them into simpler forms.

34. False. The large intestine is wider and shorter than the small intestine.

35. False : The stomach is like a flattened J-shaped bag.

36. False. Canines are used for piercing and tearing of food.

37. True

38.

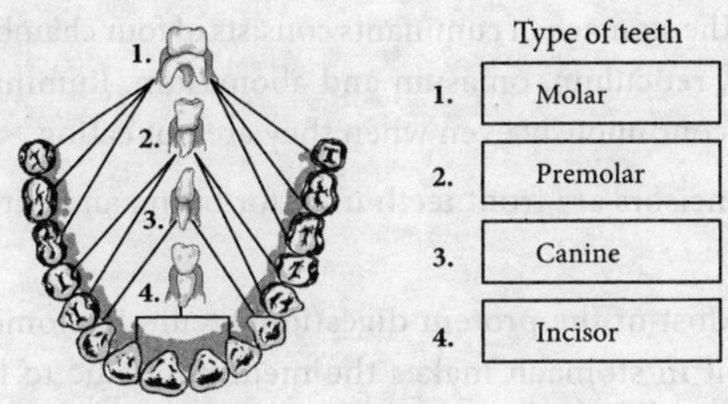

39.

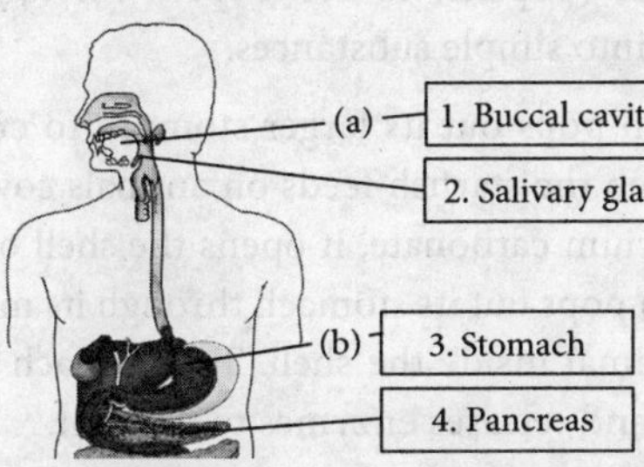

40. (b) : Ruminants are the hooved, plant-eating (grass) mammals which include cattle (cow, buffalo), goat, sheep, deer, camel, yak, etc. Stomach of these animals consists of four chambers – rumen, reticulum, omasum and abomasum.

41. (a)

42. (a) : Ruminants are able to digest cellulose as they contain bacteria and other microbes in their stomach which assist in the digestion of cellulose. Human beings cannot digest cellulose as they do not have cellulose-digesting bacteria in their stomach or intestine.

43. (d) : Ruminants are the hooved mammals (*e.g.*, cattle, deer, goat, etc.) which possess a unique digestive system. Their stomach consists of four chambers — rumen, reticulum, omasum and abomasum. During grazing, they quickly swallow plenty of grass without much chewing. The food is partially chewed and mixed with saliva. This partially chewed food is then sent to rumen, where it is stored temporarily. When the animal is resting, the partly chewed food (called cud) is brought back into the mouth (or buccal cavity) in small lumps and the animal chews it further. This process is called rumination. Ruminants are able to digest cellulose material of plants due to the presence of cellulose digesting bacteria in rumen of their stomach.

44. (a) **45. (b)**

46. rumination **47.** carbohydrate

48. rumen **49.** ruminants

50. rumen

51.

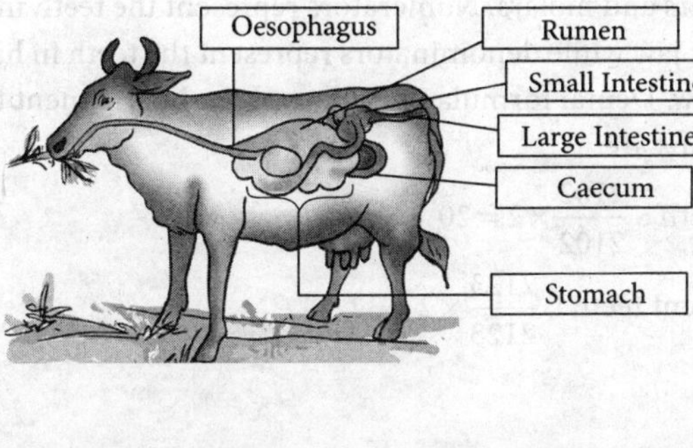

52. (b) **53. (d)**

54. (a) : *Amoeba* forms finger like projections called pseudopodia or false feet for movement and capture of food.

55. (d)

56. (a) : *Amoeba* has cell membrane, a rounded dense nucleus and many small bubble-like vacuoles in its cytoplasm.

57. digestive juices

58. growth, maintenance, multiplication

59. vacuole

60. Pseudopodia

61. cell membrane, nucleus, vacuoles

62. engulfs, pseudopodia

63. single

64. Step 1 : Ingestion – *Amoeba* feeds on some microscopic organisms. When it senses food, it pushes out pseudopodia around the food particle and engulfs it. The food becomes trapped in a food vacuole.

Step 2 : Digestion – Digestive juices are secreted into the food vacuole. They act on the food and break it down into simpler substances. Gradually, the digested food are absorbed. The absorbed substances are used for growth, maintenance and multiplication.

Step 3 : Egestion – The undigested residue of the food is expelled outside by the vacuole.

65. The labelled part Y is pseudopodia.

NCERT Exemplar Problems

1. (b) : When iodine is added to starch, it turns blue-black in colour. Potato and bread are rich in starch. Therefore, boiled and mashed potato and a slice of bread turn blue-black in colour when tested with iodine. Glucose solution does not change colour because it is digestive product of starch.

2. (b) : Our teeth cut, tear and grind the food before we swallow it. There are four types of teeth in our mouth -

(i) Incisors - These are the front eight teeth, four in upper and four in lower jaw. These are well adapted for cutting and biting of food items.

(ii) Canines - There are four canines, one canine each on either side of each jaw. These teeth are well adapted to hold and tear the food.

(iii) Premolars - There are eight premolars in total, two premolars in each half of the both upper and lower jaws. These are well adapted to crush and grind food.

(iv) Molars - There are twelve molars, three in each half of the both upper and lower jaws. These are well adapted to crush and grind the food.

3. (a) : Oesophagus gently pushes food down to the stomach in a wave like action called peristalsis. No digestion takes place in oesophagus.

In large intestine, undigested food enters where water is absorbed from it. No digestion takes place in large intestine. In rectum, semi-solid residue is stored and is finally thrown out of the body through the anus in the form of faeces. No digestion takes place in rectum.

4. **(d)** : The muscles of oesophagus gently push the food down to the stomach in a wave-like action (contractions and relaxations) called peristalsis. Actually, this movement takes place throughout the alimentary canal to push the food forward.

5. **(a)** : Hydrochloric acid (HCl) present in stomach kills the harmful bacteria that enter stomach along with food and makes the medium in the stomach acidic.

6. **(c)** : Finger-like outgrowths called villi are present in small intestine. They increase the surface area of small intestine for the absorption of digested food.

7. **(a)** : Villi are the numerous, small finger-like projections present in the inner walls of the small intestine. Villi increase the surface area of small intestine for absorption of digested food due to their thin, finger-like shape. Each villus has a network of thin and small blood vessels close to its surface. The food absorbed on the surface of villus passes into the blood in the capillaries. Villi do not have any pores.

8. **(c)** : False feet or pseudopodia of *Amoeba* are used for both movement and capture of food. Exchange of gases takes place by body wall through diffusion.

9. **(b)** : The fluids secreted by the salivary glands constitute saliva. Saliva is slightly acidic. It contains a digestive enzyme called salivary amylase, which helps in the breakdown of starch (and not any other complex sugar) into simpler sugars (oligosaccharides) and not into simple sugars (monosaccharides).

10. **(b)** 11. **(a)**

12. **(a)** : Human beings do not have cellulose digesting enzymes in their bodies and are therefore unable to digest cellulose. Since it is not digested, it passes down the entire digestive tract from mouth to anus. It acts as roughage, adds bulk to the food and helps the body to easily get rid of undigested food.

A & R Corner

1. **(c)** : Liver is a reddish brown gland situated in the upper part of the abdomen on the right side.

2. **(a)** : The inner wall of small intestine have thousands of finger like outgrowths called villi. It increases the surface area for absorption of digested food.

3. **(b)**

4. **(c)** : *Amoeba* is a single-celled organism.

5. **(d)** : The stomach of ruminants consists of four chambers, *i.e.*, rumen, reticulum, omasum and abomasum. Ruminants chew food continuously even when they are not eating.

6. **(c)** : Incisors are front teeth used for biting and cutting of food.

7. **(a)** : Most of the protein digestion occurs in stomach. HCl present in stomach makes the medium acidic to help the digestive enzyme (pepsin) to act. Pepsin in stomach breakdown proteins into simple substances.

8. **(a)** : The starfish pops out its larger stomach to engulf and digest food. When the starfish feeds on animals covered by hard shells of calcium carbonate, it opens the shell of the prey animal and then pops out its stomach through its mouth to engulf the soft animal inside the shell. The stomach then goes back into body and releases enzymes to digest it.

9. **(b)**

10. **(c)** : The chemical digestion of food is done by saliva. Saliva contains an enzyme salivary amylase that helps in breakdown of starch into simple sugars.

11. **(a)** : Butterflies usually feeds on nectars of flowers. They take in food by siphoning. The tongue or proboscis is a tube like structure which extend and siphon water and nectar during feeding.

12. **(b)**

13. **(a)** : Human beings cannot digest cellulose as they do not have cellulose digesting bacteria in their stomach and intestine.

14. **(c)** : Milk teeth are 20 in number.

15. **(d)** : Bile is secreted from the liver and it is stored in the sac-like structure called gall bladder. It plays an important role in fat digestion.

Exam Corner

1. (a) 2. (a) 3. **(b)**

4. **(d)** : Lice and mosquitoes bear piercing and sucking type mouth parts as they suck the blood of human beings and other animals.

5. **(a)** : Dental formula is the number of teeth of each type in one half of each jaw, starting from incisors to molars *i.e.*, incisors, canines, premolars and molars/incisors, canines, premolars and molars. Numerators represent the teeth in half of upper jaw while denominators represent the teeth in half of lower jaw. Dental formula of milk teeth and permanent teeth of humans are:

Milk teeth : $\frac{2102}{2102} \times 2 = 20$

Permanent teeth : $\frac{2123}{2123} \times 2 = 32$

6. **(b) :** *Amoeba* is a unicellular organism, found in fresh water. It pushes out one or more finger-like projections, called pseudopodia or false feet for movements and capture of food. When it senses food, it sends out pseudopodia around the food particle and engulfs it. The food becomes trapped in a food vacuole. Digestive juices are secreted into the food vacuole. They act on the food and break it down into simpler substances. Gradually the digested food is absorbed. The absorbed substances are used for growth, maintenance and multiplication. The undigested residue of the food is expelled outside by the vacuole.

7. **(a) :** Incisors are the front teeth. These are chisel-shaped and are used for biting and cutting.

8. **(a) :** Large intestine is called large because its diameter is larger than small intestine whereas the length of large intestine is shorter than that of small intestine.

9. **(d) :** Organ A is small intestine in which food is completely digested. The digested food is absorbed into the blood and is carried to all the parts of the body *via* blood. Organ B is large intestine in which maximum absorption of water takes place. The undigested waste matter is expelled out of the body through anus in the form of faeces.

10. **(c)**

11. **(a) :** Assimilation – Utilisation of absorbed food substances to build complex substances and to produce energy.
Absorption – The digested food substances get absorbed into blood vessels form the wall of intestine.
Egestion – The removal of faecal matter through anus.

12. **(b)** 13. **(b)**

14. **(a) :** Assimilation is transport of absorbed substances *via* blood vessels to different organs of body where they are used to build complex substances required by the body. Bile breaks up fats into tiny droplets that can be digested and absorbed more easily. Amino acids are used to build new proteins.

15. **(d) :** Papillae are part of tongue. Villi are finger-like outgrowths of inner wall of small intestine. Pancreas secretes pancreatic juice that is released in small intestine. Rumen harbours anaerobic bacteria which produces enzyme (cellulase) which helps in the digestion of cellulose.

16. **(b) :** The liver produces bile juice which is stored in the gall bladder. The bile acts on fats and break them up into tiny droplets that can be digested and absorbed more easily. The digestive juices (pancreatic and intestinal juices) then act on these tiny droplets to form simpler compounds known as fatty acids and glycerol.

17. **(a) :** There are 4 incisors, 2 canines, 4 premolars and 6 molars in each jaw or we can say that there are 8 incisors, 4 canines, 8 premolars and 12 molars in the mouth of an adult human. Incisors are the front teeth. These are chisel-shaped and are used for biting and cutting. On either side of the incisors, are present sharp, pointed teeth called canines. These are used for piercing and tearing the pieces of food such as meat. Premolars and molars are present behind the canines. These are broad and strong with almost flat surface. Molars are larger than premolars. Both premolars and molars are used for crushing and grinding the food.

18. **(b) :** Fats are broken down into tiny droplets when bile mixes with partly digested food in small intestine. Fats are then digested into fatty acids and glycerol.

19. **(b) :** Proteins are completely digested into amino acids in small intestine.

20. **(d)**

21. heterotrophs 22. Canines

23. Liver, bile 24. stomach, peristalsis

25. sugars, fatty acids, glycerol, amino acids

26. Assimilation 27. wider, shorter

28. Ruminants, rumen 29. villi

30. diarrhoea 31. pseudopodia, tentacles

32. cud 33. stomach, small intestine

34. salivary glands, starch, sugars

35. rumen, reticulum, omasum, abomasum

36. mosquito 37. liver, pancreas

38. Ruminants

39. True 40. True

41. False. The digestion of food is completed in small intestine.

42. True

43. False. Digestion of food (starch) starts in buccal cavity and completes in small intestine.

44. True

45. False. During assimilation, the absorbed substances are used to build complex substances such as proteins and to release energy.

46. True

47. False. The pancreatic juice acts on carbohydrates, fats and proteins and changes them into simpler forms.

48. False. The villi increase the surface area in small intestine for absorption of digested food.

49. False. *Amoeba* captures food with the help of pseudopodia.

50. False. Digestion of starch and carbohydrates begins in buccal cavity where enzymes present in saliva partly digest them.

51. False. Saliva moistens and lubricates food and enzyme present in it (salivary amylase) digests carbohydrates.

52. False. Humans cannot digest cellulose as they do not have cellulose-digesting bacteria in their stomach or intestine.

53. True **54.** True

55. False. Glucose is oxidized into carbon dioxide and water during cellular respiration.

56. False. Liver is the largest gland in our body.

57. True

58. False. Digestion of proteins begins in stomach when digestive juice of stomach containing digestive enzymes (*e.g.* pepsin) breaks down proteins into simple substances (*i.e.*, amino acids).

59. (a) **60.** (c)

61. (i) Gall bladder. It stores bile juice secreted by liver.
(ii) Blood. Mosquitoes have their mouth parts adapted for piercing and sucking blood from the body of human beings and other animals. A mosquito sucks the blood of animals and human beings with its proboscis.
(iii) Milk teeth

62. Liver, Pancreas

63. Rumen, Abomasum

64. Crushing and grinding food

65. Stomach **66.** Pancreas

67. (i) PSEUDOPODIA
(ii) LIVER (iii) OESOPHAGUS
(iv) RUMINANTS (v) HETEROTROPHS

68. (a) : Rumination: Ruminants (*e.g.*, cattle, deer, goat etc.,) during grazing quickly swallow plenty of grass without chewing. The food is partially chewed and mixed with saliva. This partially chewed food is then sent to rumen, where it is stored temporarily. When the animal is resting, the partly chewed food (called cud) is brought back into the mouth in small lumps and the animal chews it further. This process is called rumination.
(b) Peristalsis : The muscles of oesophagus gently push food down to the stomach in a wave-like action (contractions and relaxations) called peristalsis.

69.

Assimilation	Absorption
The absorbed substances are transported *via* the blood vessels to different organs of the body where they are used to build complex substances such as the proteins required by the body. This is called assimilation.	The digested food can pass into the blood vessels in the wall of the intestine. This process is called absorption.

70. Tongue performs the following functions :
(i) The tongue helps us to taste the food.
(ii) It moves food in our mouth between the teeth for chewing.
(iii) It mixes saliva with food while chewing.
(iv) It helps us to swallow the food.

71. Pharynx is the common passage for food and air. It leads to food pipe and windpipe which run adjacent to each other. There is a flap-like structure, called epiglottis, which closes the opening of the windpipe while eating. This prevents the entry of food into the windpipe.

72. The stomach is thick-walled bag. It is flattened J-shaped structure and is the widest part of the alimentary canal. It receives food from food pipe at one end and opens into small intestine at the other end.

73.

	Milk teeth	Permanent teeth
(i)	These are first set of teeth that erupt during infancy.	These are second set of teeth that replaces the milk teeth.
(ii)	They fall of at an age of 6-8 years.	These are permanent teeth, last throughout life or fall off during old age.
(iii)	These are 20 in number, 10 in each jaw (upper and lower).	These are 32 in number, 16 in each jaw (upper and lower).
(iv)	They do not include premolar teeth. Milk teeth: $\frac{2102}{2102}\times 2=20$	There are 8 incisors, 4 canines, 8 premolars and 12 molars. Permanent teeth: $\frac{2123}{2123}\times 2=32$

74. (a) Hydrochloric acid : Hydrochloric acid (HCl) kills bacteria that enter stomach along with food and it makes the medium in the stomach acidic to help the digestive enzymes to act.
(b) Saliva : Saliva is a digestive juice, secreted by three pairs of salivary glands present in the mouth. Saliva moistens the food and makes the chewed food slippery. This helps in swallowing the food easily. Saliva contains an enzyme called salivary amylase. It helps in the breakdown of starch (complex carbohydrate) of the food into simple sugars that are easier to digest.
(c) Bile juice : Bile is not an enzyme. It does not digest the food chemically. It plays an important role in the digestion of fats. The bile breaks up fats into tiny droplets that can be digested and absorbed more easily. The digestive juices then act on these tiny droplets to form simpler compounds known as fatty acids and glycerol. Bile also helps in neutralisation of HCl of semi-solid food that comes from stomach.

75. Villi are finger like outgrowth in the inner walls of the small intestine. The villi increase the surface area for absorption of the digested food. Each villus has a network of thin and small blood vessels close to its surface. A minute blind-ended lymph vessel called lacteal also occurs in each villus of the small intestine. Digested fats are absorbed into the lacteals. The food absorbed on the surface of villus passes into the blood in the capillaries.

76. Dental plaque is a yellowish film that develops naturally on the teeth and comprises of bacteria, food components, etc. The bacteria in the plaque convert sugars of food into acids. The acids so formed dissolve the enamel and gradually damage the teeth. This is called tooth decay or dental caries. This disease destroys the structure of tooth and produces holes in it called cavities. It causes severe toothache and if not treated in time, it can lead to tooth loss.

Tooth decay can be avoided by two ways — oral hygiene (brushing, flossing , etc.) and intake of healthy food. Chocolates, sweets, soft drinks and other sugar products are the major culprits of tooth decay. Therefore, one should clean the teeth with a brush and dental floss (a special strong thread which is moved between two teeth to take out trapped food particles) at least twice a day and rinse the mouth after every meal.

77. *Amoeba* possesses finger-like projections called pseudopodia for the capturing of food. It feeds on other microscopic organisms present in its surroundings. When it senses food, it sends out pseudopodia around the food particle and engulfs it. The food becomes trapped in a food vacuole.

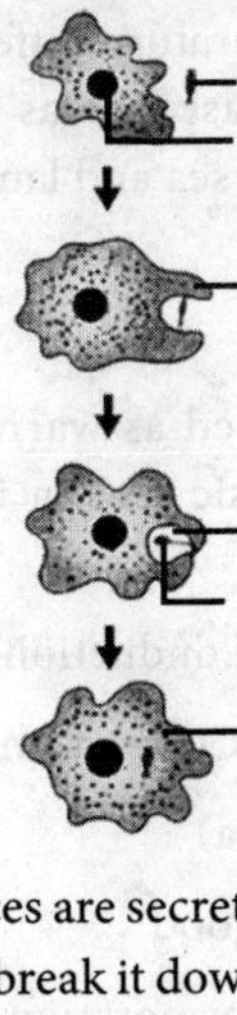

Digestive juices are secreted into the food vacuole. They act on the food and break it down into simpler substances. Gradually, the digested food is absorbed. The absorbed substances are used for growth, maintenance and multiplication. The undigested residue of the food is expelled outside by the vacuole.

78. Labelled diagram of human digestive system is as follows :

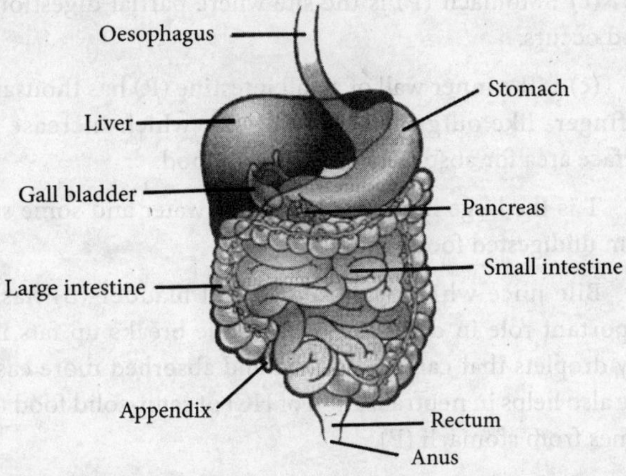

79. Digestion of food starts in mouth and gets completed in small intestine. The buccal cavity contains teeth, tongue and salivary glands. Both chemical and physical digestion takes place in mouth. The teeth cut the food into small pieces, chew and grind it. So, teeth helps in physical digestion. Salivary glands produces saliva that contains an enzyme called salivary amylase. The amylase enzyme digests the starch present in food into sugar, thereby helping in chemical digestion. Stomach churns and digests the food that comes from oesophagus. In stomach, mechanical digestion of food occurs by alternate contraction and expansion of stomach wall. Also, in stomach, chemical digestion of food takes place when the food is mixed with digestive juice of stomach. Inner lining of stomach secretes mucus, HCl and digestive enzymes. HCl kills bacteria that enter stomach along with food and makes the medium in the stomach acidic to help the digestive enzymes to act. Digestive enzymes of stomach (*e.g.*, pepsin) cause breakdown of proteins into amino acids. Partial digestion of food occurs in stomach and this semidigested food then enters small intestine. Small intestine is the region where complete digestion of food takes place. It receives the bile juice from liver and pancreatic juice from pancreas and secretes several digestive juices of its own. Thus, when the partly digested food from stomach reaches the small intestine, it is mixed with bile, pancreatic juice and intestinal juice; and the complete digestion of all the components of food takes place.

80. (a) Oral Rehydration Solution (ORS) is a type of fluid replacement used as a treatment for dehydration. It involves boiled and cooled water mixed with sugar and salt.

(b) There is no change in colour on adding iodine solution to well chewed rice because starch has been converted into simple sugars during chewing by the action of salivary amylase.

(c) Human beings cannot digest cellulose as they do not have cellulose digesting bacteria in their stomach or intestine.

(d) If we talk while eating or we eat in hurry, the epiglottis may not close and entry of food particles in the windpipe may result in choking, coughing, or hiccups.

81. **(a) :** Stomach (P) is the widest and small intestine (R) is the longest portion of alimentary canal.

82. **(c)** : Stomach (P) is the site where partial digestion of food occurs.

83. **(c)** : The inner wall of small intestine (R) has thousands of finger- like outgrowths called villi, which increase the surface area for absorption of digested food.

84. T is the large intestine. It absorbs water and some salts from undigested food material.

85. Bile juice which is stored in gall bladder (S) has an important role in digestion of fats. Bile breaks up fats into tiny droplets that can be digested and absorbed more easily. Bile also helps in neutralisation of HCl of semi-solid food that comes from stomach (P).

86. **(a)** : Partly digested food gets stored in rumen (label 1).

87. **(c)** : Label 2 is caecum, a sac like structure between oesophagus and small intestine in animals like horses and rabbits.

88. (c)

89. Label 3 is small intestine.

90. Ruminants like cattle, buffalo, sheep, deer etc., possess this type of digestive system.

91. Iodine solution

92. Starch

93. We detect the presence of starch (X) by observing change of colour in test tubes A and B.

94. When iodine solution (Y) is added to boiled rice in test tube A, it turns blue-black due to presence of starch in rice. In test tube B, there is no change in colour as the starch present in the rice has been acted upon by saliva and changes into simple sugars.

95. The conclusion drawn from above experiment is that the saliva breaks down starch into sugars.
Here, in test tube A starch is present in rice as enzyme salivary amylase has not acted upon it whereas in test tube B starch present in rice has been acted upon by salivary amylase present in saliva and has changed into simple sugars.

3 Heat

Practice Corner

1. (a) **2.** (d) **3.** (c) **4.** 4.184
5. False **6.** False **7.** True **8.** (a)
9. (c) **10.** (b) **11.** (c) **12.** (d)
13. clinical thermometer **14.** 35 °C
15. 94 °F to 108 °F **16.** Mercury
17. Hundred **18.** 0 K
19. Kelin

20. False. A clinical thermometer reads temperature from 35 °C to 42 °C.

21. True **22.** False
23. True **24.** True
25. True

26. (d) **27.** (c) **28.** (a) **29.** (d)
30. (a) **31.** True **32.** False **33.** True
34. A→Bulb; B→Mercury
35. (b) **36.** (d) **37.** (d)

38. **(a)** : Wooden ruler and rubber gloves, both are poor conductors of heat.

39. (d) **40.** (c) **41.** (b) **42.** (d)
43. (c) **44.** (d) **45.** (b) **46.** (b)
47. (b) **48.** (b)
49. radiation **50.** poor
51. insulators **52.** conduction
53. expand, cooling **54.** Decrease
55. Closely packed **56.** False
57. False

58. False. Radiation does not require any medium for the heat to flow.

59. True **60.** True **61.** True
62. True **63.** False

64. Pressure difference and temperature difference are the two causes behind the wind in coastal areas due to which transfer of heat takes place between sea and land.

65. Figure (a) – Land breeze
Figure (b) – Sea breeze

66. Convection currents are formed as warm air rises up and cool air settles down. The basic reason is the uneven temperature of atmosphere.

67. Conduction **68.** Conduction
69. Convection **70.** Convection
71. (b) **72.** (d) **73.** (a)
74. warmer **75.** good
76. light, dark **77.** evaporation
78. True **79.** True **80.** True

81. The silver coating on the inner surface of bottle prevents heat transfer by radiation, the vacuum between its double wall prevents heat by convection and the thinness of the glass wall stops heat entering or leaving the flask by conduction.

NCERT Exemplar Problems

1. (a)

2. (b) : So, heat from his body would not escape to the surroundings.

3. (c) : Celcius (°C) and Fahrenheit (°F) are two different scales used for the measurement of temperature.

4. (a) 5. (a) 6. (a)

7. (c) : Normal human body temperature is 37 °C.

A&R Corner

1. (b) : Heat energy always travels from hotter object to colder objects.

2. (c) : Heat always flows from hotter object to colder object.

3. (c) : Air above the sea is cold.

4. (b) : Thermal energy ∝ mass

5. (c) : Heat flows from hotter body to the colder body.

6. (b) : Both correct. Reason R is not the correct explanation of Assertion A.

7. (d) : The range of clinical thermometer is 32 °C to 45 °C.

8. (d) : The air in room can go from one place to another by convection. Both are false.

9. (b) : Both are true but reason is not correct explanation of assertion.

10. (a) : As copper is the best conductor of heat, it gains maximum amount of heat so that the water boils faster as compared to other vessel.

Exam Corner

1. (d) 2. (d) 3. (b)

4. (a) 5. (c)

6. True 7. True 8. True

9. True 10. True

11. (i)-T;(ii)-S;(iii)-Q;(iv)-R;(v)-P

12. $°F = \left(°C \times \frac{9}{5} + 32\right) = \left(45 \times \frac{9}{5} + 32\right) = 113\ °F$

13. $K = °C + 273.15 = 67 + 273.15 = 340.15\ K$

14. $°F = \left(°C \times \frac{9}{5} + 32\right) = \left(95 \times \frac{9}{5} + 32\right) = 203\ °F$

15. $°C = K - 273.15 = 105 - 273.15 = -168.15\ °C$

16. $°F = (K - 273.15) \times \frac{9}{5} + 32 = (99 - 273.15) \times \frac{9}{5} + 32$
$= -281.47\ °F$

17. Conduction 18. Heating

19. Digital thermometer

20. Thermal expansion

21. Alcohol

22. (i) Mercury is a shiny element which makes it easily visible through the glass.
(ii) It expands uniformly for every degree rise in temperature and remains liquid at room temperature.

23. The molecules in a solid are only free to vibrate about their fixed positions. For convection to take place, the molecules need to move carrying the heat with them. Hence, convection cannot take place in solids.

24.

Conductors	Insulators
The materials which allow heat to pass through them easily are known as conductors of heat. *e.g.*, aluminium, iron and copper.	The materials which do not allow heat to pass through them easily are known as insulators of heat. *e.g.*, plastic and wood.

25. The heating coil of the kettle is always placed near the bottom as the water at the bottom of the kettle will be heated by the heating coil. The hot water rises up and the cold water at the top sinks. A convection current is formed so that all the water becomes warm eventually.

26. The expansion produced in a substance on heating is called thermal expansion. On heating, the constituent particles gain energy and start vibrating rapidly and spread out. As a result, the substance expands.

27. Light coloured clothes reflect most of the heat that fall on them and we feel more comfortable wearing them in summer. Dark clothes absorb more heat so we feel comfortable with dark coloured clothes in winter.

28. (i) The thermometer must be washed, preferably with an antiseptic lotion like dettol or spirit or at least with clean water and dried with a clean dry cloth before every use.
(ii) The thermometer should be given two or three soft jerks to bring the mercury in the capillary, well below 37 °C.
(iii) While giving the jerks, care should be taken so that the thermometer does not hit any other object in the surrounding, otherwise its delicate bulb is likely to break.

29. (i) Conduction : The process of transfer of heat from the hotter end to the colder end of an object without any movement of constituents in the object is known as conduction.
(ii) Convection : The process of transfer of heat in which the molecules themselves carry energy from a hotter region to a colder region is called convection.
(iii) Radiation : In this process, heat is directly transferred from one body to another. It does not require any material medium for the transfer of heat.

30. The freezing point of water is referred to as the lower fixed point. The boiling point of water is referred to as the upper fixed point. The upper and the lower fixed points on different temperature scales are given as follows:

	Celsius Scale	Fahrenheit Scale	Kelvin Scale
Lower fixed point	0 °C	32 °F	~273 K
Upper fixed point	100 °C	212 °F	~373 K

31. The fibres of wool have the property of trapping air in between them. In trapping the air, woollen clothes do not allow the heat to flow away from the body, which would then become cold. Besides, wool is poor conductor of heat, so this property further prevents heat from leaving the body.

32.

	Heat	Temperature
1.	It is a form of energy.	It is a thermal condition of body.
2.	It flows from one object to other object when there is a difference in temperature.	It is a quantity that indicates whether or not and in which direction heat will flow.
3.	It is total amount of internal energy of a body.	It is proportional to average kinetic energy of the molecules of a body.
4.	In the transmission of heat, total amount of heat remains unchanged.	In the transmission of heat, temperature does not remain same.
5.	It is a cause.	It is an effect.
6.	Its SI unit is Joule.	Its SI unit is Kelvin (K).

33. Sea breeze : In coastal areas, when the land and the sea absorb heat from the sun during the day, the land heats up faster than the sea. The air above the land becomes hot and moves up, and cooler air from over the sea moves in to take its place. This is called a sea breeze.

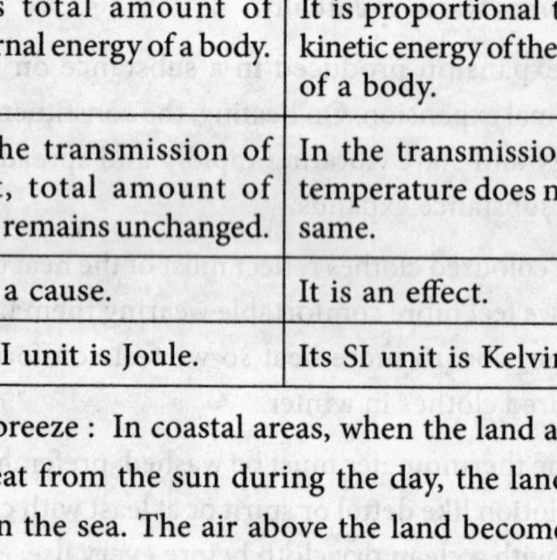

Land breeze : At night, the air above the land cools faster than the air above the sea, and air moves out from over the land towards the sea. This is called a land breeze.

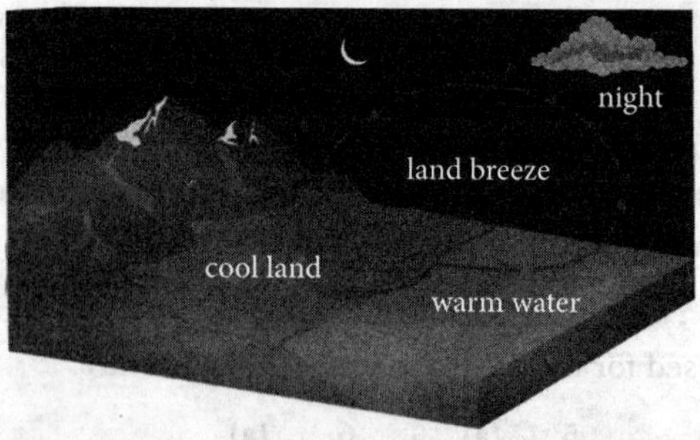

34. It is used by doctors to measure the temperature of the human body. Thermometric liquid used in this thermometer is mercury. It has a stem with an inner capillary tube and a bulb containing mercury. The capillary tube has a small bend in it. This bend prevents the mercury from getting back into the bulb after the thermometer is taken out from a patient's mouth. This enables the doctor to read the thermometer. To reuse it, it has to be given a slight jerk which brings the mercury back into the bulb by flowing past the bend. It is marked from 94 °F to 108 °F and each degree is divided into five small equal parts. For measuring the body temperature, the thermometer bulb is kept under the tongue or in the armpit for about one minute. The normal temperature of a healthy person is 98.6 °F. These days, clinical thermometers are also marked in celsius scale from 35 °C to 42 °C. The normal temperature of human being is 37 °C.

35. (i) An ice-box is made of double wall and the space between the walls is filled with some non-conducting material to provide heat insulation, so that the loss of heat can be minimized.

(ii) We don't need more range as before an after that, the human body cannot survive.

(iii) Materials which are good conductor of heat as well as electricity must have free electrons for energy transfer. But water contains molecules which move far apart on heating. Hence, water acts as insulator of heat whereas metals like silver are good conductor of heat and electricity as they have free electrons.

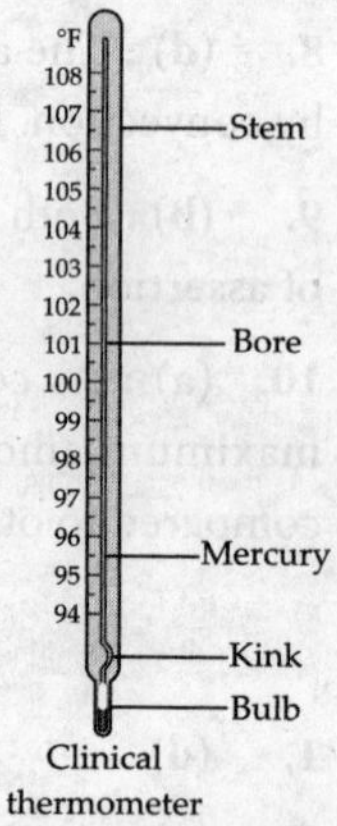

Clinical thermometer

(iv) The metal rim is heated in furnance to expand it and then putting it on the wooden wheel. Eventually, it cools down and makes a firm fit.

36. **(a) :** The lower fixed point of clinical thermometer is 35°C.

37. **(b) :** The range of clinical thermometer is 35 °C – 42 °C or 94 °F – 108 °F.

38. **(c) :** The normal temperature of human body is 37 °C or 98.6 °F,

39. **(c) :** Kink in the clinical thermometer is used to prevent the back flow of mercury into thermometer bulb.

40. Radiation is the fastest mode the heat transfer.

41. In the process of convection, the molecular motion takes place.

42. The solids can be heated by the process of conduction.

43. It is because the silver is a metal and has large number of free electrons.

4 Acids, Bases and Salts

Practice Corner

1. **(c) :** Curd and tamarind are sour in taste and acidic in nature.

2. **(b) :** Soap is basic in nature, rest all are acidic.

3. **(c) :** Acids are corrosive in nature while bases are soapy to touch.

4. (a) **5.** (d)

6. True

7. False. Tamarind contains tartaric acid.

8. True

9. False. Curd contains lactic acid.

10. False. Grapes contain tartaric acid.

11. False. Bases which are soluble in water are called alkalies.

12. False. Potassium hydroxide is a strong base.

13. Formic acid **14.** Amino acid

15. DNA **16.** Carbonic acid

17. Sulphuric acid

18.

19.

20.
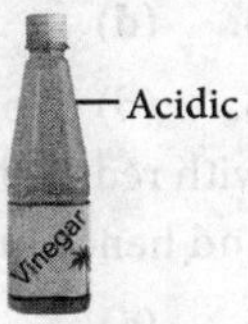

21.
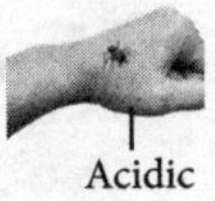

22.

23.

24.
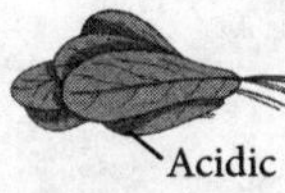

25.
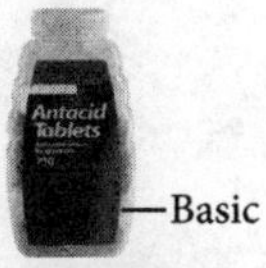

26.

27.

28.
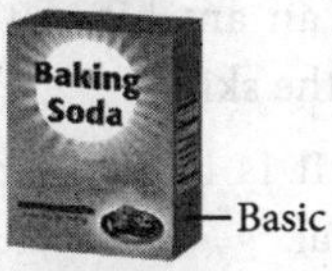

29.

30.

31.
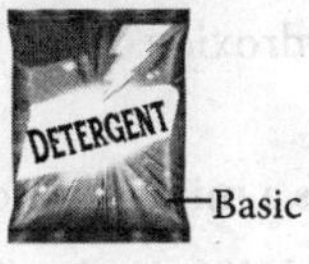

32.

33. magenta **34.** acidic, neutral

35. Acid rain **36.** red, blue

37. red **38.** no **39.** red

40. **(b) :** Phenolphthalein remain colourless with neutral solution.

41. **(c)**

42. **(a) :** Soap solution is basic in nature and phenolphthalein gives pink colour in basic medium.

43. **(b)**

44. **(b) :** China rose indicator turns magenta with acidic solution.

45. **(b) :** Neutral solutions do not show any change in colour with China rose indicator.

46. True

47. False. Phenolphthalein is colourless in acidic solution.

48. False. Phenolphthalein is a synthetic acid-base indicator.

49. False. Sodium hydroxide gives pink colour with phenolphthalein.

50. True

S.No.	Solution	Effect on turmeric solution	Effect on China rose indicator	Inference
51.	Milk of magnesia	Turns red	Turns green	Basic
52.	Orange juice	No effect	Turns dark pink	Acidic
53.	Vinegar	No effect	Turns dark pink	Acidic
54.	Soda water	No effect	Turns dark pink	Acidic
55.	Salt solution	No effect	No effect	Neutral

S.No.	Solution	Effect on red litmus paper	Effect on blue litmus paper	Inference
56.	Lemon juice	No effect	Turns red	Acidic
57.	Soap solution	Turns blue	No effect	Basic
58.	Apple juice	No effect	Turns red	Acidic
59.	Vinegar	No effect	Turns red	Acidic
60.	Baking soda solution	Turns blue	No effect	Basic
61.	Sugar solution	No effect	No effect	Neutral
62.	Distilled water	No effect	No effect	Neutral
63.	Common salt solution	No effect	No effect	Neutral

64. Phenolphthalein **65.** Turmeric solution

66. Neutral substance **67.** China rose solution

68. Red cabbage indicator

69. Neutralisation, acid, base, water, salt, heat, temperature,

70. Calcium sulphate **71.** Salt

72. NaCl **73.** KBr

74. $NaNO_3$

75. False. Heat is always evolved in a neutralisation reaction.

76. False. The reaction mixture becomes hot when dilute sulphuric acid is added to lime water as a neutralisation reaction takes place.

77. True **78.** True

79. True. NaCl is formed when a neutralisation reaction occurs between HCl (strong acid) and NaOH (strong base).

80. (b) **81.** (d)

82. (a) **83.** (b)

84. (d)

85. (i) – (T), (ii) – (S), (iii) – (Q), (iv) – (P), (v) – (R)

86. Magnesium hydroxide

87. Sodium bicarbonate

88. Zinc carbonate

89. Calcium oxide

90. Calcium hydroxide

NCERT Exemplar Problems

1. **(b) :** The correct way of making a solution of acid in water is to add acid to water. It is an exothermic reaction and a large amount of heat is produced if water is added to acid.

2. **(c) :** Salt and water are produced as a result of neutralisation reaction. *e.g.*,

$$NaOH + HCl \rightarrow NaCl + H_2O$$

3. **(b) :** Turmeric paste is yellow in colour. So it remains yellow in acid and changes its colour to red in base.

4. **(d) :** Phenolphthalein remains colourless in acidic solution and turns pink in basic solution.

5. **(a) :** Organic matter is to be added to a basic soil to neutralise the base and improve its quality.

6. **(c) :** Litmus, a natural dye used as an indicator is extracted from lichen.

7. **(d) :** Neutralisation is a chemical and irreversible change. The salt and water formed are new products and cannot be converted back to acid and base.

8. **(a) :** Basic solutions change the colour of turmeric indicator from yellow to red.

9. **(d) :** Curd and vinegar contain lactic acid and acetic acid respectively.

10. **(c) :** Colour of the phenolphthalein does not change with acidic or neutral solution.

11. **(c) :** Turmeric is an acid-base indicator. It is yellow in acidic solution and red in basic solution.

A&R Corner

1. **(c) :** Lemon and orange contain citric acid.

2. (a) **3.** (a) **4.** (a)

5. **(c) :** Acids ar diluted by adding acids to water.

6. (b)

7. **(d) :** Bases give green colour in China rose indicator and pink colour in phenolphthalein solution.

8. (b)

9. **(d) :** A farmer adds quick lime to acidic soil because quick lime neutralises the excess of acid present in soil.

10. (a)

Exam Corner

1. **(b) :** Both water and sodium hydroxide solution will not show any change with blue litmus.

2. **(d) :** Neutral and acidic solutions do not show any change with red litmus paper.

3. **(a) :** Window cleaner and lime water are basic solutions which turn China rose indicator green.

4. (d)

5. **(d) :** Soda water is acidic in nature and hence turns red with red cabbage indicator. Window cleaner is basic in nature and hence turns green with red cabbage indicator.

6. (a) **7.** (a) **8.** (d)

9. **(a) :** Formic acid is an organic acid while rest others are inorganic mineral acids.

10. proteins **11.** basic salt

12. lactic **13.** hydrochloric

14. Organic **15.** acidic

16. False **17.** True

18. True **19.** False

20. False. When an ant bites it injects an acidic liquid, (formic acid) into the skin.

21. Lime water. It is basic in nature while other three solutions are neutral.

22. Magnesium hydroxide. It is a weak base while other two are strong bases.

23. Nitric acid. It is a mineral acid, rest all are organic acids.

24. Carbonic acid. It is a weak acid, rest all are strong acids.

25.

Acids	Bases
(i) Acids are sour in taste.	Bases are bitter in taste.
(ii) Acids turn blue litmus red.	Bases turn red litmus blue.
(iii) pH of acids is always less than 7.	pH of bases is always greater than 7.
(iv) Acids release H^+ ions in their aqueous solutions.	Bases release OH^- ions in their aqueous solutions.

26. Blue litmus paper will turn red. Aerated soft drink is acidic in nature.

27. An indicator is a substance which shows change in colour when added to an acidic or basic solution.
Natural indicators : Turmeric solution, China rose indicator
Synthetic indicators : Methyl orange, phenolphthalein

28. Soap is basic in nature so, when a turmeric stain on white dress comes in contact with soap, it turns red.

29. Neutralisation : An exothermic reaction between an acid and a base to form salt and water is called neutralisation.

$$\underset{\text{Hydrochloric acid (Acid)}}{HCl} + \underset{\text{Sodium hydroxide (Base)}}{NaOH} \rightarrow \underset{\text{Sodium chloride (Salt)}}{NaCl} + \underset{\text{Water}}{H_2O}$$

30. (a)

Substances	pH value	Nature
I	13.9	Basic
II	9.8	Basic
III	2.5	Acidic
IV	4.7	Acidic
V	7.0	Neutral

(b) Increasing order of acidity of the given substances is
I < II < V < IV < III

31. *W* is basic.
X is neutral.
Y is basic.
Z is acidic.

32. Solution (I) : Solution will show red colour. Both acid and base are strong, so after neutralisation, solution will be still basic as NaOH is in excess.
Solution (II) : Solution will show red colour as it is a mixture of two strong acids.
Solution (III) : Solution will remain colourless as acid is in excess.
Solution (IV) : Solution will be magenta in colour as acid is in excess.

33. lichens, purple, acidic, red, basic, blue, litmus, paper, litmus.

34. (a) acidic, dark pink, basic, green
(b) Lime water – Test tube (III)
Acetic acid – Test tube (I)
Common salt – Test tube (II)

35. Examples of neutralisation reaction in our day-to-day life :
(i) Excess of acid in stomach causes acidity and indigestion. It is treated by neutralising the acid with a mild base like milk of magnesia.
(ii) Ant sting contains formic acid which causes inflammation. It is treated by rubbing calamine lotion which is basic in nature and neutralises the acid.
(iii) The bacteria present in mouth produce acids which leads to tooth decay. It is prevented by brushing the teeth with toothpaste which contains bases resulting in neutralisation of the acid.

36. Acidity of a base : Number of replaceable hydroxyl groups (OH^- ions) present in a base is called its acidity.
Monoacidic base : NaOH (Sodium hydroxide)
Diacidic base : $Ca(OH)_2$ (Calcium hydroxide)
Triacidic base : $Al(OH)_3$ (Aluminium hydroxide)

37. Basicity of an acid : Number of replaceable hydrogen atoms present in a molecule of an acid is called basicity of an acid.
Monobasic acid : HCl (Hydrochloric acid)
Dibasic acid : H_2SO_4 (Sulphuric acid)
Tribasic acid : H_3PO_4 (Phosphoric acid)

38. Shobit can easily identify the two chemicals with the help of indicators provided.
Methyl orange, phenolphthalein and China rose indicator when added to hydrochloric acid, it will change the colour to red, colourless and magenta respectively.
With sodium hydroxide solution, methyl orange will give yellow colour, phenolphthalein will give pink colour while China rose indicator will give green colour.

39.

S. No.	pH values	China rose indicator	Phenol-phthalein indicator	Red litmus paper	Nature
1.	3.7	Magenta	Colourless	Red	Acidic
2.	9.5	Green	Pink	Blue	Basic
3.	7.0	Pink	Colourless	Red	Neutral

40.

Sample	Phenol-phthalein indicator	China rose indicator	Nature
A (Toothpaste)	Pink	Green	Basic
B (Curd)	Colourless	Magenta	Acidic

41. A : 12.8, B : 7.0, C : 5.5, D : 2.1, E : 9.4
Significance of pH scale:

(i) The strength of an acid and a base is measured by pH scale.
(ii) Lesser the pH of a solution, more will be its acidic strength.
(iii) Higher the pH of a solution, more will be its basic strength.

42.

S.No.	Sample	Colour of China rose	Colour of methyl orange	Nature
(i)	Orange juice	Magenta	Red	Acidic
(ii)	Lime water	Green	Yellow	Basic
(iii)	Sugar solution	Pink	Orange	Neutral
(iv)	Curd	Magenta	Red	Acidic
(v)	Soap solution	Green	Yellow	Basic

43.

S. No.	Solution	Effect on turmeric solution	Effect on China rose indicator	Inference
(i)	Glucose solution	No effect	No effect	Neutral
(ii)	Nitric acid	No effect	Turns dark pink	Acidic
(iii)	Sodium hydroxide	Turns red	Turns green	Basic

44. (a) Solution (I) can be either an acid or a neutral solution. Solution (II) can be a base.
(b) If excess of solution (I) is added again, the solution becomes colourless and if excess of solution (II) is added again, solution becomes pink in colour.
(c) The process is called neutralisation.

45.

S. No.	Indicator	Colour in acidic medium	Colour in basic medium	Colour in neutral medium
(a)	Blue litmus	Red	Blue	Blue
(b)	Red litmus	Red	Blue	Red
(c)	China rose	Magenta	Green	Pink
(d)	Turmeric	Yellow	Red	Yellow
(e)	Methyl orange	Red	Yellow	Orange
(f)	Phenol-phthalein	Colourless	Pink	Colourless

46. Observations (a to e) are summarised in the table.

Indicator	Soda water (I)	Glucose solution (II)	Lime water (III)
Red litmus paper	Red (No change)	Red (No change)	Blue
Blue litmus paper	Red	Blue (No change)	Blue (No change)
Methyl orange indicator	Red	Orange (No change)	Yellow
Turmeric paper	Yellow (No change)	Yellow (No change)	Red
Phenol-phthalein solution	Colourless	Colourless	Pink
China rose indicator	Magenta	Pink (No change)	Green

47. (a) Sour substances contain acids which react with metals to form salt and hydrogen gas. Hence, sour substances should not be kept in metallic containers.
(b) Food particles (specially sugary particles) stuck in the teeth are decomposed by bacteria present in the mouth which produces acids and causes tooth decay. Hence, we should brush our teeth after meals.
(c) Bee sting is acidic (it injects formic acid into the skin) hence, it is neutralised by baking soda which is basic in nature. Wasp sting is basic hence, it is neutralised by vinegar.

48.

S. No.	Indicator	Potassium sulphate	Sodium carbonate	Ammonium sulphate
(i)	Red litmus paper	No effect	Blue	No effect
(ii)	Blue litmus paper	No effect	No effect	Red
(iii)	Phenol-phthalein indicator	Colourless	Pink	Colourless
(iv)	Methyl orange indicator	No effect	Yellow	Red
(v)	China rose indicator	No effect	Green	Magenta
(vi)	Turmeric solution	No effect	Red	Yellow
(vii)	Red cabbage solution	No effect	Green	Red

49.

S. No.	Sample	Methyl orange	China rose	Phenol-phthalein
(i)	Washing soda	Yellow	Green	Pink
(ii)	Shampoo	Yellow	Green	Pink
(iii)	Distilled water	No change	No change	Colourless
(iv)	Milk of magnesia	Yellow	Green	Pink
(v)	Sulphuric acid	Red	Magenta	Colourless

(a) Acidic substances : Sulphuric acid
(b) Basic substances : Washing soda, shampoo, milk of magnesia
(c) Neutral substances : Distilled water

50.

S. No.	Solution	Effect on red litmus paper	Effect on blue litmus paper	Inference
(i)	Lime water	Turns blue	No effect	Basic
(ii)	Detergent solution	Turns blue	No effect	Basic

(iii)	Milk of magnesia	Turns blue	No effect	Basic
(iv)	Aerated drink	No effect	Turns red	Acidic
(v)	Shampoo	Turns blue	No effect	Basic
(vi)	Washing soda solution	Turns blue	No effect	Basic
(vii)	Window cleaner	Turns blue	No effect	Basic

51. (a) **Indigestion :** Indigestion is caused by excess of acid in stomach. It is treated by neutralising the acid with a mild base. Antacids like milk of magnesia contain mild bases.

(b) **Ant bite :** An ant bite injects formic acid into our skin which causes pain and inflammation. The acid is neutralised by bases like sodium bicarbonate or zinc carbonate (calamine solution).

(c) **Acidic soil :** Excessive use of fertilisers makes the soil acidic which is not good for plants. To neutralise the acidity of the soil, some bases like slaked lime or quick lime is added to it.

(d) **Basic soil :** Organic matter is added to soil to treat excess basicity. Bacterial decomposition of organic matter releases acids which neutralise the basicity of soil.

(e) **Factory wastes:** Factory wastes are neutralised by adding basic substances before allowing them to flow into water bodies as they contain acids.

52. **(d) :** Neutralisation reaction is used in treatment of ant bite, indigestion and factory wastes.

53. **(a) :** The aqueous solution of sodium hydroxide (NaOH) is basic in nature as NaOH dissociates to give hydroxide ions (OH^-) in its aqueous solution. Therefore, it turns red litmus blue.

$$NaOH_{(aq)} \rightleftharpoons Na^+_{(aq)} + OH^-_{(aq)}$$

54. **(d) :** Sodium hydroxide is not used in the treatment of indigestion as it is a strong base that can burn the mouth and walls of stomach. Neutralisation is an exothermic process. When an ant bites, it injects formic acid into the skin.

55. **(d) :** A neutralisation reaction between limewater, $[Ca(OH)_2]$ and sulphuric acid (H_2SO_4) produces calcium sulphate ($CaSO_4$) and water (H_2O) as shown below :

$$Ca(OH)_2 + H_2SO_4 \rightarrow CaSO_4 + 2H_2O$$

56. **(b) :** $NaHCO_3$ is a mild base and will neutralise the acid. KOH is much stronger which is corrosive in nature. Moreover its reaction with acid will produce much heat which can also damage the skin.

57. The pink colour of the solution disappears and the solution becomes colourless.

58. The blue litmus paper turns red as sour milk contains lactic acid.

59. NaCl solution is neutral. No colour change is observed in this case.

60. A China rose indicator turns green when it is added to milk of magnesia. Hence, it is basic.

5 Physical and Chemical Changes

Practice Corner

1. **(d) :** Dissolving salt in water and stretching of a rubber band are physical changes.

2. **(b) :** A physical change is generally reversible.

3. **(c) :** Burning of paper is a chemical change, rest all are physical changes.

4. **(c) :** Melting of wax and condensation of steam are physical-reversible changes while slaking of lime is a chemical-irreversible change and plucking of leaves is a physical-irreversible change.

5. **(d) :** Breaking of a flower vase is a physical-irreversible change.

6.

P

7.
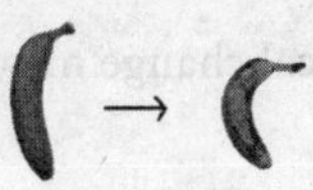
C

8.
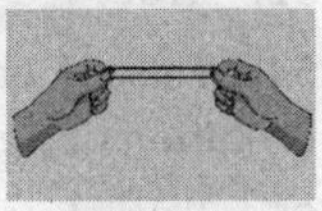
P

9.

P

10.

P

11.

P

12.

C

13.

P

14.

P

15.

C

16.

P

S.No.	Changes	Property of the substance which undergoes a change
17.	Folding a paper to make paper boat	Shape and size
18.	Heating an iron nail	Colour
19.	Making a paste of chalk from its dust	Shape
20.	Cutting a log of wood	Shape
21.	Melting of ice-cream	State

22. False **23.** False

24. False **25.** False

26. Melting of ice **27.** Cutting of wood

28. Shredding of paper **29.** Inflating a balloon

30. Vaporisation of water **31.** Condensation

32. Evaporation

33. (b) 34. (c)

35. (b) : $\underset{\text{Lime water}}{Ca(OH)_2} + \underset{\text{Carbon dioxide}}{CO_2} \rightarrow \underset{\text{Calcium carbonate}}{CaCO_3} + \underset{\text{Water}}{H_2O}$

36. (c) : Reaction will not take place as copper is less reactive than iron.

37. (a) 38. (d) 39. (b)

40. calcium carbonate 41. carbon dioxide

42. blue, green, iron sulphate, copper

43. carbon dioxide 44. rust (iron oxide)

45. iron sulphate 46. Burning of wood

47. Neutralisation reaction

48. Burning of a candle

49. Bursting fire crackers 50. True

51. False. Sound may be produced during a chemical change.

52. True 53. True

54. False. A chemical change may be accompanied with the evolution of a gas.

55. False. Explosion of a firework is a chemical change.

56. True

57. Neutralisation 58. Oxidation

59. Chemical change 60. Reduction

61. Precipitation

62. (c) 63. (c) 64. (b) 65. (d)

66. (d)

67. Rusting, chemical, oxygen, water, moisture, air, high

68. Paint, grease, metal, zinc, galvanisation, salty.

69. (a) : Crystallisation is the process in which a substance is dissolved in a solvent to get crystals of pure substance.

70. (d) : Salt can be obtained from sea water by evaporation and crystallisation.

71. (c) : Rusting is a chemical and irreversible change.

72. Evaporation 73. blue

74. True 75. True

NCERT Exemplar Problems

1. (d) : Melting of wax is a physical change. All other changes are chemical changes.

2. (b) : Cooking of vegetables is a chemical change.

3. (d) : A chemical change may involve change in colour, temperature, smell or evolution of gas, heat, etc.

4. (c) : When milk changes to curd it becomes semi solid. The taste of milk changes and the change is irreversible but there is no change in colour. It remains white only.

5. (d) : Painting can prevent rusting and the objects look more beautiful.

6. (d) : Iron pillar near Qutub Minar in Delhi is famous for its stability because it has not rusted over a long period.

7. (a) : During galvanisation iron is coated with zinc in order to prevent it from rusting.

8. (a) : Mixing of sugar in water is a physical change and crystals of sugar can be separated from a supersaturated solution hence it is a reversible change.

9. (a) : Heat may be given out or absorbed during a chemical reaction.

10. (c) : Dissolution of copper sulphate powder in water in presence of sulphuric acid is a physical change. On cooling this hot solution, the crystals of copper sulphate are separated. This is also a physical change.

A&R Corner

1. (b) 2. (a) 3. (a)

4. (c) : Rusting is an irreversible chemical change.

5. (d) : Rust is iron oxide (hydrated). Iron is coated with zinc to prevent rusting.

6. (b)

7. (d) : Setting of curd is an irreversible chemical change as properties of milk and curd are completely different.

8. (a)

9. (c) : Crystals of pure sugar separate from saturated solution on cooling.

10. (a)

Exam Corner

1. (c) 2. (d) 3. (b) 4. (d)

5. (c) : Ba and Mg are atoms while H_2 and CO_2 are molecules.

6. (d) : Burning of a candle and burning of LPG in kitchen involve both physical and chemical changes.

7. (a)

8. (c) : In a double displacement reaction, two compounds react by exchanging their ions to form two new compounds.

9. (b) : Cl_2 is removing H_2 from H_2S hence, it is an oxidizing agent.

10. (a) (I) **Irreversible-physical changes** - cutting a log of wood into pieces, punching a hole in a paper.

(II) **Chemical change** - Breaking down of ozone, lime water turning milky, digestion of food.

(III) **Reversible- physical change** - Melting of glaciers.

11. (d) : Carbon dioxide and sulphur dioxide both turn lime water milky.

12. (c) : Iron (Fe)(u) reacts with H_2O and O_2(v) present in moist air to form rust $Fe_2O_3 \cdot xH_2O$(w).

13. True 14. True

15. False. Reaction of magnesium and oxygen gives magnesium oxide.

16. True

17. False. Carbon dioxide gas is produced when acetic acid reacts with sodium hydrogencarbonate.

18. True

19. False. Magnesium burns with a dazzling white flame.

20. False. Carbon dioxide gas turns lime water milky.

21. False. Most of the chemical changes are irreversible.

22. (i) MgO (T) (ii) $FeSO_4 + Cu$ (S)
(iii) Fe_2O_3 (U) (iv) $Mg(OH)_2$ (Q)
(v) $CH_3COONa + CO_2 + H_2O$ (P)
(vi) $CaCO_3 + H_2O$ (R)

23. (i)-(Q), (ii)-(S), (iii)-(P), (iv)-(R)

24. (i)-(S), (ii)-(P), (iii)-(Q), (iv)-(R)

25. (i)-(R), (ii)-(P), (iii)-(S), (iv)-(Q)

26. magnesium hydroxide

27. saturated, crystallisation

28. physical **29.** Carbon dioxide

30. Hydrogen **31.** Physical change

32. Rust **33.** Decomposition

34. Galvanisation **35.** Crystallisation

36. $\underset{\text{Magnesium}}{2Mg} + \underset{\text{Oxygen}}{O_2} \rightarrow \underset{\text{Magnesium oxide}}{2MgO}$

37. $\underset{\text{Iron}}{Fe} + \underset{\text{Moist air}}{O_2 + H_2O} \rightarrow \underset{\text{Ferric oxide (Rust)}}{Fe_2O_3}$

38. $\underset{\text{Carbon dioxide}}{CO_2} + \underset{\text{Lime water}}{Ca(OH)_2} \rightarrow \underset{\text{Calcium carbonate}}{CaCO_3} + \underset{\text{Water}}{H_2O}$

39. $\underset{\text{Iron}}{Fe} + \underset{\text{Copper sulphate}}{CuSO_4} \rightarrow \underset{\text{Iron sulphate}}{FeSO_4} + \underset{\text{Copper}}{Cu}$

40. $\underset{\text{Zinc}}{Zn} + \underset{\text{Hydrochloric acid}}{2HCl_{(dil.)}} \rightarrow \underset{\text{Zinc chloride}}{ZnCl_2} + \underset{\text{Hydrogen}}{H_2}$

41. $\underset{\text{Acetic acid (Vinegar)}}{CH_3COOH} + \underset{\text{Sodium hydrogen carbonate (Baking soda)}}{NaHCO_3} \rightarrow \underset{\text{Sodium acetate (Salt)}}{CH_3COONa} + \underset{\text{Water}}{H_2O} + \underset{\text{Carbon dioxide}}{CO_2}$

42. $\underset{\text{Magnesium oxide (Ash)}}{MgO} + \underset{\text{Water}}{H_2O} \rightarrow \underset{\text{Magnesium hydroxide}}{Mg(OH)_2}$

43. $\underset{\text{Sodium hydroxide (Base)}}{NaOH} + \underset{\text{Hydrochloric acid (Acid)}}{HCl} \rightarrow \underset{\text{Sodium chloride (Salt)}}{NaCl} + \underset{\text{Water}}{H_2O}$

44. Burning of magnesium in air

45. Addition of oxygen **46.** Physical change

47. Decomposition **48.** Sublimation

49. Chemical, heat, light, absorbed, chemical, heat, rust iron, rusting.

50.

Physical change	Chemical change
(i) It is a temporary change.	It is a permanent change.
(ii) It is mostly reversible change.	It is mostly irreversible change.
(iii) No new substances are formed during a physical change.	New substances are formed during a chemical change.
(iv) It involves change in shape, size, colour and state.	It involves change in chemical composition.

51. When a pinch of baking soda is added to vinegar, bubbles of carbon dioxide gas are evolved with hissing sound. The gas produced is carbon dioxide which can be tested by bringing a burning matchstick near the mouth of the test tube which gets extinguished.

$\underset{\text{Acetic acid (Vinegar)}}{CH_3COOH} + \underset{\text{Sodium hydrogen carbonate (Baking soda)}}{NaHCO_3} \rightarrow \underset{\text{Sodium acetate (Salt)}}{CH_3COONa} + \underset{\text{Water}}{H_2O} + \underset{\text{Carbon dioxide}}{CO_2}$

52. Whenever a more reactive metal is added to a salt solution, the less reactive metal is displaced from its salt solution. The reaction is known as displacement reaction. When iron is dipped in copper sulphate solution, a displacement reaction takes place. Iron being more reactive than copper displaces copper from copper sulphate solution. This copper can be deposited on the iron.

$\underset{\text{Copper sulphate (Blue)}}{CuSO_4} + \underset{\text{Iron}}{Fe} \rightarrow \underset{\text{Iron sulphate (Green)}}{FeSO_4} + \underset{\text{Copper (Brown deposit)}}{Cu}$

53. (a) Cut vegetables and fruits turn brown when exposed to air due to oxidation. The exposed layer of vegetables and fruits reacts with oxygen present in the atmosphere and gets oxidised as a result of which they turn brown. It is a chemical-irreversible change as new substance is formed.

(b) Crystallisation takes place when a saturated solution is left for cooling. It is a physical-reversible change as no new substance is formed.

54. Alloying: Alloying is a process in which two or more metals or a metal and a non-metal are mixed in molten state to improve the properties of the metals. Iron gets rusted in moist air. Iron is mixed with a small amount of carbon and metals like chromium or manganese to make stainless steel. Stainless steel does not get rusted. Other examples of alloys are brass, bronze, duralumin etc.

Galvanisation: Galvanisation is the process of depositing a layer of zinc on iron. The coating of zinc does not allow the iron article to come in contact with air and moisture and thus prevents it from getting rusted.

55. Burning of candle is both a physical and a chemical change. A candle is made up of a substance called paraffin wax, which is a hydrocarbon. When a candle is lighted, the wax around the wick melts (physical change) and vapours are formed which catch fire and form the flame of a candle (chemical change).

$\underset{\text{(Hydrocarbon)}}{Wax} + O_2 \rightarrow \underset{\text{(Soot)}}{C} + H_2O + CO_2$

56. Chemical equation for rusting of iron is

$$\underset{\text{(Iron)}}{Fe} + \underset{\text{(Oxygen)}}{O_2} + \underset{\text{(Water)}}{H_2O} \rightarrow \underset{\text{(Rust)}}{Fe_2O_3 \cdot xH_2O}$$

57. Painting, greasing or coating an article with metal prevents the contact of iron with moisture and oxygen.

58. Rusting of iron articles is faster in coastal areas than in deserts because coastal areas are more humid.

59. Galvanisation: The process of depositing a layer of zinc on iron is called galvanisation. At homes, iron pipes used to carry water are galvanised.

60. Yes, mixing iron with other metals prevent rusting. Stainless steel is made by mixing iron with carbon and metals like chromium, nickel and manganese. This process is called alloying.

61. (a) Burning of paper C
(b) Tearing of paper P
(c) Melting of ice P
(d) Inflating a balloon P
(e) Stretching of rubber band P
(f) Folding a paper to make paper boat P
(g) Burning of wood C
(h) Cutting of wood P
(i) Rusting of iron C
(j) Baking a cake C

62. (a) Crystallisation
(b) It is a physical change as no new substance is formed and crystals can be redissolved to make the solution.
(c) To prepare pure crystals of copper sulphate, a few drops of sulphuric acid are added to a cup of water and then the water is boiled. Then, powdered copper sulphate is added to it with continuous stirring. When the solution becomes saturated, it is filtered and left undisturbed. When the solution gets cooled, pure crystals separate out at the bottom of the container.
(d) The process is used to obtain salt from sea water.

63. (a) (i) Crystals are solids in their purest forms that have definite geometrical shapes.
(ii) Crystallisation is the process in which pure crystals of a substance are separated from its saturated solution.
(b) To get crystals of pure sugar, the sugar is dissolved in minimum amount of water and heated to get its saturated solution. Solution is filtered to remove any impurities present in the sugar. Crystals of pure sugar separate out from the filtrate on cooling the solution.

64. The reaction in which two compounds react by exchanging their ions to form two new compounds is called double displacement reaction.
Precipitation reaction: The reaction in which two compounds react in their aqueous state to form an insoluble product, which appears in the form of a precipitate is called a precipitation reaction.
Aqueous solutions of sodium chloride and silver nitrate react to form a white precipitate of silver chloride.

$$\underset{\text{Sodium chloride}}{NaCl} + \underset{\text{Silver nitrate}}{AgNO_3} \rightarrow \underset{\text{Silver chloride (white ppt.)}}{AgCl\downarrow} + \underset{\text{Sodium nitrate}}{NaNO_3}$$

Neutralisation reaction: An acid reacts with a base and the ions are exchanged to form salt and water.

$$\underset{\text{Hydrochloric acid (Acid)}}{HCl} + \underset{\text{Sodium hydroxide (Base)}}{NaOH} \rightarrow \underset{\text{Sodium chloride (Salt)}}{NaCl} + \underset{\text{Water}}{H_2O}$$

65. A chemical equation is the representation of a chemical reaction through symbols and chemical formulae in which number of atoms of each element on the reactant side is equal to that on the product side.
Steps for balancing the chemical equation:
(i) Write down the symbols and formulae of the reactants on the left hand side and those of the products on the right hand side of an arrow.
(ii) Count the atoms of each kind on both sides of the arrow.
(iii) Make the number of atoms of each kind, equal on both sides by using proper coefficients.
For example,

$$CH_4 + O_2 \xrightarrow{\text{Heat}} CO_2 + H_2O$$

C = 1 C = 1
H = 4 H = 2
O = 2 O = 3

$$CH_4 + 2O_2 \xrightarrow{\text{Heat}} CO_2 + 2H_2O$$

C = 1 C = 1
H = 4 H = 4
O = 4 O = 4

66. When dil. hydrochloric acid is added to calcium carbonate, carbon dioxide gas is evolved.
When carbon dioxide gas is passed through a test tube containing lime water, it forms a white solid substance called calcium carbonate. This turns the solution milky.

$$\underset{\text{Calcium carbonate}}{CaCO_3} + \underset{\text{Hydrochloric acid}}{2HCl_{(dil.)}} \rightarrow \underset{\text{Calcium chloride}}{CaCl_2} + \underset{\text{Water}}{H_2O} + \underset{\text{Carbon dioxide}}{CO_2}$$

$$\underset{\text{Lime water}}{Ca(OH)_2} + \underset{\text{Carbon dioxide}}{CO_2} \rightarrow \underset{\text{Calcium carbonate}}{CaCO_3} + \underset{\text{Water}}{H_2O}$$

67. Burning of a substance in the presence of oxygen is called combustion. It is a chemical change as new substances like carbon dioxide and water are formed during combustion. Take a small piece of magnesium ribbon. Hold it with a pair of tongs and heat it on the burner. The magnesium ribbon burns with a dazzling white flame. It forms a powdery ash when it is burnt completely. A new substance is formed after burning magnesium. This powdery ash is known as magnesium oxide.

Magnesium + Oxygen → Magnesium oxide

$$2Mg + O_2 \rightarrow 2MgO$$

Thus, burning of magnesium in air is a chemical change due to formation of a new compound magnesium oxide.

68. Crystallisation is the process in which pure crystals of a substance are separated from its saturated solution. It is a physical-reversible change as no new substance is formed during crystallisation and crystals can be redissolved to make the solution.

Dissolve copper sulphate in half a beaker of water. Add a few drops of dilute sulphuric acid. Heat the solution and keep adding more copper sulphate till a saturated solution is formed and no more copper sulphate can be added to it. Filter the solution in a china dish and keep the filtrate undisturbed for some time. As the solution cools it becomes a supersaturated solution. Blue crystals of copper sulphate separate out at the bottom of china dish.

69. Rusting is a chemical change which takes place in the presence of air and moisture.

Rust is a reddish-brown powder deposited on iron objects which is formed by reaction of iron with air and water present in the atmosphere. It is hydrated iron oxide.

Iron + Oxygen + Water → Rust (Hydrated iron oxide)

$$\underset{}{Fe} + \underbrace{O_2 + H_2O}_{\text{From atmosphere}} \rightarrow \underset{\text{Hydrated iron oxide}}{Fe_2O_3.xH_2O}$$

There are two main factors which are responsible for rusting of iron :

(i) Presence of air or oxygen.

(ii) Presence of water or moisture.

Both these factors have to be present for iron to get rusted. If any of these *i.e.*, either air or water are absent, rusting will not take place.

Rusting can be prevented by painting, greasing, galvanisation and alloying.

70. Take three test tubes and put 2 iron nails in each test tube. Put some calcium chloride in test tube marked as (I) and put cork on the test tube. Put some boiled water in test tube marked as (II) and cover the surface of water with oil and cork the test tube. In test tube (III) put some tap water and put the cork. Keep the test tubes for a few days.

In test tube (I) the nails are not rusted because there is no moisture due to calcium chloride. There is no rusting in test tube (II) because the layer of oil on water prevents air to come in contact with nails. The nails in test tube (III) get rusted because they are exposed to both water and air. Hence, rusting requires both air and water.

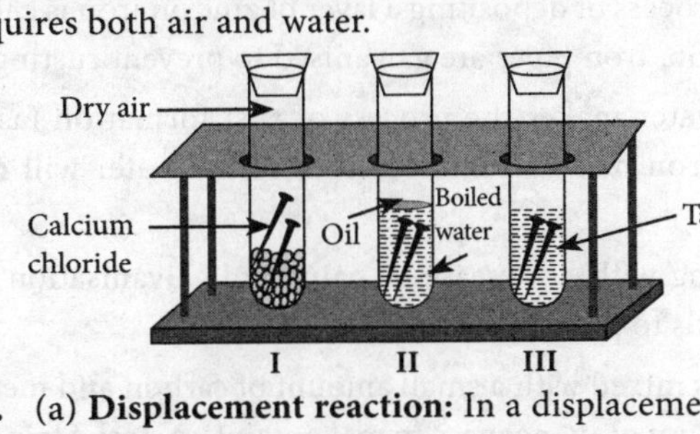

71. (a) **Displacement reaction:** In a displacement reaction, one element displaces another element from a compound and takes its place. A more reactive element displaces a less reactive element from a compound in solution form.

If a piece of copper wire is dipped in silver nitrate solution, it gets coated with silver, and the colour of the solution changes to bluish due to the formation of copper nitrate.

$$\underset{\text{Silver nitrate}}{2AgNO_3} + \underset{\text{Copper}}{Cu} \rightarrow \underset{\text{Copper nitrate}}{Cu(NO_3)_2} + \underset{\text{Silver}}{2Ag}$$

(b) **Oxidation reaction:** Oxidation reaction involves addition of oxygen or removal of hydrogen from a substance.

When carbon reacts with oxygen to form carbon dioxide, it is said to be oxidised by gaining oxygen.

$$\underset{\text{Carbon}}{C} + \underset{\text{Oxygen}}{O_2} \rightarrow \underset{\text{Carbon dioxide}}{CO_2\uparrow}$$

When hydrogen sulphide reacts with chlorine, hydrogen sulphide is said to be oxidised to sulphur by loss of hydrogen.

$$\underset{\text{Hydrogen sulphide}}{H_2S} + \underset{\text{Chlorine}}{Cl_2} \rightarrow \underset{\text{Sulphur}}{S} + \underset{\text{Hydrogen chloride}}{2HCl}$$

(c) **Combination reaction:** In a combination reaction, two or more reactants combine to form a product.

Nitrogen reacts with hydrogen to form ammonia.

$$\underset{\text{Nitrogen}}{N_2} + \underset{\text{Hydrogen}}{3H_2} \rightarrow \underset{\text{Ammonia}}{2NH_3\uparrow}$$

(d) **Reduction reaction:** Reduction reaction involves addition of hydrogen or removal of oxygen from a substance.

When hydrogen is passed over heated black copper oxide, the latter changes to reddish-brown copper metal. Here, copper oxide is said to be reduced to copper by loss of oxygen.

$$\underset{\text{Hydrogen}}{H_2} + \underset{\text{Copper oxide}}{CuO} \rightarrow \underset{\text{Copper}}{Cu} + \underset{\text{Water}}{H_2O}$$

Chlorine reacts with hydrogen in the presence of diffused light to form hydrogen chloride. Chlorine is said to be reduced to hydrogen chloride by gain of hydrogen.

$$\underset{\text{Chlorine}}{Cl_2} + \underset{\text{Hydrogen}}{H_2} \rightarrow \underset{\text{Hydrogen chloride}}{2HCl}$$

(e) **Decomposition reaction:** In a decomposition reaction, single reactant breaks down into two or more simpler products.

When calcium hydroxide is heated, calcium oxide and steam are produced.

$$\underset{\text{Calcium hydroxide}}{Ca(OH)_2} \rightarrow \underset{\text{Calcium oxide}}{CaO} + \underset{\text{Water (Steam)}}{H_2O}$$

72. (a) A shiny copper vessel turns green after some time due to formation of green coloured basic copper carbonate.

(b) Iron when comes in contact with oxygen and water undergoes rusting. Hence, it is coated with zinc.

(c) In coastal areas climate is humid hence, iron rusts faster.

73. (a) It is a chemical-irreversible change. A new substance is formed which cannot be converted back to magnesium ribbon.

(b) The powdery ash formed after burning magnesium ribbon is magnesium oxide which does not resemble with magnesium ribbon.

The chemical equation for this reaction is as follows :

$$\underset{\text{Magnesium}}{Mg} + \underset{\text{Oxygen}}{O_2} \rightarrow \underset{\text{Magnesium oxide}}{MgO}$$

(c) When magnesium oxide is dissolved in water, a new substance called magnesium hydroxide is formed.

The chemical equation is

$$\underset{\text{Magnesium oxide}}{MgO} + \underset{\text{Water}}{H_2O} \rightarrow \underset{\text{Magnesium hydroxide}}{Mg(OH)_2}$$

It is also a chemical change as a new substance is formed. The new compound formed (magnesium hydroxide) is basic in nature. The basic nature can be tested by red litmus paper which will turn blue in this solution.

74. (a) It is a chemical change as new substances are formed.

(b) Yes, colour of the solution changes from blue to green. Copper sulphate is blue in colour. When iron blade is dipped in this solution, iron displaces copper from the solution and green coloured solution of iron sulphate is formed.

(c) Yes, there is a brown deposit on the iron blade. The brown deposit is copper which gets displaced from the solution and deposits on the iron blade.

(d) $$\underset{\text{Copper sulphate (Blue)}}{CuSO_4} + \underset{\text{Iron}}{Fe} \rightarrow \underset{\text{Iron sulphate (Green)}}{FeSO_4} + \underset{\text{Copper (Brown deposit)}}{Cu}$$

75. (a) '*X*' is carbon dioxide, the gas evolved when vinegar is mixed with baking soda.

(b) It is a chemical change as new substances are formed.

(c) The chemical reaction is

$$\underset{\text{Vinegar (Acetic acid)}}{CH_3COOH} + \underset{\text{Baking soda (Sodium bicarbonate)}}{NaHCO_3} \rightarrow \underset{\text{Sodium acetate}}{CH_3COONa} + \underset{\text{Water}}{H_2O} + \underset{\text{Carbon dioxide}}{CO_2}$$

(d) When gas '*X*' is passed through lime water, lime water turns milky due to formation of calcium carbonate.

Carbon dioxide (CO_2) + Lime water [$Ca(OH)_2$]
→ Calcium carbonate ($CaCO_3$) + Water (H_2O)

(e) It is a neutralisation reaction.

76. (a) Figure (I) represents mixture of iron filings and sulphur powder which can easily be separated by magnetic separation. Hence, it is a physical change.

Figure (II) represents heating of iron filings and sulphur powder mixture to form iron sulphide which is a chemical change as a new substance is formed which has properties totally different from iron and sulphur.

(b) Characteristics of a physical change:

(i) No new substance is formed.

(ii) The properties of substances remain same after a physical change.

(iii) Only physical properties like appearance, texture, colour, smell, etc. change.

(iv) Physical changes are generally reversible.

Characteristics of a chemical change:

(i) Chemical changes are generally irreversible.

(ii) One or more new substances are formed.

(iii) New substances have properties different from the original substances.

(iv) Heat, light or both may be produced during a chemical change.

77. (a) It is a chemical change. No, it cannot be reversed.

(b) Gas '*X*' is hydrogen gas.

(c) $$\underset{\text{Zinc}}{Zn} + \underset{\text{Sulphuric acid}}{H_2SO_{4(dil.)}} \rightarrow \underset{\text{Zinc sulphate}}{ZnSO_4} + \underset{\text{Hydrogen}}{H_2}$$

(d) It will get extinguished.

(e) Yes, the test tube feels warm after this experiment because heat is evolved in this reaction.

78. (a) Tearing of paper is a physical-irreversible change.

(b) Making an aeroplane or a paper boat by folding a paper is a physical-reversible change.

(c) Three characteristics of a physical change:

(i) No new substance is formed.

(ii) Only physical properties of the substance get changed.

(iii) Most of the physical changes are reversible in nature.

79. (a) Steam gets condensed on the pan.

(b) These changes are physical changes as only change in state is taking place and no new substance is formed.

(c) These changes are reversible as state of water can be changed by heating or cooling.

(d) State of the substance

80. **(d)** : Melting of ice and sublimation of naphthalene are physical changes.

81. **(d)** : Shredding of paper is a physical and irreversible change whereas digestion of food is a chemical-irreversible change.

82. **(b)**

83. **(c)** : Reaction of vinegar with baking soda (neutralisation reaction) and respiration are also exothermic processes.

84. **(b)** : Ripening of fruits and slaking of lime are chemical irreversible change whereas dissolution of glucose is a physical reversible change.

85. Higher the content of moisture in air, higher will be the rate of rusting, which means if it is more humid, the rate of rusting increases.

86. The process of depositing a layer of zinc on iron is called galvanisation. Iron pipes are galvanised to prevent rusting.

87. Salt water makes the process of rust formation faster. Thus, the iron nail half immersed in saline water will rust faster.

88. Coating with oil, grease or paint and galvanisation are two methods to prevent rusting.

89. Iron is mixed with a small amount of carbon and metals like chromium or manganese to make stainless steel. Stainless steel does not get rusted.

90. The chemical formula of rust is $Fe_2O_3 \cdot xH_2O$.

6 Respiration in Organisms

Practice Corner

1. (d)

2. (a) : During vigorous muscular activities, like fast running, brisk walking or heavy exercise, more energy is needed. Therefore, demand for oxygen also increases, but oxygen supply to muscles remains unchanged. Due to this temporary deficiency of oxygen, skeletal muscles respire anaerobically and glucose partially breaks down to lactic acid releasing energy. Accumulation of lactic acid leads to muscle cramps.

3. (c) : When breakdown of glucose into carbon dioxide and water occurs in the body cells, in the presence of oxygen, it is called aerobic respiration. A large amount of energy is released during this process. Majority of animals and plants perform aerobic respiration.

4. (d) : In yeasts, glucose breaks down into ethyl alcohol and carbon dioxide.

$$\text{Glucose} \xrightarrow[\text{of oxygen}]{\text{In the absence}} \text{Ethyl alcohol + Carbon dioxide + Energy}$$

5. (b) : We breathe out air rich in carbon dioxide. In aerobic respiration, food (glucose) is broken down into carbon dioxide and water using oxygen.

6. (b) : Sometimes during heavy physical exercise, your body cannot get enough oxygen to produce the required energy. To get the additional energy, anaerobic respiration occurs in your muscle cells, during which partial breakdown of glucose occurs and lactic acid is produced. The accumulation of lactic acid in muscles causes muscular cramps.

$$\text{Glucose} \xrightarrow[\text{of oxygen in muscle cells}]{\text{In the absence}} \text{Lactic acid + Energy}$$

7. (d) : Cellular respiration takes place all the time in all organisms.

8. (b)

9. energy, respiration, carbon dioxide, water, oxygen, cellular respiration.

10. aerobic, anaerobic, presence, absence.

11. False. Cellular respiration takes place in all the cells of all organisms.

12. False. In yeast, glucose is broken down into ethyl alcohol and carbon dioxide.

13. True 14. True

15. False. Inhaled air is rich in oxygen.

16. True 17. True

18. False. The muscle cramps occur when muscle cells respire anaerobically. The partial breakdown of glucose produces lactic acid, accumulation of which causes cramps.

19. 1. Anaerobic respiration

2. $\text{Glucose} \xrightarrow[\text{of oxygen}]{\text{In the absence}} \text{Lactic acid + Energy}$

20. (b) : On an average, an adult human being at rest breathes in and out 15–18 times in a minute. During heavy exercise, the breathing rate can increase upto 25 times per minute.

21. (c) : The breathing rate does not remain the same under all conditions. It increases when we need more energy, *i.e.*, while walking, running or exercising. It slows down when we are taking complete rest doing no work. When breathing rate slows down to the extent that we do not get sufficient oxygen, we feel sleepy or drowsy. Thus, breathing rate changes according to the requirement of oxygen by the body.

22. (b) 23. (b)

24. (b) : Breathing is a physical (or mechanical) process. It involves taking in air rich in oxygen (inhalation) and giving out air rich in carbon dioxide (exhalation). It occurs outside the cells and does not release energy. Respiration is a biochemical process which occurs inside the cells. It involves oxidation of food (glucose) to release carbon dioxide, water and energy.

25. inhalation, exhalation 26. 15-18

27. increases 28. Breathing 29. breathe

30. (d) 31. (b)

32. (a) : Both oesophagus and trachea open into pharynx. Thus, it serves as a common passage for both food and air.

33. (b)

34. (c) : Space in the chest cavity decreases during exhalation. During inhalation, diaphragm moves down.

35. (c)

36. (b) : Here, P and Q represent inhalation and exhalation respectively. During exhalation (Q), the space in our chest cavity reduces in size which pushes air out of the lungs.

37. (d) : In the given experimental set up, when the rubber sheet is pulled down, the space inside the bell jar increases and the air pressure decreases. Air from the open end of the Y-tube rushes in to fill the cavity. This expands the small balloons. This is similar to the expansion of lungs during inhalation.

38. (a)

39. (d) : In the given figure, I represents trachea, II represents bronchus, III represents bronchiole and IV represents alveoli (or air sacs). Exchange of gases takes place in the alveoli, which are surrounded by blood vessels.

40.

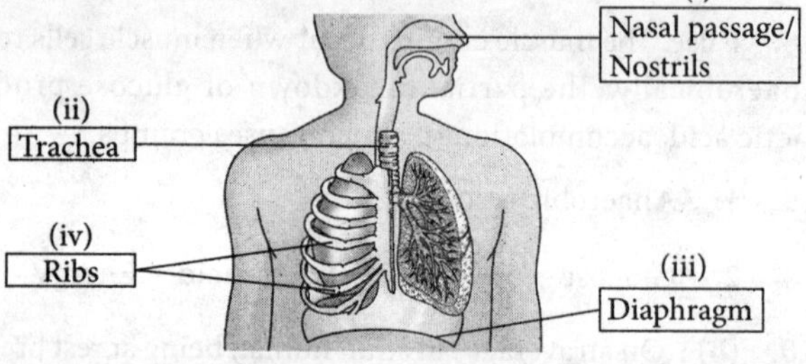

41. Diaphragm **42.** Lungs, chest cavity

43. lungs, cancer **44.** diaphragm, ribcage **45.** Sneeze

46. False. Breathing involves the movement of diaphragm and ribcage.

47. True

48. False. Our lungs are surrounded by ribs.

49. False. Our lungs contract during exhalation.

50. True

51. False. During inhalation, from the nasal cavity, the air reaches our lungs through the windpipe.

52. **(a)** **53.** **(b)**

54. **(b) :** Exhaled air contains carbon dioxide which reacts with lime water forming $CaCO_3$ which is milky in appearance.

55. **(c)**

56 1. Lime water is a solution of calcium hydroxide, $Ca(OH)_2$. Carbon dioxide released during expiration dissolves in water to form carbonic acid (H_2CO_3). H_2CO_3 and $Ca(OH)_2$ react to form calcium carbonate ($CaCO_3$) and water. Calcium carbonate is insoluble and forms a precipitate. This precipitate causes lime water to turn milky

2. Inhaled air contains more oxygen and less carbon dioxide than the exhaled air. Inhaled air contains approximately 21% of oxygen and 0.04% of carbon dioxide. Exhaled air contains approximately 16.4% of oxygen and 4.4% of carbon dioxide.

57. mixture, gases, oxygen, carbon dioxide, 21%, 0.04%, 16.4%, 4.4%

58. **(c)**

59. **(d) :** Insects (*e.g.*, cockroach) possess small openings called spiracles on the sides of their bodies.

60. **(d) :** Frogs respire through skin when under water and through buccopharyngeal cavity and lungs when on land.

61. **(a)**

62. **(b) :** Animals like elephants, lions, cows, goats, frogs, lizards, snakes, birds have lungs in their chest cavities.

63. **(b)** **64.** **(a)**

65. lungs **66.** Earthworm, frog

67. Cockroach, spiracles

68. Frogs, skin

69. tracheal tubes

70. False. Snakes breathe through lungs.

71. False. Insects such as cockroach and grasshopper have small openings called spiracles on the sides of their body.

72. False. Exchange of gases in cockroaches takes place through tracheae.

73. True **74.** True

75. **(b) :** In fish, gills serve as the respiratory organs. Gills are the projections of skin and are richly supplied with blood capillaries. Oxygen dissolved in water diffuses into the blood capillaries and carbon dioxide from blood capillaries diffuses into water.

76. **(b)** **77.** **(c)**

78. 1. Gills

2. In fish, gills serve as the respiratory organs. Gills are the projections of skin and are richly supplied with blood capillaries. Oxygen dissolved in water diffuses into the blood capillaries and carbon dioxide from blood capillaries diffuses into water.

79. True

80. False. Gills are well-supplied with a network of blood vessels.

81. True **82.** True **83.** True

84. **(b) :** Stomata are the small openings present mainly on the surface of leaves. Stomata help in gaseous exchange during photosynthesis and respiration in plants. Loss of water during the process of transpiration in plants also occurs mainly through stomata.

85. **(d)**

86. **(a) :** Plants do not have any specialised respiratory organs. The exchange of carbon dioxide and oxygen in plants occurs through small pores called stomata present mainly on the surface of leaves. Root cells of plants also need oxygen to generate energy. They get this oxygen from air trapped between soil particles. Lenticels (small pores) present on the bark of stem also help in gaseous exchange in plants.

87. **(a) :** (i) Woody plants- lenticels (iii) Lizard- lungs

88. **(d)**

89. **(d) :** The structures shown in the given figure are stomata. Stomata are mainly present on the leaf surfaces. They may also be present on young green stems but are not present in the roots.

90. False. All living organisms respire to get the energy needed for their survival.

91. False. Stomata are present on the surface of leaves.

92. True

93. False. Plants respire through stomata, lenticels and root cells.

94. False. The breakdown of glucose in the plant cells is similar to that in other living beings.

95.

Plant parts	Roles in respiration
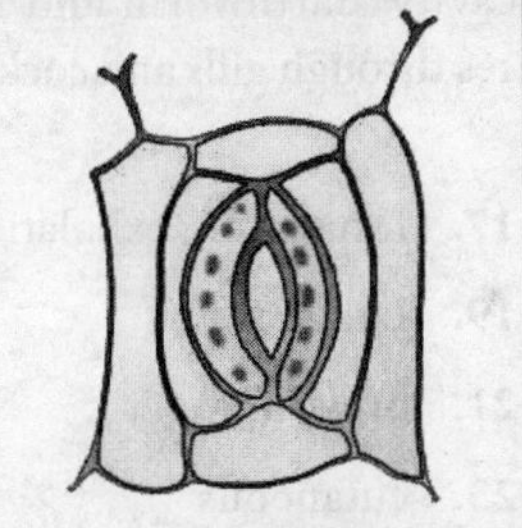 Stomata	Stomata 1. In plants, the exchange of oxygen and carbon dioxide occurs through stomata. 2. Each stoma is guarded with guard cell, which controls opening and closing of stomata depending on light and water availability.
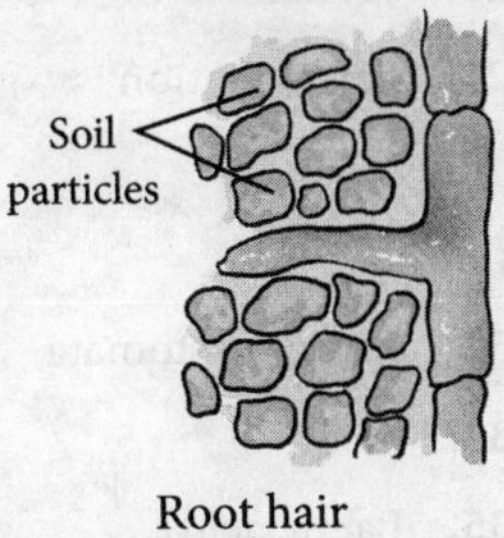 Root hair	Root hair Root cells get oxygen from the air trapped between soil particles.

NCERT Exemplar Problems

1. **(d)** : When we do heavy exercise our body does not get enough oxygen to produce the required energy. To get additional energy, anaerobic respiration occurs within our muscle cells. In this process, there occurs partial breakdown of glucose to produce lactic acid. The accumulation of lactic acid in the body causes muscular cramps.

2. **(c)** : Yeast (fungi) respires anaerobically and yields ethyl alcohol and carbon dioxide. Due to the production of ethyl alcohol, yeast is used in brewing industry. This process of anaerobic respiration in yeast is called as fermentation.

3. **(a)** : During exhalation, the diaphragm moves up and ribs move downwards and inwards, decreasing the space in the chest cavity, this increases the air pressure inside the lungs and forces the air out of the lungs.

4. **(c)** : Breathing means taking in air rich in oxygen and giving out air rich in carbon dioxide with the help of respiratory organs. The taking in of oxygen-rich air into the body is called inhalation and giving out of carbon dioxide - rich air is known as exhalation.

5. **(b)** : Fish use gills for exchange of gases. Gills are richly supplied with thin blood vessels called capillaries. As water enters through the mouth it flows over the gills. The blood in the capillaries absorbs oxygen dissolved in water, and gives out carbon dioxide into the water.

6. **(d)** : The skin of the earthworm and the frog feels moist and slimy on touching. It is because in earthworms and frogs, exchange of gases takes place by diffusion through the moist body surface.

A & R Corner

1. **(a)** : Internal respiration occurs in the body cells. It involves exchange of gases between the blood and the body cells and use of oxygen by the body cells to oxidise food and release energy.

2. **(b)**

3. **(d)** : During anaerobic respiration, glucose is not completely oxidised into carbon dioxide and water. It is broken down either into ethyl alcohol and carbon dioxide or into lactic acid.

4. **(d)** : During inhalation, the ribs move upward and outward, and the diaphragm moves down. This increases the volume of thoracic cavity.

5. **(b)**

6. **(b)** : The skin of earthworm feels moist and slimy on touching. The exchange of gases takes place by diffusion through the moist outer surface.

7. **(b)** : Fish use gills for exchange of gases. Gills are richly supplied with thin blood vessels called capillaries.

8. **(a)** : Lenticels are the small pores or openings present on the bark of the stems. Gaseous exchange between the atmosphere and the cells takes place through these lenticels.

9. **(b)**

10. **(b)** : Breathing rate is a term used for number of times a person breathes in a minute. It is measured when a person is at rest and involves counting the number of breaths in one minute by counting how many times the chest rises.

11. **(c)** : Alveoli have very thin walls and are richly supplied with blood capillaries.

12. **(c)** : Inhaled air contains oxygen (21%) and carbon dioxide (0.04%).

13. **(c)** : Breathing occurs inside the lungs in mammals and respiration occurs at cellular level.

14. **(b)**

15. **(c)** : Diaphragm plays an important role in both inspiration and expiration.

Exam Corner

1. **(b)** : Lenticels are the pores present in the stems of woody plants which allow exchange of gases between the atmosphere and internal tissues.

2. **(c)** : Each stoma is surrounded by two kidney-shaped guard cells. The expansion and contraction of the guard cells which depend on the availability of water and light, result in opening and closing of the stomata.

3. **(b) :** Respiration through skin is called cutaneous respiration. In earthworm, exchange of gases takes place by diffusion through the moist outer surface.

4. **(c) :** Gills are the projections of skin made up of a large number of gill filaments, and are richly supplied with blood capillaries.

5. **(b) :** Haemoglobin is the red coloured pigment present in blood. It combines with oxygen to form a temporary compound called oxyhaemoglobin. It is in this form that oxygen is carried through blood to different body cells. On reaching the cells, oxyhaemoglobin dissociates to release the trapped oxygen and the released oxygen diffuses into the cells.

6. **(b) :** The alveoli are air sacs that are richly supplied with blood vessels. Alveoli are present at end of respiratory tubes, it is the site for the exchange of gases.

7. **(a) :** In anaerobic respiration, glucose is broken down without the use of oxygen with the release of energy. Anaerobic respiration occurs in some bacteria, yeast and some parasitic flatworms. The products of anaerobic respiration are either lactic acid (in skeletal muscles of mammals) or ethyl alcohol and CO_2 (in yeasts). As compared to aerobic respiration, the process of anaerobic respiration is faster and produces lesser amount of energy.

8. **(b) :** When a person breathes in (during inspiration), diaphragm becomes flat and gets lowered by the contraction of its muscles. Ribs move upward and outward, thereby increasing the volume of thoracic cavity.

9. **(a)**

10. **(a) :** The process of anaerobic respiration which yields either ethyl alcohol and carbon dioxide (in yeast) or lactic acid (in skeletal muscles of mammals) is also called fermentation.

11. **(b) :** The windpipe branches into two smaller tubes called bronchi (*singular*-bronchus). Each bronchus enters into its respective lung. Inside the lungs, the bronchi divide and redivide into bronchioles which further divide and finally end in air sacs or alveoli. In unicellular organisms, such as *Amoeba* and *Paramecium*, exchange of gases occurs by diffusion through the cell membrane.

12. **(c) :** Lenticels are present in stem of woody plants. Stomata are tiny pores present in the leaves for gaseous exchange.

13. **(a) :** The mucus and the hair present inside the nose trap dirt, dust particles and disease-causing germs, and prevent them from entering the respiratory system. We do not get clean air if we breathe through our mouth instead of our nose. Therefore, we should always breathe through the nose as it will protect us from catching infections.

14. **(a) :** During inhalation, the ribs move upward and outward, and the diaphragm moves down (becoming flat). This increases the volume of thoracic cavity. The lungs, being elastic, also increase in size, and the air pressure in the lungs decreases. Air from the atmosphere having higher pressure rushes into lungs through the respiratory passage. Hence, the lungs get filled with fresh air.

15. **(b) :** Frog respires through lungs, through skin as well as through buccopharyngeal cavity. Earthworm and *Hydra* respires through skin, fish respires through gills and cockroach respires through spiracles.

16. diffusion **17.** inhalation, exhalation

18. tracheae, lungs **19.** Lactic acid

20. alveoli **21.** breathing

22. inhaled, exhaled **23.** cutaneous

24. aerial roots **25.** bronchi

26. oxyhaemoglobin **27.** Fermentation

28. increases

29. ethyl alcohol, carbon dioxide

30. oxygen, anaerobic **31.** lenticels, stomata

32. blood vessels **33.** hair

34. single-celled, beer, wine **35.** Lactic acid

36. False. Although respiration takes place all the time, the rate of photosynthesis during the day is much greater than the rate of respiration. Thus, the oxygen released by plants during photosynthesis is much more than the oxygen consumed during respiration. During the night, photosynthesis does not take place due to the absence of sunlight. Only respiration takes place during the night.

37. False. Mucus and hair present inside the nose trap dirt, dust and germs and prevent them from entering the respiratory system.

38. False. The rate of exchange of gases in plants is much slower than in animals.

39. False. Respiration through skin is called cutaneous respiration.

40. True **41.** True **42.** True

43. True. Root cells of plants also need oxygen to generate energy. They get this oxygen from air trapped between soil particles.

44. False. When a frog is under water, it respires through the skin whereas on land, it respires through lungs.

45. False. The windpipe branches into two smaller tubes called bronchi.

46. True **47.** True

48. False. Earthworm respires only through its moist skin.

49. False. Reaction that takes place during cellular respiration is similar to the reaction that occurs in combustion.

50. False. Lungs are present in the chest cavity which are surrounded by ribs on the sides.

51. True **52.** True

53. False. The size of the chest decreases during exhalation.

54. False. Muscle cramps are due to the accumulation of lactic acid in the muscle cells as a result of anaerobic respiration.

55. False. Plants carry out respiration all the time.

56. 1. Inhalation has been shown in the given figure.
2. During inhalation, the ribs move upward and outward, and the diaphragm moves down. This increases the volume of thoracic cavity. The lungs, being elastic, also increase in size, and the air pressure in the lungs decreases. Air from atmosphere having higher pressure rushes into the lungs through the respiratory passage. Hence, the lungs get filled with fresh air.

57. In set up A, oxygen gas collects in the tube. This is because in the presence of sunlight, photosynthesis occurs, during which the plant uses carbon dioxide and water to produce oxygen.
In set up B, the apparatus is covered with a black box, therefore photosynthesis cannot occur in the absence of sunlight. Here, the plant is undergoing respiration during which it uses oxygen and produces carbon dioxide and water.
Although the process of respiration is also taking place in set up A, but the rate of photosynthesis is much more than the rate of respiration, so that net result is release of oxygen.

58. Aerobic respiration, Anaerobic respiration

59. Earthworm, Frog

60. Oxygen, Carbon dioxide

61. Carbon dioxide, Water

62. Stomata, Lenticels

63. (i) Diaphragm (ii) ribcage

64. Earthworm. It respires through its skin. The other three respire through lungs.

65. Glucose. The other three are end products of glucose oxidation (respiration).

66. Lungs. Lungs are respiratory organ of humans and many animals. The other three are respiratory organs of plants.

67. Skin. In humans, skin is not a respiratory organ. The other three are part of respiratory system of humans.

68. Stomata. It is a respiratory organ of plants. The other three are respiratory organs of animals.

69. Lenticels are small pores present on the back of the stem that help in gaseous exchange in plants.

70. In the process of breathing air is taken up through nostrils. Then passes into the nasal cavity reaching the lungs. The dust, pollens and smoke particles get trapped in the hair present in the nasal cavity. Sometimes, foreign particles get past the nasal cavity and irritate the lining of nasal cavity which result in a forceful expulsion of air in the form of sneeze.

71.

S.No.	Breathing	Respiration
1.	It involves intake of oxygen and release of carbon dioxide.	Respiration is a more complex process of oxidation of food in body cells to release energy.
2.	It is a physical (or mechanical) process which involves exchange of gases.	It is a biochemical process which involves oxidation of food with release of energy.
3.	It involves breathing organs, *e.g.*, lungs in mammals.	It occurs at cellular level.

72. (a) Fermentation : This process of anaerobic respiration which yields either ethyl alcohol and carbon dioxide (in yeast) or lactic acid (in skeletal muscles of mammals) is also called fermentation.
(b) Stomata : In plants, the exchange of oxygen and carbon dioxide occurs through small pores called stomata (*singular*: stoma) present on the surface of leaves.

73. In earthworm, exchange of gases takes place by diffusion through the moist outer surface. The skin of earthworm feels moist and slimy on touching. The exchange of carbon dioxide and oxygen occurs between air and blood in the skin. Respiration through skin is called cutaneous respiration.

74.

	Aerobic respiration	Anaerobic respiration
1.	Occurs in the presence of oxygen.	Occurs in the absence of oxygen.
2.	Glucose is completely oxidised.	Glucose is broken down incompletely.
3.	End products are carbon dioxide and water.	End products are either ethyl alcohol and carbon dioxide or lactic acid.
4.	More energy is produced.	Very little energy is produced.
5.	Occurs in most of the plants and animals.	Occurs in few organisms like yeast, some bacteria and some parasitic worms.

75. Insects (*e.g.*, cockroach) possess small openings called spiracles on the sides of their bodies. These spiracles are connected to fine tubes called tracheae. The tracheae are further branched into smaller tubes called tracheoles that are in contact with the body cells. Oxygen rich air rushes through spiracles into the tracheae and tracheoles, and reaches every cell of the body. Similarly, carbon dioxide from the cells goes into the tracheoles and the tracheae, and moves out through spiracles. In this way, exchange of gases occurs through tracheae and, hence is called tracheal respiration.

76. Exchange of gases in fish takes place by gills. As water enters through the mouth of the fish, it flows over the gills, which are richly supplied with blood capillaries. Oxygen dissolved in water diffuses into the blood capillaries, while carbon dioxide present in capillary blood diffuses into water. The oxygenated blood from capillaries is taken to heart and pumped to different parts of the body, while the carbon dioxide rich blood from body tissues is taken to gills for the exchange of gases.

77.

	Inhalation		Exhalation
1.	During inhalation, the ribs move upward and outward, and the diaphragm moves down (becoming flat). This increases the volume of thoracic cavity.	1.	During exhalation, the ribs move downward and inward, and the diaphragm moves up (again becoming dome shaped).
2.	The lungs increase in size, and the air pressure in the lungs decreases.	2.	The lungs decrease in size and the air pressure in the lungs increases
3.	Air from the atmosphere having higher pressure rushes into the lungs.	3.	The air from the lungs having higher pressure is pushed out.

78. The air we breathe in eventually reaches the alveoli of the lungs, where exchange of gases takes place. The alveoli are richly supplied with blood vessels (called alveolar capillaries). Oxygen present in the air we breathe in, goes into the blood contained in alveolar capillaries. Carbon dioxide present in the blood (as a waste product of respiration) passes out of the blood in the alveoli.

79. $2 \rightarrow 6 \rightarrow 3 \rightarrow 1 \rightarrow 5 \rightarrow 4$

80. The breakdown of food (glucose) in the body cells, with the release of carbon dioxide (CO_2), water (H_2O), and energy is referred to as respiration or cellular respiration.
Respiration is a biochemical process that involves :
(i) intake of oxygen from the environment
(ii) oxidation of food (glucose) with the help of oxygen taken in
(iii) production of energy, carbon dioxide and water
(iv) elimination of carbon dioxide.
Respiration is of two main types: aerobic respiration and anaerobic respiration.
When breakdown of glucose into carbon dioxide and water occurs in the body cells, in the presence of oxygen, it is called aerobic respiration. A large amount of energy is released during this process. Majority of animals and plants perform aerobic respiration.

$$\underset{\text{Glucose}}{C_6H_{12}O_6} + \underset{\text{Oxygen}}{6O_2} \longrightarrow \underset{\text{Carbon dioxide}}{6CO_2} + \underset{\text{Water}}{6H_2O} + \text{Energy}$$

When glucose is broken down without the use of oxygen, it is called anaerobic respiration. Organisms that can survive and obtain energy in the absence of oxygen are called anaerobes (or anaerobic organisms). During anaerobic respiration, glucose is not completely broken down into carbon dioxide and water. It is broken down either into ethyl alcohol and carbon dioxide or into lactic acid. Very little amount of energy is released during anaerobic respiration. Anaerobic respiration occurs in yeast, some bacteria and parasitic flatworms.

81. Breathing is a mechanical process which involves inhalation and exhalation. These processes occur due to the movement of the muscles of the diaphragm and the rib cage.
Inhalation : During inhalation, the ribs move upward and outward, and the diaphragm moves down. This increases the volume of thoracic cavity. The lungs, being elastic, also increase in size, and the air pressure in the lungs decreases. Air from the atmosphere having higher pressure rushes into lungs through nostrils and the respiratory passage. Hence, the lungs get filled with fresh air.
Exhalation: During exhalation, ribs move downward and inward, and the diaphragm moves up. This decreases the volume of thoracic cavity so that the air pressure inside the lungs increases. Air from the lungs is pushed outside.
Mechanism of breathing in humans is as follows

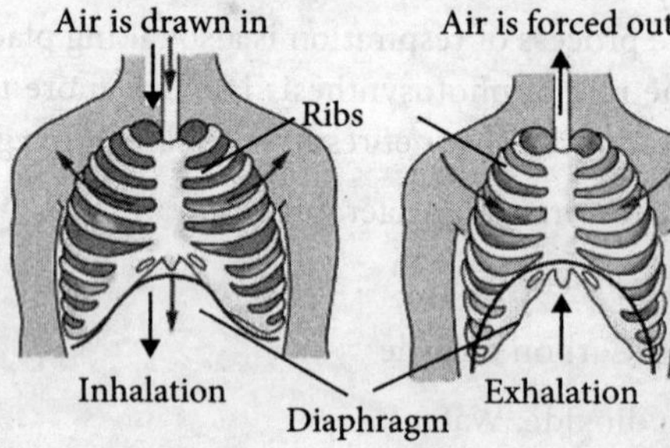

82. In plants, the exchange of oxygen and carbon dioxide occurs through small pores called stomata (*singular*: stoma) present on the surface of leaves. Each stoma is guarded by two kidney-shaped guard cells. The expansion and contraction of guard cells, which depends on light and water availability, results in opening and closing of the stomata. Lenticels (small pores) present on the bark of the stem also help in gaseous exchange in plants. Root cells of plants also respire, so they also need oxygen to generate energy. They get this oxygen from air trapped between soil particles.

83. Through the following activity, we can show that exhaled air has more carbon dioxide than inhaled air.
Take two test tubes, each of them half-filled with lime water. Using two-holed stoppers, glass tubes and clips, set up the apparatus as shown in figure. Use the rubber tube at the middle to breathe in and out through the mouth. As you suck in air through the rubber tube, open clip X and close clip Y. The inhaled air passes through lime water in test tube A. As you exhale through the rubber tube, open clip Y and close

clip X. The exhaled air passes through lime water in test tube B. Exhaled air has more carbon dioxide than inhaled air as shown in below experiment

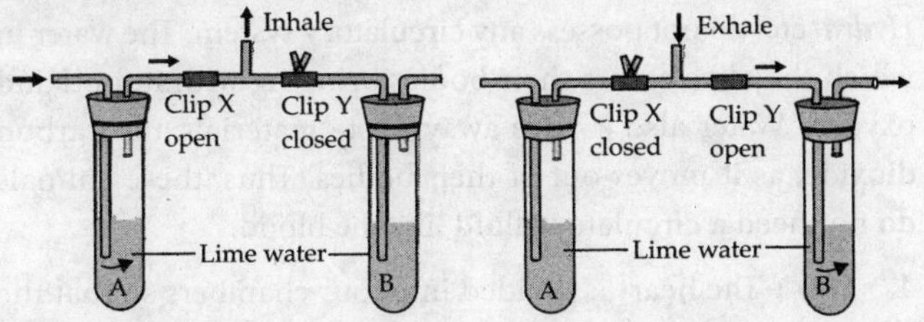

Lime water turns more milky in test tube B with clip Y open. In test tube A, lime water turns milky only to a negligible amount. This shows that less amount of CO_2 is present in inhaled air whereas more amount of CO_2 is present in exhaled air.

84. Human respiratory system consists of the nostrils, nasal cavity, pharynx, larynx, trachea, bronchi and lungs. The lungs are situated in a space within the chest called the chest cavity (or thoracic cavity). The walls of the thoracic cavity are supported by ribs. The floor of the cavity is made of a sheet of muscles called the diaphragm.

Human respiratory system is as follows

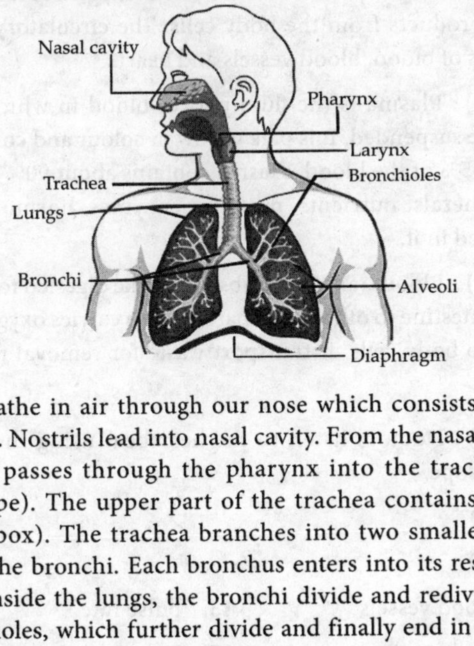

We breathe in air through our nose which consists of two nostrils. Nostrils lead into nasal cavity. From the nasal cavity, the air passes through the pharynx into the trachea (or windpipe). The upper part of the trachea contains larynx (voice box). The trachea branches into two smaller tubes called the bronchi. Each bronchus enters into its respective lung. Inside the lungs, the bronchi divide and redivide into bronchioles, which further divide and finally end in air sacs or alveoli, where exchange of gases occurs.

85. (a) When we inhale dust-laden air, dust particles are captured by the hair of the nostrils. Sometimes, they get past the nostril hair in the nasal cavity, and irritate the lining of the cavity. As a result we sneeze. Sneezing expels these foreign particles from the inhaled air so that dust free, clean air enters our body.

(b) Yeast is a single-celled organism. It respires anaerobically and yields ethyl alcohol and carbon dioxide. The yeast cells are, therefore, used to make wine and beer in brewing industry. Yeasts are also used to raise dough in baking industry due to the production of carbon dioxide.

(c) Our body needs energy for all activities, which is provided by oxidation of food during respiration. During intense physical activities like running, there is larger demand of energy to perform these activities. Hence, more oxygen is required to meet this extra demand of energy. Therefore, an athlete breathes faster and deeper than usual after finishing the race so as to provide extra oxygen and hence extra energy to the body.

(d) We should not overwater potted plants, because in that case, the water replaces the air in the soil and the roots cannot breathe. This affects the growth of plants.

(e) During respiration, plants take in oxygen and give out carbon dioxide. Although respiration takes place all the time, the rate of photosynthesis during the day is much higher than the rate of respiration. Thus, the oxygen released by plants during photosynthesis is much more than the oxygen consumed during respiration. During the night, however, photosynthesis does not take place, due to the absence of sunlight. Only respiration takes place during the night. Plants therefore take in oxygen and release only carbon dioxide at night. That is the reason, it is advised not to sleep under the tree at night.

86. (c) : The given figures represent mechanism of breathing in human beings. X shows inhalation and Y shows exhalation.

87. (b) : The process Y is exhalation. During exhalation, the ribs move downward and inward, and the diaphragm moves upward.

88. (b) : During the process Y (exhalation), the diaphragm move upwards and becomes dome shaped.

89. (d) : During inhalation (X), the ribs move upward and outward, and the diaphragm moves down. This increases the volume of thoracic cavity. The lungs being elastic, also increase in size, and the air pressure in the lungs decreases. Air from the atmosphere having higher pressure rushes into the lungs through the respiratory passage. Hence, the lungs get filled with fresh air.

90. (a) : During exhalation (Y), when ribs and diaphragm return to their original position, the volume of thoracic cavity decreases and so also of lungs. This increases the air pressure inside the lungs.

91. (b) : During the process P (aerobic respiration) food is broken down into carbon dioxide and water, and energy is released which is stored in the form of ATP.

$C_6H_{12}O_6 + 6O_2 \rightarrow 6CO_2 + 6H_2O$ + Energy

92. (c) : The organisms that can respire in the absence of oxygen are called anaerobes. Organisms like yeast, some bacteria and parasitic flatworms perform this kind of respiration.

93. (d) : The process Q is anaerobic respiration which occurs in the absence of oxygen. In the absence of oxygen, glucose partially breaks into carbon dioxide and ethyl alcohol. In humans, the process Q (anaerobic respiration) takes place when a muscle undergoes extreme contraction due to vigrous exercise and produces lactic acid.

94. The process P(aerobic respiration) occurs in body cells, in which food breaks down in the presence of oxygen into carbon dioxide and water. The CO_2 formed during cellular respiration is expelled out during breathing. The confirmation of CO_2 production can be done by blowing air gently into the glass of lime water with the help of straw. The lime water turns milky. This is because while blowing air, we exhale carbon dioxide gas which turns lime water milky.

95. Sometimes during heavy physical exercise our body cannot get enough oxygen to produce the required energy. To get the additional energy anaerobic respiration (Q) occurs in our body cells during which partial breakdown of glucose occurs and is converted into lactic acid. Accumulation of lactic acid leads to muscle fatigue.

96. Organism X, *i.e.*, earthworm shows cutaneous respiration. The skin of earthworm feels moist and slimy on touching. It is because the exchange of CO_2 and O_2 occurs between air and blood through skin.

97. Organism Y (Cockroach) possess small openings on the sides of their bodies called spiracles.

98. In cockroach (Y) spiracles are present on the sides of their body. Spiracles rushes oxygen rich air into the tracheae and tracheoles which provide oxygen rich air to every cell of the body. Similarly, carbon dioxide from the body cells enters the tracheoles and through tracheae, moves out of the body through spiracles. Here, the exchange of gases takes place through tracheae hence it is called tracheal respiration.

99. Frog also exhibits cutaneous respiration through skin in under water like earthworm (X).

100. In fish (Z), gills serve as the respiratory organ and help to obtain oxygen from dissolved water, whereas in earthworm (X), the diffusion of gases occurs through the moist outer surface of skin.

7 Transportation in Animals and Plants

Practice Corner

1. **(b) :** Red blood cells (RBCs) or erythrocytes are biconcave, disc shaped structures which contain a red-coloured pigment called haemoglobin. Due to the presence of haemoglobin pigment, RBCs are red in colour and impart red colour to the blood.

2. **(b) :** When you place the middle and index fingers of your right hand on the inner side of your left wrist, you will feel some throbbing movements. This throbbing is called pulse, which is due to the blood rushing through the artery. Pulse is a regular jerk of an artery. The number of pulses per minute is called the pulse rate.

3. **(c) :** Simple aquatic multicellular organisms *e.g.* sponges, *Hydra*, etc. do not possess any circulatory system. The water in which they live enters their bodies bringing with it food and oxygen. Water also carries away waste materials and carbon dioxide, as it moves out of their bodies. Thus, these animals do not need a circulatory fluid like the blood.

4. **(a) :** The heart is divided into four chambers so that the oxygenated blood and deoxygenated blood remain separate and do not mix. The two upper chambers are called the atria (*singular: atrium*) or auricles and the two lower chambers are called the ventricles.

5. **(a) :** The vena cava (main veins) bring deoxygenated blood from all parts of the body (except lungs) to the right atrium. The right atrium pumps this blood into the right ventricle, which then pumps it into the pulmonary artery. The pulmonary artery transfers the blood to the lungs for oxygenation.

6. **(c) :** Circulatory system is the life support system that provides our body cells with food and oxygen. It takes away waste products from the body cells. The circulatory system consists of blood, blood vessels and heart.

7. **(d) :** Plasma is the fluid part of blood in which blood cells are suspended. It is pale yellow in colour and constitutes about 55% of the blood. Plasma contains about 90% water. It has minerals, nutrients, proteins, enzymes, hormones, etc. dissolved in it.

8. **(d) :** Blood transports substances like digested food from small intestine to other body parts. It also carries oxygen from lungs to body cells. It transport waste for removal from the body.

9. **(b) :** Doctors listen to the heartbeat using the device stethoscope.

10. **(a)**

11. **(b)**

12. Blood vessels
13. pulse rate
14. Veins
15. Pulmonary vein
16. chest cavity
17. pulse
18. capillaries
19. heartbeat
20. ventricles
21. Arteries

22. S, the pulmonary vein carries oxygen-rich blood from lungs to heart and P, the pulmonary artery carries carbon dioxide-rich blood from heart to lungs.

23. Q (vein) carries carbon dioxide rich blood from organs to the heart and R (artery) carries oxygen-rich blood from heart to the body organs.

24. (b) : Human excretory system consists of a pair of kidneys, a pair of ureters, urinary bladder, urethra and urinary opening. Urine passes from the kidneys through two tubes called ureters into an elastic sac called the urinary bladder, where it is stored temporarily until it is excreted from the body through urinary opening located at the end of urethra.

25. (b) : Urine is the waste product removed by the kidneys. It consists of 95% water, 2.5% urea, and 2.5% other waste products.

26. (a) : The kidneys consist of about one million coiled tubes called nephrons. Nephrons are the tiny filtering units of the kindney. They filter out excess water, salts and urea from blood.

27. (b) **28.** (a)

29. uric acid **30.** dialysis

31. 1 – 1.8 **32.** excretion

33. water, salts

34. False. The main excretory product in snakes is uric acid.

35. True **36.** True

37. False. Blood reaching our kidneys contains both useful and harmful substances. Only harmful substances have to be removed from our body.

38. False. The percentage of water in human urine in 95%.

39. False. In human beings, urine is stored in the urinary bladder.

40. True

41. False. The wastes in our body are dissolved in blood and are removed as urine.

42. False. Ureters carry urine from kidneys to urinary bladder.

43.

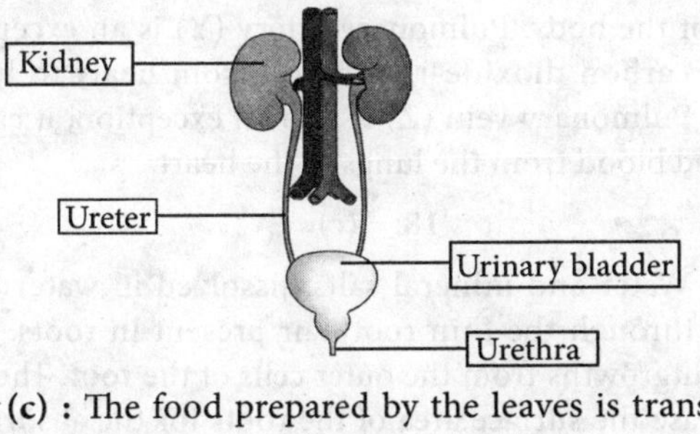

44. (c) : The food prepared by the leaves is transported to all parts of the plant through the cells of phloem. This process is known as translocation. Phloem has elongated cells called sieve tubes through which the contents of phloem can move in the upward as well as downward direction.

45. (b) : The process of losing water in the form of water vapour from the aerial parts of a plant is known as transpiration. Transpiration of water from leaves creates a suction pull, which pulls water and minerals up the plant from the roots to great heights of trees.

46. (a) **47.** (c)

48. (a) : Plants absorb water and mineral nutrients from the soil through the roots.

49. Xylem, phloem, vascular, stomata, leaves

50. True

51. False. The root hair increases the surface area of roots for the absorption of water.

52. False. Xylem forms a continuous network of channels that connects roots to the leaves through the stems and branches.

53. True **54.** True **55.** True

56. A suction pull is generated.

57. Transpiration.

58. Significance of transpiration–

(i) It helps the water to reach great heights in the tall trees.

(ii) It cools down the plant.

NCERT Exemplar Problems

1. (c) : Human excretory system comprises of a pair of kidneys, a pair of ureters, a urinary bladder, a urethra and urinary opening. Urine passes from the kidneys through two tubes called ureters into an elastic sac called the urinary bladder. The urinary bladder stores the urine temporarily, which is then excreted through the urethra.

2. (b) : Phloem tissue consists of a group of specialised cells. Sieve tubes are elongated tubular conducting channels of phloem through which food is transported. The contents of phloem can move in the upward as well as in the downward direction. Therefore, they form a two-way traffic in plants.

3. (d) : Capillaries have thin walls, they pick up carbon dioxide and other wastes from every cell and pass them into the alveoli and kidneys respectively. They also pick up oxygen and digested food from the alveoli and small intestine respectively and pass them to each and every body cell for cellular respiration.

4. (c) : Lips do not secrete sweat because of the absence of sweat glands.

5. (c) : The root cells absorb water and mineral salts continuously from the soil. The evaporation of water from the leaf surfaces during the process of transpiration produces a suction force (transpiration pull) that causes the water to move upwards.

6. (c) : Most aquatic animals, *e.g.*, bony fish, *Hydra*, leech, crocodile etc. excrete the waste as ammonia gas, which easily dissolves in water. These animals are referred to as ammonotelic animals and excretion of ammonia is termed as ammonotelism.

A & R Corner

1. **(b) :** Blood is a fluid connective tissue, which has cells of various kinds (RBCs, WBCs and Platelets) suspended in fluid part. Blood helps in transport of O_2, CO_2 and food materials.

2. **(a)**

3. **(a) :** Platelets are the tiny fragments of special cells formed in the bone marrow, clotting of blood becomes very important whenever there is an injury, to prevent excessive blood loss.

4. **(c) :** The throbbing movements correspond to the blood being pumped by the heart in the artery. This throbbing is called pulse.

5. **(a)**

6. **(d) :** Simple aquatic multicellular organisms, like sponges, *Hydra* etc. do not possess any circulatory system. The water in which sponges and *Hydra* live brings food and oxygen as it enters their bodies.

7. **(a) :** The partition between atrium and ventricle as auriculo – ventricular septum, helps to avoid mixing of blood rich in oxygen with the blood rich in carbon dioxide.

8. **(c) :** Urea is the major excretory product in humans while aquatic animals like fishes excrete cell waste as ammonia.

9. **(c) :** Plants need to transport the food from leaves and water and minerals from roots to all other parts of the plant.

10. **(a)** 11. **(a)**

12. **(c) :** Xylem is the vascular tissue which transports water and minerals from the roots. Phloem is meant for the transport of food to all parts of the plant.

13. **(c) :** The walls of ventricles are thicker than the auricles because, ventricles have to pump the blood to all parts of the body during their contraction and the back flow of blood is prevented by the presence of valves in the heart.

14. **(b)** 15. **(a)**

Exam Corner

1. **(b) :** Plasma is a fluid that contains minerals, nutrients, proteins, enzymes, hormones, etc. dissolved in it.

2. **(d) :** Transportation of food and water across the plant body is carried out through well-developed transport system called vascular system. The vascular system comprises of vascular tissues – xylem and phloem.

3. **(d)** 4. **(c)**

5. **(c) :** Veins are the blood vessels which carry carbon dioxide-rich (deoxygenated) blood from the body organs back to the heart. Veins have thin elastic walls. The diameter of veins is greater than that of arteries. These are superficially placed. The blood pressure in the veins is low. There are a series of valves present in veins, which help to prevent back flow, and allow blood to flow only towards the heart.

6. **(a) :** Aorta is a part of circulatory system.

7. **(b) :** Arteries branch into finer and smaller blood vessels called capillaries, which join to form veins. Capillaries are the smallest blood vessels, that connect arteries to veins. They have very thin walls, through which oxygen, digested food, carbon dioxide, waste products etc. are exchanged between the blood and the body cells.

8. **(c)**

9. **(d) :** Most aquatic animals, *e.g.*, sponges, *Hydra*, bony fish, leech, crocodile, etc. excrete the cell waste as ammonia, which directly dissolves in water. Animals which excrete ammonia are called ammonotelic animals and excretion of ammonia is termed as ammonotelism.
Nephrons are the fine filtering units of the kidney. They filter out excess water, salt and urea from the blood.

10. **(a) :** The vena cava (main veins) bring deoxygenated blood from all parts of the body to the right atrium. The right atrium pumps this blood into the right ventricle, which then pumps it into the pulmonary artery. This artery takes the blood to the lungs for oxygenation.
The oxygenated blood is received by the left atrium through the two pairs of pulmonary veins (one pair each from the right and left lung). It is then pumped into the left ventricle. The left ventricle, in turn, pumps the blood into the aorta (main artery), through which it is supplied to the rest of the body.

11. **(d)** 12. **(c)**

13. **(d) :** RBC transports O_2 to various body cells and take CO_2 from the body cells to the lungs where it is breathed out. WBC protects us from diseases by destroying harmful bacteria and other foreign materials. Platelets block the flow of blood, prevent blood loss and help in blood clotting. Plasma is the fluid part of the blood in which all the blood cells are suspended.

14. **(a)** 15. **(b)**

16. **(d) :** Arteries carry oxygen-rich blood from heart to all parts of the body. Pulmonary artery (Y) is an exception, it carries carbon dioxide-rich blood from heart to lungs. Similarly, Pulmonary vein (Z) is also an exception, it carries oxygenated blood from the lungs to the heart.

17. **(b)** 18. **(c)**

19. **(c) :** Water and mineral salts dissolved in water enter the plant through the thin root hair present in roots. Root hair are outgrowths from the outer cells of the root. The root hair increase the surface area of the roots for the absorption of water and mineral salts.

20. **(a) :** Arteries have thick elastic walls to allow stretching, and to deal with the high pressure of blood coming from the heart. Arteries are usually deep seated.

21. **(b) :** A doctor uses the stethoscope as a device to amplify the sound of the heart. It consists of a chest piece that carries a sensitive diaphragm, two ear pieces and a tube joining the parts. Doctors can get clues about the condition of your heart by listening through a stethoscope.

22. (b) **23.** (b) **24.** (b)

25. Platelets

26. Haemoglobin **27.** pulse

28. vascular tissue **29.** RBCs

30. urine **31.** transpiration

32. False. White blood cells are slightly larger in size then red blood cells and can move on their own.

33. False. Auricles have comparatively thinner walls than ventricles.

34. False. Pulse in the throbbing movement felt at our wrist which is caused due to expansion of arteries.

35. False. Ventricles are the two lower chambers of the heart with thick muscular walls.

36. True **37.** True **38.** True

39. True **40.** True **41.** True

42. False. Animals such as sponges and *Hydra* do not possess any circulatory and excretory system.

43. False. Pulmonary vein is the only vein that carries oxygen-rich blood from lungs to the heart.

44. True

45. False. Human urine contains 2.5% of urea.

46. A - Root hair, B - Xyelm vessels

47. Transpiration pull

48. (d) **49.** (b)

50. RBC, WBC, platelets, plasma, blood vessels, artery, vein, oxygen-rich, carbon dioxide-rich, capillaries, pump.

51. phloem and xylem.

52. Kidneys

53. Right auricle and left auricle.

54. Pulmonary artery carries carbon dioxide-rich blood to the lungs and pulmonary vein carries oxygen-rich blood to the heart respectively in human beings.

55. The valves prevent the backflow of blood and septum prevents mixing of oxygen-rich and carbon dioxide-rich blood in the heart.

56. Excretion **57.** Right ventricle

58. Phloem **59.** Prepare food

60. Cell membrane

61. (a) The walls of the different chambers of the heart are made of special muscles called cardiac muscles. These muscles contract and relax rhythmically to pump the blood. This rhythmic contraction and relaxation of different chambers produces the heartbeat. One complete contraction and relaxation of the heart is called one heartbeat.

(b) Pulse rate – The throbbing movement that is felt when you place the middle and index fingers of your right hand on the innerside of your wrist is called pulse. It is caused due to the blood rushing through the artery. The number of pulses per minute is called the pulse rate.

62.

S.No.	Arteries	Veins
1.	They are thick walled vessels with narrow lumen.	They are thin walled vessels with wide lumen.
2.	They carry blood away from the heart.	They bring blood towards the heart.
3.	They are situated in the deeper regions of the body.	Veins are superficial in nature.
4.	Walls of arteries are impermeable to gases and other substances.	Walls of veins are also impermeable.
5.	Arteries carry oxygenated blood, except the pulmonary artery.	Veins carry deoxygenated blood, except the pulmonary vein.

63. Some land animals like birds, lizards, snakes, etc. with less water availability excrete a semi-solid, white coloured compound *i.e.* uric acid. Some animals convert ammonia to urea in the liver and excrete urea as a waste product *e.g.* frogs, toads, man and all other mammals. Most aquatic animals like bony fish, crocodiles, etc. excrete cell waste as ammonia which directly dissolves in water.

64. Kidney is the main excretory organ of human body. It removes the waste material out of the body. Hence, if kidneys fail to function properly, the wastes will keep on accumulating in the body, which in turn, would damage the internal organs of the body. This can even lead to the death of the person. Such a person can survive only under the following conditions-

(i) Periodic removal of wastes from blood through dialysis.

(ii) Replacement of the damaged kidney with a healthy one by a process called kidney transplantation.

65.

S.No.	Xylem	Phloem
1.	It transports water and minerals.	It transports food that is synthesised in the leaves.
2.	Contents of xylem move only in the upward direction.	Contents of the phloem move both upward and downward direction.
3.	Xylem has elongated cells called xylem vessels.	Phloem has elongated cells called sieve tubes.
4.	The upward movement of sap taking place in xylem is called ascent of sap.	The food prepared by leaves transported to all parts of the plant through phloem is called translocation.

66. Blood contains a red coloured pigment called haemoglobin. It is the presence of this haemoglobin in RBCs that makes them red in colour.

Haemoglobin combines with oxygen to form oxyhaemoglobin and transports it to various cells of the body. When blood reaches the body cells, oxyhaemoglobin dissociates releasing oxygen and haemoglobin. The oxygen is used by the cells for respiration. Haemoglobin then becomes available to transport oxygen again. Haemoglobin also combines with carbon dioxide and transports it from the body cells to the lungs, where it is breathed out.

67. The walls of a heart are made up of special muscles called cardiac muscles. These muscles contract and relax rhythmically to pump the blood. This rhythmic contraction and relaxation of different chambers produces the heartbeat. Pulse is the throbbing felt at various points of our body like neck, wrist, back of the knee, etc. due to the blood rushing through the artery. It is caused due to a regular jerk of an artery.

68. The heart has four chambers—two upper chambers are called auricles and two lower chambers are called ventricles. The left chambers of the heart are completely separated from right chambers of the heart, to prevent the mixing of oxygen-rich and carbon dioxide-rich blood.
The vena cava (main veins) bring deoxygenated blood from all parts of the body to the right atrium. The right atrium pumps this blood into the right ventricle, which then pumps it into the pulmonary artery. This artery takes the blood to the lungs for oxygenation.
The oxygenated blood is received by the left atrium through the pulmonary veins (2 each from the right and left lungs). It is then pumped into the left ventricle, which in turn, pumps the blood into the aorta (main artery), through which it is supplied to all parts of the body.
The circulation of blood can be illustrated by the following flow chart :

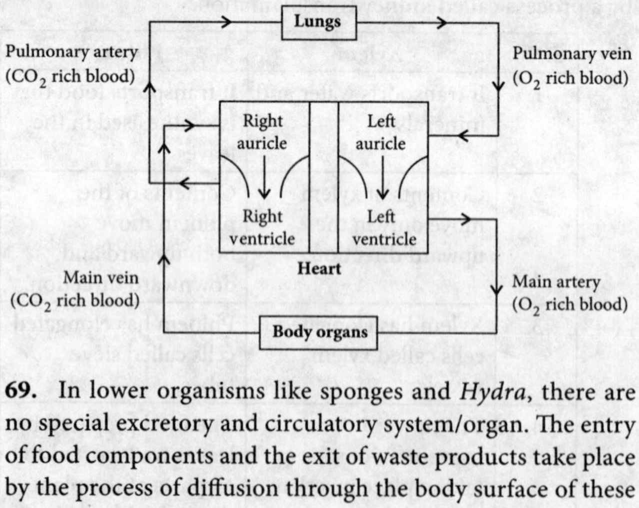

69. In lower organisms like sponges and *Hydra*, there are no special excretory and circulatory system/organ. The entry of food components and the exit of waste products take place by the process of diffusion through the body surface of these organisms.

70. Importance of transpiration in plants:
(i) It creates a suction pull (transpiration pull) due to which water and minerals rise high up in the tall trees. Thus, it helps in ascent of sap.
(ii) Transpiration helps to cool the plant, due to evaporation of water.

71.

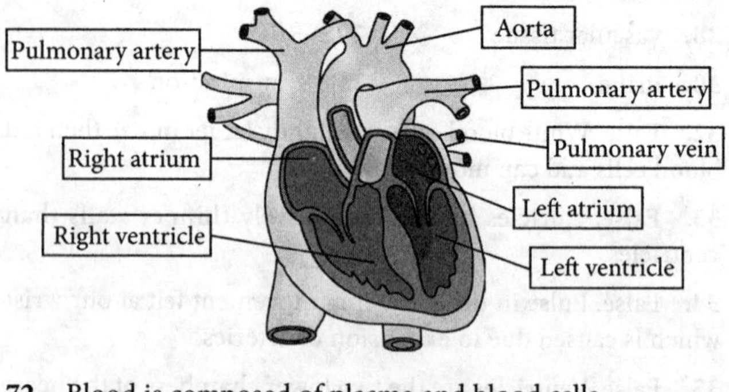

72. Blood is composed of plasma and blood cells.
Plasma is the fluid part of blood in which blood cells are suspended. Blood cells are of three types:
(i) Red blood cells (RBCs) contain haemoglobin to transport O_2 to various cells of the body. They also help to take CO_2 from the body cells to the lungs, where it can be breathed out.
(ii) White blood cells (WBCs) help to protect against diseases by destroying harmful bacteria and other foreign materials.
(iii) Blood platelets help the blood to clot, whenever there is a wound on the body.

73. There are three types of blood vessels — arteries, veins and capillaries.
Arteries : Arteries carry oxygen-rich (oxygenated) blood from the heart and distribute it to all parts of the body. Pulmonary artery is an exception as it carries carbon dioxide-rich (deoxygenated) blood from the heart to the lungs. Arteries have thick elastic walls to allow stretching, and to deal with the high pressure of blood coming from the heart. Arteries are usually deep seated.
Veins : Veins are the blood vessels which carry carbon dioxide-rich (deoxygenated) blood from the body organs back to the heart. Pulmonary vein is an exception as it carries oxygenated blood from the lungs to the heart. Veins have thin elastic walls. The diameter of veins is greater than that of arteries. These are superficially placed. The blood pressure in the veins is low. There are a series of valves present in veins, which help to prevent back flow, and allow blood to flow only towards the heart.
Capillaries : Arteries branch into finer and smaller blood vessels called capillaries, which join to form veins. Capillaries are the smallest blood vessels, that connect arteries to veins. They have very thin walls, through which oxygen, digested food, carbon dioxide, waste products etc. are exchanged between the blood and the body cells.

74. The vena cava (main veins) bring deoxygenated blood from all parts of the body (except lungs) to the right atrium. The right atrium pumps this blood into the right ventricle, which then pumps it into the pulmonary artery.

The pulmonary artery transfers the blood to the lungs for oxygenation.
The oxygenated blood is received by the left atrium through two pairs of pulmonary veins (1 pair from right lung and 1 pair from left lung). It is then pumped into the left ventricle. The left ventricle, in turn, pumps the blood into the aorta (main artery), through which it is supplied to the rest of the body.

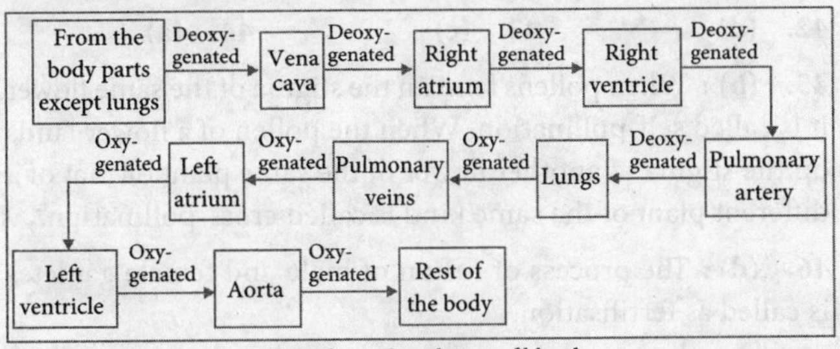

Flow chart: Circulation of blood

The deoxygenated blood from the different body parts again enters the right side of the heart, and is pumped to the lungs through pulmonary artery, where it gives up its carbon dioxide, and picks up oxygen. This oxygen-rich blood then travels back to the left side of the heart, and is again sent to the different parts of the body. In this way, the process is repeated again and again, and blood circulates through the body, 72 times in a minute, same as the heart beat rate and pulse rate.

75. The excretory system in higher animals and in humans consists of a pair of kidneys, a pair of ureters, a urinary bladder, a urethra and a urinary opening.
Kidneys consist of a large number of coiled tubes called nephrons. Each kidney contains about one million nephrons. Nephrons are the tiny filtering units of the kidney. They filter out excess water, salts and urea from the blood as it passes through them. The clean and purified blood leaves the kidneys, and continues circulating in the body.
The wastes removed by the kidneys are in the form of a liquid called urine. It passes from the kidneys through ureters into the urinary bladder, where it is stored temporarily until it is excreted from the body through urinary opening located at the end of urethra.
Sweat glands present in our skin also help to eliminate excretory wastes such as salts, urea, etc. and help to keep the body cool.

76. Plants possess a well-developed vascular system which performs following functions:

– Transportation of water and minerals from roots to the top of the plant through xylem.
– Transportation of food synthesised in the leaves to various plant parts upto the roots through phloem.

Transpiration from the surface of leaves builds a transpiration pull that helps in the transportation of water and minerals from roots to the top of plant.

77. (a) The right side of the heart consists of right atrium and right ventricle which contain carbon dioxide-rich blood and the left side of the heart consists of left atrium and left ventricle which contain oxygen-rich blood. The right side of the heart is completely separated from the left side with the help of a partition called septum, so that the two types of blood do not mix.
(b) Blood in the heart flows only in one direction because heart has a number of valves that do not allow the blood flow in any other direction.
(c) In xylem, water moves only in upward direction due to the suction pull created by transpiration. In case of phloem, food is transported to downward parts of the plant and when leaves are shed, stored food in root is transported upward to the upper parts of the plant.

78. (b) : A-represents deoxygenated blood (carbon dioxide rich) which comes from the all body parts to heart and B represents oxygenated blood (oxygen rich) which comes from lungs to the heart for further distribution to the body.

79. (b) : II-pulmonary artery.
III-pulmonary vein.

80. (c) : I-represents-vena cava *i.e.*, superior and inferior vena cava which bring deoxygenated blood from all parts of the body to the heart for oxygenation. IV represents aorta which supplies blood to all part of the body

81. (c) **82. (d)**

83. (b) : X – represents stomata.

84. (c) : I-represents open type of stomatal pore and II-represents closed type of stomatal pore.

85. (a)

86. The two functions of stomata (*X*) are:
(i) The exchange of gases in plants occurs through stomata.
(ii) The excess water in plants evaporates through stomata by the process of transpiration.

87. (a) : Transpiration is the process of loss of water in the form of water vapour from the aerial parts of a plant. It transports water and dissolved minerals from the roots to the top of the plant by creating a suction pull called transpiration pull.

88. (d)

89. (a) : P – represents kidneys which are the main excretory organs in humans.

90. (b)

91. (a) : R – represents ureters which transport urine from kidneys to bladder.

92. The urinary bladder(s) temporarily stores urine until it is eliminated through urethra.

8 Reproduction in Plants

Practice Corner

1. (a) 2. (a)

3. (b) : Cutting is done in vegetative part of a plant to grow plant while others are asexual reproduction methods.

4. (c) : *Bryophyllum* has buds in the margins of leaves and when leaf falls on moist soil, it give rise to a new plant.

5. (b) 6. (c) 7. (b)

8. (a) : New plants can also grow from roots, and the plants produced by vegetative propagation take less time to grow and bear flowers and fruits earlier than those produced from seeds.

9. (d) : In sweet potato, roots give rise to a new plant. In turmeric, ginger and potato, eyes with bud can give rise to new plant.

10. (b)

11. (b) : Grafting is an artificial method of vegetative propagation. Cutting of stem from one plant and joining it on the stem with roots of other plant as done in case of mango.

12. (b) : Flower is not a vegetative part of a plant. It is a reproductive part of a plant. Spores are also asexual reproductive bodies.

13. (b)

14. (a) : Vegetative propagation is a type of asexual reproduction in which new plants are produced from vegetative parts of plant like roots, stems, leaves and buds.

15. vegetative 16. node

17. budding 18. seeds

19. flower, leaf 20. algae

21. reproduction 22. Yeast

23. Flowers 24. True

25. False. In vegetative propagation, new plants are exact copies of the parent plant.

26. False 27. True

28. False. Both parents are involved in the sexual reproduction.

29. True 30. True

31. False. In *Dahlia*, reproduction takes place through roots.

32. True 33. Sprouting from an 'eye'

34. *Hydra* 35. Spore formation

36. Asexual reproduction

37. (a)

38. (b) : Corn, papaya and cucumber produce unisexual flowers where as mustard, rose and *Petunia* have bisexual flowers.

39. (b)

40. (c) : Cucumber produced unisexual flowers.

41. (b) : Anther is a part of male reproductive system of a flower called stamen.

42. (d) 43. (c) 44. (a)

45. (b) : When pollens land on the stigma of the same flower it is called self-pollination. When the pollen of a flower lands on the stigma of another flower of the same plant or that of a different plant of the same kind is called cross-pollination.

46. (d) : The process of fusion of male and female gametes is called as fertilisation.

47. (b) 48. (a)

49. (b) : Flower contains male and female reproductive cells and so play role in sexual reproduction.

50. (b)

51. (c) : *Petunia* flowers have both pistil and stamen together.

52. (b) : In cross-pollination, pollen grains of a flower lands on the stigma of another flower of the different plant of same kind.

53. (d) : It is complete flower as it has both pistil and stamen in a single flower.

54. zygote 55. egg

56. Pollen grains 57. pollination

58. embryo 59. bisexual

60. coat 61. unisexual

62. False. In cross pollination, pollen grains are transferred from anther of one flower to the stigma of flower of the same plant or the different plant.

63. True

64. False. Pistil of a flower consists of a style, stigma and ovary. Stamen of flower consists of anther and filament.

65. True

66. False. Colourful petals attract the insects.

67. False. Insects help during cross-pollination. No agent is required for self-pollination.

68. The given figures show the process of fertilisation.

69. On reaching the stigma, pollen grain germinates and produces a thin pollen tube. It extends through the style, reaches the ovary and enters the ovule. The pollen tube contains two male gametes. One of the male gametes fuses with the female gamete and forms a zygote. The process of fusion of a male and a female gamete to form a zygote is called fertilisation.

70. (d)

71. (c) : After fertilisation, the ovary grows into a fruit.

72. (b)

73. (c) : The seed contains an embryo enclosed in a protective seed coat.

74. (c)

75. fruit

76. mango, orange

77. ovules

78. True

79. False. After fertilisation, ovary develops into fruit and the other floral parts such as petals, sepals and stamen, etc., fall off.

80. False. Orange have seeds with seed coat.

81. False. Embryo is present inside the seed and is enclosed in a protective seed coat.

82. (b)

83. (d) : Seeds and fruits of plants are carried away by wind, water and animals.

84. (d)

85. (a)

86. (c)

87. (d) : Plants get benefit by seed dispersal. It prevents overcrowding and also the competition between the plants and its seedlings for water minerals and sunlight. It also helps the plants to invade new habitats.

88. (a) : Fruits of some plants burst with sudden jerks. This results in scattering of seeds for away from parent plant, *i.e.*, in case of balsam, castor, pea, etc.

89. (d) : Pistil consists of stigma, style and ovary. Growth of new plant depends on seed dispersal. Fruit is the ripened ovary. Bisexual flowers are complete flowers. Seeds of *Urena* are dispersed by animals.

90. animals

91. hairy

92. explosion or sudden jerk

93. winged

94. hooks

95. True

96. False. Coconuts are fibrous fruit of coconut trees.

97. True

98. False. *Xanthium* has spiny seeds with hooks that are carried by animals to distant places.

99. True

100. (a) (i) Hairy seeds of madar (aak).
(ii) Spiny seeds of *Xanthium*.
(iii) Winged seeds of maple.
(b) The seeds of aak (madar) and maple are dispersed by wind and the seeds of *Xanthium* are dispersed to distant places by animals.

NCERT Exemplar Problems

1. (b) : Sexual reproduction is the process of development of new organisms through the formation and fusion of gametes. The organs specialised to perform sexual reproduction in flowering plants are flowers. After fertilisation ovary changes into fruit and ovules change into seeds. Seeds produce new plants.

2. (c) : In fragmentation, parent body breaks down into two or more fragments. Each body fragment develops into an organism. Fragmentation is asexual mode of reproduction and plant body can be fragmented into many parts and each part can develop into new plant so, through this method algae spread rapidly.

3. (a) : Wings of maple and drumstick seeds help them to fly in air, so they are carried to long distances by wind.

4. (c) : Eye of potato is the vegetative bud which arises from nodes of stem tuber and when this bud or eye is placed in soil, it produces new plantlets. Likewise *Bryophyllum* leaf also has vegetative buds on leaf margins which when placed in soil produce new plantlets.

5. (c) : Ovaries of different flowers may have one ovule *e.g.*, wheat, paddy, mango to many ovules, *e.g.*, papaya, watermelon, etc.

6. (a) : It is not necessary to have two plants for sexual reproduction to take place. In self pollinated plants, single plant can perform sexual reproduction.
Besides insects, many other agents carry out pollination, *i.e.*, bats, snails, birds, wind, water, etc.

7. (c) : The transfer of pollen grains from the anther to the stigma is called pollination. Pollen grains are immobile, they cannot move by themselves to reach the stigma. An external agency is required for this.

A & R Corner

1. (d) : Sexual reproduction is the most common method of reproduction in plants which involves two parents, *i.e.*, one male and one female.

2. (b)

3. (d) : *Vallisneria* is water - pollinated plant and its male flowers present in groups to form inflorescence.

4. (b)

5. (d) : Tuberous roots of *Dahlia*, sweet potato and *Asparagus* become swollen due to food stored in them. In *Oxalis*, vegetative propagation occurs by sub-aerial stems.

6. (b) : *Spirogyra* is a multicellular green algae found in freshwater ponds and in slow streams. In *Spirogyra* reproduction occurs by the process of fragmentation. In fragmentation the body of parent organism breaks into two or more fragments each of which can produce an offspring.

7. **(b)**

8. **(d) :** Stamen is the male reproductive organ of flower. It consists of long slender sterile filament and upper swollen fertile anther. Stigma and style are the parts of pistil.

9. **(b) :** Rhizomes are underground stems of ginger and turmeric which bears buds. The buds grow to give rise to new plants.

10. **(b) :** Callus is an unorganised mass of rapidly dividing cells of tissues which differentiate into root and shoot in (tissue culture) nutrient medium containing plant hormones.

11. **(c) :** In grafting, the features of two plants are combined. Stem cutting with buds of one plant called scion, is kept over the cut stem of another plant called the stock. The scion and stock are firmly tied together. After sometime, the tissues of the stock and scion join together to form one plant. The stock supplies the essential nutrients to the scion.

12. **(a) :** Fertilisation is the process of fusion of male gamete and the female gamete resulting in the production of the zygote.

13. **(b)**

14. **(c) :** The flowers which contain either only the stamen or only the pistil are called unisexual flowers. For, *e.g.*, maize, papaya, cucumber, date palm, etc. The flowers which contain both stamens as well as pistils are called bisexual flowers, *e.g.*, mustard, rose, *Petunia*, etc.

15. **(c) :** Vegetative organs take part in nutrition, growth and maintenance of plant body, *e.g.*, roots, stem and leaves. Reproductive organs take part in formation of new plants, *e.g.*, flowers.

Exam Corner

1. **(a) :** Asexual reproduction involves only one parent and the offspring produced are identical to the parent plant. Sexual reproduction involves two parents and so offsprings produced are not identical to the parents and show variations.

2. **(b) :** To carry out a fair test in order to find out the effect of overcrowding on the growth of plants, the type of soil used, the size of pots used and other environmental conditions should be kept same. However, the number of plants should be kept different in the two pots.

3. **(d) :** Bright colour and sweet fragrance attracts the insects that carry out pollution.

4. **(b)**

5. **(d) :** Structure 'X' represents a stage of pollen grain after pollination but before fertilisation. After landing of pollen on the stigma, a thin tube grows out of pollen. It grows till it reaches the ovule and release the male gamete, that further contribute to the process of fertilisation.

6. **(b)**

7. **(c) :** Tissue culture is a method of artificial propagation of plants from a small plant tissue placed in a nutrient medium.

8. **(a)**

9. **(d) :** It is grafting. Grafting is an artificial method of vegetative propagation a type of asexual reproduction in which a stem cutting of one plant is kept over the cut stem of another plant. They both are tied firmly together. After sometimes, they form one plant.

10. **(b) :** Budding occurs naturally in yeast where a buldge-like structure called bud from parent give rise to the new individual.

11. **(b)** 12. **(c)**

13. **(a) :** Sunflower is brightly colour flower that attracts insects and thus it is pollinated by insects. Grasses have light weight seeds that are easily blown by wind whereas *Vallisneria* is a water plant with floating seeds that are pollinated by water.

14. **(d)** 15. **(c)** 16. **(a)**

17. asexual reproduction 18. sexual

19. scion, stock 20. Vegetative propagation.

21. buds 22. Nectar

23. unisexual 24. True

25. False. Brightly colour flowers that produce nectar are mainly insect pollinated.

26. True 27. True

28. True : Sexual reproduction is the fusion of male and female gametes. As both parents are involved, the offsprings have the mixture of both parental genes.

29. True 30. True

31. False. Ovule grows into seed whereas ovary grows into fruit.

32. False. Pollen grain germinates on stigma and produces a pollen tube in the pistil. Pollen tube connects the pollen grain with the ovule for the fusion of male and female gametes.

33. False. Grafting is an artificial method of vegetative propagation where a twig of one plant is placed over the stem of another plant and tied together.

34. True 35. True

36. False. Stamen is the male reproductive part whereas pistil is the female reproductive part of a flower.

37. True 38. True

39. False. Yeast is a unicellular organism that reproduces by budding.

40. True

41. False. Asexual reproduction takes place through spores. Seeds are produced in sexual reproduction.

42. False. Tuberous roots of *Dahlia* give rise to new plant.

43. False. Leaf margins of *Bryophyllum* has buds that can grow into new plants.

44. (a)

45. Vegetative propagation, Fragmentation

46. Moss, Ferns **47.** *Xanthium, Urena*

48. Mustard, Rose **49.** Potato, Ginger

50. *Bryophyllum* – It reproduces by leaf bud while others reproduce by 'eye' with a bud in it.

51. Walnut – It is hard fruit while others are fleshy and juicy.

52. Flowers – It is the reproductive part of a plant while others are vegetative part of a flower.

53. Corn – It is an incomplete or unisexual flower while others are complete or bisexual flowers.

54. *Spirogyra* – It reproduces through fragmentation while others reproduce through spore formation.

55. (a) The fusion of male and female gametes (to form a zygote) is called fertilisation.
(b) The transfer of pollen grain from the anther of the stigma of either the same flower/different flower of same plant of different plants of same species is called pollination.
(c) The early growth of a plant from its seed is called germination.

56. Tissue culture is a method of artificial propagation where a piece of tissue (called explant) is cut from the growing tip of a plant and kept in a nutrient medium containing hormones that make the cells divide to form a group of cells. This unorganised cell mass called callus. When roots develop, the callus is transferred to a new medium containing hormones. The cells of callus in this nutrient medium divide and differentiate into roots and shoot and form a new plant let. The plantlets so formed can now be grown in pots filled with soil. This method of growing plants is also referred to micropropation.

57.

S.No.	Self-pollination	Cross-pollination
(a)	In self-pollination, pollen grain of a flower reaches to the stigma of same flower.	In cross-pollination, the transfer of pollen grains from the anthers of a flower to the stigma of another flower on different plant of the same species.
(b)	No pollinating agent is required.	Pollinating agent like wind, air or insects are required.
(c)	It occurs only in bisexual flowers.	It occurs in unisexual flowers.
(d)	It does not lead to genetic variation in the next generation.	It leads to genetic variation in the next generation.

58.

S.No.	Asexual reproduction	Sexual reproduction
(a)	Plants can give rise to new plants without seeds.	New plants are obtained from seeds.
(b)	The new individual comes from a single parent.	Two parents are required to produce an individual.
(c)	No sex cells are required.	It takes place with the help of specialised sex cells.
(d)	Characters of the new individual are same as that of the parent.	New individual has the characters of both the parents.

59. Flowers are so colourful because coloured flower petals assist in attracting insects, birds and small mammals to the flower for pollination.

60. Cutting is a process in which a piece of vegetative part, usually stem of a plant is selected and is rooted in the soil that ultimately grows into a new plant. Whereas grafting is practised in those plants which do not produce roots readily. In this process, cutting of a plant is attached to the piece of another rooted plant. The cutting called a scion while the rooted plant is called a stock.

61. The process of fusion of the male gamete (released by pollen tube) with the female gamete inside the ovule to form a zygote is called fertilisation. After fertilisation, ovary matures into fruit and the ovules mature into seeds. The seed contains a developing embryo (formed from zygote), protected in seed coats. The seed germinates under suitable conditions of water, oxygen, temperature, etc.

62. Spore formation occurs in bacteria and fungi. Spores are tiny, spherical bodies covered by hard protective coat to withstand unfavourable conditions. They germinate under favourable conditions to develop into new plants. It occurs in moss and ferns. Whereas in budding, a bud occurs on the body of the parent organism. This bud increases in size and eventually breaks off from the parent, *e.g.*, yeast.

63. Germination is the early growth of a plant from its seed. A seed contains developing embryo in it. The embryo is present in the resting stage and begins to grow only under favourable conditions. Under suitable conditions like sufficient moisture, oxygen and warmth, the enzymes present in the seed start functioning and change the stored food into soluble form. This helps in the growth of radicle and plumule. The radicle starts growing first and pushes down in the soil. It becomes the root. Then the plumule starts growing. It pushes up and grows into the shoot and leaves. The leaves start to make food by photosynthesis and thus, the plant manufactures its own food.

64. On reaching the stigma, pollen grain germinates and produces a thin pollen tube. It extends through the style, reaches the ovary and enters the ovule. The pollen tube contains two male gametes. One of the male gametes fuses with the female gamete and forms a zygote. The process of fusion of a male and a female gamete to form a zygote is called fertilisation.

65. Potatoes are the underground stems called tubers. They are swollen because they store food in them. Potato tubers possess scars or depressions called 'eyes'. Each eye represents a node in which small buds are present. These buds can give rise to new plants.

66. Importance of seed dispersal are:

(i) It prevents competition between the plant and its own seedlings for sunlight, water and minerals.

(ii) It also prevents such competition between the seedlings.

(iii) It also enables the plants to invade new habitats for wider distribution.

Dispersal of seeds: Seeds of a plant are dispersed in various ways such as:

(i) By winds: Winged seeds such as those of drumstick and maple, light seeds of grasses or hairy seeds of *madar* (aak) and hairy fruit of sunflower get blown off with the wind to far away places.

(ii) By water: Some seeds are dispersed by water. These fruits usually have the floating ability in the form of spongy or fibrous outer coat as in coconut.

(iii) By animals: Some seeds are dispersed by animals, especially spiny seeds with hooks which get attached to the body of animals and are carried to distant places. Examples are *Xanthium and Urena*.

(iv) By humans: Human beings carry various fruits to long distances with them and thus helping in seed dispersal.

(v) Some seeds are dispersed when the fruits burst with sudden jerks. The seeds are scattered far from the parent plant. This happens in the case of castor and balsam.

67. The process of growing new plants by artificial methods is known as artificial propagation. Some of these methods are as follows :

(a) Cutting: In this method, a healthy young branch of a plant having leaf buds is cut off and planted in moist soil. The cutting develops roots and grows into a new plant. This method is used to propagate plants like rose, *Bougainvillea* and sugarcane.

(b) Layering: In this method, a young branch is bent towards the ground and covered with moist soil forming a layer. After sometime, roots develop from the covered part. The branch is then cut off from the parent plant and allowed to grow into a new plant. This method is commonly done in jasmine, vines, cherry, strawberry, etc.

(c) Grafting: In this method, stem cutting with buds of one plant, (scion) is kept over the cut stem of another plant, (stock). The scion and the stock are then firmly tied together. After sometime, the tissues of the stock and scion join together to form one plant.

(d) Tissue culture: In tissue culture method, a small piece of tissue (called explant) is cut off from the growing tip of a plant. The cells of this tissue are then grown in suitable nutrient medium under controlled conditions of temperature, humidity, etc. The cells of the tissue divide rapidly and form an unorganised cell mass called callus.

The cells of callus divide and differentiate into roots and shoot and form a new plantlet. The plantlets so formed can now be grown in pots filled with soil. *Chrysanthemum, Asparagus*, orchids are grown and developed by tissue culture method.

68. Grafting is an artificial method of vegetative propagation in plants. It is used in horticulture to develop new varieties of ornamental plants and fruit trees. In this method, cutting with buds of one plant, called the scion, is kept over the cut stem of another plant, called the stock. The scion and the stock are then firmly tied together.

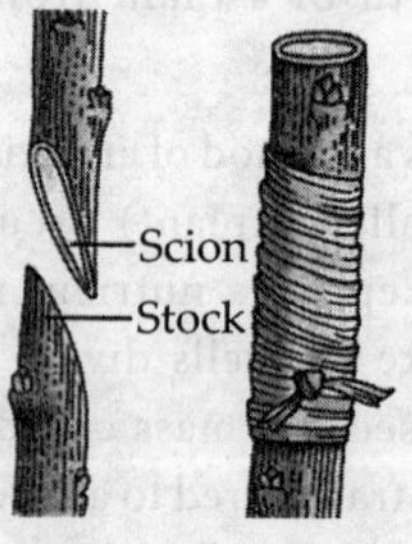

The care is to be taken that stock has an extensive root system under the soil. After sometime, the tissues of the stock and scion join together to form one plant. The stock supplies the essential nutrients to the scion. This is a common method to develop new varieties of apple, guava, mango, etc. By grafting, the features of two are combined to have superior characteristics of both the plants in the new plant.

69. The process of transfer of pollen grains from the anther of a flower to the stigma of a flower is known as pollination. Pollination leads to fertilisation because for fertilisation to occur, the pollen grains from the stamen must first be transferred to the stigma of the pistil. On reaching the stigma, pollen grain grows out into a thin pollen tube. It extends through the style, reaches the ovary and enters the ovule. The pollen tube contains two male gametes. One of the male gametes fuses with the female gamete present in the ovule and forms a zygote. The process of fusion of a male and a female gamete to form a zygote is called fertilisation.

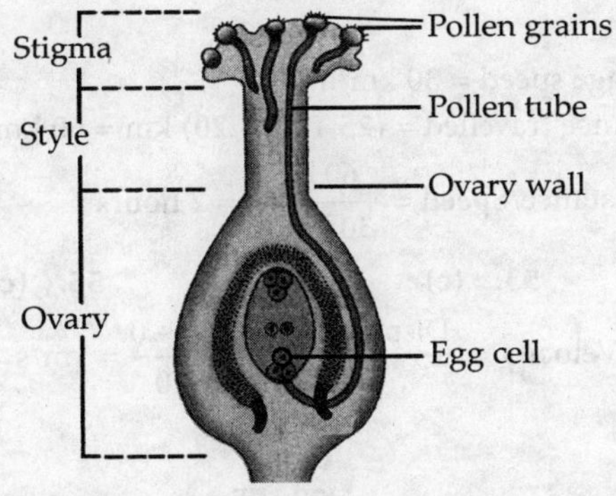

70. Labelled diagram of a bisexual flower is as follows:

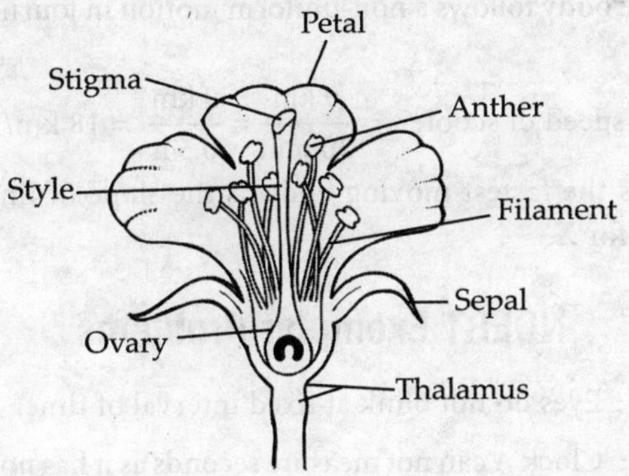

A typical flower has a broad base or thalamus (receptacle) over which are borne four whorls of floral leaves — sepals, petals, stamens and carpels. Stamens and carpels (or pistils) are the male and female reproductive parts of a flower respectively.
Sepals form the outermost whorl of a flower which are usually green in colour. They protect the flower in bud condition.
Petals are present on inner side of sepals. These are coloured to attract insects, birds etc., to help in pollination.
Stamen : Each stamen consists of the anther and a long slender stalk called the filament. Pollen grains are formed inside the anther. Pollen grains produce male gametes.
Pistil : The carpel or pistil consists of three parts — stigma, style, and ovary. Stigma is present at the top and is sticky. The style is a long tube that connects the stigma to the ovary. Ovary is the basal swollen portion. One or more ovules are present in the ovary. The female gamete or egg cell is formed inside the ovule.

71. (i) Colourful and scented petals attracts various insects, birds and small mammals to the flower for pollination. Insects get attracted easily to the colourful petals and hence pollinate flowers.
(ii) Pollen grains have a tough protective coat which prevents them from drying up since they are carried by wind or water. It also protect them from harsh climatic conditions.
(iii) Same kind of plants grow in different places as seeds or fruits of these plants are scattered to different areas by various agents such as wind, water, animals, etc. The seeds or fruits are scattered over a large area in order to find an available space for their germination.
(iv) Drumstick has winged seeds that are easily blown off with the wind to far away places.

72. **(a) :** In the given figure P, Q, R and S represent pollen grain, stigma, ovule and style respectively. Stigma, style and ovary forms the female reproductive part of flower. Ovary develops into fruit and ovule (R) develops into seed. Style(s) is a long tube that connects the stigma to the ovary.

73. **(c) :** Pollen grain (P) – Formed inside the anther
Stigma (Q) – Landing platform for pollen grains
Ovule (R) – Site where female gamete is formed
Style (S) – Connects stigma to the ovary

74. **(c) :** P (Pollen grain) produces male gametes and R (ovule) produces female gamete. The fusion of male gamete with female gamete is called fertilisation.

75. **(a) :** In *Petunia* male and female reproductive parts of flower are present in same flower hence, it is bisexual.

76. **(c) :** Wind pollinated flowers have feathery and long stigma.

77. **(b) :** X is showing tuberous roots of sweet potato which become swollen due to food stored in them.

78. **(b) :** Y represents the ginger rhizome, which bear buds, which grows and give rise to new plants.

79. **(d) :** Ginger and turmeric possess rhizomes which are the main underground stems that bear buds and these buds grow to give rise to new plants.

80. *Bryophyllum*, *Begonia*.

81. Z is the potato tuber. Potato is an underground stem tuber and posses scars or depressions called eyes. Each eye represents a bud which can develop into new plant.

82. A (Insect-pollinated flower) – Orchids
B (Wind-pollinated flower) – Maize
C (Water-pollinated flower) – *Vallisneria*

83. A is insect pollinated flower. These flowers possess following features:
(i) Flowers are big and brightly coloured.
(ii) Have nectaries that produce plenty of nectar.
(iii) Produce odour which may be pleasant or foul.
(iv) Have sticky stigma and sticky pollen grains.

84. In *Vallisneria* (C), which is a water- pollinated flower, male flowers do not occur singly but are present in group to form inflorescence. Pollination takes place by the agency of water. The male flowers detach from the inflorescence and rise to the water surface where they float. The female flowers have long stalks which enable them to reach the water surface. The male flowers are carried by water currents towards female flowers where they release their pollens and in this way pollination takes place.

85. Due to small petal size, the stamens and the pistils are well exposed to the wind, making wind pollination easier.

9 Motion and Time

Practice Corner

1. (c) 2. (c) 3. (b)
4. True
5. False. A car moving at a constant speed shows uniform motion. 6. True

S.No.	Slower	Faster
7.	Boat	Ship
8.	Road roller	Train
9.	Motor bike	Helicopter
10.	Scooter	Van
11.	Kid's scooty	Bus

12. (b) 13. (c)
14. (c) : pounds per square inch is the unit of pressure.
15. (a) 16. (b) 17. (d)
18. True 19. True
20. False. If the speed of an object moving along a straight line keeps changing, its motion is said to be non-uniform.
21. True
22. (a) 23. (b) 24. (d) 25. (a)
26. (a) 27. (a) 28. (c) 29. (a)
30. periodic motion 31. bob
32. oscillatory 33. time period
34. True 35. True
36. True 37. False
38. True 39. True
40. Pendulum (iii) has larger average time period as the length of the string is the largest. The time period of the pendulum is directly proportional to the length of the string.
41. (a) : Speed = $\frac{\text{Distance}}{\text{Time}} \Rightarrow \text{Time} = \frac{300 \text{ km}}{50 \text{ km/h}} = 6 \text{ h}$
42. (a)
43. (c) : An odometer is used to measure the distance travelled by a vehicle.
44. (b) : Distance = speed × time
45. (b)
46. (a) : $90 \text{ km/hr} \times \frac{5}{18} = 25 \text{ m/s}$
47. (c) : Velocity have direction.
48. speedometer 49. distance
50. m/s
51. Average speed = 30 km/h
Total distance travelled = (25 + 15 + 20) km = 60 km
Time = Distance/Speed = $\frac{60 \text{ km}}{30 \text{ km/h}} = 2 \text{ hours}$
52. (c) 53. (c) 54. (a) 55. (c)
56. (b) : Velocity = $\frac{\text{Displacement}}{\text{Time}} = \frac{70-0}{70} = 1 \text{m/s}$
57. (a)
58. True 59. True
60. The body follows a non-uniform motion in journey from *O* to *F*.
Average speed of scooter = $\frac{9 \text{ km}}{30 \text{ min}} = \frac{9 \text{ km}}{0.5 \text{ h}} = 18 \text{ km/h}$
61. *X* is the fastest moving body as the slope of line is the steepest for *X*.

NCERT Exemplar Problems

1. (d) : Eyes do not blink at fixed interval of time.
2. (c) : Clock *A* can not measure seconds as it has no second hand. Clocks *A* and *B* both have minute hands, so time interval of 5 minutes can be measured by both of them.
3. (a) : Distance time graph for uniform motion shows a straight line. Slope is same for both table *A* and table *B*.
4. (b) : Speed = $\frac{\text{Distance}}{\text{Time}} = \frac{54 \times 1000}{90 \times 60} = 10 \text{ m/s}$
5. (c)
6. (a)
7. (d) : Time taken by the bob to move from
A to *O* = $t_1 + t_2 = t_{AO} = t_{OA}$
Similarly, $t_{OB} = t_1 + t_2 = t_{BO}$
So, time period = $t_{AO} + t_{OB} + t_{BO} + t_{OA} = 4(t_1 + t_2)$
8. (a)
9. (b) : Average speed = $\frac{\text{Total distance}}{\text{Time taken}} = \frac{(3+3) \text{ km}}{\left(\frac{1}{2}+\frac{1}{3}\right) \text{h}}$
$= \frac{(3+3) \text{ km}}{\left(\frac{1}{2}+\frac{1}{3}\right) \text{h}}$
$= \frac{6}{5/6} = \frac{36}{5} = 7.2 \text{ km/h}$

A&R Corner

1. (a) : A century is equal to 100 years.
2. (b) : Time period is independent of displacement.
3. (b) : Greater is the velocity, more is displacement covered.

4. **(b) :** The motion of earth around sun is not oscillatory as it is not a to and fro motion about a fixed point.

5. **(c) :** Odometer measure the total distance travelled.

6. **(b) :** Assertion and reason both are true but the reason is not the correct explanation of assertion.

7. **(a) :** The slope of graph is zero which shows no change in position of a body at rest. Assertion and reason both are true and the reason is correct explanation of assertion.

8. **(a) :** Both are true and reason is the correct explanation is assertion.

9. **(c) :** Assertion is true but the reason is false as the time period of the pendulum does not depend on the mass of pendulum.

10. **(b) :** Both are true and reason is not the correct explanation of assertion.

Exam Corner

1. (b) **2.** (b) **3.** (d)

4. (c) : Distance = Speed × Time $= 2 \times \frac{18}{5} \times \frac{1}{2}$ km = 3.6 km

5. (c) : A week have 7 days.

6. True **7.** True

8. False. The time period of a pendulum depends on the length of the string attached to the bob.

9. False. Displacement is the shortest distance between initial and final position.

10. True

11. (i)-T; (ii)-P; (iii)-R; (iv)-Q; (v)-S

12. Digital clock

13. Motion of a simple pendulum

14. Motion of the Earth around the Sun

15. Motion of the Earth on its own axis

16. Motion of a car which covers a distance of 1 metre in each second.

17. Amplitude **18.** Stopwatch

19. Odometer

20. Motion **21.** Measurement

22. (a)

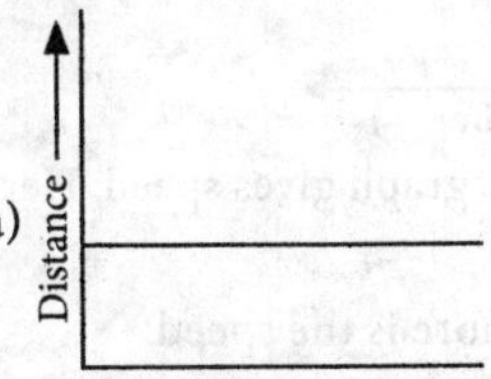

(b)

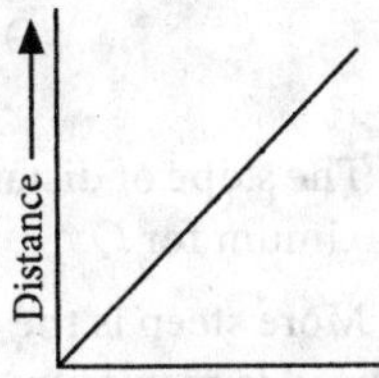

23. Distance = 7200 m
Time = 1 min = 60 seconds

Speed $= \frac{\text{Distance}}{\text{Time}} = \frac{7200}{60} = 120$ m/s

24. The total distance covered by an object divided by the total time taken is called average speed.
Average speed = Total distance covered/Total time taken

25. For a uniform motion, the velocity of an object remains constant. So, even after 10 seconds, the body will continue to move with a velocity of 20 m/s.

26. The main limitation of sundial is that it can be used only in the presence of sunlight and not at night or not in cloudy or rainy days.

27.

Uniform motion	Non-uniform motion
If an object is moving along a straight line with a constant speed then the motion of object is called uniform motion. Bus moving at constant speed is an example of uniform motion.	If the speed of an object moving along a straight line keeps changing, its motion is said to be non-uniform motion. For example, movement of bus or car.

28. Total distance travelled by the car in 5 hours = 50 km + 45 km + 65 km + 70 km + 75 km = 305 km

$\therefore$ Average speed $= \frac{\text{Total distance}}{\text{Total time taken}} = \frac{305 \text{ km}}{5 \text{ h}} = 61$ km/h

29. Distance-time graph for non-uniform motion

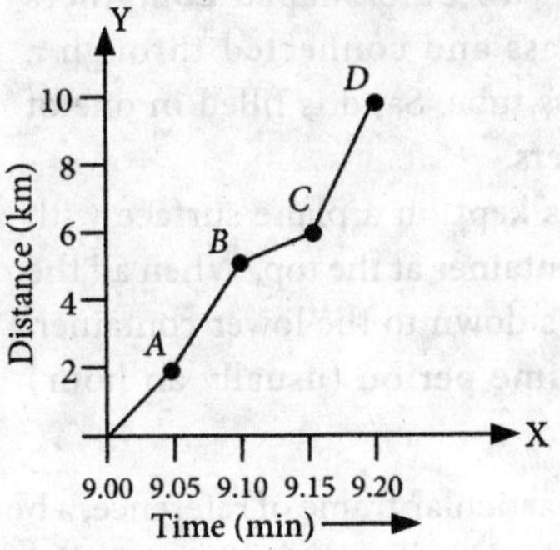

30. Distance travelled by car A = 15,360 m = 15.360 km
Time taken = 3 hours

Speed of car $A = \frac{\text{Distance}}{\text{Time}} = \frac{15.360 \text{ km}}{3 \text{ h}} = 5.12$ km/h

Distance travelled by car B = 56 km
Time taken = 7 hours

Speed $= \frac{\text{Distance}}{\text{Time}} = \frac{56 \text{ km}}{7 \text{ h}} = 8$ km/h

Thus, car B was moving faster.

31. A simple pendulum consists of a rod or thread attached at a pivot point fixed to a rigid support and a small mass (a metal bob) at the other end. When the bob attached to the thread is pulled to a side and released, it swings down due to the effect of gravity. The pendulum then moves back and forth at fixed intervals.

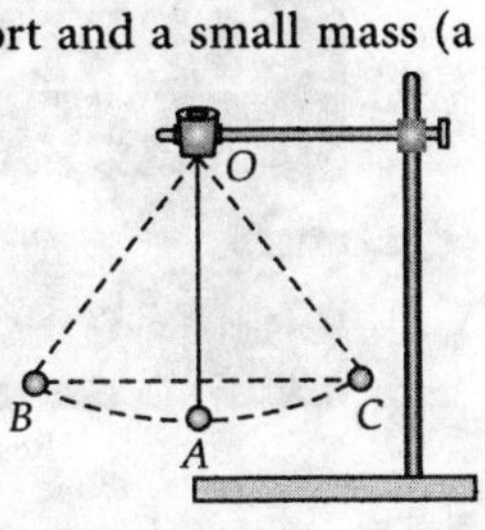

This back and forth motion of a simple pendulum is an example of periodic or oscillatory motion.

In figure, O is the point of support of the pendulum and A is the rest or mean position. B and C are the two extreme positions. The movement of the pendulum from one extreme position B to another extreme position C and then back to B completes one oscillation.

The path of the oscillation can be either way— B-A-C-A-B or A-C-A-B-A.

The time taken by the pendulum to complete one oscillation is referred to as the time period and is denoted by T.

32. Sundial : It measures time by the position of the Sun. It has a stick put in the centre of a circular disc. The position and length of the shadow of the stick on the dial gives an indication of time. The limitation of this instrument is that it cannot function during cloudy weather and at night.

Water clock : In a water clock, water is allowed to flow out from a hole made at the bottom of a bowl-shaped container into another bowl kept below. The emptying of the water filled bowl to different levels corresponds to specific time period.

Sand clock : Sand clock or hourglass consists of two bulb-shaped containers made of glass and connected through a narrow glass tube. Sand is filled in one of the containers.

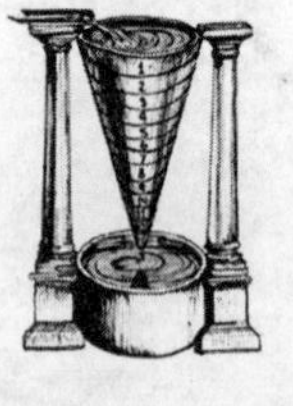

The clock is kept on a plane surface with the filled container at the top. When all the sand trickles down to the lower container, a definite time period (usually an hour) is over.

33. For a particular frame of reference, a body may be at rest, but for some other frame of reference, the same body may be in motion.

Consider two persons sitting in a moving train. For each of them the other is at rest while the train itself is in motion. Therefore, you may say that a person seated in a moving train is at rest.

A person on the ground sees the train along with both the persons and objects in it in motion. For him the two persons are in motion.

Rest and motion are relative

A person seated in a moving train is at rest in relation to any other person (body) in the same train, but is in motion in relation to any other person (body) outside the train. Similarly, the person on the road is in motion with reference to a person viewing him from the moving train.

34. (i) The displacement of an object can be either equal to or less than the distance travelled by the object, because the displacement is the shortest distance between initial and final positions of the object while distance travelled is the length of the actual path traversed by the object.

(ii) Ancient clocks like the sand clock, the water clock, were somewhat crude types of clocks. They only gave an approximation of a duration of time. So, they were abandoned and modern watches were discovered.

(iii) Because the measurement of time was done in terms of distance and mass. Mechanical clocks were designed which used to measure time in terms of weight. Accuracy in measuring length and mass enabled us to measure time with more accuracy and precision.

35. (a) : Distance in one round = circumference of circular path

$= 2 \times \pi \times R = 2 \times \frac{22}{7} \times 70 = 440$ m

36. (b) : Displacement from A to C

= Length AC = diameter

$= 2 \times 70 = 140$ m

37. (c) : Distance from $A \rightarrow B \rightarrow C \rightarrow D$

$= \frac{3}{4} \times \text{Circumference} = \frac{3}{4} \times 2\pi R$

$= \frac{3}{4} \times 2 \times \frac{22}{7} \times 70$

time, 10 s

speed $= \frac{330}{10} = 33$ m/s

38. (d) : Displacement in one complete round is zero.

So, average velocity $= \frac{\text{Total distance}}{\text{Total time}} = 0$ m/s

39. For non uniform motion, the graph is not a straight line. Therefore, graph for non-uniform motion is,

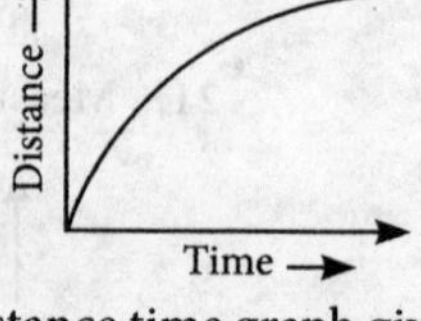

40. The slope of distance time graph gives speed. Here slope is maximum for Q.

41. More steep is the slope, more is the speed.

So, speed is maximum for OA.

Maximum speed $= \frac{100}{5} = 20$ m/s

42. Avg. speed maximum $= \frac{\text{Total distance}}{\text{Total time}} = \frac{150}{20} = 7.5$ m/s

10 Electric Current and its Effects

Practice Corner

1. (d)
2. (d)
3. (d) : A switch or a key can be placed anywhere in the circuit.
4. (a) : The current flows from the positive terminal to the negative terminal of the battery in an electric circuit.
5. (b)
6. (a)
7. (c)
8. cells
9. positive, negative
10. filament
11. switch
12. False. A group of two or more than two cells is known as battery.
13. True
14. False. —||--||— is the symbol of a battery.
15. False. Electric current flows in a closed circuit.
16. True
17. Battery
18. Switch in 'OFF' position
19. Bulb
20. Switch in 'ON' position
21. Electric wire
22. Electric cell
23. (a)
24. (b)
25. (d)
26. (a)
27. (b)
28. (d)
29. (b)
30. (a)
31. (b) : nichrome
32. Miniature Circuit Breaker
33. increased
34. False. A fuse is an application of heating effect of current.
35. False
36. True
37. False
38. True
39. True
40. (a), (e), (f)
41. (b), (c), (d)
42. (c)
43. (c)
44. Hans Christian Oersted
45. deflection
46. magnet
47. North-South
48. True
49. True
50. False. A compass needle shows deflection only when electric current is passed through it.
51. As the switch is opened in this case, therefore, there is no flow of current in the circuit. Thus, a compass needle when brought near this device, does not show any deflection.
52. (b)
53. (a) : An electromagnet shows magnetism only in the presence of electricity.
54. (c)
55. (b)
56. electromagnet
57. decrease
58. electromagnet
59. True
60. False. It is a temporary magnet.
61. True
62. False
63. True
64. (d) : Iron is the only magnetic material, the rest of the materials given are not magnetic materials. Hence, the core becomes an induced magnet when it is placed inside the coil and therefore, it produces the strongest electromagnet.
65. electromagnet
66. magnetic
67. electric bell
68. True
69. True
70. False. An electric bell works in the presence of electricity.
71. False. When the electromagnet pulls the iron strip, it breaks the circuit and current stops flowing through the coil.
72. Spring
73. Soft iron armature
74. Adjusting screw
75. Striker
76. Gong
77. Electromagnet

NCERT Exemplar Problems

1. (a) : A current carrying wire acts as a magnet with a magnetic field around it, the strength of which depends upon the amount of current passing through it.
2. (c)
3. (c) : As soon as the switch is 'ON', current can be found everywhere in the circuit.
4. (b)
5. (d)

A&R Corner

1. (b) : For the conduction of heat and electricity, it is true that the electrons are responsible.
2. (c) : The melting point of tungsten is very high.
3. (a) : Both are true
4. (b) : Both are true but the reason is not the correct explanation of assertion.
5. (d) : Wire is not charged when the current flows through it.
6. (c) : The electrons moves from lower potential region to higher potential region.

7. **(c) :** Different ratings of fuse used for different amount of current to flow.

8. **(a)**

9. **(b) :** Both are true but reason is not the correct explanation of assertion.

10. **(b) :** Both are true reason is not the correct explanation of assertion.

Exam Corner

1. **(a) :** Batteries are the power sources that provide energy. Too much electric current flowing through a bulb will cause the filament in the bulb to melt.

2. **(d)**

3. **(d) :** Except wooden ruler, all are magnetic materials.

4. **(d)** 5. **(b)**

6. True 7. False

8. False 9. True

10. True

11. (i)-R; (ii)-P; (iii)-S; (iv)-T; (v)-Q

12. Solenoid 13. Voltmeter

14. Battery 15. Fuse

16. Circuit diagram

17.

18. 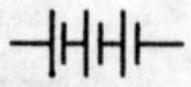

19. 

20. 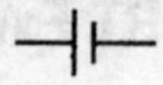

21. 

22. The bulb will not glow as there is no source of current connected in the circuit.

23. MCBs (Miniature circuit breakers) are switches which automatically turn off when current in a circuit exceeds the safe limit. We turn them on and the circuit is once again complete.

24.

Fuse	Heating Wire
(a) It has low melting point.	(a) It has high melting point.
(b) It melts or breaks when a large amount of current flows through it.	(b) It withstands when a large amount of current flows through it.
(c) It is made up of tin-lead alloy.	(c) It is made up of constantan.

25. The wire or component or device gets hot when an electric current passes through it. This is known as heating effect of the electric current.

26. Electric bulbs have a filament made of tungsten. This filament gets so hot when an electric current flows through it that it glows. So, an electric bulb gets hot as well.

27. The heat developed in a conductor due to the passage of electric current depends on the following factors :
(i) current flowing through the conductor
(ii) time of passage of current
(iii) nature of conductor
(iv) physical characteristics of conductor (e.g., length and thickness).

28. Battery is a combination of two or more cells. This can be constructed by placing cells properly on cell holder such that the positive terminal of one cell is connected to the negative terminal of the other. A piece of wire is connected to each of the two metal clips on the cell holder.

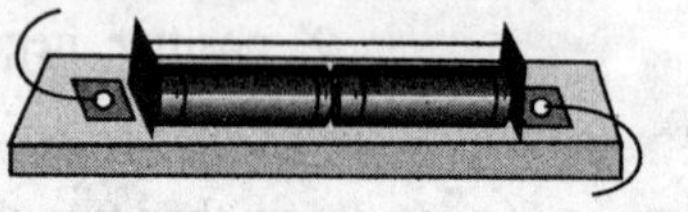

29. Fuse is a safety device which prevents our houses, appliances and electric circuits from electrical hazards at the time of the short circuiting or overloading. The fuse works on the basis of heating effects of the electric current. If by an accident the current exceeds a certain limit this device becomes overheated and melts which breaks the circuit and supply of electricity is stopped. In this way, it helps in prevention of damage.

30. Electric iron works on the basis of heating effect of electricity. When an electric current passes through the wires they become hot. Electric iron contains a coil of wire. This coil of wire is called an element. When these appliances are switched on after connecting to the electric supply, their elements become red hot and give out heat.

31. Electric bell consists of an iron striker around which is wound a wire. When current is passed by pressing button, the wire turns into a temporary magnet. The hammer is attracted towards gong to make sound. When this strikes, the current is disconnected automatically. It happens due to shift arrangement in it. The magnetic property of wire is lost and it comes back to its original position through a spring. In this way, we get separated hammering resulting in ringing of an electric bell.

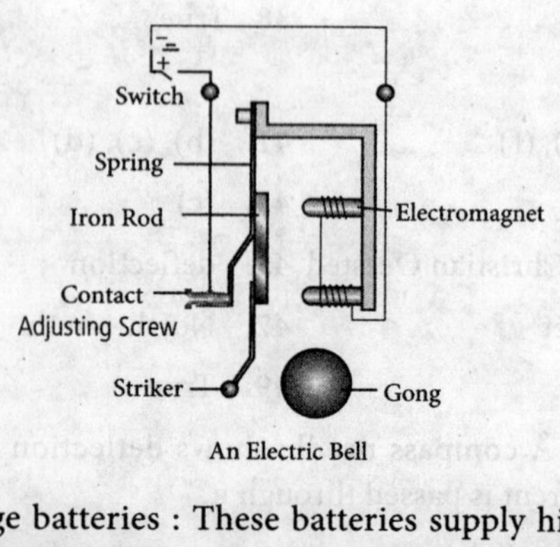

An Electric Bell

32. Storage batteries : These batteries supply high electric current for long duration. These are advantageous as these can be charged again and again and the batteries are not replaced with new ones very frequently.

Applications of storage batteries :

(i) They are used in motor cars and railway carriages for lighting the head camps.

(ii) They are also used to start the engines of cars and buses etc.

33. When current is passed through a coil of wire wrapped around an iron rod, then the coil behaves like a magnet. One end of coil acts as north pole and other end acts as south pole. When the electric current is switched off, the coil generally loses its magnetism. Such coils are called electromagnets. The electromagnets are very strong and their power can be increased so they are very important.

Two important applications (uses) of electromagnets are :

(i) They are used in electric bells, telegraphs, telephones and speakers etc.

(ii) They are used in cranes to lift heavy loads of scrap iron or iron sheets.

34. (i) Tungsten has high melting point and high resistance. So, it can heat up easily and bulb glows withstanding with high temperature.

(ii) This is because the resistance of a heater wire is high, whereas that of the connecting wire is extremely low.

(iii) We should never touch a lighted electric bulb as it may be very hot and our hand may get burnt badly.

(iv) When current passing through the wire exceeds the maximum limit, it gets heated up and due to low melting point of fuse, it melts and quickly breaks the circuit. This prevents damage to the appliances.

35. **(a) :** Electric switch cannot works on heating effect of current.

36. **(a) :** Nicrome is the mixture of nickel and chromium.

37. **(b) :** When the current increases the amount of heat produced also increase.

38. **(a) :** for heating element, the resistance should be high and high melting point.

39. The core of electromagnet is made by iron.

40. A solenoid becomes magnet when current passes through it, so it is temporary electromagnet.

41. The magnetic field of a solenoid is similar to a bar magnet.

42. When more number of cells are connected and the iron core is there, the electromagnet is strongest.

11 Light

Practice Corner

1. (a) **2.** (d)

3. (c) **4.** (c)

5. Because these holes are in straight line and light propagates in a straight line, *i.e.*, rectilinear propagation of light.

6. (a) **7.** (c) **8.** (d) **9.** (d)

10. (c) **11.** (a) **12.** (a) **13.** (a)

14. (b)

15. image **16.** Reflection

17. mirror **18.** True

19. True **20.** False

21. True **22.** True

23. True **24.** True

25. False

26. If a sharpener is kept at a distance of 10 cm in front of a mirror, then the distance between its image and the mirror will be 10 cm. Because the image in a plane mirror is always formed at the same distance from the mirror as the object is kept in front of it.

27. (a) **28.** (c)

29. True **30.** True

31. False. The correct image is 'Я'.

32. True

33. (i) ƎƆИƎIƆS (ii) SCIEИCE

34. (c) **35.** (a) **36.** (c) **37.** (c)

38. Convex, concave **39.** Concave

40. real **41.** Concave mirror

42. False. Concave mirror is used for magnified image.

43. False. Real images are obtained on a screen.

44. True. For the object position between pole and focus, the image formed is virtual.

45. (b) **46.** (b) **47.** (c)

48. (b) **49.** (d)

50. convex **51.** Concave

52. convex **53.** Convex

54. True **55.** True

56. True **57.** False

58. False. It is converging in nature.

59. False

60. Bi-convex lens is used in this magnifying glass.

61. (b) **62.** (c) **63.** (c)

64. white **65.** violet

66. back **67.** dispersion

68. Issac Newton **69.** False

70. False. White light splits into seven colors.

71. False. B stands for blue.

72.

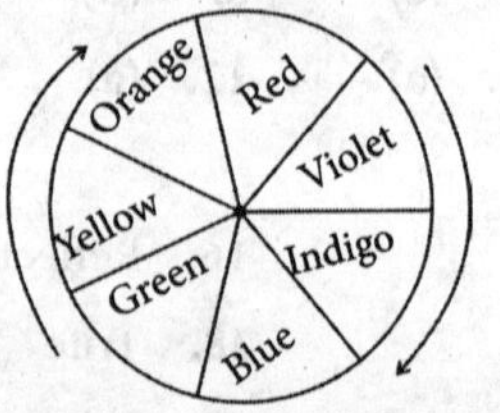

NCERT Exemplar Problems

1. **(c) :** Plane mirror forms erect and same size image while convex mirror forms erect and smaller size image.

2. **(a) :** Plane and convex mirrors forms virtual images.

3. **(b) :** Distance between object and mirror + distance between mirror and image = (0.5 + 0.5) m = 1 m

4. **(b) :** Convex mirror and concave lens form diminished images.

5. **(b) :** Rainbow appears usually after the rain when the sun is low in the sky and you can see a rainbow only when your back is towards the sun.

6. **(b)**

7. **(c)**

8. **(b) :** Image formed by a concave lens is always virtual, erect and smaller in size than the object.

A&R Corner

1. **(c) :** The speed of light changes as it passes from one medium to another.

2. **(c) :** It generally form real and inverted images.

3. **(a) :** Light travels faster in air than glass.

4. **(a) :** It given greater view of traffic.

5. **(a) :** $F = \infty$ for a plane mirror.

6. **(d) :** We can see the virtual images.

7. **(a) :** Image distance from a plane mirror = object distance from the plane mirror.

8. **(c) :** Virtual images can be formed by the converging lenses also.

9. **(b) :** Reason is not the correct explanation of assertion.

10. **(b) :** Both are true but the reason is not correct explanation of assertion.

Exam Corner

1. (a) **2.** (a) **3.** (a)

4. (a) **5.** (b)

6. True **7.** True

8. False **9.** True

10. True

11. (i)-Q; (ii)-P; (iii)-S; (iv)-T; (v)-R

12. Dispersion **13.** Reflection

14. Spectrum **15.** Retina

16. Incident ray

17. Astronomical telescope

18. Size is different for different distances from mirror.

19. Spectacles **20.** Shadow

21. Convex lens

22. When light is made to pass through prism, the light of different colours travel with different speeds. The red light travels the fastest, thus bending the least, while violet light is the slowest, bending the most.

23. Ray from X is reflected into the eye.
Ray from Y is not reflected into the eye.
Hence, the image of X is visible to the eye.

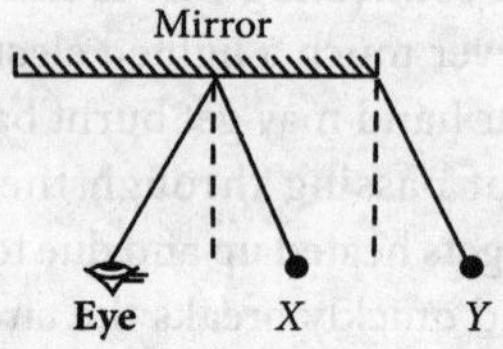

24. Type of image which can be obtained on a screen is called a real image. An image which cannot be obtained on a screen is called a virtual image.

25. If the reflecting surface of a spherical mirror is convex or outward, it is called convex mirror.
The images formed by convex lens are mostly real and inverted except when object is very close.

26. When an object is placed near the convex lens, then an enlarged image is formed. Due to this property, convex lens is used as a magnifying glass.

27. No, colour of cloth is the colour which it reflects. Since blue light does not contain any red coloured component. But yellow light ($Y = R + G$) is combination of red and green components. So, the colour of cloth will appear red.

28. A convex mirror is used as a rear view mirror in vehicles such as car, bus, truck, etc. since it forms a smaller and virtual image. It can be used to see a much larger area than the area visible by a plane mirror.

29. Reflection that takes place through a regular and smooth surface is known as regular reflection. Reflection that takes place through a rough and dull surface is known as irregular or diffused reflection.

30. An image formed by a plane mirror shows the following characteristics:

(i) Image formed in a plane mirror is upright or erect.
(ii) It is always virtual.
(iii) It is of the same size as the size of the object.
(iv) The image formed in the mirror is at the same distance behind the mirror as the object is in front of it.

31. Concave mirrors are used as shaving mirrors as these magnify the image and image is upright, when the mirror is held close. Concave mirrors are used in torches and car headlights to reflect the light of bulb to create a powerful beam of light.

Convex mirrors are used as rear view mirrors in automobiles as the images are erect and field of view is wide. However the distance of the objects in the mirror appear farther than they are.

32. Consider an object of height *AB* placed at a certain distance in front of a mirror. To understand the process of image formation by a plane mirror, we have to draw a ray diagram. In a ray diagram, first a few incident rays of light are drawn from the object to the mirror as shown in figure (a). Then reflected rays from the mirror are drawn obeying the laws of reflection as shown in figure (b). Now extend the reflected ray behind the mirror in backward direction. The image will be formed at the point where these extended reflected rays intersect. We may notice that the reflected rays appear to diverge from the image as shown in figure (c).

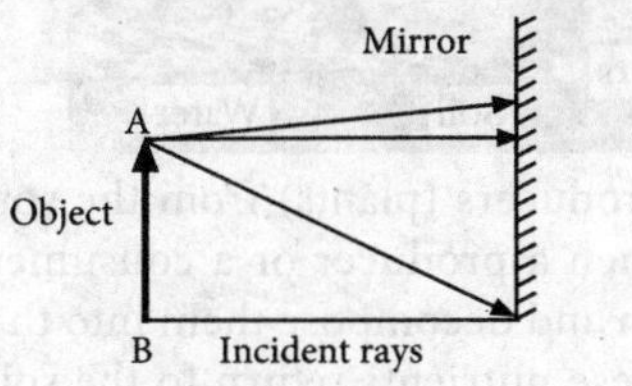

fig. (a)

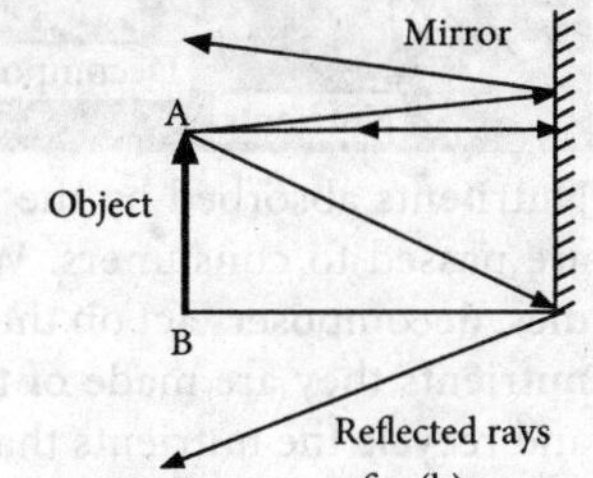

fig. (b)

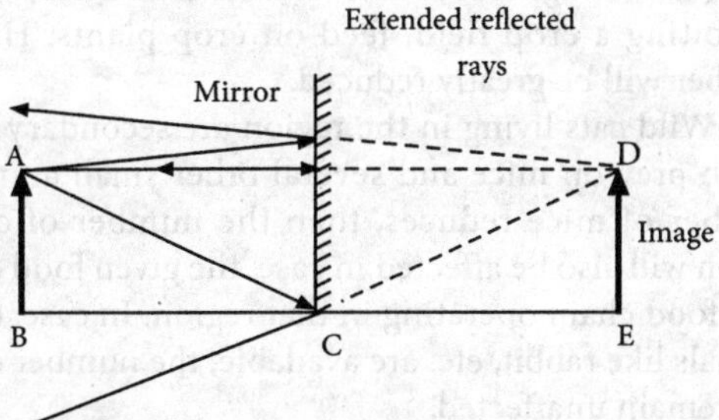

fig. (c)

33. A source of light is an object, from which light is given out. Some sources of light are natural and many others are man made sources. Sun is the most important natural source of light. An electric lamp, an oil lamp, a candle etc. are some of the many man made sources of light.

The sources of light are of two types :

(i) Self luminous : A self luminous source is that which possesses light of its own. For example, the sun, the stars, electric lamps, candles etc. are self luminous sources.

(ii) Non-luminous : A non-luminous source is that which does not possess light of its own. It receives light from an external source and scatters it to the surroundings. For example, the moon, a book, a table, a chair etc. are non-luminous sources.

34.

Concave lens	Convex lens
(a) A concave lens is thinner in the middle than at the edges. It is also known as diverging lens as it diverges the rays of light falling on it.	(a) A convex lens is thicker in the middle than at the edges. It is also known as converging lens as it converges the rays of light falling on it.
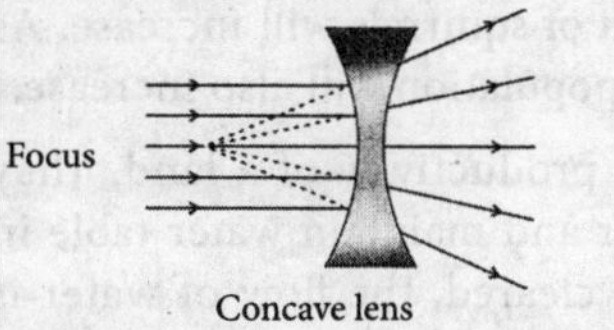	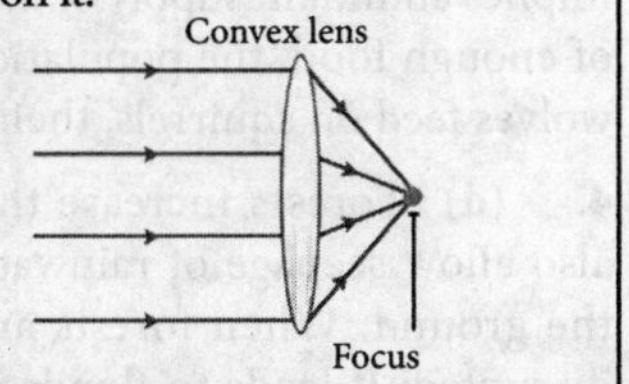
(b) It forms a virtual, erect and diminished image of all objects irrespective of their distance from the lens.	(b) It forms a real and inverted image of the object kept beyond its focal point. For an object kept between its optical centre and focus, it forms virtual, erect and a magnified image.

35. (i) Parallel rays passing through a convex lens converge to a point known as the principal focus (*F*) or real focus. In case of a diverging or concave lens, the rays of light do not actually meet, but appear to diverge from a point called the principal focus of the concave lens or virtual focus.
(ii) This is due to refraction. The rays of light meet above the object in the denser medium.
(iii) The extent of reflection depends upon the shine and smoothness of the surface. More is the shine and smoothness of the surface, more will be the reflection. That is why mirrors reflect most of the light falling on it. Therefore, for reflection, shiny surfaces are required.

36. **(b) :** As newspaper is a rough and unpolished surface, so diffused reflection takes place.

37. **(d) :** $\angle i = 0° \Rightarrow \angle r = 0°$

38. **(b) :** $\angle i = 60° \Rightarrow \angle r = 60°$

39. **(c) :** $\angle R = 35° \Rightarrow \angle S = 90° - 35° = 55°$
$\angle T = S = 55°$

40. Because rose reflects red colour so it is of red colour, actually.

41. It appears black as no colour of light is reflected by the rose.

42. The secondary colour is violet.

43. The colour obtained is cyan.

12 Forests : Our Lifeline

Practice Corner

1. (c) 2. (b)

3. (d) : In the given food chain, plant is eaten by squirrel. Squirrel is eaten by wolf and wolf is eaten by tiger to maintain the ecological balance.
If the population of tiger decreases then there will be less tigers to prey on wolves and therefore, the population of wolves will increase. Increase in the population of plants implies abundant supply of food for squirrels. In the presence of enough food, the population of squirrels will increase. As wolves feed on squirrels, their population will also increase.

4. (d) : Forests increase the productivity of a land. They also allow seepage of rainwater and maintain water table in the ground. When forests are cleared, the flow of water is disrupted. It leads to floods in some areas and droughts in others.

5. (c) : Saprotrophs are organisms that feed on dead and decaying organic matter. Mostly saprotrophs are bacteria and fungi.

6. (c) : Felling of trees in large scales will disturb the balance between carbon dioxide and oxygen gases. Increase in the amount of gases like carbon dioxide in the air will lead to global warming as these gases absorb heat and increase the temperature of the earth.

7. (c) : Forest provides food and shelter to many animals and plants. Forests release oxygen and absorb carbon dioxide. Forests maintain a balance between oxygen and carbon dioxide on the earth.

8. (a)

9. (d) : The shape of crown of tree labelled IV is extensive and covers greater area. The leaves and branches in the crown are densely packed and will not allow much of the sunlight to pass through it. This tree will be most suitable for growing along a walkway as it will provide shade and cooling effect to the pedestrians in hot sunny day.

10. (b) 11. (b)

12. (a) : Producers are green plants that make their own food from carbon dioxide and water, using the energy of sunlight. All food chains are linked. If any one food chain is disturbed, it affects other food chains. Destruction of forests or large scale is called deforestation.

13. False. All food chains are linked.

14. True 15 True

16. False. Forests allow seepage of rainwater and maintain water table in ground, hence, prevent floods and droughts.

17. False. The vegetation that grows under the shade of the canopy is known as the understorey.

18. True

19. False. The amount of carbon dioxide increases in the absence of forests.

20. False. The forest absorbs noise. Noise pollution is less near the places of forest.

21. True

22. False. Larger number of herbivores means more availability of food for carnivores.

23. Decomposers 24. Canopy

25. Herbs 26. dispersal

27. linked 28. soil, shelter

29. Forests 30. Soil

31. photosynthesis 32. bacteria, fungi

33. (i) recycling (ii) fungi
(iii) soil (iv) roots

34.

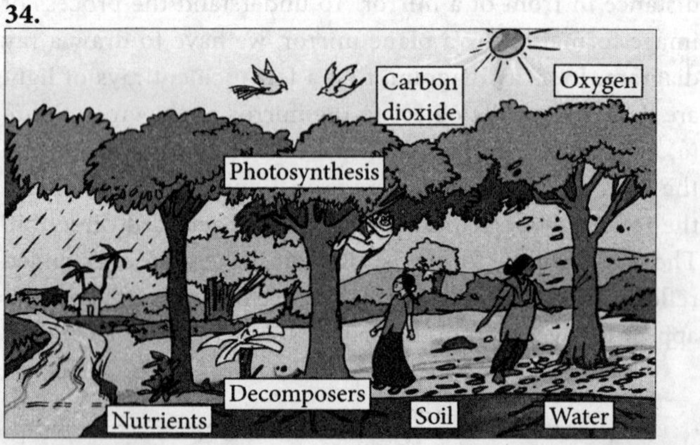

Nutritents absorbed by the producers (plants) from the soil are passed to consumers. When a producer or a consumer dies, decomposers act on them and decompose them into the nutrients they are made of these nutrients return to the soil and recycle the nutrients that have been taken from the soil.

35. (a) Drought leads to destruction of a crop plant. Mice inhabiting a crop field, feed on crop plants. Hence, their number will be greatly reduced.
(b) Wild cats living in the region are secondary consumers which prey on mice and several other small animals. If the number of mice reduces, then the number of cats in that region will also be affected in case, the given food chain is the only food chain operating in that region. In case, other small animals like rabbit, etc. are available, the number of wild cats will remain unaffected.

NCERT Exemplar Problems

1. (b) : Plants in the forest release oxygen during photosynthesis. This provides oxygen to all animals and helps to maintain the ratio of oxygen to carbon dioxide in the atmosphere.

2. (c) 3. (d)

4. (a)

5. (b) : Thermocol is not prepared from the wood obtained from forest.

6. **(c)** : Teak, *sal* and *kachnar* are the names of trees whereas porcupine is an animal.

7. **(a)**: Semal is the name of a tree and hornbill is the name of an animal.

8. **(d)** : Ginger is not found commonly in forests. It is a small plant which can be easily cultivated in crop fields.

9. **(a)**: The branchy part of a tree above stem is known as crown.

10. **(c)**: Forests prevent flooding. In a forest, raindrops do not hit the forest floor directly. The canopy layer of the forest intercepts the flow of raindrops so that rainwater falls on the leaves of trees and then drips slowly onto the forest floor. Thus, water does not collect and stagnate on the forest floor.

A & R Corner

1. **(a)**

2. **(a)** : If forests disappear, the amount of carbon dioxide in air will increase, resulting in the increase of earth's temperature.

3. **(d)** : Plants take up carbon dioxide for photosynthesis and oxygen for respiration.

4. **(c)** : Not only fungi, bacteria are also involved in the decomposition of dead plant and animal tissues. They are called decomposers.

5. **(a)**

6. **(a)** : Trees absorb CO_2 (for photosynthesis), so its concentration can be kept under control by planting more trees.

7. **(b)** 8. **(a)**

9. **(a)** : The canopy is the thickest layer and much of the sunlight and rain is stopped by the thick foliage.

10. **(c)** : The animals can disperse the seeds of certain plants and can help the forest to grow and regenerate.

11. **(a)** 12. **(a)**

13. **(a)** : Forests are called as green lungs because they help to maintain a balance between O_2 and CO_2 in the atmosphere.

14. **(c)**

15. **(c)** : The transpired water in the air contributes to the formation of cloud and rainfall.

Exam Corner

1. **(c)** : Food chain is a simple representation of energy flow in nature. Grain is a producer as it can synthesize its own food hence, it will occupy the first trophic level in a food chain. Insect are primary consumers as they directly feed on grains so they will constitute the second trophic level. Frog feeds on insect. Hence, it is secondary consumer and will form the next link of the food chain. Snake is a tertiary consumer as it feeds on frog and will occupy the highest trophic level. Hence, the correct order in which different organisms will be arranged in a food chain, is as follows:

Grain → Insect → Frog → Snake

2. **(d)** : Bacteria and fungi are consumers that feed mainly on dead remains of plants and animals, and are called decomposers. When a producer or a consumer dies, bacteria and fungi act to break down or decompose the material of its dead body into the nutrient substances it was made up of. These nutrient substances return to the soil from where they came and mix with it. From the soil, these nutrients are again absorbed by the roots of living plants. Thus, the decomposers act as recyclers and serve a very useful purpose of maintaining the balance of nutrients in the soil.
Snails, millipedes and termites are not decomposers. They are small animals.

3. **(a)**

4. **(d)** : Forests act as natural absorbers of rainwater. In a forest, raindrops do not hit the forest floor directly. The canopy layer of the forest intercepts the flow of raindrops so that rainwater falls on the leaves of trees and then drips slowly onto the forest floor. Thus, water does not collect and stagnate on the forest floor. This prevents flooding.

5. **(a)** : In the process 'X', carbon dioxide is released from both plants and animals. Hence, it is respiration. Respiration is a process that results in the release of energy, and formation of carbon dioxide and water as by products. It occurs in both plants and animals.

6. **(d)** : Forests act as natural absorbers of rainwater. In a forests, raindrops do not hit the forest floor directly. The canopy layer of forest intercepts the flow of raindrops so that rainwater falls on the leaves of the trees and then drips slowly to the forest floor. This prevents water from collecting on the forest floor and allows water to seep and thus, prevents flooding. Moreover, this helps to maintain water table throughout the year. The roots of trees in a forest bind the soil particles firmly and prevent them from getting carried away by wind or water. Hence, forests prevent soil erosion.

7. **(d)** : The understorey is a tangle of shrubs, young trees, palms and woody plants that can grow in the shade of taller trees. There are different horizontal layers in the understorey. Giant and tall trees form the uppermost layer. Below the gaint and tall trees are smaller trees, below which are the shrubs and tall grasses. The herbs form the lowest layer.

8. **(d)** : We get many things from forests. Forests yield valuable products such as timber, wood pulp (for making paper), turpentine, latex (for the manufacture of rubber), oils, spices, resin, gum, lac and medicinal plants.

9. **(d)**

10. **(d)** : Decomposers operate at all levels of food chain.

11. **(c)**

12. **(d)** : The animals which come at the end of a food chain are called as top consumers or top carnivores. These are the animals which are not preyed upon by any other animals.

13. **(c)** : Primary consumers or herbivores are animals which feed on plants or plant products. These animals occupy second trophic level.

14. **(a)**

15. (a) : The tallest trees of the rainforest are in the emergent layer. These tall trees get lot of sunlight. Some of the trees grow as tall as 200 feet.

16. (d) : Forests help to purify the atmospheric air. Trees in forests absorb CO_2 gas and release O_2 gas during the process of photosynthesis. Forests help to maintain a balance between CO_2 and O_2 in the atmosphere and are thus, referred to as 'green lungs' of the earth.

17. (b) : Canopy : The branches of tall trees form a green roof over other plants. This looks like an umbrella.
Forest floor : It is dark, damp, covered with a layer of dead and decaying leaves, fruits, seeds, twigs and herbs.

18. (a)

19. (c) : In forest, organisms are dependent on each other for their survival. If any organism is removed from the forest, many organisms would get affected.

20. (c)

21. (c) : Forests help to maintain the ratio of oxygen and carbon dioxide in the air. Trees and other plants in forests take CO_2 (for its use in photosynthesis) from atmospheric air and add O_2 to it. Therefore, in the absence of forests, the amount of carbon dioxide will increase resulting in an increase in the earth's temperature leading to global warming.

22. (d) : A food chain consists of producers, consumers and decomposers.

23. (d) : Vulture is a scavenger. It feeds on dead animals.

24. (b) : Statement (ii) is incorrect. Plants and animals in a forest are dependent on each other for their growth and survival. Plants provide oxygen, food and shelter to animals whereas animals provide CO_2 to plants for photosynthesis and help in their seed dispersal to distant places.

25. (b)

26. (b) : In nature, all food chains start with producers and they occupy the first trophic level.

27. (c) 28. (d)

29. (d)

30. (c) : Teak provides timber, fox is tertiary consumer or top consumer, eagle is not a decomposer.

31. (c) : In a rainforest, these layers are emergent layer, canopy, understorey and forest floor, starting from top to bottom.

32. (b) 33. (b)

34. (a) Vessel C. Since vessel C has least number of plantlets, the flow of water is not disrupted by them. The water flows easily and quickly over vessel C, which removes top layer of soil.
(b) Cause of soil erosion. The removal and thinning of the soil layer due to climatic and physical processes, such as high rainfall, which is greatly accelerated by certain human activities such as deforestation is called soil erosion.
(c) This experiment shows that plants bind the soil and help to prevent removal of soil *i.e.*, soil erosion. In nature, forests prevent soil erosion and control floods and droughts.

35. food chain 36. Herbivores

37. Canopy 38. Scavengers

39. Deforestation, carbon dioxide

40. rainwater

41. methane, nitrous oxide

42. primary, secondary

43. trophic level

44. soil erosion 45. Omnivores

46. Green plants, producers 47. Forest

48. Humus 49. food web

50. dependent

51. Herbivores, carnivores

52. shrubs, herbs

53. Seed dispersal

54. climate, watercycle

55. Neem, Tulsi

56. Timber, Latex

57. Bacteria, Fungi

58. Lion, Wolf

59. Deer, Goat

60. Grains → Hen → Cat

61. Grains → Mouse → Owl

62. Carrot → Rabbit → Snake → Hawk

63. Grass → Deer → Tiger → Vulture

64.

Canopy	Understorey
Canopy is a forest layer formed by branches of tall trees. It is like a roof over other plants. It looks like an umbrella. It is the thickest forest layer and much of the sunlight and rain is stopped by its thick foliage.	Understorey is a forest layer formed by vegetation that grows under the shade of the canopy. It is a tangle of shrubs, trees, and woody plants. Giant trees form the uppermost layer, smaller trees are below them, under which are shrubs and grasses. The herbs form the lowest layer.

65. Decomposers are the microorganisms (*e.g.*, bacteria and fungi) which feed on dead remains of plants and animals. They break down the material of the dead body into simple inorganic nutrients, which are then released into the soil. From the soil, these nutrients are again absorbed by the roots of living plants. In this way, decomposers help in cleaning of the environment as well as recycling of nutrients.

66. Deforestation refers to the large scale cutting down of trees on a land, where trees are re-planted whereas afforestation refers to large scale planting of trees in an area where there was no forest.

67. A food chain is sequence of organisms through which represents energy and nutrients transferred from one organism to another in a particular habitat. A number of interconnected food chains form a food web.

68. The position that an organism occupies in a food chain is called trophic level. A food chain may have many trophic levels. The first trophic level in a food chain is occupied by producers. Primary consumers occupy the second trophic level and secondary consumers occupy next higher trophic level in a food chain.

69. Forests act as natural absorber of rainwater. In a forest, raindrops do not hit the forest floor directly. The canopy layer of forest intercepts the flow of raindrops so that rainwater falls on the leaves of trees and then drips slowly onto the forest floor. Thus, forests allow rainwater to seep. This helps to maintain the water table throughout the year. In the absence of forest, rain directly hits the ground and rainwater gets collected or stagnates on ground leading to floods. Much water is wasted in this way and does not seep down to replenish the water table.

70. The organisms which are capable of synthesizing their own food using CO_2 and water in the presence of sunlight, by the process of photosynthesis are called producers or autotrophs, *e.g.*, green plants. Whereas, the organisms which directly or indirectly depend on the food prepared by plants are called consumers or heterotrophs *e.g.*, animals.

71. By harbouring greater variety of plants, the forest provides greater opportunities for food for the herbivores. Larger number of herbivores means increased availability of food for a variety of carnivores. The wide variety of animals helps the forest to regenerate and grow. Decomposers help in maintaining the supply of nutrients to the growing plants in the forest. Therefore, the forest is a 'dynamic living entity' — "full of life and vitality".

72. Animals help in pollination and seed dispersal of the plants. Seeds of some plants cling to the body of animals and are carried away to new places. This helps in the dispersal of seeds.
Animals provide nutrients to the plants. The bodies of dead and decaying animals and the droppings of animals are acted upon by microbes, which reduce them to simple inorganic compounds. These compounds get percolated into the soil and enrich the soil with nutrients which are absorbed by plants. This is called recycling of nutrients. Therefore, plants depend on animals for inorganic nutrients.

73. The consequences of deforestation are as follows:
(i) Climatic imbalance : Felling of trees in large numbers will disturb the balance between carbon dioxide and oxygen gases. Increase in the amount of gases likes carbon dioxide in the air, will lead to global warming as these gases absorb heat and increase the temperature of the earth.
(ii) Desertification : Deforestation may lead to desertification *i.e.*, spread of deserts. The Sahara Desert once used to be a lush green forest, became a desert as a result of extensive deforestation.
(iii) Soil erosion : Plant roots bind the soil particles firmly and help to prevent soil erosion. Clearing of forests removes the plant cover which leads to increased soil erosion, removes the top fertile layer of soil and leaves the area barren.

74. Due to the presence of vegetation of different heights with different types of crown, several horizontal layers are created in the rainforest. These layers are divided into different types *viz.* emergent layer, canopy, understorey and forest floor.
(i) Emergent layer - The tallest trees of the rainforest are in the emergent layer. These tall trees get lot of sunlight. Animals found in this layer include birds (such as toucan, macaw etc.), different kinds of butterflies, insects, monkeys, snakes etc.
(ii) Canopy - The branches of the tall trees form a green roof over the other plants, this is known as the canopy. The canopy looks like an umbrella. This is the thickest layer and much of the sunlight and rain is stopped by the thick foliage. Animals found in the canopy layer include many birds, monkeys, orangutans, sloths, lizards, snakes, insects, etc.
(iii) Understorey- The vegetation that grows under the shade of the canopy is known as the understorey. The understorey is a tangle of shrubs, young trees, palms and woody plants that can grow in the shade of taller trees. The herbs form the lowest layer. Animals found in understorey include various kinds of frogs, lizards, snakes, insects, butterflies, monkeys etc.
(iv) Forest floor- The forest floor is dark, damp, covered with a layer of dead and decaying leaves, fruits, seeds, twigs and herbs. Mosses and ferns grow on the forest floor where it is warm, damp, and shady. Animals found in this layer include millepedes, beetles etc. Large animals like elephants, leopards, jaguars, tapirs, rhinoceros, snakes, tigers, etc.

75. Forests are a very important renewable resource and are the wealth of our country. They are useful in the following ways:
(i) Purify air and maintain balance of O_2 and CO_2 : Plants in the forests release oxygen and absorb carbon dioxide during the process of photosynthesis. They provide O_2 to all the animals including human beings for respiration. Thus, forests help to maintain a balance between O_2 and CO_2 in the atmosphere.
(ii) Regulate climate and water cycle : Plants in the forests absorb water from the soil through their roots and release it into the air by the process of transpiration. This increases the amount of water vapour in the air, helps in cloud formation and rainfall. Increased amount of water vapour in the atmosphere also cools the surrounding air.
(iii) Provide food and shelter : By harbouring great variety of plants, the forest provides greater opportunities for food for the herbivores. Larger number of herbivores means increased availability of food for a variety of carnivores.
Animals also depend on plants for shelter and safety. Most birds make their nests on branches of trees. Monkeys, apes and bats live on trees. Some insects, such as caterpillar, ladybird, butterfly, moth, grasshopper and firefly find shelter among plants. Many people belonging to different tribes also live in forests. They depend mostly on forests for their livelihood.
(iv) Prevent soil erosion : The roots of plants bind the soil particles together and prevent soil erosion.
(v) Control floods and maintain water table : In a forest, raindrops do not hit the forest floor directly. The canopy layer

of the forest intercepts the flow of raindrops so that rainwater falls on the leaves of trees and then drips slowly onto the forest floor. Water does not collect and stagnate on the forest floor. This prevents flooding.

(vi) Provide valuable products : We get many things from forests. Forests yield valuable products such as timber, wood pulp (for making paper), turpentine, latex (for the manufacture of rubber), oils, spices, resin, gum, lac and medicinal plants.

76. (a) Green plants are called producers as they can manufacture their own food by the process of photosynthesis.
(b) Trees and other plants in forests take in CO_2 and release O_2 during the process of photosynthesis. Hence, they maintain a balance between these two gases in the atmosphere. They purify the air by adding O_2 to it and removing excess of CO_2 from it. Hence, forests are called nature's lungs.
(c) Greenhouse gases absorb infrared radiations that are re-radiated by earth's surface. This increases the average temperature of earth and its atmosphere. Carbon dioxide, methane, ozone and nitrous oxide are some greenhouse gases. The average rise in temperature changes weather patterns, melting of polar ice caps with a corresponding rise in sea level.

77. **(b) :** The transformation of A to B is due to deforestation which involves the cutting of trees on large scale.

78. **(b) :** In the absence of trees the animals will not get food and shelter, so their population will decrease.

79. **(a) :** Soil in figure B will be prone to soil erosion as there are firmly no trees which can hold the soil through their roots.

80. **(b)**

81. **(a) :** The concentration of CO_2 in the atmosphere will increase as due to the absence of trees, the CO_2 will not be utilised by the trees for photosynthesis.

82. **(a) :** Food chain (X) is a series or sequence of transfer of energy in the form of food which occurs when one organism is consumed by another organism.

83. **(a) :** Grass is an autotroph. Autotrophs are those organisms which can prepare their own food by the process of photosynthesis.

84. **(d) :** Population of grasshopper will increase as there will be no consumer which can feed on grasshoppers and the population of snake will decrease because there will be no prey population for snake to feed on.

85. **(d)**

86. Grasshopper, frog and snake are predators as well as prey. Grasshopper is a predator of grass and prey of frog. Frog is a prey of snake and predator of grasshopper and snake is a prey of eagle and predator of frog.

87. **(a)**

88. **(a) :** Maximum photosynthesis occur in layer A, which is the emergent layer of forest. In this layer, trees receive a lot of sunlight which speed up the rate of photosynthesis and increases the productivity.

89. **(d) :** Along with birds, monkeys and snakes can be found in layer A.

90. Layer D is the bottom most layer of a forest known as forest floor. It has dark coloured, nutrient rich humus which is prepared by the decaying plant and animal components. Insects like ants and beetles are commonly found here.

13 Wastewater Story

Practice Corner

1. **(b)**

2. **(b) :** Many people around the world are consuming unsafe drinking water because of lack of facility to clean water.

3. **(d)**

4. Logo shows 'Water for life' (2005-2015)
All efforts made during this decade aim to reduce the number of people who do not have access to safe drinking water.

5. True **6.** True

7. True

8. False. 'Sewage Treatment' takes place in several stages.

9. True **10.** **(c)**

11. **(d) :** Contaminated or polluted water contains microbes that can cause diseases such as typhoid, cholera, dysentery.

12. **(c)**

13. **(b)**

1.	Organic impurities	– Pesticides and herbicides
2.	Inorganic impurities	– Metals and phosphates
3.	Nutrients	– Nitrogen and phosphorus
4.	Disease causing bacteria	– Typhoid and cholera causing microorganisms

14. wastewater, rainwater, contaminants, organic, inorganic, nutrients.

15. **(b)** **16.** **(a)**

17. **(b) :** Chlorine is added to disinfect the water, it can kill the microbes are that contaminating the water.

18. **(b)** **19.** **(b)**

20. Filtration process

21. During sewage treatment, solid wastes from the sewage are first removed by passing the water through layers of sand and fine gravel.

22. **(d)** **23.** **(a)**

24. **(a) :** In the first step wastewater is passed through bar screens where large objects like rags, sticks, cans, plastic packets, napkins are removed.

25. **(b) :** Air is pumped into the clarified water to help aerobic bacteria to grow which consume human waste, food waste, soaps and other unwanted matter still remaining in clarified water.

26. **(b) :** In a grit and sand removal tank, the speed of the incoming wastewater is decreased so that solid heavy objects such as sand, grit, stones, etc. settle down at the bottom and are removed.

27. bar screens **28.** sludge

29. clarified water **30.** skimmer

31. anaerobic, biogas **32.** aerobic

33. sand drying beds **34.** Dried sludge

35. chlorine, ozone **36.** nature

37. False. From wastewater, sludge is removed with a scraper and floatable solids are removed with a skimmer.

38. True **39.** True

40. False. Biogas is used as fuel or can be used to produce electricity.

41. True **42.** True

43. False. Dried sludge is used as manure, returning organic matter and nutrients to the soil.

44. Aerator: It contains aerobic bacteria which grow rapidly and consume organic matter, soaps, detergents, etc.

45. Grit and sand removal tank: It removes heavy objects like sand, grit, stones, etc. from wastewater.

46. Sedimentation tank : Solids like faeces and floatable materials like oil and grease are removed with the help of scraper and skimmer in this tank.

47. **(d) :** Some household wastes such as fats and oils, used tea leaves, paints and solvents etc., should not be thrown into the sink. They pollute the water.

48. **(b)** **49.** **(d)**

50.

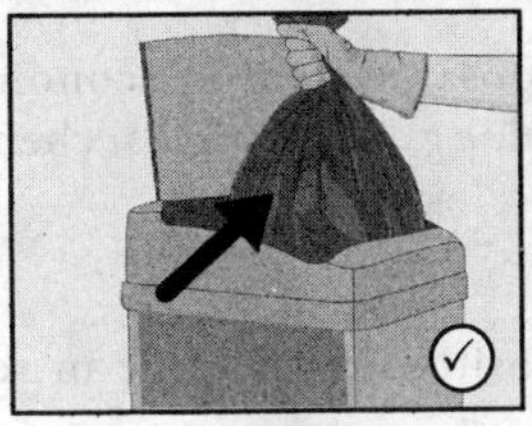

51.

52.

53. **(d)**

54. **(b) :** Malaria is not a water-borne disease.

55. **(d) :** Untreated human excreta is a health hazard. It causes water pollution and soil pollution. Both the surface water and ground water get polluted. Ground water is a source of water for wells, tube wells, etc. Thus, it becomes the most common route for water-borne diseases such as cholera, typhoid, polio, dysentery, etc.

56. **(a) :** Dysentery is a water-borne disease

57. sanitation **58.** surface water

59. Untreated human excreta

60. typhoid, polio, meningitis, hepatitis

61. **(d)**

62. **(d) :** A vermi-processing toilet is a type of toilet in which human excreta is treated by earthworms. It has been found to be a novel, low water-use toilet for safe processing of human waste, without odour and fly problem. The operation of the toilet is very simple and hygienic. The human excreta is treated with no water or small flush of water.

63. **(a) :** Untreated sewage is a major source of ground water and surface water pollution. The organic material that is discharged with sewage into water bodies uses up substantial oxygen, and thereby disturbs the ecological balance of rivers and lakes. Untreated sewage if allowed to flow directly into rivers, poses a major health risk for humans and animals as it leads to water-borne diseases.

64. Septic tanks, scavenging, biogas plant, electricity

65. **(d)** **66.** **(d)**

67. **(c) :** The government has laid down certain standards of sanitation but, unfortunately, they are not strictly enforced.

68. Figure B shows a good sanitation practice.

69. We should not scatter litter anywhere. Always throws the garbage in the dustbin. If there is no dustbin in sight, we should carry the litter home and throw it in the dustbin.

70. (i) We should not spit in public places.
(ii) We should never urinate on the roadside.

NCERT Exemplar Problems

1. **(d) :** Water discharged during daily chores-like washing clothes, flushing toilet, washing dishes, bathing etc., becomes dirty. This dirty water is called wastewater. Water trickling from a damaged tap, water coming out of a shower and water flowing in a river are not dirty and hence it is not a wastewater.

2. **(a) :** Sewage is a wastewater that includes domestic or industrial liquid wastes. It contains various dissolved and suspended impurities.

3. **(c) :** The sewage is treated to destroy the germs and reduce the contaminants. In wastewater treatment, wastewater is passed through sedimentation tank, in which organic materials settle down and are removed with scraper. This is called sludge. In separate tank, sludge is acted upon by anaerobic bacteria which produces methane, carbon dioxide, and biogas by process known as digestion.
Therefore, both sludge and biogas are products of wastewater treatment.

4. (d) : In some places there are open drains to dispose off the sewage. These drains can easily get blocked by plastic bags, and can overflow. Therefore, the problems of smell, breeding of mosquitoes, flies and germs are encountered in open drains.

5. (c) : Asthma is an air borne respiratory disease. It is caused due to an allergy to dust, pollen grains or any other allergen present in air.

6. (a) : During wastewater treatment, dis-infectant like chlorine is added to the water to kill harmful micro-organisms.

7. (b) : Sewage goes through a system of pipes, called sewers, which are linked to each other to form a network called sewerage system.

8. (c) : Various metals and phosphates are inorganic impurities of sewage, while pesticides, urea and vegetable wastes are organic impurities.

9. (d) : In wastewater treatment, waste-water is allowed to enter a grit and sand removal tank. Here, the speed of wastewater is reduced in order to allow sand, grit and pebbles to settle down.

10. (a) : Sewers are the pipes through which wastewater generated from homes, industries and hospitals flows. They are not the source of wastewater.

A & R Corner

1. (a)

2. (b) : Biogas is produced by the activity of anaerobic bacteria on the sewage.

3. (c) : Sewage treatment involves physical, chemical and biological processes from wastewater, which removes physical, chemical and biological contaminants.

4. (d) : Waste water is passed through bar screens. Large objects like rags, sticks, cans, plastic packets, napkins are removed and the speed of the incoming wastewater is decreased to allow sand, grit and pebbles to settle down in grit and sand removal tank.

5. (c) : The septic tank acts as sedimentation-cum-digestion tank.

6. (a)

7. (b) : Chlorine and ozone are used to disinfect treated water before releasing into distribution system.

8. (c) : Pesticides are used to kill pest while insecticides are used to kill insects.

9. (d) : Air is pumped into clarified water to help aerobic bacteria to grow and during aeration, oxygen is circulated throughout the water to remove foul odour.

10. (b) **11. (b)**

12. (b) : Drinking contaminated water causes large number of water borne diseases like cholera, typhoid, polio, hepatitis, etc.

13. (c) : The presence of undesirable materials in water bodies is known as water pollution.

14. (b)

15. (c) : Harmful chemicals need to be eliminated before water enters the rivers.

Exam Corner

1. (b)

2. (c) : Eucalyptus tree absorbs all the surplus wastewater from the sewage ponds rapidly and releases pure water vapour into the atmosphere through transpiration.

3. (a) **4. (d)**

5. (c) : In sedimentation tank, solids like faeces settle at bottom and are removed with the help of scrapper.

6. (a)

7. (a) : The activated sludge is about 97% water.

8. (c)

9. (d) : Organic impurities in sewage includes human and animal wastes, oil, urea, pesticides, vegetable waste, etc.

10. (d) **11. (a)**

12. (a) : Given figure represents water clarifier where faeces are removed by scrapper and floating solids like oil are removed by skimmer.

13. (b) **14. (b)**

15. (d) : Biogas use does not add to pollution.

16. (d)

17. (b) : In vermi-composting toilets, human excreta is treated by earthworms.

18. (d) **19. (a)**

20. (a) : Onsite sewage disposal system is economical alternative for sewage disposal, *e.g.*, septic tanks, chemical toilets and composting pits.

21. (d) **22. (b)**

23. (a) : Anaerobic decomposition takes place in septic tanks.

24. (b) : Sewers that carry only domestic sewage are called as sanitary sewers.

25. (a) **26. (b)**

27. (d) : Given figure represents bar screens which remove large solid materials such as rags, sticks, cans, plastic bags, napkins, etc.

28. (c) **29.** Manholes

30. clarifiers **31.** digester, anaerobic

32. aeration **33.** methane

34. water, suspended microbes

35. Anaerobic

36. ground water, surface water

37. anaerobic **38.** earthworms

39. Wastewater Treatment Plant (WWTP) or Sewage Treatment Plant (STP)

40. P – Grit and sand removal tank
Q – Sedimentation tank (clarifier)
R – Aeration tank
S – Chlorination tank

41. In the digester tank, many types of anaerobic bacteria decompose the organic matter present in sludge to produce biogas, which can be used as a fuel directly or it can be used to generate electricity. The digested sludge left after the removal of biogas is taken out, dried and used as a manure which returns nutrients to the soil.

42. False. Harmful microorganisms that can cause diseases are present in domestic waste.

43. False. Aeration tanks contain aerobic bacteria.

44. True **45.** False

46. False. Biogas is also called as gobar gas.

47. True **48.** True

49. False. In vermi-composting toilets, earthworms are used.

50. False. Pesticides and herbicides are organic impurities present in sewage.

51. True **52.** True

53. True

54. False. The speed of the influent is decreased in a grit and sand removal tank.

55. False. *Eucalyptus* trees can purify wastewater rapidly in nature.

56. True

57. False. Chemicals, medicines and insecticides should not be thrown into the sink.

58. True

59. False. Clarified water is free from plastics and oils.

60. Hospital and factories

61. Cans and plastic bags

62. Cholera and typhoid

63. Septic tank and composting toilet

64. Phosphorus and nitrogen

65. Herbicides. Herbicides are organic impurities while rest all are inorganic impurities.

66. Aeration tank. It is a biological process whereas others are physical process.

67. Sewage treatment plants. All others are alternative methods of sewage disposal system.

68. Nitrogen. Nitrogen is a nutrient present in sewage while all others are organic impurities.

69. Heat attack. Heart attack is not a water-borne disease while all others are water-borne diseases.

70. The sludge collected at the bottom of the sedimentation tank is continuously removed by scrapers. The floating materials which contain oils and grease are removed with the help of skimmer.

71. Sludge is decomposed by anaerobic bacteria resulting in the production of biogas.

72. (a) Dried sludge is used as manure, returning organic matter and nutrients to the soil.
(b) Biogas is used as a fuel directly or it can be used to generate electricity.

73. It is advised to grow *Eucalyptus* trees all along a sewage pond because they absorb all the surplus wastewater from the sewage ponds rapidly and release pure water vapour into the atmosphere through transpiration.

74. Chemicals like chlorine and ozone are added to treated water to disinfect it. The purpose of disinfection in the treatment of wastewater is to completely eliminate the harmful microorganisms present in the water.

75. Sewage is wastewater released by homes, industries, hospitals, offices and other users. It also includes rainwater that has run down the street during a storm or heavy rain. Sewage is a liquid waste. It is a complex mixture containing suspended solids, organic and inorganic impurities, nutrients, saprotrophic and disease causing bacteria and other microbes. Untreated sewage is a major source of ground water and surface water pollution. The organic material that is discharged with sewage into water bodies uses up substantial oxygen, and thereby disturbs the ecological balance of rivers and lakes. Untreated sewage if allowed to flow directly into rivers, poses a major risk for the health of humans and animals.

76. Untreated human excreta is a health hazard. It causes water pollution and soil pollution. Both the surface water and ground water get polluted. Ground water is a source of water for wells, tube wells, *etc.* Thus, it becomes the most common route for water-borne diseases such as cholera, typhoid, polio, dysentery, *etc.*

77. Cooking oil and fats if thrown into the drains, they can harden and block the pipes. Tea leaves and solid food remains choke the drains and do not allow free flow of oxygen. It also hampers with the degradation process.

78. Poor sanitation and contaminated drinking water is the cause of a large number of diseases such as cholera, typhoid, polio, meningitis, hepatitis, dysentery, etc. Untreated sewage is a major source of ground water and surface water pollution. It is important to have a proper drainage system at all the places, and hygienic sanitary conditions, which is the responsibility of both the citizens as well as the municipality.

79 Sludge is human waste (like faeces) which settles down at the bottom in the clarifier (or sedimentation tank), from where it is collected by a scraper. It is then transferred to a separate tank called digester where it is decomposed by the anaerobic bacteria. The biogas produced in the process can be used as fuel or can be used to produce electricity. The clarified water from the sedimentation tank is passed into aeration tank. In the aeration tank, the suspended microbes settle down at the bottom as activated sludge. The activated sludge is about 97% water. The water is removed by sand drying beds or machines. Dried sludge is used as manure, returning organic matter and nutrients to the soil.

80. (i) Septic tank : In septic tank, the sewage is allowed to flow into a tank in which anaerobic bacteria decompose the waste. The septic tank acts as sedimentation-cum-digestion tank. Anaerobic (in the absence of air) digestion of the settled sludge occurs in its bottom zone, and the remaining liquid has to undergo treatment in a soak pit/filter bed. This can be done in areas where the water table is very low and the rainwater from the surface also does not interfere with their functioning. Septic tanks are suitable for places where there is no sewerage system, for hospitals, isolated buildings or a cluster of 4 to 5 houses.

(ii) Composting toilet : The composting toilet is a dry toilet that uses a predominantly aerobic processing system that treats excreta, typically with no water or small volumes of flush water, *via* composting or managed aerobic decomposition.

81. A few simple housekeeping practices help to reduce the amount of wastewater produced. This can be done in following ways:

(i) Do not dispose off cooking oils and fats in the kitchen sink. They can block pipes when they harden. Throw them in dustbins.

(ii) Do not dispose off used tea leaves, solid food remains, sanitary napkins etc. in the kitchen sink or in the toilet. They clog the drains and prevent free flow of oxygen that interferes with the decomposition process. Throw them in dustbins.

(iii) Do not dispose off chemicals such as paints, medicines and insecticides in the sink. They kill microbes that clean the water.

82. Treatment of wastewater at a wastewater treatment plant involves physical, chemical, and biological processes, which remove physical, chemical and biological matter that contaminates the wastewater. Following steps are involved in treatment of wastewater :

(i) Bar screens : Wastewater is passed through bar screens which remove large objects like rags, sticks, cans, plastic packets, napkins, etc.

(ii) Grit and sand removal : Water then goes through grit and sand removal tank, where sand, grit, pebbles, etc. settle down at the bottom and are removed.

(iii) Sedimentation tank : Water is then allowed to enter in a tank where solids like faeces (called sludge) settle at the bottom and are removed with a scraper. A skimmer removes the floatable materials like oil and grease. Water so cleared is called clarified water. Sludge is collected in digesters, where it is decomposed by anaerobic bacteria resulting in the production of biogas.

(iv) Aerator : Clarified water is then passed through an aerator tank where air is pumped into the water. It helps aerobic bacteria to grow which decompose organic matter like human and animal waste. After several hours, the suspended microbes settle at the bottom of the tank as activated sludge. The water is then removed from the top. The dried activated sludge is used as manure.

(v) Chlorination : The treated water has low level of organic material and suspended matter. It is disinfected through chemicals like chlorine and ozone, before discharging it into water bodies.

83. (i) We should not scatter litter anywhere. If there is no dustbin at sight, we should carry the litter home and throw it in the dustbin.

(ii) We should realise our responsibility in maintaining the water sources in a healthy state.

(iii) Adopting good sanitation practices should be our way of life.

(iv) Whenever we come across open drains or leaky sewerage pipes or poor drainage anywhere in the city, we should approach the municipality and bring the problem into its notice.

84. (a) Oils and fats should not be thrown into the drain as they can harden and block the pipes. In an open drain the fats clog the soil pores reducing its effectiveness in filtering water.

(b) Air is pumped into clarified water in a sewage treatment plant to help aerobic bacteria to grow which consume human waste, food waste, soaps and other unwanted matter still remained in clarified water.

(c) Speed of the influent is slowed down in a grit and sand removal tank, so that the solid heavy objects such as sand, grit, stones, etc. settle down at the bottom and are removed.

85. (d)

86. (c)

87. (a) : Wastewater is passed through bar screens (A) in which large objects like rags, sticks, cans, plastic packets and napkins are removed.

88. (b) : In grit and sand removal tank (B), speed of incoming wastewater is decreased to allow sand, grit and pebbles to settle down.

89. (b) : Sludge is decomposed by anaerobic bacteria to produce biogas in separate tank.

90. (d) : Organic impurities - Human faeces, animal waste, oil, urea, pesticides, herbicides, fruit and vegetable, etc.
Inorganic impurities - Nitrates, phosphate, metals.

91. (c)

92. (b) : Network of big and small pipes, called sewers, forming the sewearage.

93 (a)

94. Phosphorus and nitrogen.